LITERATURE BY DOING

Responding to Poetry, Essays, Drama, and Short Stories

Susan Tchudi, Ph.D.
Central Michigan University
Mount Pleasant, Michigan

Stephen Tchudi, Ph.D.
Michigan State University
East Lansing, Michigan

Seymour Yesner, M.A.
Brookline High School
Brookline, Massachusetts

Joan Yesner, M.S.W.
formerly, Marshall-University
High School
Minneapolis, Minnesota

National Textbook Company
a division of *NTC Publishing Group* • Lincolnwood, Illinois USA

To our children, Stephen, Emily, Michael, Christopher, and Ruthbea, who we hope will always gain pleasure and personal growth from literature

INTERIOR PHOTO CREDITS

Laurence Risser, Minneapolis, Minnesota, pages 2, 28, 84, 104, 122, 152, 204
Photri, Marilyn Gartman Agency, Chicago, Illinois, pages 58, 176
Karen Christoffersen, NTC Publishing Group, Lincolnwood, Illinois, page 140
Seymour Yesner, Brookline, Massachusetts, page 222
Historical Pictures Services, Chicago, Illinois, page 248

COVER PHOTO CREDITS

H. Armstrong Roberts (upper left, lower left, right)
Karen Christoffersen (center)

INTERIOR BOOK DESIGN

Linda Snow Shum

Acknowledgments

"A Room Full of Leaves" from *Not What You Expected* by Joan Aiken, copyright © 1972, 1974 by Joan Aiken, reprinted by permission of Brandt & Brandt Literary Agents, Inc.

"Roommates," by Max Apple, copyright © 1987 by The New York Times Company, reprinted by permission.

"The Unknown Citizen," copyright 1940 and renewed 1968 by W. H. Auden, reprinted from *W. H. Auden: Collected Poems*, edited by Edward Mendelson, by permission of Random House, Inc.

"Equal in Paris" from *Notes of a Native Son* by James Baldwin, copyright © 1955, renewed 1983 by James Baldwin, reprinted by permission of Beacon Press.

"The Subliminal Man" by J. G. Ballard, copyright © 1961 by J. G. Ballard, reprinted by permission of the author and the author's agents, Scott Meredith Literary Agency, Inc., 845 Third Avenue, New York, NY 10022.

"Birds in Their Nest Agree" from *Women and Children First* by Sally Benson, copyright 1943 by F-R Publishing Corp., reprinted by permission of Random House, Inc.

"My Last Duchess" from *The Poems of Robert Browning*, selected by Rosemary Sprague, copyright © 1964, reprinted by permission of Harper & Row Publishers, Inc.

"Incident" from *On These I Stand* by Countee Cullen, copyright © 1925 by Harper & Brothers, copyright renewed 1953 by Ida M. Cullen, reprinted by permission of GRM Associates, Agents for the Estate of Ida M. Cullen.

"old age sticks" is reprinted from *Complete Poems, 1913–1962*, by E. E. Cummings, by permission of Liveright Publishing Corporation, copyright © 1923, 1925, 1931, 1935, 1938, 1939, 1940, 1944, 1945, 1946, 1947, 1948, 1949, 1950, 1951, 1952, 1953, 1954, 1955, 1956, 1957, 1958, 1959, 1960, 1961, 1962 by the Trustees for the E. E. Cummings Trust, copyright © 1961, 1963, 1968 by Marion Morehouse Cummings.

"The Road Not Taken" by Robert Frost, copyright 1916 by Holt, Rinehart and Winston and renewed 1944 by Robert Frost, reprinted from *The Poetry of Robert Frost*, edited by Edward Connery Lathem, by permission of Henry Holt and Company, Inc.

"Sand Hill Road" by Morton Grosser, copyright © 1966 by *Harper's Magazine*. All rights reserved. Reprinted from the April issue by special permission.

"Naming the State Bird" by Keith Gunderson from *3142 Lyndale Ave., So., Apt. 24—Prose Poems 25 Selections*, by Keith Gunderson, Minnesota Writers' Publishing House, 1975.

"The Man He Killed" from *The Complete Poems of Thomas Hardy*, edited by James Gibson, Macmillan, 1978.

"A Question of Blood" by Ernest Haycox, reprinted by permission of Ernest Haycox, Jr.

"Those Winter Sundays" is reprinted from *Angle of Ascent: New and Selected Poems*, by Robert Hayden, by permission of Liveright Publishing Corporation, copyright © 1975, 1972, 1970, 1966 by Robert Hayden.

"A Noiseless Flash" from *Hiroshima* by John Hersey. Copyright 1946, and renewed 1974 by John Hersey. Reprinted by permission of Alfred A. Knopf, Inc.

"First Offense" by Evan Hunter, copyright © 1955, renewed 1983 by Evan Hunter.

"Charles" from *The Lottery and Other Stories* by Shirley Jackson, copyright 1948, 1949 by Shirley Jackson, copyright renewed © 1976, 1977 by Laurence Hyman, Barry Hyman, Mrs. Sarah Webster, and Mrs. Joanne Schnurer, reprinted by permission of Farrar, Straus and Giroux, Inc.

"The Death of the Ball Turret Gunner" from *The Complete Poems* by Randall Jarrell, copyright © 1945, 1951, 1955 by Randall Jarrell, copyright © 1969 by Mrs. Randall Jarrell, reprinted by permission of Farrar, Straus and Giroux, Inc.

"Loneliness" by Brooks Jenkins from *Scholastic Magazine*, copyright 1935, reprinted by permission of Scholastic, Inc.

"As Best She Could" by Donald Jones, reprinted from *Medical Aid and Other Poems* by permission of author, copyright © 1967 by Donald Jones.

"Warning" copyright © Jenny Joseph, from *Rose in the Afternoon*, Dent, London, 1974, reprinted by permission of John Johnson Ltd., London.

"Counterparts" from *Dubliners* by James Joyce, copyright 1916 by B. W. Huebsch, Inc., definitive text copyright © 1967 by the Estate of James Joyce. All rights reserved. Reprinted by permission of Viking Penguin, a division of Penguin Books USA, Inc.

Commonwealth countries, including Canada, and the other countries of the Copyright Union, is subject to a royalty. All rights, including professional, amateur, motion picture, recitation, public reading, radio, television and cablevision broadcasting, and the rights of translation into foreign languages, are strictly reserved. Amateurs may produce this play upon payment of a royalty of fifteen dollars ($15) for the first performance and ten dollars ($10) for each succeeding performance, payable one week before the play is to be given, to Samuel French, Inc., at 45 West 25th Street, New York, NY 10010, or at 7623 Sunset Blvd., Hollywood, CA 90046, or if in Canada, to Samuel French (Canada) Ltd., at 80 Richmond St. E., Toronto M5C 1P1.

"The Red Wheelbarrow" by William Carlos Williams, from *Collected Poems, Volume I: 1909–1939*, copyright 1938 by New Directions Publishing Corporation.

"A Blessing" by James Wright, copyright © 1971 by James Wright, reprinted from *Collected Poems* by permission of Wesleyan University Press.

"Birds" from *Collected Poems 1942–70* by Judith Wright, copyright © 1971 by Judith Wright, reprinted by permission of Angus & Robertson Publishers.

Excerpt from *Black Boy* by Richard Wright, copyright 1937, 1942, 1944, 1945 by Richard Wright, reprinted by permission of Harper & Row, Publishers, Inc.

"Sea Lullaby" by Elinor Wylie, copyright 1921 by Alfred A. Knopf, Inc. and renewed 1949 by W. R. Benet. Reprinted from *Collected Poems of Elinor Wylie*, by permission of the publisher.

We give special thanks to two of our very helpful editors, Solveig Robinson and Sue Schumer, for their able assistance in resolving, always with equanimity, the multitude of petty problems that beset a work of this kind.

Contents

Keeping a Reading Journal   x

UNIT ONE: **People and Problems**   1

Section A. **Choices and Decisions**   3

The Road Not Taken	*Robert Frost*	4
Report on the Barnhouse Effect	*Kurt Vonnegut, Jr.*	6
Birds in Their Nest Agree	*Sally Benson*	14
Birds	*Judith Wright*	18
A Sudden Trip Home in the Spring	*Alice Walker*	20

Section B. **Community and Culture**   29

As Best She Could	*Don Jones*	30
Loneliness	*Brooks Jenkins*	32
Shooting an Elephant	*George Orwell*	34
The Long Christmas Dinner	*Thornton Wilder*	39
Chee's Daughter	*Juanita Platero and Siyowin Miller*	49

Section C. **Freedom and Justice**   59

The Man with the Hoe	*Edwin Markham*	60
The Time Factor	*Gloria Steinem*	64
The Perfidy of Maatland	*Alan Paton*	67
Equal in Paris	*James Baldwin*	73

UNIT TWO: **Passages**   83

Section A. **Discoveries**   85

Incident	*Countee Cullen*	86
Charles	*Shirley Jackson*	88
Sucker	*Carson McCullers*	92
Fifteen	*William Stafford*	98
On First Looking into Chapman's Homer	*John Keats*	100
The Red Wheelbarrow	*William Carlos Williams*	102

Section B. **Remembrances**   105

    The Centaur   *May Swenson*   106
    Naming the State Bird   *Keith Gunderson*   109
    Black Boy   *Richard Wright*   111
    My Last Duchess   *Robert Browning*   115
    Roommates   *Max Apple*   118

Section C. **Youth and Age**   123

    old age sticks   *E. E. Cummings*   124
    Those Winter Sundays   *Robert Hayden*   126
    Flight   *Doris Lessing*   128
    Ulysses   *Alfred Tennyson*   132
    Warning   *Jenny Joseph*   135
    Do not go gentle into that good
        night   *Dylan Thomas*   137

UNIT THREE: **Visionaries and Dreamers**   139

Section A. **Utopias and Dystopias**   141

    The Big Rock Candy Mountains   *Anonymous*   142
    Where I Lived, and What I
        Lived For   *Henry David Thoreau*   145
    The Unknown Citizen   *W. H. Auden*   148
    Caliban in the Coal Mines   *Louis Untermeyer*   150

Section B. **Other Worlds**   153

    A Room Full of Leaves   *Joan Aiken*   154
    Sand Hill Road   *Morton Grosser*   162
    The Subliminal Man   *J. G. Ballard*   164
    Museums   *Louis MacNeice*   174

Section C. **The Mysterious**   177

    Dr. Heidegger's Experiment   *Nathaniel Hawthorne*   178
    The Red-headed League   *Arthur Conan Doyle*   184
    Eleven Blue Men   *Berton Roueché*   197

UNIT FOUR: **Challenges**   195

Section A. **Creatures Great and Small**   205

    Thinking like a Mountain   *Aldo Leopold*   206
    A Blessing   *James Wright*   209
    The Jersey Heifer   *Peggy Harding Love*   211
    Grizzly   *John McPhee*   218

Section B. **On Native Grounds**   223

    How to Ride a Water Buffalo   *Pira Sudham*   224
    A Question of Blood   *Ernest Haycox*   228
    Girl's-Eye View of Relatives   *Phyllis McGinley*   232
    Counterparts   *James Joyce*   234
    First Offense   *Evan Hunter*   240

Section C. **Hostilities**   249

    The Sniper   *Liam O'Flaherty*   250
    The Man He Killed   *Thomas Hardy*   254
    War   *Luigi Pirandello*   256
    Dulce et Decorum Est   *Wilfred Owen*   259
    A Noiseless Flash   *John Hersey*   262
    The Death of the Ball Turret Gunner   *Randall Jarrell*   270
    Sea Lullaby   *Elinor Wylie*   272
    I Will Fight No More Forever   *Chief Joseph*   274

Glossary of Key Literary Terms   275

Keeping a Reading Journal

Everyone who keeps a journal does so for the same reason—to preserve something, to hold on to a memory or an idea and prevent its getting lost. However, the things people think worth preserving in a journal are bewildering in their variety. You'll find descriptions of trips, expense records, poems, lists, stories, reminders, drafts of letters, philosophical speculations—anything and everything.

Now we suggest that you keep a special kind of journal, a reading journal. A reading journal is a place to record your feelings, thoughts, associations, and insights into the worlds and the ideas of the writers whose works are included in this book. Writers write to share their visions. Readers read to expand their experience. Keeping a reading journal is a way to preserve your involvement with literature.

Most importantly, the reading journal is your journal. You write about the way you understand and experience the poems, stories, and essays that you read. Forget about trying to come up with the "right answer" or guessing what your teacher has in mind. Instead, this journal should be a reflection of you. Your responses may sometimes differ from those of others, and even from those of your teacher. That's fine. All it means is that you have your own point of view. Perhaps you want to find out why others responded differently, and perhaps you want to share some of your writing with them. That's up to you. But your journal should be a place where you can work through your ideas without fear of having the "wrong" answer.

What is more, you don't have to work everything out in a poem or a play before you write down a response. You can use your journal as a place to discover what you think. Writing is a good way to capture those ideas that are flitting around in your head, express them, and better understand them. If it turns out that you were wrong about something, you can always change your mind.

Your journal is also a place to experiment. Play with the ideas in the literature that you read. For example, imagine yourself as the author and think about how you might change an ending. Imagine yourself as a character and think about how you might react to an event. Create your own literature in response to the literature that you read.

Remember, your journal is for capturing ideas. Don't stop to worry about spelling and punctuation. When you go public with some writing from your journal, then you can take the time to make sure everything is written clearly and correctly.

From time to time, your teacher may wish to review your journal to learn more about you and your ideas. However, there may be entries you consider too personal to share with others. For this reason, a loose-leaf notebook is recommended as a journal. That way you can remove any material of a purely personal nature. Similarly, in reading the journals of others, you should always respect their right to privacy.

Literature by Doing provides at least one idea for a journal entry for every selection in the book. These ideas may in turn stimulate still other ideas for you to write about. Your journal will become not only a record of interesting experiences but a rich source of writing ideas on which to draw in the future.

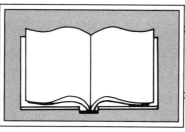
People and Problems

Section A
Choices and
Decisions

Section B
Community and
Culture

Section C
Freedom and
Justice

Choices and Decisions

*Literature provides a means by which
you may deepen your understanding of
people—their needs, their feelings, their problems,
and their solutions—
and in the process learn more
about yourself. The stories and poems
in this section introduce
you to people making choices. In some
cases you are able to see the
consequences of those choices and
in others you can only guess—
along with those involved—about what
the outcome might be.*

The Road Not Taken

Robert Frost

In this poem, the speaker must make a decision that he finds difficult. The choice he makes, he believes, will have far-reaching effects on his life.

Two roads diverged in a yellow wood,
And sorry I could not travel both
And be one traveller, long I stood
And looked down one as far as I could
To where it bent in the undergrowth;

Then took the other, as just as fair,
And having perhaps the better claim,
Because it was grassy and wanted wear;
Though as for that the passing there
Had worn them really about the same,

And both that morning equally lay
In leaves no step had trodden black.
Oh, I kept the first for another day!
Yet knowing how way leads on to way,
I doubted if I should ever come back.

I shall be telling this with a sigh.
Somewhere ages and ages hence:
Two roads diverged in a wood, and I—
I took the one less travelled by,
And that has made all the difference.

Discuss

1. Which of the following best describes the speaker's feelings about the choice he makes? What, in the poem, provides the evidence for your response?

      a. The choice is an easy one.

      b. He chooses the easier road.

      c. Both roads seemed equally interesting.

2. Do you think the speaker of the poem will return to try the other road? Why or why not?

3. What factors does the speaker take into consideration when deciding the road he will choose?

Explore

1. The speaker of a poem may be the poet or a character the poet has created, a persona. Describe the speaker of this poem. What personality traits can you infer? What do you suppose his values are?

2. What evidence is there in the poem that the two roads are more than just roads, but serve as a symbol for the idea of choice? How does the speaker lend importance to the choice he is making?

3. How would you describe the tone of this poem? What emotion do you hear in the speaker's voice? Is he excited about his choice? Disappointed? Angry? Resigned?

4. Why do you suppose the poet has chosen not to describe the results of the choice? How would the meaning of the poem be changed if you knew the results of the poet's decision?

For Your Journal

1. Think about a time when two clear choices were presented to you, and you had to decide between them. On what basis did you make your decision? How did you feel about having to make the decision? What were the consequences of your choice? Did you regret it or ever wish you had made the other choice? How do you think things might have turned out differently had you done so?

2. Create a story about the speaker of the poem. What choice is he trying to make in the poem? Which "road" does he choose? What are the consequences "ages and ages hence" of that decision? What does he feel about the choice he made? How has it "made all the difference"?

3. Tell how you make decisions. On what do you base them? How much do others influence you? To what extent do you gather information on which to make a decision? Are some of your decisions more emotional than others? Do you make decisions easily? What is easiest for you to decide? What gives you trouble?

Report on the Barnhouse Effect

Kurt Vonnegut, Jr.

In this story a scientist finds himself in conflict with the government over the ways his powerful discovery can best benefit humankind. The scientist must decide not only what's best for himself but also what he thinks is best for the world. The narrator of the story, a student of the scientist, is drawn into this web of power and placed in the position of having to make a crucial decision.

LET ME BEGIN by saying that I don't know any more about where Professor Arthur Barnhouse is hiding than anyone else does. Save for one short, enigmatic message left in my mailbox on Christmas Eve, I have not heard from him since his disappearance a year and a half ago.

What's more, readers of this article will be disappointed if they expect to learn how *they* can bring about the so-called "Barnhouse Effect." If I were able and willing to give away that secret, I would certainly be something more important than a psychology instructor.

I have been urged to write this report because I did research under the professor's direction and because I was the first to learn of his astonishing discovery. But while I was his student I was never entrusted with knowledge of how the mental forces could be released and directed. He was unwilling to trust anyone with that information.

I would like to point out that the term "Barnhouse Effect" is a creation of the popular press, and was never used by Professor Barnhouse. The name he chose for the phenomenon was *"dynamopsychism,"* or *force of the mind.*

I cannot believe that there is a civilized person yet to be convinced that such a force exists, what with its destructive effects on display in every national capital. I think humanity has always had an inkling that this sort of force does exist. It has been common knowledge that some people are luckier than others with inanimate objects like dice. What Professor Barnhouse did was to show that such "luck" was a measurable force, which in his case could be enormous.

By my calculations, the professor was about fifty-five times more powerful than a Nagasaki-type atomic bomb at the time he went into hiding. He was not bluffing when, on the eve of "Operation Brainstorm," he told General Honus Barker: "Sitting here at the dinner table, I'm pretty sure I can flatten anything on earth—from Joe Louis to the Great Wall of China."

There is an understandable tendency to look upon Professor Barnhouse as a supernatural visitation. The First Church of Barnhouse in Los Angeles has a congregation numbering in the thousands. He is godlike in neither appearance nor intellect. The man who disarms the world is single, shorter than the average American male, stout, and averse to exercise. His I.Q. is 143, which is good but certainly not sensational. He is quite mortal, about to celebrate his fortieth birthday, and in good health. If he is alone now, the isolation won't bother him too much. He was quiet and shy when I knew him, and seemed to find more companionship in books and music than in his associations at the college.

Neither he nor his powers fall outside the sphere of Nature. His dynamopsychic radiations are subject to many known physical laws that apply in the field of radio. Hardly a person has not now heard the snarl of "Barnhouse static" on his home receiver. The radiations are affected by sunspots and variations in the ionosphere.

However, they differ from ordinary broadcast waves in several important ways. Their total energy can be brought to bear on any single point the professor chooses, and that energy is undiminished by distance. As a weapon, then, dynamopsychism has an impressive advantage over bacteria and atomic bombs, beyond the fact that it costs nothing to use: it enables the professor to single out critical individuals and objects instead of slaughtering whole populations in the process of maintaining international equilibrium.

As General Honus Barker told the House Military Affairs Committee: "Until someone finds Barnhouse, there is no defense against the Barnhouse Effect." Efforts to "jam" or block the radiations have failed. Premier Slezak could have saved himself the fantastic expense of his "Barnhouse-proof" shelter. Despite the shelter's twelve-foot-thick lead armor, the premier has been floored twice while in it.

There is talk of screening the population for men potentially as powerful dynamopsychically as the professor. Senator Warren Foust demanded funds for this purpose last month, with the passionate declaration: "He who rules the Barnhouse Effect rules the world!" Commissar Kropotnik said much the same thing, so another costly armaments race, with a new twist, has begun.

This race at least has its comical aspects. The world's best gamblers are being coddled by governments like so many nuclear physicists. There may be several hundred persons with dynamopsychic talent on earth, myself included. But, without knowledge of the professor's technique, they can never be anything but dice-table despots. With the secret, it would probably take them ten years to become dangerous weapons. It took the professor that long. He who rules the Barnhouse Effect is Barnhouse and will be for some time.

Popularly, the "Age of Barnhouse" is said to have begun a year and a half ago, on the day of Operation Brainstorm. That was when dynamopsychism became significant politically. Actually, the phenomenon was discovered in May, 1942, shortly after the professor turned down a direct commission in the Army and enlisted as an artillery private. Like X-rays and vulcanized rubber, dynamopsychism was discovered by accident.

From time to time Private Barnhouse was invited to take part in games of chance by his barrack mates. He knew nothing about the games, and usually begged off. But one evening, out of social grace, he agreed to shoot craps. It was terrible or wonderful that he played, depending upon whether or not you like the world as it now is.

"Shoot sevens, Pop," someone said.

So "Pop" shot sevens—ten in a row to bankrupt the barracks. He retired to his bunk and, as a mathematical exercise, calculated the odds against his feat on the back of a laundry slip. His chances of doing it, he found, were one in almost ten million! Bewildered, he borrowed a pair of dice from the man in the bunk next to his. He tried to roll sevens again, but got only the usual assortment of numbers. He lay back for a moment, then resumed his toying with the dice. He rolled ten more sevens in a row.

He might have dismissed the phenomenon with a low whistle. But the professor instead mulled over the circumstances surrounding his two lucky streaks. There was one single factor in common: on both occasions, *the same thought train had flashed through his mind just before he threw the dice.* It was that thought train which aligned the professor's brain cells into what has since become the most powerful weapon on earth.

———————■———————

The soldier in the next bunk gave dynamopsychism its first token of respect. In an understatement certain to bring wry smiles to the faces of the world's dejected demagogues, the soldier said, "You're hotter'n a two-dollar pistol, Pop." Professor Barnhouse was all of that. The dice that did his bidding weighed but a few grams, so the forces involved were minute; but the unmistakable fact that there were such forces was earth-shaking.

Professional caution kept him from revealing his discovery immediately. He wanted more facts and a body of theory to go with them. Later, when the atomic bomb was dropped in Hiroshima, it was fear that made him hold his peace. At no time were his experiments, as Premier Slezak called them, "a bourgeois plot to shackle the true democracies of the world." The professor didn't know where they were leading.

In time, he came to recognize another startling feature of dynamopsychism: *its strength increased with use.* Within six months, he was able to govern dice thrown by men the length of a barracks distant. By the time of his discharge in 1945, he could knock bricks loose from chimneys three miles away.

Charges that Professor Barnhouse could have won the last war in a minute, but did not care to do so, are perfectly senseless. When the war ended, he had the range and power of a 37-millimeter cannon, perhaps—certainly no more. His dynamopsychic powers graduated from the small-arms class only after his discharge and return to Wyandotte College.

I enrolled in the Wyandotte Graduate School two years after the professor had rejoined the faculty. By chance, he was assigned as my thesis adviser. I was unhappy about the assignment, for the professor was, in the eyes of both colleagues and students, a somewhat ridiculous figure. He missed classes or had lapses or memory during lectures. When I arrived, in fact, his shortcomings had passed from the ridiculous to the intolerable.

"We're assigning you to Barnhouse as a sort of temporary thing," the dean of social studies told me. He looked apologetic and perplexed. "Brilliant man, Barnhouse, I guess. Difficult to know since his return, perhaps, but his work before the war brought a great deal of credit to our little school."

When I reported to the professor's laboratory for the first time, what I saw was more distressing than the gossip. Every surface in the room was covered with dust; books and apparatus had not been disturbed for months. The professor sat napping at his desk when I entered. The only signs of recent activity were three overflowing ashtrays, a pair of scissors, and a morning paper with several items clipped from its front page.

As he raised his head to look at me, I saw that his eyes were clouded with fatigue. "Hi," he said, "just can't seem to get my sleeping done at night." He lighted a cigarette, his hands trembling slightly. "You the young man I'm supposed to help with a thesis?"

"Yes, sir," I said. In minutes he converted my misgivings to alarm.

"You an overseas veteran?" he asked.

"Yes, sir."

"Not much left over there, is there?" He frowned. "Enjoy the last war?"

"No, sir."

"Look like another war to you?"

"Kind of, sir."

"What can be done about it?"

I shrugged. "Looks pretty hopeless."

He peered at me intently. "Know anything about international law, the U.N., and all that?"

"Only what I pick up from the papers."

"Same here," he sighed. He showed me a fat scrapbook packed with newspaper clippings. "Never used to pay any attention to international politics. Now I study them the way I used to study rats in mazes. Everybody tells me the same thing—'Looks hopeless.' "

"Nothing short of a miracle—" I began.

"Believe in magic?" he asked sharply. The professor fished two dice from his vest pocket. "I will try to roll twos," he said. He rolled twos three times in a row. "One chance in about 47,000 of that happening. There's a miracle for you." He beamed for an instant, then brought the interview to an end, remarking that he had a class which had begun ten minutes ago.

He was not quick to take me into his confidence, and he said no more about his trick with the dice. I assumed they were loaded, and forgot about them. He set me the task of watching male rats cross electrified metal strips to get to food or female rats—an experiment that had been done to everyone's satisfaction in the nineteen-thirties. As though the pointlessness of my work were not bad enough, the professor annoyed me further with irrelevant questions. His favorites were: "Think we should have dropped the atomic bomb on Hiroshima?" and "Think every new piece of scientific information is a good thing for humanity?"

———————■———————

However, I did not feel put upon for long. "Give those poor animals a holiday," he said one morning, after I had been with him only a month. "I wish you'd help me look into a more interesting problem—namely, my sanity."

I returned the rats to their cages.

"What you must do is simple," he said, speaking softly. "Watch the inkwell on my desk. If you see nothing happen to it, say so, and I'll go quietly—relieved, I might add—to the nearest sanitarium."

I nodded uncertainly.

He locked the laboratory door and drew the blinds, so that we were in twilight for a moment. "I'm odd, I know," he said. "It's fear of myself that's made me odd."

"I've found you somewhat eccentric, perhaps, but certainly not—"

"If nothing happens to that inkwell, 'crazy as a bedbug' is the only description of me that will do," he interrupted, turning on the overhead lights. His eyes narrowed. "To give you an idea of how crazy,

I'll tell you what's been running through my mind when I should have been sleeping. I think maybe I can save the world. I think maybe I can make every nation a *have* nation, and do away with war for good. I think maybe I can clear roads through jungles, irrigate deserts, build dams overnight."

"Yes, sir."

"Watch the inkwell!"

Dutifully and fearfully I watched. A high-pitched humming seemed to come from the inkwell; then it began to vibrate alarmingly, and finally to bound about the top of the desk, making two noisy circuits. It stopped, hummed again, glowed red, then popped in splinters with a blue-green flash.

Perhaps my hair stood on end. The professor laughed gently. "Magnets?" I managed to say at last.

"Wish to heaven it were magnets," he murmured. It was then that he told me of dynamopsychism. He knew only that there was such a force; he could not explain it. "It's me and me alone—and it's awful."

"I'd say it was amazing and wonderful!" I cried.

"If all I could do was make inkwells dance, I'd be tickled silly with the whole business." He shrugged disconsolately. "But I'm no toy, my boy. If you like, we can drive around the neighborhood, and I'll show you what I mean." He told me about pulverized boulders, shattered oaks, and abandoned farm buildings demolished within a fifty-mile radius of the campus. "Did every bit of it sitting right here, just thinking—not even thinking hard."

He scratched his head nervously. "I have never dared to concentrate as hard as I can for fear of the damage I might do. I'm to the point where a mere whim is a blockbuster." There was a depressing pause. "Up until a few days ago, I've thought it best to keep my secret for fear of what use it might be put to," he continued. "Now I realize that I haven't any more right to it than a man has a right to own an atomic bomb."

He fumbled through a heap of papers. "This says about all that needs to be said, I think." He handed me a draft of a letter to the Secretary of State.

Dear Sir:

I have discovered a new force which costs nothing to use, and which is probably more important than atomic energy. I should like to see it used most effectively in the cause of peace, and am,

therefore, requesting your advice as to how this might best be done.

Yours truly,
A. Barnhouse.

"I have no idea what will happen next," said the professor.

There followed three months of perpetual nightmare, wherein the nation's political and military great came at all hours to watch the professor's tricks.

We were quartered in an old mansion near Charlottesville, Virginia, to which we had been whisked five days after the letter was mailed. Surrounded by barbed wire and twenty guards, we were labeled "Project Wishing Well," and were classified as Top Secret.

For companionship we had General Honus Barker and the State Department's William K. Cuthrell. For the professor's talk of peace-through-plenty they had indulgent smiles and much discourse on practical measures and realistic thinking. So treated, the professor, who had at first been almost meek, progressed in a matter of weeks toward stubbornness.

He had agreed to reveal the thought train by means of which he aligned his mind into a dynamopsychic transmitter. But, under Cuthrell's and Barker's nagging to do so, he began to hedge. At first he declared that the information could be passed on simply by word of mouth. Later he said that it would have to be written up in a long report. Finally, at dinner one night, just after General Barker had read the secret orders for Operation Brainstorm, the professor announced, "The report may take as long as five years to write." He looked fiercely at the general. "Maybe twenty."

The dismay occasioned by this flat announcement was offset somewhat by the exciting anticipation of Operation Brainstorm. The general was in a holiday mood. "The target ships are on their way to the Caroline Islands at this very moment," he declared ecstatically. "One hundred and twenty of them! At the same time, ten V-2s are being readied for firing in New Mexico, and fifty radio-controlled jet bombers are being equipped for a mock attack on the Aleutians. Just think of it!" Happily he reviewed his orders. "At exactly 1100 hours next Wednesday, I will give you the order to *concentrate*; and you, professor, will think as hard as you can about sinking the target ships, destroying the V-2s before they hit the ground, and knocking down the bombers before they reach the Aleutians! Think you can handle it?"

The professor turned gray and closed his eyes. "As I told you before, my friend, I don't know what I can do." He added bitterly, "As for this Operation Brainstorm, I was never consulted about it, and it strikes me as childish and insanely expensive."

General Barker bridled. "Sir," he said, "your field is psychology, and I wouldn't presume to give you advice in that field. Mine is national defense. I have had thirty years of experience and success, Professor, and I'll ask you not to criticize my judgment."

The professor appealed to Mr. Cuthrell. "Look," he pleaded, "isn't it war and military matters we're all trying to get rid of? Wouldn't it be a whole lot more significant and lots cheaper for me to try moving cloud masses into drought areas, and things like that? I admit I know next to nothing about international politics, but it seems reasonable to suppose that nobody would want to fight wars if there were enough of everything to go around. Mr. Cuthrell, I'd like to try running generators where there isn't any coal or water power, irrigating deserts, and so on. Why, you could figure out what each country needs to make the most of its resources, and I could give it to them without costing American taxpayers a penny."

"Eternal vigilance is the price of freedom," said the general heavily.

Mr. Cuthrell threw the general a look of mild distaste. "Unfortunately, the general is right in his own way," he said. "I wish to heaven the world were ready for ideals like yours, but it simply isn't. We aren't surrounded by brothers, but by enemies. It isn't a lack of food or resources that has us on the brink of war—it's a struggle for power. Who's going to be in charge of the world, our kind of people or theirs?"

The professor nodded in reluctant agreement and arose from the table. "I beg your pardon, gentlemen. You are, after all, better qualified to judge what is best for the country. I'll do whatever you say." He turned to me. "Don't forget to wind the restricted clock and put the confidential cat out," he said gloomily, and ascended the stairs of his bedroom.

———■———

For reasons of national security, Operation Brainstorm was carried on without the knowledge of the American citizenry which was paying the bill. The observers, technicians, and military men involved in the activity knew that a test was under way—a test of what, they had no idea. Only thirty-seven key men, myself included, knew what was afoot.

In Virginia, the day for Operation Brainstorm was unseasonably cool. Inside, a log fire crackled in the fireplace, and the flames were reflected in the polished metal cabinets that lined the living room. All that remained of the room's lovely old furniture was a Victorian love seat, set squarely in the center of the floor, facing three television receivers. One long bench had been brought in for the ten of us privileged to watch. The television screens showed, from left to right, the stretch of desert which was the rocket target, the guinea-pig fleet, and a section of the Aleutian sky through which the radio-controlled bomber formation would roar.

Ninety minutes before H-hour the radios announced that the rockets were ready, that the observation ships had backed away to what was thought to be a safe distance, and that the bombers were on their way. The small Virginia audience lined up on the bench in order of rank, smoked a great deal, and said little. Professor Barnhouse was in his bedroom. General Barker bustled about the house like a woman preparing Thanksgiving dinner for twenty.

At ten minutes before H-hour the general came in, shepherding the professor before him. The professor was comfortably attired in sneakers, gray flannels, a blue sweater, and a white shirt open at the neck. The two of them sat side by side on the love seat. The general was rigid and perspiring; the professor was cheerful. He looked at each of the screens, lighted a cigarette and settled back.

"Bombers sighted!" cried the Aleutian observers.

"Rockets away!" barked the New Mexico radio operator.

All of us looked quickly at the big electric clock over the mantel, while the professor, a half-smile on his face, continued to watch the television sets. In hollow tones, the general counted away the seconds remaining. "Five . . . four . . . three . . . two . . . one . . . *Concentrate!*"

Professor Barnhouse closed his eyes, pursed his lips, and stroked his temples. He held the position for a minute. The television images were scrambled, and the radio signals were drowned in the din of Barnhouse static. The professor sighed, opened his eyes, and smiled confidently.

"Did you give it everything you had?" asked the general dubiously.

"I was wide open," the professor replied.

The television images pulled themselves together, and mingled cries of amazement came over the radios tuned to the observers. The Aleutian sky was streaked with the smoke trails of bombers screaming down in flames. Simultaneously, there appeared high over the rocket target a cluster of white puffs, followed by faint thunder.

General Barker shook his head happily. "By George!" he crowed. "Well, sir, by George, by George, by George!"

"Look!" shouted the admiral seated next to me. "The fleet—it wasn't touched!"

"The guns seem to be drooping," said Mr. Cuthrell.

We left the bench and clustered about the television sets to examine the damage more closely. What Mr. Cuthrell had said was true. The ships' guns curved downward, their muzzles resting on the steel decks. We in Virginia were making such a hullabaloo that it was impossible to hear the radio reports. We were so engrossed, in fact, that we didn't miss the professor until two short snarls of Barnhouse static shocked us into sudden silence. The radios went dead.

We looked around apprehensively. The professor was gone. A harassed guard threw open the front door from the outside to yell that the professor had escaped. He brandished his pistol in the direction of the gates, which hung open, limp and twisted. In the distance, a speeding government station wagon topped a ridge and dropped from sight into the valley beyond. The air was filled with choking smoke, for every vehicle on the grounds was ablaze. Pursuit was impossible.

"What in God's name got into him?" bellowed the general.

Mr. Cuthrell, who had rushed out onto the front porch, now slouched back into the room, reading a penciled note as he came. He thrust the note into my hands. "The good man left this billet-doux under the door knocker. Perhaps our young friend here will be kind enough to read it to you gentlemen, while I take a restful walk through the woods."

"*Gentlemen,*" I read aloud, "*As the first super-weapon with a conscience, I am removing myself from your national defense stockpile. Setting a new precedent in the behavior of ordnance, I have humane reasons for going off. A. Barnhouse.*"

Since that day, of course, the professor has been systematically destroying the world's armaments, until there is now little with which to equip an army other than rocks and sharp sticks. His activities haven't exactly resulted in peace, but have, rather, precipitated a bloodless and entertaining sort of war that might be called the "War of the Tattletales." Every nation is flooded with enemy agents whose sole mission is to locate military equipment, which is promptly wrecked when it is brought to the professor's attention in the press.

Just as every day brings news of more armaments pulverized by dynamopsychism, so has it brought rumors of the professor's whereabouts. During last week alone, three publications carried articles proving variously that he was hiding in an Inca ruin in the Andes, in the sewers of Paris, and in the unexplored lower chambers of Carlsbad Caverns. Knowing the man, I am inclined to regard such hiding places as unnecessarily romantic and uncomfortable. While there are numerous persons eager to kill him, there must be millions who would care for him and hide him. I like to think that he is in the home of such a person.

One thing is certain: at this writing, Professor Barnhouse is not dead. Barnhouse static jammed broadcasts not ten minutes ago. In the eighteen months since his disappearance, he has been reported dead some half-dozen times. Each report has stemmed from the death of an unidentified man resembling the professor, during a period free of the static. The first three reports were followed at once by renewed talk of rearmament and recourse to war. The saber-rattlers have learned how imprudent premature celebrations of the professor's demise can be.

Many a stouthearted patriot has found himself prone in the tangled bunting and timbers of a smashed reviewing stand, seconds after having announced that the arch-tyranny of Barnhouse was at an end. But those who would make war if they could, in every country in the world, wait in sullen silence for what must come—the passing of Professor Barnhouse.

———◼———

To ask how much longer the professor will live is to ask how much longer we must wait for the blessing of another world war. He is of short-lived stock: his mother lived to be fifty-three, his father to be forty-nine; and the life-spans of his grandparents on both sides were of the same order. He might be expected to live, then, for perhaps fifteen years more, if he can remain hidden from his enemies. When one considers the number and vigor of these enemies, however, fifteen years seems an extraordinary length of time, which might better be revised to fifteen days, hours, or minutes.

The professor knows that he cannot live much longer. I say this because of the message left in my mailbox on Christmas Eve. Unsigned, typewritten on a soiled scrap of paper, the note consisted of ten sentences. The first nine of these, each a bewildering tangle of psychological jargon and references to obscure texts, made no sense to me at first reading. The tenth, unlike the rest, was simply constructed and contained no large words—but its irrational content made it the most puzzling and bizarre sentence of all. I nearly threw the note away, thinking it a colleague's warped notion of a practical joke. For some reason, though, I added it to the clutter on top of my desk, which included, among other mementos, the professor's dice.

It took me several weeks to realize that the message really meant something, that the first nine sentences, when unsnarled, could be taken as instructions. The tenth still told me nothing. It was only last night that I discovered how it fitted in with the rest. The sentence appeared in my thoughts last night, while I was toying absently with the professor's dice.

I promised to have this report on its way to the publishers today. In view of what has happened, I am obliged to break that promise, or release the report incomplete. The delay will not be a long one, for one of the few blessings accorded a bachelor like myself is the ability to move quickly from one abode to another, or from one way of life to another. What property I want to take with me can be packed in a few hours. Fortunately, I am not without substantial private means, which may take as long as a week to realize in liquid and anonymous form. When this is done, I shall mail the report.

I have just returned from a visit to my doctor, who tells me my health is excellent. I am young, and, with any luck at all, I shall live to a ripe old age indeed, for my family on both sides is noted for longevity.

Briefly, I propose to vanish.

Sooner or later, Professor Barnhouse must die. But long before then I shall be ready. So, to the saber-rattlers of today—and even, I hope, of tomorrow—I say: Be advised. Barnhouse will die. But not the Barnhouse Effect.

Last night, I tried once more to follow the oblique instructions on the scrap of paper. I took the professor's dice, and then, with the last, nightmarish sentence flitting through my mind, I rolled fifty consecutive sevens.

Good-by.

Discuss

1. How does the narrator's attitude toward Professor Barnhouse change over the course of the story? How do his views of Barnhouse compare with others in the story?

2. According to the narrator, there are advantages of dynamopsychism over bacteria and atomic weapons as a military tool. Which statement best characterizes its superiority?

   a. Dynamopsychism cannot be copied by other nations trying to gain world superiority.

   b. Sites of destruction can be pinpointed with dynamopsychism, to avoid loss of lives and valuable property.

   c. It is easier for governments to control the use of dynamopsychism than bacteria or atomic weapons.

3. How does Professor Barnhouse believe that his power can save the world? Compare his views for the use of dynamopsychism with those of Mr. Cuthrell and General Barker. On what basis do the government officials disagree with Professor Barnhouse?

Explore

1. At the beginning of the story, the narrator is an outsider and a stranger to Professor Barnhouse. But by the end he is Barnhouse's supporter and confidante. How does this shift in the narrator's role affect your sympathies? How might you feel if the story were told from the point of view of a third-person narrator (someone outside the story)? How might your reactions differ if Barnhouse told the story?

2. What does the title of the story mean? For whom is the report written? How is the story like a government or public report? How does it differ? Why do you suppose Vonnegut uses this device?

3. This story is science fiction, based on a "what if" situation rather than on reality. As in much science fiction, there is enough reality in the story to make it involving and believable. Which aspects of the story are believable? Which ones are based on life as you know it? What, in the story, do you think is possible? On what basis do you draw your conclusions?

4. Did the ending of the story surprise you? Why do you think the narrator makes the decision he does? What do you come to know about his personality earlier in the story to make this ending believable?

For Your Journal

1. With whom do your sympathies lie—Professor Barnhouse or General Barker? With whom do you agree on the source of war? Provide evidence for your viewpoint.

2. Imagine yourself with the powers of the Barnhouse Effect. How would you use your power?

3. Assume that you are Professor Barnhouse at the end of the story. Write a letter to the General and the Secretary of State explaining why you took the course you did.

Birds in Their Nest Agree

Sally Benson

In the following story a mother and her grown-up daughter struggle to sort out their relationship but never directly address their real problems. The mother, having devoted her life to her daughter, reflects on that decision. Both she and her daughter question whether the decision was a good one.

Mrs. Armstrong moved the upholstered chair away from the radio and replaced it with the straight, high-backed one that stood in front of the desk. Although it was her intention to turn on the radio so low that she would be able to hear it only by sitting very close to it, she did not immediately do this. Upstairs, Anna was still moving about as she dressed and it would be some minutes before she would be ready to leave. She was running in to New York for the day to have lunch and dinner and then go to the theatre with Peggy Masters and her husband, who were in town for a week. It was not usual for Anna to be away from home a whole day, and Mrs. Armstrong wanted her to have a picture to carry away with her when she walked out of the house into the bright autumn sunshine: a picture of her mother, looking very tiny and forlorn, her shoulders stooped as she leaned forward trying to catch the faint notes of a radio program.

She began to wander aimlessly about the small, overcrowded room, noting with satisfaction that everything was in its place—the magazines in order on the gate-legged table, the plants watered, the tidies freshly pressed and neatly pinned to the plum-colored velvet of the chairs. The radiator was turned on, and with the sun pouring through the two front windows the room was very warm. The furniture was too heavy and gave the impression of having occupied a more spacious place. There was precision in the way the ornaments were arranged, a mathematical accuracy possible only to a woman on whose hands time rested heavily.

Hearing Anna's heavy tread above, she frowned. It did not seem right that Anna should have grown from a pretty child to a large, robust woman of thirty. Practically overnight, it seemed, too. Thinking back to the days when she had been busy creating a home for her, and to the bustle and stir of a hundred small activities, she felt betrayed. She had neglected her own friends for the child, she reasoned. She had picked up the threads of her life after her husband's death and done everything for Anna. And there was nothing to warn her in those full days that one day it would all be over and she would become an elderly lady living in a mediocre suburb with her unmarried daughter. A faint hope lingered that this lull, this deadly lull, was only temporary. It seemed incredible that there was no child to get ready for school, no clock to watch so as to have lunch on the dot, no small clothes to wash. It had never occurred to her while Anna was growing up that a time would come when she herself would have to live with maturity.

She went over and sat in the chair, very still, her face curiously dead, as though for years no inner emotion had quickened it. She was so far away in some dim, confused past that she did not see Anna until she reached the foot of the stairs. At the sight of her, Mrs. Armstrong's mouth sagged a little at the corners and she seemed to become smaller.

Anna was looking well. She was a tall, thickly built woman, and she had about her a certain compactness. Her clothes were not smart, yet she was so neatly put together that she looked almost handsome in them. She had an unfortunate manner of addressing her mother, a teasing inflection in her voice, that had nothing light or humorous about it. "Well, am I all right?" she asked.

Mrs. Armstrong surveyed her critically. "I think your slip shows just a little, on the left."

Anna pulled at the shoulders of her dress and adjusted a strap. "Better?"

"I suppose so," her mother answered, and sighed.

A flicker of uneasiness crossed Anna's face. "I tell you what," she suggested a little hurriedly. "Why don't you put on your hat and coat and walk to the station with me? You can pick up something for your dinner on the way back, something you really like and not something you think I like."

For a moment Mrs. Armstrong did not answer. She looked out of the window into the golden sunshine and then she turned again toward Anna. A dreadful feeling of inertia filled the room. "I don't think I will," she said. "You run along."

In the bright light her hair shone white and soft, curling a little at the nape of her neck. Her hands were small, but they were the hands of a woman who relentlessly spared herself nothing; they showed faint signs of burns and the nails were cut short. Anna noted with a pang that the cuffs of her mother's dress were quite worn.

"I hate to leave you here alone," she said. "If I'd thought, I'd have asked Peggy if I could bring you. She wouldn't have minded. I mean, she probably would have loved it."

Mrs. Armstrong's shoulders straightened slightly. "I can live without Peggy Masters," she answered tartly.

Anna moved her body impatiently. "Oh, Mother! Of course you can! I just thought it might be fun for you. You always liked Peggy."

"I don't like her and I don't dislike her." Mrs. Armstrong said. "I certainly don't *approve* of her."

Anna gave an annoyed little laugh. "Not *approve?*" she asked. "Well, that's the silliest thing I ever heard of! What on earth is there about Peggy not to approve *of?*"

Mrs. Armstrong groped in the jumble of her mind for an answer. "I may be old-fashioned," she said, "but I must say I don't approve of a woman who goes flying about the country and leaves her children with a hired nurse. It may be all very well, yet I assure you I wouldn't have done it."

"You might have been better off if you had," Anna said. The minute the words were out of her mouth, her face flushed and her lips moved as though making an effort to swallow what she had said. But it was too late.

Her mother made herself even smaller in the chair. "Yes, I suppose I've been a fool," she agreed.

"I didn't say you'd been a fool. You know I didn't."

"Not in so many words, maybe."

Anna glanced anxiously toward the clock and then back at her mother. She stood, hesitating and uncomfortable. "It's a lovely day," she said. "You oughtn't to sit here alone. Wouldn't you like to go to a movie or something?"

"No," Mrs. Armstrong answered. "No."

She turned and looked out the window once more. The day was so clear that everything outside seemed to be either in bright sunlight or shadow. Even the people who passed the house had a definite, active look. Street sounds were sharp and pleasing.

Inside the room there was a close stillness which was not disturbed by the faint, feminine rustle of the two women.

"No," Mrs. Armstrong repeated. "I'll be all right. You run along."

Anna stood for a moment watching her mother sitting there in the sunlight, her hair white with faint tinges of yellow, two red marks on her small nose where her pince-nez pinched it, her eyes nondescript with the faded blue of age, her back a delicate curve, and only the faint movement of her feet betraying a constant and deep-seated impatience.

She began to pull on her gloves slowly. "Well, I better run along or I'll be late," she said. The animation that had been in her face when she came down the stairs was there no longer and her walk was heavier. She walked toward her mother and, stooping, kissed her lightly.

"Good-bye," she said.

She closed the front door gently and started down the walk. As she reached the street she turned and looked back at the window. Her mother had not moved and there was something about her immobility and the way the curtains framed her slight figure in its black dress that made her look not quite real but more like a painting of a mother.

Discuss

1. Which statement best sums up Mrs. Armstrong's feelings about the past?

   a. Mrs. Armstrong enjoyed her time as the mother of a young child and wishes that she could relive that time.

   b. Mrs. Armstrong misses devoting her life to someone who needed her.

   c. Mrs. Armstrong hated motherhood and is relieved that her child finally grew up.

2. Why does Anna regret telling her mother that she might have been better off leaving her child with a nurse? What reaction does her mother have to that remark? Why?

3. Which statement best summarizes the meaning of this story? Why do you think so?

   a. Adult children should not live with their parents.

   b. It can be difficult to adapt to changes in roles developed over time.

   c. You can never tell how children are going to turn out on the basis of their childhood behavior.

Explore

1. Think about the home in which the Armstrongs live. How does the appearance of the house reflect the people who live there? How does the description of the setting affect your response to the story?

2. How do you learn about characters' feelings and intentions in this story? What does the narrator tell you about the thoughts and perceptions of the characters? Why is Mrs. Armstrong so unhappy? How do her feelings affect your sympathies in the story? With whom do your sympathies lie and why?

3. Most of the story takes place in the house, with only a brief glimpse of the outside. Compare the description of the outside with the more detailed description of the inside of the house. How do those pictures symbolize the lives of the two women?

4. You learn a great deal about Mrs. Armstrong through the descriptions of her appearance, her mannerisms, and her gestures. Sum up her personality on the basis of these descriptions.

5. What does the last line of the story mean? How does Anna's view of her mother as a painting symbolize the nature of their relationship?

6. What does the title of the story mean?

For Your Journal

1. Have you ever known anyone who is a "martyr," someone who suffers loudly over the sacrifices he or she has made for others but pretends to endure quietly? Describe that person, how he or she expresses martyrdom, and your reactions to that behavior.

2. What future do you see for the relationship between Mrs. Armstrong and her daughter? Will they continue in the same way? What might happen to change the ways they feel or what they do?

3. Imagine your relationship with your parents when you become an adult. How will it change from the way it is now? How will they feel about you as an adult? How will they and you view your childhood?

Birds

Judith Wright

The speaker in the following poem is struggling with conflicts that are disrupting her life. She describes the ease with which birds live and explores the difficulty that people have being what they want to be.

Whatever the bird is, is perfect in the bird.
Weapon kestrel hard as a blade's curve,
thrush round as a mother or a full drop of water,
fruit-green parrot wise in his shrieking swerve—
all are what bird is and do not reach beyond bird.

Whatever the bird does is right for the bird to do—
cruel kestrel dividing in his hunger the sky,
thrush in the trembling dew beginning to sing,
parrot clinging and quarrelling and veiling his queer eye—
all these are as birds are and good for birds to do.

But I am torn and beleaguered by my own people.
The blood that feeds my heart is the blood they gave me,
and my heart is the house where they gather and fight for
     dominion—
all different, all with a wish and a will to save me,
to turn me into the ways of other people.

If I could leave their battleground for the forest of a bird
I could melt the past, the present and the future in one
and find the words that lie behind all these languages.
Then I could fuse my passions into one clear stone
and be simple to myself as the bird is to the bird.

Discuss

1. What pictures does the poem present of the birds in the first two stanzas? Do you think the speaker admires birds? If so, in what ways?

2. In the third stanza, the speaker describes herself. What is going on in the speaker's life? How does the speaker respond?

3. What does "simple to myself" mean to the speaker? What is the value of simplicity and how would she achieve it?

Explore

1. Why do you suppose the poet chose birds to represent simplicity? What kind of simplicity do they represent? How might the poem have differed if the poet had used fish or cats or snails to represent simplicity?

2. In the first stanza the poet uses similes, comparisons using "as" or other indicators, to provide pictures of the birds. What image do you have of each bird on the basis of these comparisons? How do the descriptions of their actions in stanza two reinforce your view?

3. In the third stanza "heart" and "blood" are metaphors, words that take on new meanings by being compared indirectly to other things. What are the new, figurative meanings of "heart" and "blood"? How does their use affect the strength of her message?

4. In the last stanza how is the word "languages" used? Why does the poet contrast "languages" with "words"? How do their meanings differ?

5. In the last stanza, what does the speaker believe she could accomplish in the forest of a bird? Analyze the simile used to compare her goals with the bird's simplicity.

For Your Journal

1. Write about a time when you wished to escape from a conflict or the pressures of others controlling you. What did you do to maintain your sense of self?

2. If you were to choose an animal that represents your own goals and hopes, what would that animal be? What are your hopes? How does that animal symbolize them?

3. Animals are often used to symbolize human traits, as in Aesop's fables. Write about some of the associations you make with animals and human beings.

A Sudden Trip Home in the Spring

Alice Walker

The following story is about a young woman who lives in different worlds and doesn't quite feel a part of either of them. As a southern black in an almost all-white school, Sarah is—though admired and complimented—an oddity. At home, her family finds her goals and values difficult to understand. In the course of the story, she reaches some new insights about who she is.

SARAH WALKED SLOWLY OFF the tennis court, fingering the back of her head, feeling the sturdy dark hair that grew there. She was popular. As she walked along the path toward Talfinger Hall, her friends fell into place around her. They formed a warm, jostling group of six. Sarah, because she was taller than the rest, saw the messenger first. "Miss Davis," he said, standing still until the group came abreast of him, "I've got a telegram for ye." Brian was Irish and always quite respectful. He stood with his cap in his hand until Sarah took the telegram. Then he gave a nod that included all the young ladies before he turned away. He was young and good-looking, though annoyingly servile, and Sarah's friends twittered.

"Well, open it!" someone cried, for Sarah stood staring at the yellow envelope, turning it over and over in her hand.

"Look at her," said one of the girls, "isn't she beautiful! Such eyes, and hair and *skin!*"

Sarah's tall, caplike hair framed a face of soft brown angles, high cheekbones, and large, dark eyes. Her eyes enchanted her friends because they always seemed to know more, and to find more of life amusing, or sad, than Sarah cared to tell.

Her friends often teased Sarah about her beauty; they loved dragging her out of her room so that their boy friends, naïve and worldly young men from Princeton and Yale, could see her. They never guessed she found this distasteful. She was gentle with her friends, and her outrage at their tactlessness did not show. She was most often in-clined to pity them, though embarrassment sometimes drove her to fraudulent expressions. Now she smiled and raised eyes and arms to heaven. She acknowledged their unearned curiosity as a mother endures the prying impatience of a child. Her friends beamed love and envy upon her as she tore open the telegram.

"He's dead," she said.

Her friends reached out for the telegram, their eyes on Sarah.

"It's her father," one of them said softly. "He died yesterday. Oh, Sarah," the girl whimpered, "I'm so sorry!"

"Me too." "So am I." "Is there anything we can do?"

But Sarah had walked away, head high and neck stiff.

"So graceful!" one of her friends said.

"Like a proud gazelle," said another. Then they all trooped to their dormitories to change for supper.

Talfinger Hall was a pleasant dorm. The common room just off the entrance had been made into a small modern-art gallery with some very good original paintings, lithographs, and collages. Pieces were constantly being stolen. Some of the girls could not resist an honest-to-God Chagall, signed (in the plate) by his own hand, though they could have afforded to purchase one from the gallery in town. Sarah Davis' room was next door to the gallery, but her walls were covered with inexpensive Gauguin reproductions, a Reubens ("The Head of a Negro"), a Modigliani, and a Picasso. There was a full wall of her own drawings, all of black women. She found black men impossible to draw or to paint; she could not bear to trace defeat onto blank pages. Her women figures were matronly, massive of arm, with a weary victory showing in their eyes. Surrounded by Sarah's drawings was a red SNCC[1] poster of an old man holding a small girl whose face nestled in his shoulder. Sarah often felt she was the little girl whose face no one could see.

To leave Talfinger even for a few days filled Sarah with fear. Talfinger was her home now; it suited her better than any home she'd ever known. Perhaps she loved it because in winter there was a fragrant fireplace and snow outside her window. When hadn't she dreamed of fireplaces that really warmed, snow that almost pleasantly froze? Georgia seemed far away as she packed; she did not want to leave New York, where, her grandfather had liked to say, "the devil hangs out and catches young gals by the front of their dresses." He had always believed the South the best place to live on earth (never mind that certain people invariably marred the landscape), and swore he expected to die no more than a few miles from where he had been born. There was tenacity even in the gray frame house he lived in, and in scrawny animals on his farm who regularly reproduced. He was the first person Sarah wanted to see when she got home.

There was a knock on the door of the adjoining bathroom, and Sarah's suite mate entered, a loud Bach Concerto just finishing behind her. At first she stuck just her head into the room, but seeing Sarah fully dressed she trudged in and plopped down on the bed. She was a heavy blond girl with large, milk-white legs. Her eyes were small and her neck usually gray with grime.

"My, don't you look gorgeous," she said.

"Ah, Pam," said Sarah, waving her hand in disgust. In Georgia she knew that even to Pam she would be just another ordinarily attractive *colored* girl. In Georgia there were a million girls better looking. Pam wouldn't know that, of course, she'd never been to Georgia; she'd never even seen a black person to speak to—that is, before she met Sarah. One of her first poetic observations about Sarah was that she was "a poppy in a field of winter roses." She had found it weird that Sarah did not own more than one coat.

"Say, listen, Sarah," said Pam, "I heard about your father. I'm sorry. I really am."

"Thanks," said Sarah.

"Is there anything we can do? I thought, well, maybe you'd want my father to get somebody to fly you down. He'd go himself but he's taking mother to Madeira this week. You wouldn't have to worry about trains and things."

Pamela's father was one of the richest men in the world, though no one ever mentioned it. Pam only alluded to it at times of crisis, when a friend might benefit from the use of a private plane, train, or ship; or, if someone wanted to study the characteristics of a totally secluded village, island, or mountain, she might offer one of theirs. Sarah could not comprehend such wealth, and was always annoyed because Pam didn't look more like a billionaire's daughter. A billionaire's daughter, Sarah thought, should really be less horsy and brush her teeth more often.

"Gonna tell me what you're brooding about?" asked Pam.

Sarah stood in front of the radiator, her fingers resting on the window seat. Down below, girls were coming up the hill from supper.

"I'm thinking," she said, "of the child's duty to his parents after they are dead."

"Is that all?"

"Do you know," asked Sarah, "about Richard Wright and his father?"

Pamela frowned. Sarah looked down at her.

"Oh, I forgot," she said with a sigh, "they don't teach Wright here. The poshest school in the U.S. and the girls come out ignorant." She looked at her watch, saw she had twenty minutes before her train. "Really," she said almost inaudibly, "why Tears Eliot, Ezratic Pound, and even Sara Teacake, and no Wright?" She and Pamela thought e. e. cummings very clever with his perceptive spelling of great literary names.

"Is he a poet, then?" asked Pam. She adored poetry, all poetry. Half of America's poetry she had, of course, not read, for the simple reason that she had never heard of it.

"No," said Sarah, "he wasn't a poet." She felt weary. "He was a man who wrote, a man who had trouble with his father." She began to walk about the room, and came to stand below the picture of the old man and the little girl.

"When he was a child," she continued, "his father ran off with another woman, and one day when Richard and his mother went to ask him for money to buy food, he laughingly rejected them. Richard, being very young, thought his father Godlike—big, omnipotent, unpredictable, undependable, and cruel; entirely in control of his universe; just like God. But, many years later, after Wright had become a famous writer, he went down to Mississippi to visit his father. He found, instead of God, just an old, watery-eyed field hand, bent from plowing, his teeth gone, smelling of manure. Richard realized that the most daring thing his 'God' had done was run off with that other woman."

"So?" asked Pam. "What 'duty' did he feel he owed the old man?"

"So," said Sarah, "that's what Wright wondered as he peered into that old, shifty-eyed Mississippi Negro face. What was the duty of the son of a destroyed man? The son of a man whose vision had stopped at the edge of fields that weren't even his. Who was Wright without his father? Was he Wright the great writer? Wright the Communist? Wright the French farmer? Wright whose wife could never accompany him to Mississippi? Was he, in fact, still his father's son? Or was he freed by his father's desertion to be nobody's son, to be his own father? Could he disavow his father and live? And if so, live as what? As whom? And for what purpose?"

"Well," said Pam, swinging her hair over her shoulders and squinting her small eyes, "if his father rejected him I don't see why Wright even bothered to go see him again. From what you've said, Wright earned the freedom to be whoever he wanted to be. To a strong man a father is not essential."

"Maybe not," said Sarah, "but Wright's father was one faulty door in a house of many ancient rooms. Was that one faulty door to shut him off forever from the rest of the house? That was the question. And though he answered this question eloquently in his work, where it really counted, one can only wonder if he was able to answer it satisfactorily—or at all—in his life."

"You're thinking of his father more as a symbol of something, aren't you?" asked Pam.

"I suppose," said Sarah, taking a last look around her room. "I see him as a door that refused to open, a hand that was always closed. A fist."

Pamela walked with her to one of the college limousines, and in a few minutes she was at the station. The train to the city was just arriving.

"Have a nice trip," said the middle-aged driver courteously as she took her suitcase from him. But, for about the thousandth time since she'd seen him, he winked at her.

Once away from her friends, she did not miss them. The school was all they had in common. How could they ever know her if they were not allowed to know Wright? she wondered. She was interesting, "beautiful," only because they had no idea what made her, charming only because they had no idea from where she came. And where they came from, though she glimpsed it—in themselves and in F. Scott Fitzgerald—she was never to enter. She hadn't the inclination or the proper ticket.

II

Her father's body was in Sarah's old room. The bed had been taken down to make room for the flowers and chairs and casket. Sarah looked for a long time into the face, as if to find some answer to her questions written there. It was the same face, a dark, Shakespearean head framed by gray, woolly hair and split almost in half by a short, gray mustache. It was a completely silent face, a shut face. But her father's face also looked fat, stuffed, and ready to burst. He wore a navy-blue suit, white shirt, and black tie. Sarah bent and loosened the tie. Tears started behind her shoulder blades but did not reach her eyes.

"There's a rat here under the casket," she called to her brother, who apparently did not hear her, for he did not come in. She was alone with her father, as she had rarely been when he was alive. When he was alive she had avoided him.

"Where's that girl at?" her father would ask. "Done closed herself up in her room again," he would answer himself.

For Sarah's mother had died in her sleep one night. Just gone to bed tired and never got up. And Sarah had blamed her father.

Stare the rat down, thought Sarah; surely that will help. *Perhaps it doesn't matter whether I misunderstood or never understood.*

"We moved so much, looking for crops, a place to *live*," her father had moaned, accompanied by Sarah's stony silence. "The moving killed her. And now we have a real house, with *four* rooms, and a mailbox on the *porch*, and it's too late. She gone. *She* ain't here to see it." On very bad days her father would not eat at all. At night he did not sleep.

Whatever had made her think she knew what love was or was not?

Here she was, Sarah Davis, immersed in Camusian philosophy, versed in many languages, a poppy, of all things, among winter roses. But before she became a poppy she was a native Georgian sunflower, but still had not spoken the language they both knew. Not to him.

Stare the rat down, she thought, and did. The rascal dropped his bold eyes and slunk away. Sarah felt she had, at least, accomplished something.

Why did she have to see the picture of her mother, the one on the mantel among all the religious doodads, come to life? Her mother had stood stout against the years, clean gray braids shining across the top of her head, her eyes snapping, protective. Talking to her father.

"He called you out your name, we'll leave this place today. Not tomorrow. That be too late. Today!" Her mother was magnificent in her quick decisions.

"But what about your garden, the children, the change of schools?" Her father would be holding, most likely, the wide brim of his hat in nervously twisting fingers.

"He called you out your name, we go!"

And go they would. Who knew exactly where, before they moved? Another soundless place, walls falling down, roofing gone; another face to please without leaving too much of her father's pride at his feet. But to Sarah then, no matter with what alacrity her father moved, foot-dragging alone was visible.

The moving killed her, her father had said, but the moving was also love.

Did it matter now that often he had threatened their lives with the rage of his despair? That once he had spanked the crying baby violently, who later died of something else altogether . . . and that the next day they moved?

"No," said Sarah aloud, "I don't think it does."

"Huh?" It was her brother, tall, wiry, black, deceptively calm. As a child he'd had an irrepressible temper. As a grown man he was tensely smooth, like a river that any day will overflow its bed.

He had chosen a dull gray casket. Sarah wished for red. Was it Dylan Thomas who had said something grand about the dead offering "deep, dark defiance"? It didn't matter; there were more ways to offer defiance than with a red casket.

"I was just thinking," said Sarah, "that with us Mama and Daddy were saying NO with capital letters."

"I don't follow you," said her brother. He had always been the activist in the family. He simply directed his calm rage against any obstacle that might exist, and awaited the consequences with the same serenity he awaited his sister's answer. Not for him the philosophical confusions and poetic observations that hung his sister up.

"That's because you're a radical preacher," said Sarah, smiling up at him. "You deliver your messages in person with your own body." It excited her that her brother had at last imbued their childhood Sunday sermons with the reality of fighting for change. And saddened her that no matter how she looked at it this seemed more important than Medieval Art, Course 201.

III

"Yes, Grandma," Sarah replied. "Cresselton is for girls only, and *No*, Grandma, I am not pregnant."

Her grandmother stood clutching the broad, wooden handle of her black bag, which she held, with elbows bent, in front of her stomach. Her eyes glinted through round, wire-framed glasses. She spat into the grass outside the privy. She had insisted that Sarah accompany her to the toilet while the body was being taken into the church. She had leaned heavily on Sarah's arm, her own arm thin and the flesh like crepe.

"I guess they teach you how to really handle the world," she said. "And who knows, the Lord is everywhere. I would like a whole lot to see a great-grand. You don't specially have to be married, you know. That's why I felt free to ask." She reached into her bag and took out a Three Sixes bottle, which she proceeded to drink from, taking deep, swift swallows with her head thrown back.

"There are very few black boys near Cresselton," Sarah explained, watching the corn liquor leave the bottle in spurts and bubbles. "Besides, I'm really caught up now in my painting and sculpturing . . . " Should she mention how much she admired Giacometti's work? No, she decided. Even if her grandmother had heard of him, and Sarah was positive she had not, she would surely think his statues much too thin. This made Sarah smile and remember how difficult it had been to convince her grandmother that even if Cresselton had not given her a scholarship she would have managed to go there anyway. Why? Because she wanted somebody to teach her to paint and to sculpture, and Cresselton had the best teachers. Her grandmother's notion of a successful granddaughter was a married one, pregnant the first year.

"Well," said her grandmother, placing the bottle with dignity back into her purse and gazing pleadingly into Sarah's face, "I sure would 'preshate a great-grand." Seeing her granddaughter's smile, she heaved a great sigh, and, walking rather haughtily over the stones and grass, made her way to the church steps.

As they walked down the aisle, Sarah's eyes rested on the back of her grandfather's head. He was sitting on the front middle bench in front of the casket, his hair extravagantly long and white and softly kinked. When she sat down beside him, her grandmother sitting next to him on the other side, he turned toward her and gently took her hand in his. Sarah briefly leaned her cheek against his shoulder and felt like a child again.

IV

They had come twenty miles from town, on a dirt road, and the hot spring sun had drawn a steady rich scent from the honeysuckle vines along the way. The church was a bare, weatherbeaten ghost of a building with hollow windows and a sagging door. Arsonists had once burned it to the ground, lighting the dry wood of the walls with the flames from the crosses they carried. The tall, spreading red-oak tree under which Sarah had played as a child still dominated the churchyard, stretching its branches widely from the roof of the church to the other side of the road.

After a short and eminently dignified service, during which Sarah and her grandfather alone did not cry, her father's casket was slid into the waiting hearse and taken the short distance to the cemetery, an overgrown wilderness whose stark white stones appeared to be the small ruins of an ancient civilization. There Sarah watched her grandfather from the corner of her eye. He did not seem to bend under the grief of burying a son. His back was straight, his eyes dry and clear. He was simply and solemnly heroic, a man who kept with pride his family's trust and his own grief. *It is strange,* Sarah thought, *that I never thought to paint him like this, simply as he stands; without anonymous, meaningless people hovering beyond his profile; his face turned proud and brownly against the light.* The defeat that

had frightened her in the faces of black men was the defeat of black forever defined by white. But that defeat was nowhere on her grandfather's face. He stood like a rock, outwardly calm, the grand patriarch of the Davis family. The family alone defined him, and he was not about to let them down.

"One day I will paint you, Grandpa," she said as they turned to go. "Just as you stand here now, with just," she moved closer and touched his face with her hand, "just the right stubborn tenseness of your cheek. Just that look of Yes and No in your eyes."

"You wouldn't want to paint an old man like me," he said, looking deep into her eyes from wherever his mind had been. "If you want to make me, make me up in stone."

The completed grave was plump and red. The wreaths of flowers were arranged all on one side, so that from the road there appeared to be only a large mass of flowers. But already the wind was tugging at the rose petals and the rain was making dabs of faded color all over the green-foam frames. In a week, the displaced honeysuckle vines, the wild roses, the grapevines, the grass, would be back. Nothing would seem to have changed.

V

"What do you mean, come *home?*" Her brother seemed genuinely amused. "We're all proud of you. How many black girls are at that school? Just *you?* Well, just one more besides you, and she's from the North. That's really something!"

"I'm glad you're pleased," said Sarah.

"Pleased! Why, it's what Mama would have wanted, a good education for little Sarah; and what Dad would have wanted too, if he could have wanted anything after Mama died. You were always smart. When you were two and I was five you showed me how to eat ice cream without getting it all over me. First, you said, nip off the bottom of the cone with your teeth, and suck the ice cream down. I never knew *how* you were supposed to eat the stuff once it began to melt."

"I don't know," she said; "sometimes you can want something a whole lot, only to find out later that it wasn't what you *needed* at all."

Sarah shook her head, a frown coming between her eyes. "I sometimes spend *weeks,*" she said, "trying to sketch or paint a face that is unlike every other face around me, except, vaguely, for one. Can I help but wonder if I'm in the right place?"

Her brother smiled. "You mean to tell me you spend *weeks* trying to draw one face, and you still wonder whether you're in the right place? You must be kidding!" He chucked her under the chin and laughed out loud. "You learn how to draw the face," he said, "then you learn how to paint me and how to make Grandpa up in stone. Then you can come home or go live in Paris, France. It'll be the same thing."

It was the unpreacher-like gaiety of his affection that made her cry. She leaned peacefully into her brother's arms. She wondered if Richard Wright had had a brother.

"You are my door to all the rooms," she said; "don't ever close."

And he said, "I won't," as if he understood what she meant.

VI

"When will we see you again, young woman?" he asked later as he drove her to the bus stop.

"I'll sneak up one day and surprise you," she said.

At the bus stop, in front of a tiny service station, Sarah hugged her brother with all her strength. The white station attendant stopped his work to leer at them, his eyes bold and careless.

"Did you ever think," said Sarah, "that we are a very old people in a very young place?"

She watched her brother from a window on the bus; her eyes did not leave his face until the little station was out of sight and the big Greyhound lurched on its way toward Atlanta. She would fly from there to New York.

VII

She took the train to the campus.

"My," said one of her friends, "you look wonderful! Home sure must agree with you!"

"Sarah was home?" someone who didn't know asked. "Oh, *great*, how was it?"

Well, how was it? went an echo in Sarah's head. The noise of the echo almost made her dizzy.

"How was it?" she asked aloud, searching for, and regaining, her balance.

"How was it?" She watched her reflection in a pair of smiling hazel eyes.

"It was fine," she said slowly, returning the smile, thinking of her grandfather. "Just fine."

The girl's smile deepened. Sarah watched her swinging along toward the back tennis courts, hair blowing in the wind.

Stare the rat down, thought Sarah; *and whether it disappears or not, I am a woman in the world. I have buried my father, and shall soon know how to make my grandpa up in stone.*

Discuss

1. Sarah refers to the U.S. author Richard Wright a number of times. Which statement best describes what she feels she has in common with him?

   a. Both Sarah and Richard Wright attended all-white schools and felt like outsiders.

   b. Both Sarah and Richard Wright felt alienated from their fathers.

   c. Both Sarah and Richard Wright felt anger that the white world did not appreciate their art.

2. Which statement best characterizes the attitudes of Sarah's classmates toward her?

   a. Sarah is a curiosity; their polite treatment of her grows out of a feeling of superiority or discomfort in her presence.

   b. Sarah's classmates resent her obvious intellectual superiority; they are outwardly polite to her, but inwardly jealous.

   c. Sarah's classmates see her as an equal and readily allow her into their worlds.

3. Why does Sarah sketch only black women and not black men? What makes her decide that she would like to draw her grandfather?

Explore

1. In this story the author uses irony to show the differences between Sarah's world in Georgia and Sarah's world at college. Read the entry on irony in the Glossary of Key Literary Terms, and describe the contradictions in Sarah's life. What are the ironies in her relationships with her friends? What ironies do you see in her work as an artist? Is Sarah aware of any of these ironies? How do you know?

2. At one point in the story, Sarah asks to come home for good, but her brother discourages her. Why does she want to come home? Why does she decide to return to school?

3. Describe Sarah's relationships with her brother, her grandmother, and her grandfather. What insights do those relationships give you into her character, the kind of person she is?

4. "Stare the rat down" has several meanings in the story. What are they, and how do they contribute to Sarah's level of understanding?

5. What is Richard Wright's significance to Sarah? How does his life contribute to the discoveries that Sarah makes? What does Sarah learn in the course of the story?

For Your Journal

1. Do you think children have a duty to parents after the parents are dead? If so, what is that duty?

2. In this story Sarah struggles in a new situation in order to learn what she wants to know. Have you ever been in a situation in which you felt uncomfortable or different? What was the cause of your discomfort? How did you resolve it?

3. Write a description of Sarah's life ten years after the time of the story as you envision it. What do you think would have become of Sarah? Do you think she would have stayed in school? Would she have succeeded as an artist? Would she have had lasting relationships with her college friends?

Community and Culture

What is a culture? It is the
pattern of beliefs, customs,
social forms, and behavior of people
living in a community. The two poems,
the essay, the play, and the story
in this section show people—
both real and imagined—
whose lives are limited, defined, and
challenged by the cultures and
communities in which they live.
Some of these people find themselves
in alien cultures, cultures where
they are not understood or supported,
cultures they must reject. Some find
that the culture they live in provides
a starting point for them to
establish who they are. Others find
that the culture provides insights
into larger human issues.

As Best She Could

Don Jones

The culture of those in power is sometimes unyielding when faced
by the needs of a person from a different culture. In the following
poem, seeking help from a government agency takes its toll on a
proud but poverty-stricken old woman.

Old widow crazed with hunger, you came in crippled,
your backcountry eyes bright and furtive, your voice
careening between a whimper and wild thin laughter.

I saw you take the edge of the chair and cower
as the social worker cut through your explanations,
your patches of self-respect, with her curt queries.

Terrible your smile when asked about your holdings
in bonds, in bank accounts, in property,
your look when reminded of life insurance lapsed.

She wouldn't believe you lived as best you could
on the meager uncertain amount your daughters sent you
and paid no rent to an old and kindly landlord.

She took your naked terror of death for greed
and probable fraud, denied you, sent you off
for written proofs from daughters out of state.

Their misspelt notes came in some three weeks later,
your card for medical care went out, but soon
came back from Public Health a cancellation.

No blame attached, the regulations followed,
your death quite likely in any case, but still
I see you rise and quiver away, your stiff heart
pounding with baffled rage, with stifled pride.

Discuss

1. Which word do you think best describes the attitude of the social worker toward the old woman? Why do you think so?

   a. Suspicious

   b. Sympathetic

   c. Pitying

2. Why does the old woman come to the social service agency? What tells you that this is not a typical act for her?

3. You know that the woman in this poem is old. What else can you tell about her social class, education, and background?

Explore

1. In this poem the poet chooses to personalize the scene by having an observer, the "I" of the poem, address the observed, the old woman. What effect does the poet achieve by referring to the old woman as "you"? How would the poem be different if the poet described her in the third person, as "she"?

2. What is the poet's attitude toward the old woman and the events that occur in the poem? How do you know?

3. Describe the emotions that the old woman is feeling. What phrases and images does the poet use to show this woman's feelings?

4. What is the poet's attitude toward the social service agency and the social worker? Is the poem neutral, critical, or sympathetic toward them? Why do you think so?

For Your Journal

1. What is your reaction to the events in this poem? How do the events and people in the poem coincide with your view of welfare and welfare recipients? To what extent do your past experiences and values affect your response to the poem? In what ways does the poet's attitude create a response in you?

2. Write the dialogue that you think occurred between the old woman and the social worker. Try to capture the language of the characters that the poet has created with this poem.

3. Write a letter to the social service agency represented in this poem, telling its people your reaction to the way they handled this case.

Loneliness

Brooks Jenkins

In this poem the narrator recalls a brief visit with an old man and reaching a new understanding.

I was about to go, and said so;
And I had almost started for the door.
But he was all alone in the sugar-house,
And more lonely than he'd ever been before.
We'd talked for half an hour, almost,
About the price of sugar, and how I like my school,
And he had made me drink some syrup hot,
Telling me it was better that way than when cool.

And I agreed, and thanked him for it,
And said good-bye, and was about to go.
Want to see where I was born?
He asked me quickly. How to say no?

The sugar-house looked over miles of valley.
He pointed with a sticky finger to a patch of snow
Where he was born. The house, he said, was gone.
I can understand these people better, now I know.

Discuss

1. Which statement best characterizes the relationship between the two people in the poem? How do you know?

   a. They know very little about each other and have shared rather superficial information.

   b. The younger person visits the older person frequently to keep him company in his lonely job.

   c. They have grown up in the same community and understand each other's experiences very well.

2. What is the setting of this poem? Of what significance is it to the meaning of the poem?

Explore

1. What do you know about the speaker of the poem? How do you learn what you know?

2. What is the attitude of the speaker of the poem toward the man he visits? Does the speaker like him? Respect him? Feel sorry for him? Tolerate him? What makes you think so?

3. Why do you think the speaker wants to say no when the man asks, "Do you want to see where I was born?" How does the speaker's attitude change after seeing the place?

4. What does the speaker "know" in the last line of the poem? What does the title of the poem have to do with what the speaker learns in the course of the poem?

5. Notice the form of the poem. What is the poem's rhyme scheme (pattern of rhyme for the last syllable of each line)? What do you notice about the grouping of the stanzas? Why do you suppose the poet uses this form and rhyme scheme?

For Your Journal

1. Have you ever formed a relationship with a person whose life and past differed from your own? Describe that experience and what you learned from it.

2. Have you ever entertained an older person who felt alone? If so, how did that person express loneliness? What was your response?

Shooting an Elephant

George Orwell

George Orwell describes his experience of working as a British police officer in Burma, now the Union of Myanmar. The resentment that the Burmese feel toward the British government is expressed in their attitude toward all British officials, and Orwell finds he must respond to their resentment in an unusual act.

IN MOULMEIN, in Lower Burma, I was hated by large numbers of people—the only time in my life that I have been important enough for this to happen to me. I was sub-divisional police officer of the town, and in an aimless, petty kind of way anti-European feeling was very bitter. No one had the guts to raise a riot, but if a European woman went through the bazaars alone somebody would probably spit betel juice[1] over her dress. As a police officer I was an obvious target and was baited whenever it seemed safe to do so. When a nimble Burman tripped me up on the football field and the referee (another Burman) looked the other way, the crowd yelled with hideous laughter. This happened more than once. In the end the sneering yellow faces of young men that met me everywhere, the insults hooted after me when I was at a safe distance, got badly on my nerves. The young Buddhist priests were the worst of all. There were several thousand of them in the town and none of them seemed to have anything to do except stand on street corners and jeer at Europeans.

All this was perplexing and upsetting. For at that time I had already made up my mind that imperialism was an evil thing and the sooner I chucked up my job and got out of it the better. Theoretically—and secretly, of course—I was all for the Burmese and all against their oppressors, the British. As for the job I was doing, I hated it more bitterly than I can perhaps make clear. In a job like that you see the dirty work of Empire at close quarters. The wretched prisoners huddling in the stinking cages of the lock-ups, the grey, cowed faces of the long-term convicts, the scarred buttocks of the men who had been flogged with bamboos—all these oppressed me with an intolerable sense of guilt. But I could get nothing into perspective. I was young and ill-educated and I had had to think out my problems in the utter silence that is imposed on every Englishman in the East. I did not even know that the British Empire is dying,[2] still less did I know that it is a great deal better than the younger empires that are going to supplant it. All I knew was that I was stuck between my hatred of the empire I served and my rage against the evil-spirited little beasts who tried to make my job impossible. With one part of my mind I thought of the British Raj as an unbreakable tyranny, as something clamped down, in *saecula saeculorum*,[3] upon the will of prostrate peoples; with another part I thought that the greatest joy in the world would be to drive a bayonet into a Buddhist priest's guts. Feelings like these are the normal by-products of imperialism; ask any Anglo-Indian official, if you can catch him off duty.

One day something happened which in a roundabout way was enlightening. It was a tiny incident in itself, but it gave me a better glimpse than I had had before of the real nature of imperialism—the real motives for which despotic govern-

[1]**betel juice:** saliva turned brownish-red from areca nuts and betel palm leaves, chewed as a stimulant in parts of Southeast Asia.

[2]**British Empire is dying:** Burma became independent on January 4, 1948.

[3]**saecula saeculorum:** *Lat.*, generations of generations or ages of ages.

ments act. Early one morning the sub-inspector at a police station the other end of the town rang me up on the 'phone and said that an elephant was ravaging the bazaar. Would I please come and do something about it? I did not know what I could do, but I wanted to see what was happening and I got on to a pony and started out. I took my rifle, an old .44 Winchester and much too small to kill an elephant, but I thought the noise might be useful *in terrorem*.[4] Various Burmans stopped me on the way and told me about the elephant's doings. It was not, of course, a wild elephant, but a tame one which had gone "must."[5] It had been chained up, as tame elephants always are when their attack of "must" is due, but on the previous night it had broken its chain and escaped. Its mahout,[6] the only person who could manage it when it was in that state, had set out in pursuit, but had taken the wrong direction and was now twelve hours' journey away, and in the morning the elephant had suddenly reappeared in the town. The Burmese population had no weapons and were quite helpless against it. It had already destroyed somebody's bamboo hut, killed a cow and raided some fruit-stalls and devoured the stock; also it had met the municipal rubbish van and, when the driver jumped out and took to his heels, had turned the van over and inflicted violences upon it.

The Burmese sub-inspector and some Indian constables were waiting for me in the quarter where the elephant had been seen. It was a very poor quarter, a labyrinth of squalid bamboo huts, thatched with palmleaf, winding all over a steep hillside. I remember that it was a cloudy, stuffy morning at the beginning of the rains. We began questioning the people as to where the elephant had gone and, as usual, failed to get any definite information. That is invariably the case in the East; a story always sounds clear enough at a distance, but the nearer you get to the scene of events the vaguer it becomes. Some of the people said that the elephant had gone in one direction, some said that he had gone in another, some professed not even to have heard of any elephant. I had almost made up my mind that the whole story was a pack of lies, when we heard yells a little distance away. There was a loud, scandalized cry of "Go away, child! Go away this instant!" and an old

woman with a switch in her hand came round the corner of a hut, violently shooing away a crowd of naked children. Some more women followed, clicking their tongues and exclaiming; evidently there was something that the children ought not to have seen. I rounded the hut and saw a man's dead body sprawling in the mud. He was an Indian, a black Dravidian coolie,[7] almost naked, and he could not have been dead many minutes. The people said that the elephant had come suddenly upon him round the corner of the hut, caught him with its trunk, put its foot on his back and ground him into the earth. This was the rainy season and the ground was soft, and his face had scored a trench a foot deep and a couple of yards long. He was lying on his belly with arms crucified and head sharply twisted to one side. His face was coated with mud, the eyes wide open, the teeth bared and grinning with an expression of unendurable agony. (Never tell me, by the way, that the dead look peaceful. Most of the corpses I have seen looked devilish.) The friction of the great beast's foot had stripped the skin from his back as neatly as one skins a rabbit. As soon as I saw the dead man I sent an orderly to a friend's house nearby to borrow an elephant rifle. I had already sent back the pony, not wanting it to go mad with fright and throw me if it smelt the elephant.

The orderly came back in a few minutes with a rifle and five cartridges, and meanwhile some Burmans had arrived and told us that the elephant was in the paddy fields[8] below, only a few hundred yards away. As I started forward practically the whole population of the quarter flocked out of the houses and followed me. They had seen the rifle and were all shouting excitedly that I was going to shoot the elephant. They had not shown much interest in the elephant when he was merely ravaging their homes, but it was different now that he was going to be shot. It was a bit of fun to them, as it would be to an English crowd; besides they wanted the meat. It made me vaguely uneasy. I had no intention of shooting the elephant—I had merely sent for the rifle to defend myself if necessary—and it is always unnerving to have a crowd following you. I arched down the hill, looking and feeling a fool, with the rifle over my shoulder and an ever-growing army of people jostling at my heels. At the bottom, when you got away from the huts, there was a metalled road and beyond that a

---

[4]*in terrorem*: *Lat.*, in fear.
[5]**"must"**: pun on *musth*, a state of violent behavior that occurs naturally and periodically in male elephants.
[6]**mahout**: elephant keeper.

[7]**coolie**: unskilled laborer.
[8]**paddy fields**: unharvested rice plots.

miry waste of paddy fields a thousand yards across, not yet ploughed but soggy from the first rains and dotted with coarse grass. The elephant was standing eight yards from the road, his left side towards us. He took not the slightest notice of the crowd's approach. He was tearing up bunches of grass, beating them against his knees to clean them and stuffing them into his mouth.

I had halted on the road. As soon as I saw the elephant I knew with perfect certainty that I ought not to shoot him. It is a serious matter to shoot a working elephant—it is comparable to destroying a huge and costly piece of machinery—and obviously one ought not to do it if it can possibly be avoided. And at that distance, peacefully eating, the elephant looked no more dangerous than a cow. I thought then and I think now that his attack of "must" was already passing off; in which case he would merely wander harmlessly about until the mahout came back and caught him. Moreover, I did not in the least want to shoot him. I decided that I would watch him for a little while to make sure that he did not turn savage again, and then go home.

But at that moment I glanced round at the crowd that had followed me. It was an immense crowd, two thousand at the least and growing every minute. It blocked the road for a long distance on either side. I looked at the sea of yellow faces above the garish clothes—faces all happy and excited over this bit of fun, all certain that the elephant was going to be shot. They were watching me as they would watch a conjurer about to perform a trick. They did not like me, but with the magical rifle in my hands I was momentarily worth watching. And suddenly I realized that I should have to shoot the elephant after all. The people expected it of me and I had got to do it; I could feel their two thousand wills pressing me forward, irresistibly. And it was at this moment, as I stood there with the rifle in my hands, that I first grasped the hollowness, the futility of the white man's dominion in the East. Here was I, the white man with his gun, standing in front of the unarmed native crowd—seemingly the leading actor of the piece; but in reality I was only an absurd puppet pushed to and fro by the will of those yellow faces behind. I perceived in this moment that when the white man turns tyrant it is his own freedom that he destroys. He becomes a sort of hollow, posing dummy, the conventionalized figure of a sahib.[9] For

[9]**sahib:** master or gentleman; originally a title like "Sir".

it is the condition of his rule that he shall spend his life in trying to impress the "natives," and so in every crisis he has got to do what the "natives" expect of him. He wears a mask, and his face grows to fit it. I had got to shoot the elephant. I had committed myself to doing it when I sent for the rifle. A sahib has got to act like a sahib; he has got to appear resolute, to know his own mind and do definite things. To come all that way, rifle in hand, with two thousand people marching at my heels, and then to trail feebly away, having done nothing—no, that was impossible. The crowd would laugh at me. And my whole life, every white man's life in the East, was one long struggle not to be laughed at.

But I did not want to shoot the elephant. I watched him beating his bunch of grass against his knees, with that preoccupied grandmotherly air that elephants have. It seemed to me that it would be murder to shoot him. At that age I was not squeamish about killing animals, but I had never shot an elephant and never wanted to. (Somehow it always seems worse to kill a *large* animal.) Besides, there was the beast's owner to be considered. Alive, the elephant was worth at least a hundred pounds; dead, he would only be worth the value of his tusks, five pounds, possibly. But I had got to act quickly. I turned to some experienced-looking Burmans who had been there when we arrived, and asked them how the elephant had been behaving. They all said the same thing: he took no notice of you if you left him alone, but he might charge if you went too close to him.

It was perfectly clear to me what I ought to do. I ought to walk up to within, say, twenty-five yards of the elephant and test his behavior. If he charged, I could shoot; if he took no notice of me, it would be safe to leave him until the mahout came back. But also I knew that I was going to do no such thing. I was a poor shot with a rifle and the ground was soft mud into which one would sink at every step. If the elephant charged and I missed him, I should have about as much chance as a toad under a steam-roller. But even then I was not thinking particularly of my own skin, only of the watchful yellow faces behind. For at that moment, with the crowd watching me, I was not afraid in the ordinary sense, as I would have been if I had been alone. A white man mustn't be frightened in front of "natives"; and so, in general, he isn't frightened. The sole thought in my mind was that if anything went wrong those two thousand Burmans would see me pursued, caught, trampled on and reduced to a grinning corpse like that Indian up the hill. And if that happened it was quite probable that some of them would laugh. That would never do. There was only one alternative. I shoved the cartridges into the magazine and lay down on the road to get a better aim.

The crowd grew very still, and a deep, low, happy sigh, as of people who see the theatre curtain go up at last, breathed from innumerable throats. They were going to have their bit of fun after all. The rifle was a beautiful German thing with cross-hair sights. I did not then know that in shooting an elephant one should shoot to cut an imaginary bar running from ear-hole to ear-hole. I ought, therefore, as the elephant was sideways on, to have aimed straight at his ear-hole; actually I aimed several inches in front of this, thinking the brain would be further forward.

When I pulled the trigger I did not hear the bang or feel the kick—one never does when a shot goes home—but I heard the devilish roar of glee that went up from the crowd. In that instant, in too short a time, one would have thought, even for the bullet to get there, a mysterious, terrible change had come over the elephant. He neither stirred nor fell, but every line of his body had altered. He looked suddenly stricken, shrunken, immensely old, as though the frightful impact of the bullet had paralysed him without knocking him down. At last, after what seemed a long time—it might have been five seconds, I dare say—he sagged flabbily to his knees. His mouth slobbered. An enormous senility seemed to have settled upon him. One could have imagined him thousands of years old. I fired again into the same spot. At the second shot he did not collapse but climbed with desperate slowness to his feet and stood weakly upright, with legs sagging and head drooping. I fired a third time. That was the shot that did for him. You could see the agony of it jolt his whole body and knock the last remnant of strength from his legs. But in falling he seemed for a moment to rise, for as his hind legs collapsed beneath him he seemed to tower upward like a huge rock toppling, his trunk reaching skywards like a tree. He trumpeted, for the first and only time. And then down he came, his belly towards me, with a crash that seemed to shake the ground even where I lay.

I got up. The Burmans were already racing past me across the mud. It was obvious that the elephant would never rise again, but he was not dead. He was breathing very rhythmically with long rattling gasps, his great mound of a side painfully rising and falling. His mouth was wide open—I could see far down into caverns of pale pink throat. I waited a long time for him to die, but his breathing did not weaken. Finally I fired my two remaining shots into the spot where I thought his heart must be. The thick blood welled out of him like red velvet, but still he did not die. His body did not even jerk when the shots hit him, the tortured breathing continued without a pause. He was dying, very slowly and in great agony, but in some world remote from me where not even a bullet could damage him further. I felt that I had got to put an end to that dreadful noise. It seemed dreadful to see the great beast lying there, powerless to move and yet powerless to die, and not even to be able to finish him. I sent back for my small rifle and poured shot after shot into his heart and down his throat. They seemed to make no impression. The tortured gasps continued as steadily as the ticking of a clock.

In the end I could not stand it any longer and went away. I heard later that it took him half an hour to die. Burmans were bringing dahs and baskets even before I left, and I was told they had stripped his body almost to the bones by the afternoon.

Afterwards, of course, there were endless discussions about the shooting of the elephant. The owner was furious, but he was only an Indian and could do nothing. Besides, legally I had done the right thing, for a mad elephant has to be killed, like a mad dog, if its owner fails to control it. Among the Europeans opinion was divided. The older men said I was right, the younger men said it was a damn shame to shoot an elephant for killing a coolie, because an elephant was worth more than any damn Coringhee coolie. And afterwards I was very glad that the coolie had been killed; it put me legally in the right and it gave me a sufficient pretext for shooting the elephant. I often wondered whether any of the others grasped that I had done it solely to avoid looking a fool.

Discuss

1. Which statement best sums up Orwell's attitude toward British rule in Burma?

    a. As a police officer, Orwell felt loyal to Britain and its objectives.

    b. Orwell felt that the Burmese were morally superior to the British and ought to be free to determine their own destiny.

    c. Orwell opposed British imperialism, despite his low regard for the Burmese.

2. Describe the treatment of Orwell by the Burmese people. What is the source of their hostility?

3. What does Orwell take into consideration when deciding whether to kill the elephant? On what basis, finally, does he make his decision? What are his reservations?

4. Which statement best reflects Orwell's reasons for telling this story?

    a. He wants to show the effects on someone who is put in the position of ruling others.

    b. He wants to show how he became opposed to killing animals.

    c. He wants to show how Europeans were able to gain the admiration of the Burmese.

Explore

1. Orwell mentions his fear of being laughed at several times in this essay. What larger threat is represented by being laughed at? Under what circumstances might a person be ridiculed by the natives?

2. Why are the Burmese so involved in the pursuit of the elephant? What do you suppose is the source of their pleasure and interest?

3. Orwell goes into detail about the death of the elephant. Why? What function does this scene serve in the account?

4. Describe Orwell's character and personality as revealed in this essay. What is important to him? What are his social and political values? How would you characterize his sense of self? Do you think he feels proud of himself? Why or why not?

For Your Journal

1. Describe some alternatives that Orwell might have had. Which ones do you think would have been preferable to the decision he made? Why? What do you imagine you would have done if you had been in Orwell's place?

2. Have you ever been confronted by a situation in which none of the choices you had was a good one? How did you decide what to do? What were the results of your choice?

3. Pretend you are Orwell just after the events in the essay. Write a letter to your superiors justifying the action you took.

4. Write a description of Orwell's action from the point of view of one of the Burmese observers.

The Long Christmas Dinner
Thornton Wilder

A Christmas dinner provides the backdrop for showing a family and its traditions over a ninety-year period. Family members adopt, adapt, and reject one another's cultures.

The dining-room of the Bayard home. Close to the footlights a long dining table is handsomely spread for Christmas dinner. The carver's place with a great turkey before it is at the spectator's right.

A door, left back, leads into the hall.

At the extreme left, by the proscenium pillar, is a strange portal trimmed with garlands of fruits and flowers. Directly opposite is another edged and hung with black velvet. The portals denote birth and death.

Ninety years are to be traversed in this play which represents in accelerated motion ninety Christmas dinners in the Bayard household. The actors are dressed in inconspicuous clothes and must indicate their gradual increase in years through their acting. Most of them carry wigs of white hair which they adjust upon their heads at the indicated moment, simply and without comment. The ladies may have shawls concealed beneath the table that they gradually draw up about their shoulders as they grow older.

Throughout the play the characters continue eating imaginary food with imaginary knives and forks.

There is no curtain. The audience arriving at the theatre sees the stage set and the table laid, though still in partial darkness. Gradually the lights in the auditorium become dim and the stage brightens until sparkling winter sunlight streams through the dining room windows.

Enter LUCIA. *She inspects the table, touching here a knife and there a fork. She talks to a servant girl who is invisible to us.*

LUCIA. I reckon we're ready now, Gertrude. We won't ring the chimes today. I'll just call them myself.

She goes into the hall and calls:
Roderick. Mother Bayard. We're all ready. Come to dinner.

Enter RODERICK *pushing* MOTHER BAYARD *in a wheel chair.*

MOTHER BAYARD. . . . and a new horse too, Roderick. I used to think that only the wicked owned two horses. A new horse and a new house and a new wife!

RODERICK. Well, Mother, how do you like it? Our first Christmas dinner in the new house, hey?

MOTHER BAYARD. Tz-Tz-Tz! I don't know what your dear father would say!

LUCIA. Here, Mother Bayard, you sit between us.
RODERICK *says grace.*

MOTHER BAYARD. My dear Lucia, I can remember when there were still Indians on this very ground, and I wasn't a young girl either. I can remember when we had to cross the Mississippi on a new-made raft. I can remember when St. Louis and Kansas City were full of Indians.

LUCIA. (*tying a napkin around* MOTHER BAYARD'S *neck*). Imagine that! There!—What a wonderful day for our first Christmas dinner: a beautiful sunny morning, snow, a splendid sermon. Dr. McCarthy preaches a splendid sermon. I cried and cried.

RODERICK. (*extending an imaginary carvingfork*). Come now, what'll you have, Mother? A little sliver of white?

LUCIA. Every least twig is wrapped around with ice. You almost never see that. Can I cut it up for you, dear? (*over her shoulder*) Gertrude, I forgot the jelly. You know,—on the top shelf.—Mother Bayard, I found your mother's gravy-boat while we were moving. What was her name, dear? What were all your names? You were . . . a . . . Genevieve Wainright. Now your mother—

MOTHER BAYARD.   Yes, you must write it down somewhere. I was Genevieve Wainright. My mother was Faith Morrison. She was the daughter of a farmer in New Hampshire who was something of a blacksmith too. And she married young John Wainright—

LUCIA. (*memorizing on her fingers*).   Genevieve Wainright. Faith Morrison.

RODERICK.   It's all down in a book somewhere upstairs. We have it all. All that kind of thing is very interesting. Come, Lucia, just a little wine. Mother, a little red wine for Christmas day. Full of iron. "Take a little wine for thy stomach's sake."[1]

LUCIA.   Really, I can't get used to wine! What would my father say? But I suppose it's all right.
    Enter COUSIN BRANDON *from the hall. He takes his place by* LUCIA.

COUSIN BRANDON. (*rubbing his hands*).   Well, well, I smell turkey. My dear cousins, I can't tell you how pleasant it is to be having Christmas dinner with you all. I've lived out there in Alaska so long without relatives. Let me see, how long have you had this new house, Roderick?

RODERICK.   Why, it must be. . . .

MOTHER BAYARD.   Five years. It's five years, children. You should keep a diary. This is your sixth Christmas dinner here.

LUCIA.   Think of that, Roderick. We feel as though we had lived here twenty years.

COUSIN BRANDON.   At all events it still looks as good as new.

RODERICK. (*over his carving*).   What'll you have, Brandon, light or dark?—Frieda, fill up Cousin Brandon's glass.

LUCIA.   Oh, dear, I can't get used to these wines. I don't know what my father'd say, I'm sure. What'll you have, Mother Bayard?
    During the following speeches MOTHER BAYARD'S *chair, without any visible propulsion, starts to draw away from the table, turns toward the right, and slowly goes toward the dark portal.*

MOTHER BAYARD.   Yes, I can remember when there were Indians on this very land.

LUCIA. (*softly*).   Mother Bayard hasn't been very well lately, Roderick.

MOTHER BAYARD.   My mother was a Faith Morrison. And in New Hampshire she married a young John Wainright, who was a Congregational minister. He saw her in his congregation one day. . . .

LUCIA.   Mother Bayard, hadn't you better lie down, dear?

MOTHER BAYARD.   . . . and right in the middle of his sermon he said to himself: "I'll marry that girl." And he did, and I'm their daughter.

LUCIA. (*half rising and looking after her with anxiety*): Just a little nap, dear?

MOTHER BAYARD.   I'm all right. Just go on with your dinner. I was ten, and I said to my brother—
    She goes out. A very slight pause.

COUSIN BRANDON.   It's too bad it's such a cold dark day today. We almost need the lamps. I spoke to Major Lewis for a moment after church. His sciatica[2] troubles him, but he does pretty well.

LUCIA. (*dabbing her eyes*).   I know Mother Bayard wouldn't want us to grieve for her on Christmas day, but I can't forget her sitting in her wheel chair right beside us, only a year ago. And she would be so glad to know our good news.

RODERICK. (*patting her hand*).   Now, now. It's Christmas. (*Formally*) Cousin Brandon, a glass of wine with you, sir.

COUSIN BRANDON. (*half rising, lifting his glass gallantly*).   A glass of wine with you, sir.

LUCIA.   Does the Major's sciatica cause him much pain?

COUSIN BRANDON.   Some, perhaps. But you know his way. He says it'll be all the same in a hundred years.

LUCIA.   Yes, he's a great philosopher.

RODERICK.   His wife sends you a thousand thanks for her Christmas present.

LUCIA.   I forget what I gave her.—Oh, yes, the workbasket!
    Through the entrance of birth comes a nurse wheeling a perambulator trimmed with blue ribbons. LUCIA *rushes toward it, the men following.*
    O my wonderful new baby, my darling baby! Who ever saw such a child! Quick, nurse, a boy or a girl? A boy! Roderick, what shall we call him? Really, nurse, you've never seen such a child!

[1]**"Take a little wine"**: I Tim. 5:23

[2]**sciatica:** back pain.

RODERICK.   We'll call him Charles after your father and grandfather.

LUCIA.   But there are no Charleses in the Bible, Roderick.

RODERICK.   Of course, there are. Surely there are.

LUCIA.   Roderick!—Very well, but he will always be Samuel to me.—What miraculous hands he has! Really, they are the most beautiful hands in the world. All right, nurse. Have a good nap, my darling child.

RODERICK.   Don't drop him, nurse. Brandon and I need him in our firm.

> *Exit nurse and perambulator into the hall. The others return to their chairs,* LUCIA *taking the place left vacant by* MOTHER BAYARD *and* COUSIN BRANDON *moving up beside her.* COUSIN BRANDON *puts on his white hair.*

Lucia, a little white meat? Some stuffing? Cranberry sauce, anybody?

LUCIA. (*over her shoulder*).   Margaret, the stuffing is very good today.—Just a little, thank you.

RODERICK.   Now something to wash it down. (*Half rising*) Cousin Brandon, a glass of wine with you, sir. To the ladies, God bless them.

LUCIA.   Thank you, kind sirs.

COUSIN BRANDON.   Pity it's such an overcast day today. And no snow.

LUCIA.   But the sermon was lovely. I cried and cried. Dr. Spaulding does preach such a splendid sermon.

RODERICK.   I saw Major Lewis for a moment after church. He says his rheumatism comes and goes. His wife says she has something for Charles and will bring it over this afternoon.

> *Enter nurse again with perambulator. Pink ribbons. Same rush toward the left.*

LUCIA.   O my lovely new baby! Really, it never occurred to me that it might be a girl. Why, nurse, she's perfect.

RODERICK.   Now call her what you choose. It's your turn.

LUCIA.   Looloolooloo. Aië. Aië. Yes, this time I shall have my way. She shall be called Genevieve after your mother. Have a good nap, my treasure.

> *She looks after it as the nurse wheels the perambulator into the hall.*

Imagine! Sometime she'll be grown up and say "Good morning, Mother. Good morning, Father."—Really, Cousin Brandon, you don't find a baby like that every day.

COUSIN BRANDON.   *And the new factory.*

LUCIA.   A new factory? Really? Roderick, I shall be very uncomfortable if we're going to turn out to be rich. I've been afraid of that for years.—However, we mustn't talk about such things on Christmas day. I'll just take a little piece of white meat, thank you. Roderick, Charles is destined for the ministry. I'm sure of it.

RODERICK.   Woman, he's only twelve. Let him have a free mind. *We* want him in the firm, I don't mind saying. Anyway, no time passes as slowly as this when you're waiting for your urchins to grow up and settle down to business.

LUCIA.   I don't want time to go any faster, thank you. I love the children just as they are.—Really, Roderick, you know what the doctor said: One glass a meal. (*Putting her hand over his glass*) No, Margaret, that will be all.

> RODERICK *rises, glass in hand. With a look of dismay on his face he takes a few steps toward the dark portal.*

RODERICK.   Now I wonder what's the matter with me.

LUCIA.   Roderick, do be reasonable.

RODERICK. (*tottering, but with gallant irony*).   But, my dear, statistics show that we steady, moderate drinkers. . . .

LUCIA. (*rises, gazing at him in anguish*).   Roderick! My dear! What . . . ?

RODERICK. (*returns to his seat with a frightened look of relief*).   Well, it's fine to be back at table with you again. How many good Christmas dinners have I had to miss upstairs? And to be back at a fine bright one, too.

LUCIA.   O my dear, you gave us a very alarming time! Here's your glass of milk.—Josephine, bring Mr. Bayard his medicine from the cupboard in the library.

RODERICK.   At all events, now that I'm better I'm going to start doing something about the house.

LUCIA.   Roderick! You're not going to change the house?

RODERICK.   Only touch it up here and there. It looks a hundred years old.

> CHARLES *enters casually from the hall. He kisses his mother's hair and sits down.*

LUCIA.   Charles, you carve the turkey, dear. Your father's not well.—You always said you hated carving, though you *are* so clever at it.

> *Father and son exchange places.*

CHARLES.   It's a great blowy morning, mother. The wind comes over the hill like a lot of cannon.

LUCIA.   And such a good sermon. I cried and cried. Mother Bayard loved a good sermon so. And she used to sing the Christmas hymns all around the year. Oh, dear, oh, dear, I've been thinking of her all morning!

RODERICK.   Sh, Mother. It's Christmas day. You mustn't think of such things.—You mustn't be depressed.

LUCIA.   But sad things aren't the same as depressing things. I must be getting old: I like them.

CHARLES.   Uncle Brandon, you haven't anything to eat. Pass his plate, Hilda . . . and some cranberry sauce. . . .

Enter GENEVIEVE. *She kisses her father's temple and sits down.*

GENEVIEVE.   It's glorious. Every least twig is wrapped around with ice. You almost never see that.

LUCIA.   Did you have time to deliver those presents after church, Genevieve?

GENEVIEVE.   Yes, Mama. Old Mrs. Lewis sends you a thousand thanks for hers. It was just what she wanted, she said. Give me lots, Charles, lots.

RODERICK.   (*rising and starting toward the dark portal*).   Statistics, ladies and gentlemen, show that we steady, moderate. . . .

CHARLES.   How about a little skating this afternoon, Father?

RODERICK.   I'll live till I'm ninety.

LUCIA.   I really don't think he ought to go skating.

RODERICK.   (*at the very portal, suddenly astonished*).   Yes, but . . . but . . . not yet!

He goes out.

LUCIA. (*dabbing her eyes*).   He was so young and so clever, Cousin Brandon. (*Raising her voice for* COUSIN BRANDON's *deafness*) I say he was so young and so clever.—Never forget your father, children. He was a good man.—Well, he wouldn't want us to grieve for him today.

CHARLES.   White or dark, Genevieve? Just another sliver, Mother?

LUCIA. (*putting on her white hair*).   I can remember our first Christmas dinner in this house, Genevieve. Twenty-five years ago today. Mother Bayard was sitting here in her wheel chair. She could remember when Indians lived on this very spot and when she had to cross the river on a new-made raft.

CHARLES AND GENEVIEVE.   She couldn't have, Mother. That can't be true.

LUCIA.   It certainly was true—even I can remember when there was only one paved street. We were very happy to walk on boards. (*Louder, to* COUSIN BRANDON) We can remember when there were no sidewalks, can't we, Cousin Brandon?

COUSIN BRANDON. (*delighted*).   Oh, yes! And those were the days.

CHARLES AND GENEVIEVE. (*sotto voce*).[3](*This is a family refrain.*)   Those were the days.

LUCIA.   . . . and the ball last night, Genevieve? Did you have a nice time? I hope you didn't *waltz*, dear. I think a girl in our position ought to set an example. Did Charles keep an eye on you?

GENEVIEVE.   He had none left. They were all on Leonora Banning. He can't conceal it any longer, Mother. I think he's engaged to marry Leonora Banning.

CHARLES.   I'm not engaged to marry anyone.

LUCIA.   Well, she's very pretty.

GENEVIEVE.   I shall never marry, Mother—I shall sit in this house beside you forever, as though life were one long, happy Christmas dinner.

LUCIA.   O my child, you mustn't say such things!

GENEVIEVE (*playfully*).   You don't want me? You don't want me?

LUCIA *bursts into tears.*

Why, Mother, how silly you are! There's nothing sad about that—what could possibly be sad about that.

LUCIA (*drying her eyes*).   Forgive me. I'm just unpredictable, that's all.

CHARLES *goes to the door and leads in* LEONORA BANNING.

LEONORA (*kissing* LUCIA's *temple*).   Good morning, Mother Bayard. Good morning, everybody. It's really a splendid Christmas day today.

CHARLES.   Little white meat? Genevieve, Mother, Leonora?

LEONORA.   Every least twig is encircled with ice.—You never see that.

CHARLES (*shouting*).   Uncle Brandon, another?—Rogers, fill my uncle's glass.

LUCIA (*to* CHARLES).   Do what your father used to do. It would please Cousin Brandon so. You know—(*pretending to raise a glass*)—"Uncle Brandon, a glass of wine—"

[3]**sotto voce** (*sot ō vō chĕ*): It., in a low tone.

CHARLES (*rising*).   Uncle Brandon, a glass of wine with you, sir.

BRANDON.   A glass of wine with you, sir. To the ladies, God bless them every one.

THE LADIES.   Thank you, kind sirs.

GENEVIEVE.   And if I go to Germany for my music I promise to be back for Christmas. I wouldn't miss that.

LUCIA.   I hate to think of you over there all alone in those strange pensions.[4]

GENEVIEVE.   But, darling, the time will pass so fast that you'll hardly know I'm gone. I'll be back in the twinkling of an eye.

> *Enter Left, the nurse and perambulator. Green ribbons.*

LEONORA.   Oh, what an angel! The darlingest baby in the world. Do let me hold it, nurse.

> *But the nurse resolutely wheels the perambulator across the stage and out the dark door.*

Oh, I did love it so!

> LUCIA *goes to her, puts her arm around* LEONORA's *shoulders, and they encircle the room whispering—*LUCIA *then hands her over to* CHARLES *who conducts her on the same circuit.*

GENEVIEVE (*as her mother sits down,—softly*).   Isn't there anything I can do?

LUCIA (*raises her eyebrows, ruefully*).   No, dear. Only time, only the passing of time can help in these things.

> CHARLES *and* LEONORA *return to the table.*

Don't you think we could ask Cousin Ermengarde to come and live with us here? There's plenty for everyone and there's no reason why she should go on teaching the First Grade for ever and ever. She wouldn't be in the way, would she, Charles?

CHARLES.   No, I think it would be fine.—A little more potato and gravy, anybody? A little more turkey, Mother?

> BRANDON *rises and starts slowly toward the dark portal.* LUCIA *rises and stands for a moment with her face in her hands.*

COUSIN BRANDON (*muttering*).   It was great to be in Alaska in those days. . . .

GENEVIEVE (*half rising, and gazing at her mother in fear*).   Mother, what is . . . ?

LUCIA (*hurriedly*).   Hush, my dear. It will pass.—Hold fast to your music, you know. (*As* GENEVIEVE *starts toward her*) No, no. I want to be alone for a few minutes.

[4]**pensions:** variation of *pensiones* (It.), hotels or boarding houses.

She turns and starts after COUSIN BRANDON *toward the Right.*

CHARLES.   If the Republicans collected all their votes instead of going off into cliques among themselves, they might prevent his getting a second term.

GENEVIEVE.   Charles, Mother doesn't tell us, but she hasn't been very well these days.

CHARLES.   Come, Mother, we'll go to Florida for a few weeks.

> *Exit* BRANDON.

LUCIA (*smiling at* GENEVIEVE *and waving her hand*).   Don't be foolish. Don't grieve.

> *She clasps her hands under her chin; her lips move, whispering; she walks serenely into the portal.*
> GENEVIEVE *stares after her, frozen.*
> *At the same moment the nurse and perambulator enter from the Left. Pale yellow ribbons.*
> LEONORA *rushes to it.*

LEONORA.   O my darlings . . . twins . . . Charles, aren't they glorious! Look at them. Look at them.

GENEVIEVE (*sinks down on the table her face buried in her arms*).   But what will I do? What's left for me to do?

CHARLES (*bending over the basket*).   Which is which?

LEONORA.   I feel as though I were the first mother who ever had twins.—Look at them now!—But why wasn't Mother Bayard allowed to stay and see them!

GENEVIEVE (*rising suddenly distraught, loudly*).   I don't want to go on. I can't bear it.

CHARLES (*goes to her quickly*). (*They sit down. He whispers to her earnestly, taking both her hands.*) But Genevieve, Genevieve! How frightfully Mother would feel to think that . . . Genevieve!

GENEVIEVE (*shaking her head wildly*).   I never told her how wonderful she was. We all treated her as though she were just a friend in the house. I thought she'd be here forever.

LEONORA (*timidly*).   Genevieve darling, do come one minute and hold my babies' hands. We shall call the girl Lucia after her grandmother,—will that please you? Do just see what adorable little hands they have.

> GENEVIEVE *collects herself and goes over to the perambulator. She smiles brokenly into the basket.*

GENEVIEVE.   They are wonderful, Leonora.

LEONORA.   Give him your finger, darling. Just let him hold it.

CHARLES.   And we'll call the boy Samuel.—Well, now everybody come and finish your dinners. Don't drop them, nurse; at least don't drop the boy. We need him in the firm.

LEONORA (*stands looking after them as the nurse wheels them into the hall*).   Someday they'll be big. Imagine! They'll come in and say "Hello, Mother!" (*She makes clucking noises of rapturous consternation.*)

CHARLES.   Come, a little wine, Leonora, Genevieve? Full of iron. Eduardo, fill the ladies' glasses. It certainly is a keen, cold morning. I used to go skating with Father on mornings like this and Mother would come back from church saying—

GENEVIEVE (*dreamily*).   I know: saying "Such a splendid sermon. I cried and cried."

LEONORA.   Why did she cry, dear?

GENEVIEVE.   That generation all cried at sermons. It was their way.

LEONORA.   Really, Genevieve?

GENEVIEVE.   They had had to go since they were children and I suppose sermons reminded them of their fathers and mothers, just as Christmas dinners do us. Especially in an old house like this.

LEONORA.   It really is pretty old, Charles. And so ugly, with all that ironwork filigree and that dreadful cupola.

GENEVIEVE.   Charles! You aren't going to change the house!

CHARLES.   No, no. I won't give up the house, but great heavens! it's fifty years old. This Spring we'll remove the cupola and build a new wing toward the tennis courts.

From now on GENEVIEVE *is seen to change. She sits up more straightly. The corners of her mouth become fixed. She becomes a forthright and slightly disillusioned spinster.* CHARLES *becomes the plain business man and a little pompous.*

LEONORA.   And then couldn't we ask your dear old Cousin Ermengarde to come and live with us? She's really the self-effacing kind.

CHARLES.   Ask her now. Take her out of the First Grade.

GENEVIEVE.   We only seem to think of it on Christmas day with her Christmas card staring us in the face.

Enter Left, nurse and perambulator. Blue ribbons.

LEONORA.   Another boy! Another boy! Here's a Roderick for you at last.

CHARLES.   Roderick Brandon Bayard. A regular little fighter.

LEONORA.   Goodbye, darling. Don't grow up too fast. Yes, yes. Aïë, aïë, aïë—stay just as you are.—Thank you, nurse.

GENEVIEVE (*who has not left the table, repeats dryly*).   Stay just as you are.

Exit nurse and perambulator. The others return to their places.

LEONORA.   Now I have three children. One, two, three. Two boys and a girl. I'm collecting them. It's very exciting. (*Over her shoulder*) What, Hilda? Oh, Cousin Ermengarde's come! Come in, cousin.

She goes to the hall and welcomes COUSIN ERMENGARDE *who already wears her white hair.*

ERMENGARDE (*shyly*).   It's such a pleasure to be with you all.

CHARLES (*pulling out her chair for her*).   The twins have taken a great fancy to you already, Cousin.

LEONORA.   The baby went to her at once.

CHARLES.   Exactly how are we related, Cousin Ermengarde?—There, Genevieve, that's your specialty.—First a little more turkey and stuffing, Mother? Cranberry sauce, anybody?

GENEVIEVE.   I can work it out; Grandmother Bayard was your. . . .

ERMENGARDE.   Your Grandmother Bayard was a second cousin of my Grandmother Haskins through the Wainrights.

CHARLES.   Well it's all in a book somewhere upstairs. All that kind of thing is awfully interesting.

GENEVIEVE.   Nonsense. There are no such books. I collect my notes off gravestones, and you have to scrape a good deal of moss—let me tell you—to find one great-grandparent.

CHARLES.   There's a story that my Grandmother Bayard crossed the Mississippi on a raft before there were any bridges or ferryboats. She died before Genevieve or I were born. Time certainly goes very fast in a great new country like this. Have some more cranberry sauce, Cousin Ermengarde.

ERMENGARDE (*timidly*).   Well, time must be passing very slowly in Europe with this dreadful, dreadful war going on.

CHARLES.   Perhaps an occasional war isn't so bad after all. It clears up a lot of poisons that collect in nations. It's like a boil.

ERMENGARDE.   Oh, dear, oh dear!

CHARLES (*with relish*).   Yes, it's like a boil.—Ho! ho! Here are your twins.

The twins appear at the door into the hall. SAM *is wearing the uniform of an ensign.[5]* LUCIA *is fussing over some detail on it.*

LUCIA.   Isn't he wonderful in it, Mother?

CHARLES.   Let's get a look at you.

SAM.   Mother, don't let Roderick fool with my stamp album while I'm gone.

LEONORA.   Now, Sam, do write a letter once in a while. Do be a good boy about that, mind.

SAM.   You might send some of those cakes of yours once in a while, Cousin Ermengarde.

ERMENGARDE (*in a flutter*).   I certainly will, my dear boy.

CHARLES.   If you need any money, we have agents in Paris and London, remember.

SAM.   Well, goodbye. . . .

SAM *goes briskly out through the dark portal, tossing his unneeded white hair through the door before him.* LUCIA *sits down at the table with lowered eyes.*

ERMENGARDE (*after a slight pause, in a low, constrained voice, making conversation*).   I spoke to Mrs. Fairchild for a moment coming out of church. Her rheumatism's a little better, she says. She sends you her warmest thanks for the Christmas present. The workbasket, wasn't it?—It was an admirable sermon. And our stained-glass window looked so beautiful, Leonora, so beautiful. Everybody spoke of it and so affectionately of Sammy. (LEONORA'S *hand goes to her mouth.*) Forgive me, Leonora, but it's better to speak of him than not to speak of him when we're all thinking of him so hard.

LEONORA (*rising, in anguish*).   He was a mere boy. He was a mere boy, Charles.

CHARLES.   My dear, my dear.

LEONORA.   I want to tell him how wonderful he was. We let him go so casually. I want to tell him how we all feel about him.—Forgive me, let me walk about a minute.—Yes, of course, Ermengarde—it's best to speak of him.

LUCIA (*in a low voice to Genevieve*).   Isn't there anything I can do?

GENEVIEVE.   No, no. Only time, only the passing of time can help in these things.

LEONORA, *straying about the room finds herself near the door to the hall at the moment that her son* RODERICK *enters. He links his arm with hers and leads her back to the table.*

---

[5]**ensign**: junior naval officer.

RODERICK.   What's the matter, anyway? What are you all so glum about? The skating was fine today.

CHARLES.   Sit down, young man. I have something to say to you.

RODERICK.   Everybody was there. Lucia skated in the corners with Dan Creighton the whole time. When'll it be, Lucia, when'll it be?

LUCIA.   I don't know what you mean.

RODERICK.   Lucia's leaving us soon, Mother. Dan Creighton, of all people.

CHARLES (*ominously*).   Roderick, I have something to say to you.

RODERICK.   Yes, Father.

CHARLES.   Is it true, Roderick, that you made yourself conspicuous last night at the Country Club—at a Christmas Eve dance, too?

LEONORA.   Not now, Charles, I beg of you. This is Christmas dinner.

RODERICK (*loudly*).   No, I didn't.

LUCIA.   Really, Father, he didn't. It was that dreadful Johnny Lewis.

CHARLES.   I don't want to hear about Johnny Lewis. I want to know whether a son of mine. . . .

LEONORA.   Charles, I beg of you. . . .

CHARLES.   The first family of this city!

RODERICK (*rising*).   I hate this town and everything about it. I always did.

CHARLES.   You behaved like a spoiled puppy, sir, an ill-bred spoiled puppy.

RODERICK.   What did I do? What did I do that was wrong?

CHARLES.   You were drunk and you were rude to the daughters of my best friends.

GENEVIEVE (*striking the table*).   Nothing in the world deserves an ugly scene like this. Charles, I'm ashamed of you.

RODERICK.   Great God, you gotta get drunk in this town to forget how dull it is. Time passes so slowly here that it stands still, that's what's the trouble.

CHARLES.   Well, young man, we can employ your time. You will leave the university and you will come into the Bayard factory on January second.

RODERICK (*at the door into the hall*).   I have better things to do than to go into your old factory. I'm going somewhere where time passes, my God!

He goes out into the hall.

LEONORA (*rising*).   Roderick, Roderick, come here just a moment.—Charles, where can he go?

LUCIA (*rising*).   Sh, Mother. He'll come back. Now I have to go upstairs and pack my trunk.

LEONORA.   I won't have any children left!

LUCIA.   Sh, Mother. He'll come back. He's only gone to California or somewhere.—Cousin Ermengarde has done most of my packing—thanks a thousand times, Cousin Ermengarde. (*She kisses her mother.*) I won't be long.

> She runs out into the hall.
> GENEVIEVE and LEONORA *put on their white hair.*

ERMENGARDE.   It's a very beautiful day. On the way home from church I stopped and saw Mrs. Foster a moment. Her arthritis comes and goes.

LEONORA.   Is she actually in pain, dear?

ERMENGARDE.   Oh, she says it'll all be the same in a hundred years!

LEONORA.   Yes, she's a brave little stoic.

CHARLES.   Come now, a little white meat, Mother?—Mary, pass my cousin's plate.

LEONORA.   What is it, Mary?—Oh, here's a telegram from them in Paris! "Love and Christmas greetings to all." I told them we'd be eating some of their wedding cake and thinking about them today. It seems to be all decided that they will settle down in the East, Ermengarde. I can't even have my daughter for a neighbor. They hope to build before long somewhere on the shore north of New York.

GENEVIEVE.   There is no shore north of New York.

LEONORA.   Well, East or West or whatever it is.
> *Pause.*

CHARLES.   My, what a dark day.
> *He puts on his white hair. Pause.*
> How slowly time passes without any young people in the house.

LEONORA.   I have three children somewhere.

CHARLES (*blunderingly offering comfort*).   Well, one of them gave his life for his country.

LEONORA (*sadly*).   And one of them is selling aluminum in China.

GENEVIEVE (*slowly working herself up to a hysterical crisis*).   I can stand everything but this terrible soot everywhere. We should have moved long ago. We're surrounded by factories. We have to change the window curtains every week.

LEONORA.   Why, Genevieve!

GENEVIEVE.   I can't stand it. I can't stand it any more. I'm going abroad. It's not only the soot that comes through the very walls of this house; it's the *thoughts*, it's the thought of what has been and what might have been here. And the feeling about this house of the years *grinding away*. My mother died yesterday—not twenty-five years ago. Oh, I'm going to live and die abroad! Yes, I'm going to be the American old maid living and dying in a pension in Munich or Florence.

ERMENGARDE.   Genevieve, you're tired.

CHARLES.   Come, Genevieve, take a good drink of cold water. Mary, open the window a minute.

GENEVIEVE.   I'm sorry. I'm sorry.
> *She hurries tearfully out into the hall.*

ERMENGARDE.   Dear Genevieve will come back to us, I think.
> *She rises and starts toward the dark portal.*
> You should have been out today, Leonora. It was one of those days when everything was encircled with ice. Very pretty indeed.
> *CHARLES rises and starts after her.*

CHARLES.   Leonora, I used to go skating with Father on mornings like this.—I wish I felt a little better.

LEONORA.   What! Have I got two invalids on my hands at once? Now, Cousin Ermengarde, you must get better and help me nurse Charles.

ERMENGARDE.   I'll do my best.
> ERMENGARDE *turns at the very portal and comes back to the table.*

CHARLES.   Well, Leonora, I'll do what you ask. I'll write the puppy a letter of forgiveness and apology. It's Christmas day. I'll cable it. That's what I'll do.
> *He goes out the dark door.*

LEONORA (*drying her eyes*).   Ermengarde, it's such a comfort having you here with me. Mary, I really can't eat anything. Well, perhaps, a sliver of white meat.

ERMENGARDE (*very old*).   I spoke to Mrs. Keene for a moment coming out of church. She asked after the young people.—At church I felt very proud sitting under our windows, Leonora, and our brass tablets. The Bayard aisle,—it's a regular Bayard aisle and I love it.

LEONORA.   Ermengarde, would you be very angry with me if I went and stayed with the young people a little this Spring?

ERMENGARDE.   Why, no. I know how badly they want you and need you. Especially now that they're about to build a new house.

LEONORA.   You wouldn't be angry? This house is yours as long as you want it, remember.

ERMENGARDE.   I don't see why the rest of you dislike it. I like it more than I can say.

LEONORA.   I won't be long. I'll be back in no time and we can have some more of our readings-aloud in the evening.

She kisses her and goes into the hall.

ERMENGARDE, *left alone, eats slowly and talks to* MARY.

ERMENGARDE.   Really, Mary, I'll change my mind. If you'll ask Bertha to be good enough to make me a little eggnog. A dear little eggnog.—Such a nice letter this morning from Mrs. Bayard, Mary. Such a nice letter. They're having their first Christmas dinner in the new house. They must be very happy. They call her Mother Bayard, she says, as though she were an old lady. And she says she finds it more comfortable to come and go in a wheel chair.—Such a dear letter. . . . And Mary, I can tell you a secret. It's still a great secret, mind! They're expecting a grandchild. Isn't that good news! Now I'll read a little.

She props a book up before her, still dipping a spoon into a custard from time to time. She grows from very old to immensely old. She sighs. The book falls down. She finds a cane beside her, and soon totters into the dark portal, murmuring:

"Dear little Roderick and little Lucia."

Note: Copies of this play, in individual paper covered acting editions, are available from Samuel French, Inc., 45 W. 25th St., New York, N.Y. 10010 or 7623 Sunset Blvd., Hollywood, Calif. 90046 or in Canada Samuel French, (Canada) Ltd., 80 Richmond Street East, Toronto M5C 1P1, Canada.

Discuss

1. A number of phrases are repeated again and again throughout the play. What are some of those phrases? What function do they have in the play? How do they reflect the meaning of the play?

2. Which statement best summarizes the play? Why do you think so?

  a. Nothing in life ever changes.

  b. Family ties are weakening and children respect traditions less than they used to.

  c. Life is always renewing itself.

Explore

1. What sorts of devices show the passage of time? Why do you suppose the playwright uses those methods? What is their effect?

2. Although the play takes place over a ninety-year period, you always see the characters at Christmas dinner. Why? What point is the playwright making with this setting?

3. Throughout the play a few references are made to events and people outside the family. What are those references and what function do they serve in the play?

4. The men and the women in the play focus on different issues and talk about different problems. Compare and contrast concerns of the two sexes.

5. Compare the end of the play with the beginning of the play. What significance do the similarities and differences give to the meaning of the play?

6. On page 45 is the following stage direction: SAM *goes briskly out through the dark portal, tossing his unneeded white hair through the door before him.* What is the meaning of Sam's tossing the white hair?

7. The stage directions for the play call for little in the way of scenery or props. Moreover, the play is not broken into scenes, but is a single scene taking in the ninety-year period, with characters simply appearing and disappearing on stage as they come into existence or die. What is the effect of this sort of staging? Should the play have been longer? Why or why not?

8. At the end of the play Ermengarde is left alone in the house. Why do you suppose the play ends with her rather than with Mother Bayard in the new house?

For Your Journal

1. There are many family phrases and family traditions that appear in this story. Do you have such customs in your family? If so, describe some of them. To whom are they most important? In what ways do you see family phrases or traditions as an adult? Do you think you will continue them?

2. Like the Bayards, many families have their black sheep, the child who rebels. Was there a black sheep in your family's past? Who was the black sheep? How did this child deviate from the family?

3. How important is the family tree to your family? Is it written down? Does someone keep records? What significance does that hold for you? For other members of your family?

Chee's Daughter

Juanita Platero and Siyowin Miller

Chee is caught between two cultures—the culture of his parents and that of
his in-laws, which is threatening him with the loss of his only child.

THE HAT TOLD THE STORY, the big, black, drooping
Stetson. It was not at the proper angle, the proper
rakish angle for so young a Navaho. There was no
song, and that was not in keeping either. There
should have been at least a humming, a faint, all-
to-himself "he he he heya," for it was a good horse
he was riding, a slender-legged, high-stepping
buckskin that would race the wind with light knee-
urging. This was a day for singing, a warm winter
day, when the touch of the sun upon the back be-
lied the snow high on distant mountains.

Wind warmed by the sun touched his high-
boned cheeks like flicker feathers, and still he rode
on silently, deeper into Little Canyon, until the red
rock walls rose straight upward from the stream bed
and only a narrow piece of blue sky hung above.
Abruptly the sky widened where the canyon walls
were pushed back to make a wide place, as though
in ancient times an angry stream had tried to go all
ways at once.

This was home—this wide place in the canyon—levels of jagged rock and levels of rich red
earth. This was home to Chee, the rider of the
buckskin, as it had been to many generations before him.

He stopped his horse at the stream and sat
looking across the narrow ribbon of water to the
bare-branched peach trees. He was seeing them
each springtime with their age-gnarled limbs trans-
figured beneath veils of blossom pink; he was seeing them in autumn laden with their yellow fruit,
small and sweet. Then his eyes searched out the
indistinct furrows of the fields beside the stream,
where each year the corn and beans and squash
drank thirstily of the overflow from summer rains.
Chee was trying to outweigh today's bitter betrayal

of hope by gathering to himself these reminders of
the integrity of the land. Land did not cheat! His
mind lingered deliberately on all the days spent
here in the sun caring for the young plants, his
songs to the earth and to the life springing from
it— ". . . In the middle of the wide field . . . Yellow Corn Boy . . . He has started both ways . . . ,"
then the harvest and repayment in full measure.
Here was the old feeling of wholeness and of oneness with the sun and earth and growing things.

Chee urged the buckskin toward the family
compound where, secure in a recess of overhanging
rock, was his mother's dome-shaped hogan, red
rock and red adobe like the ground on which it
nestled. Not far from the hogan was the half-circle
of brush like a dark shadow against the canyon
wall—corral for sheep and goats. Farther from the
hogan, in full circle, stood the horse corral made of
heavy cedar branches sternly interlocked. Chee's
long thin lips curved into a smile as he passed his
daughter's tiny hogan squatted like a round Pueblo
oven beside the corral. He remembered the summer day when together they sat back on their heels
and plastered wet adobe all about the circling wall
of rock and the woven dome of piñon twigs. How
his family laughed when the Little One herded the
bewildered chickens into her tiny hogan as the first
snow fell.

Then the smile faded from Chee's lips and his
eyes darkened as he tied his horse to a corral post
and turned to the strangely empty compound.
"Someone has told them," he thought, "and they
are inside weeping." He passed his mother's deserted loom on the south side of the hogan and
pulled the rude wooden door toward him, bowing
his head, hunching his shoulders to get inside.

His mother sat sideways by the center fire, her feet drawn up under her full skirts. Her hands were busy kneading dough in the chipped white basin. With her head down, her voice was muffled when she said, "The meal will soon be ready, son."

Chee passed his father sitting against the wall, hat over his eyes as though asleep. He passed his older sister who sat turning mutton ribs on a crude wire grill over the coals, noticed tears dropping on her hands. "She cared more for my wife than I realized," he thought.

Then because something must be said sometime, he tossed the black Stetson upon a bulging sack of wool and said, "You have heard, then." He could not shut from his mind how confidently he had set the handsome new hat on his head that very morning, slanting the wide brim over one eye; he was going to see his wife and today he would ask the doctors about bringing her home; last week she had looked so much better.

His sister nodded but did not speak. His mother sniffled and passed her velveteen sleeve beneath her nose. Chee sat down, leaning against the wall. "I suppose I was a fool for hoping all the time. I should have expected this. Few of our people get well from the coughing sickness. But *she* seemed to be getting better."

His mother was crying aloud now and blowing her nose noisily on her skirt. His father sat up, speaking gently to her.

Chee shifted his position and started a cigarette. His mind turned back to the Little One. At least she was too small to understand what had happened, the Little One who had been born three years before in the sanitarium where his wife was being treated for the coughing sickness, the Little One he had brought home to his mother's hogan[1] to be nursed by his sister whose baby was a few months older. As she grew fat-cheeked and sturdy-legged, she followed him about like a shadow; somehow her baby mind had grasped that of all those at the hogan who cared for her and played with her, he—Chee—belonged most to her. She sat cross-legged at his elbow when he worked silver at the forge; she rode before him in the saddle when he drove the horses to water; often she lay wakeful on her sheep-pelts until he stretched out for the night in the darkened hogan and she could snuggle warm against him.

Chee blew smoke slowly and some of the sadness left his dark eyes as he said, "It is not as bad as it might be. It is not as though we are left with nothing."

[1]**hogan:** Navaho dwelling constructed of earth and logs.

Chee's sister arose, sobs catching in her throat, and rushed past him out the doorway. Chee sat upright, a terrible fear possessing him. For a moment his mouth could make no sound. Then: "The Little One! Mother, where is she?"

His mother turned her stricken face to him. "Your wife's people came after her this morning. They heard yesterday of their daughter's death through the trader at Red Sands."

Chee started to protest but his mother shook her head slowly. "I didn't expect they would want the Little One either. But there is nothing you can do. She is a girl child and belongs to her mother's people; it is custom."

Frowning, Chee got to his feet, grinding his cigarette into the dirt floor. "Custom! When did my wife's parents begin thinking about custom? Why, the hogan where they live doesn't even face the East!" He started toward the door. "Perhaps I can overtake them. Perhaps they don't realize how much we want her with us. I'll ask them to give my daughter back to me. Surely they won't refuse."

His mother stopped him gently with her outstretched hand. "You couldn't overtake them now. They were in the trader's car. Eat and rest, and think more about this."

"Have you forgotten how things have always been between you and your wife's people?" his father said.

That night, Chee's thoughts were troubled—half-forgotten incidents became disturbingly vivid—but early the next morning he saddled the buckskin and set out for the settlement of Red Sands. Even though his father-in-law, Old Man Fat, might laugh, Chee knew that he must talk to him. There were some things to which Old Man Fat might listen.

Chee rode the first part of the fifteen miles to Red Sands expectantly. The sight of sandstone buttes near Cottonwood Spring reddening in the morning sun brought a song almost to his lips. He twirled his reins in salute to the small boy herding sheep toward many-colored Butterfly Mountain, watched with pleasure the feathers of smoke rising against tree-darkened western mesas[2] from the hogans sheltered there. But as he approached the familiar settlement sprawled in mushroom growth along the highway, he began to feel as though a scene from a bad dream was becoming real.

Several cars were parked around the trading store which was built like two log hogans side by

[2]**mesas:** high flat-topped hills.

side, with red gas pumps in front and a sign across the tarpaper roofs: *Red Sands Trading Post—Groceries Gasoline Cold Drinks Sandwiches Indian Curios.* Back of the trading post an unpainted frame house and outbuildings squatted on the drab, treeless land. Chee and the Little One's mother had lived there when they stayed with his wife's people. That was according to custom—living with one's wife's people—but Chee had never been convinced that it was custom alone which prompted Old Man Fat and his wife to insist that their daughter bring her husband to live at the trading post.

Beside the Post was a large hogan of logs, with brightly painted pseudo-Navaho designs on the roof—a hogan with smoke-smudged windows and a garish blue door which faced north to the highway. Old Man Fat had offered Chee a hogan like this one. The trader would build it if he and his wife would live there and Chee would work at his forge making silver jewelry where tourists could watch him. But Chee had asked instead for a piece of land for a cornfield and help in building a hogan far back from the highway and a corral for the sheep he had brought to this marriage.

A cold wind blowing down from the mountains began to whistle about Chee's ears. It flapped the gaudy Navaho rugs which were hung in one long bright line to attract tourists. It swayed the sign *Navaho Weaver at Work* beside the loom where Old Man Fat's wife sat hunched in her striped blanket, patting the colored thread of a design into place with a wooden comb. Tourists stood watching the weaver. More tourists stood in a knot before the hogan where the sign said: *See Inside a Real Navaho Home 25¢.*

Then the knot seemed to unravel as a few people returned to their cars; some had cameras; and there against the blue door Chee saw the Little One standing uncertainly. The wind was plucking at her new purple blouse and wide green skirt; it freed truant strands of soft dark hair from the meager queue[3] into which it had been tied with white yarn.

"Isn't she cunning!" one of the women tourists was saying as she turned away.

Chee's lips tightened as he began to look around for Old Man Fat. Finally he saw him passing among the tourists collecting coins.

Then the Little One saw Chee. The uncertainty left her face and she darted through the

[3] **queue:** hair tied in a braid.

crowd as her father swung down from his horse. Chee lifted her in his arms, hugging her tight. While he listened to her breathless chatter, he watched Old Man Fat bearing down on them, scowling.

As his father-in-law walked heavily across the gravelled lot, Chee was reminded of a statement his mother sometimes made: "When you see a fat Navaho, you see one who hasn't worked for what he has."

Old Man Fat was fattest in the middle. There was indolence in his walk even though he seemed to hurry, indolence in his cheeks so plump they made his eyes squint, eyes now smoldering with anger.

Some of the tourists were getting into their cars and driving away. The old man said belligerently to Chee, "Why do you come here? To spoil our business? To drive people away?"

"I came to talk with you," Chee answered, trying to keep his voice steady as he faced the old man.

"We have nothing to talk about," Old Man Fat blustered and did not offer to touch Chee's extended hand.

"It's about the Little One." Chee settled his daughter more comfortably against his hip as he weighed carefully all the words he had planned to say. "We are going to miss her very much. It wouldn't be so bad if we knew that *part* of each year she could be with us. That might help you too. You and your wife are no longer young people and you have no young ones here to depend upon." Chee chose his next words remembering the thriftlessness of his wife's parents, and their greed. "Perhaps we could share the care of this little one. Things are good with us. So much snow this year will make lots of grass for the sheep. We have good land for corn and melons."

Chee's words did not have the expected effect. Old Man Fat was enraged. "Farmers, all of you! Long-haired farmers! Do you think everyone must bend his back over the short-handled hoe in order to have food to eat?" His tone changed as he began to brag a little. "We not only have all the things from cans at the trader's, but when the Pueblos come past here on their way to town we buy their salty jerked mutton, young corn for roasting, dried sweet peaches."

Chee's dark eyes surveyed the land along the highway as the old man continued to brag about being "progressive." *He* no longer was tied to the land. He and his wife made money easily and could *buy* all the things they wanted. Chee realized too late that he had stumbled into the old argument between himself and his wife's parents. They had never understood his feeling about the land—that a man took care of his land and it in turn took care of him. Old Man Fat and his wife scoffed at him, called him a Pueblo farmer, all during that summer when he planted and weeded and harvested. Yet they ate the green corn in their mutton stews, and the chili paste from the fresh ripe chilis, and the tortillas from the cornmeal his wife ground. None of this working and sweating in the sun for Old Man Fat, who talked proudly of his easy way of living—collecting money from the trader who rented this strip of land beside the highway, collecting money from the tourists.

Yet Chee had once won that argument. His wife had shared his belief in the integrity of the earth, that jobs and people might fail one but the earth never would. After that first year she had turned from her own people and gone with Chee to Little Canyon.

Old Man Fat was reaching for the Little One. "Don't be coming here with plans for my daughter's daughter," he warned. "If you try to make trouble, I'll take the case to the government man in town."

The impulse was strong in Chee to turn and ride off while he still had the Little One in his arms. But he knew his time of victory would be short. His own family would uphold the old custom of children, especially girl children, belonging to the mother's people. He would have to give his daughter up if the case were brought before the Headman of Little Canyon, and certainly he would have no better chance before a strange white man in town.

He handed the bewildered Little One to her grandfather who stood watching every movement suspiciously. Chee asked, "If I brought you a few things for the Little One, would that be making trouble? Some velvet for a blouse, or some of the jerky she likes so well . . . this summer's melon?"

Old Man Fat backed away from him. "Well," he hesitated, as some of the anger disappeared from his face and beads of greed shone in his eyes. "Well," he repeated. Then as the Little One began to squirm in his arms and cry, he said, "No! No! Stay away from here, you and all your family."

The sense of his failure deepened as Chee rode back to Little Canyon. But it was not until he sat with his family that evening in the hogan, while the familiar bustle of meal preparing went on about him, that he began to doubt the wisdom of the things he'd always believed. He smelled the coffee boiling and the oily fragrance of chili powder dusted into the bubbling pot of stew; he watched his mother turning round crusty fried bread in the small black skillet. All around him was plenty—a half of mutton hanging near the door, bright strings of chili drying, corn hanging by the braided husks, cloth bags of dried peaches. Yet in his heart was nothing.

He heard the familiar sounds of the sheep outside the hogan, the splash of water as his father filled the long drinking trough from the water barrel. When his father came in, Chee could not bring himself to tell a second time of the day's happenings. He watched his wiry, soft-spoken father while his mother told the story, saw his father's queue of graying hair quiver as he nodded his head with sympathetic exclamations.

Chee's doubting, acrid thoughts kept forming: Was it wisdom his father had passed on to him or was his inheritance only the stubbornness of a long-haired Navaho resisting change? Take care of the land and it will take care of you. True, the land had always given him food, but now food was not enough. Perhaps if he had gone to school he would have learned a different kind of wisdom, something to help him now. A schoolboy might even be able to speak convincingly to this government man whom Old Man Fat threatened to call, instead of sitting here like a clod of earth itself—Pueblo farmer indeed. What had the land to give that would restore his daughter?

In the days that followed, Chee herded sheep. He got up in the half-light, drank the hot coffee his mother had ready, then started the flock moving. It was necessary to drive the sheep a long way from the hogan to find good winter forage. Sometimes Chee met friends or relatives who were on their way to town or to the road camp where they hoped to get work; then there was friendly banter and an exchange of news. But most of the days seemed endless; he could not walk far enough or fast enough from his memories of the Little One or from his bitter thoughts. Sometimes it seemed his daughter trudged beside him, so real he could almost hear her footsteps—the muffled pad-pad of little feet clad in deerhide. In the glare of a snow bank he would see her vivid face, brown eyes sparkling. Mingling with the tinkle of sheep bells he heard her laughter.

When, weary of following the small sharp hoof marks that crossed and recrossed in the snow, he sat down in the shelter of a rock, it was only to be reminded that in his thoughts he had forsaken his brotherhood with the earth and sun and growing things. If he remembered times when he had flung himself against the earth to rest, to lie there in the sun until he could no longer feel where he left off and the earth began, it was to remember also that now he sat like an alien against the same earth; the belonging-together was gone. The earth was one thing and he was another.

It was during the days when he herded sheep that Chee decided he must leave Little Canyon. Perhaps he would take a job silversmithing for one of the traders in town. Perhaps, even though he spoke little English, he could get a job at the road camp with his cousins; he would ask them about it.

Springtime transformed the mesas. The peach trees in the canyon were shedding fragrance and pink blossoms on the gentled wind. The sheep no longer foraged for the yellow seeds of chamiso but ranged near the hogan with the long-legged new lambs, eating tender young grass.

Chee was near the hogan on the day his cousins rode up with the message for which he waited. He had been watching with mixed emotions while his father and his sister's husband cleared the fields beside the stream.

"The boss at the camp says he needs an extra hand, but he wants to know if you'll be willing to go with the camp when they move it to the other side of the town?" The tall cousin shifted his weight in the saddle.

The other cousin took up the explanation. "The work near here will last only until the new cut-off beyond Red Sands is finished. After that, the work will be too far away for you to get back here often."

That was what Chee had wanted—to get away from Little Canyon—yet he found himself not so interested in the job beyond town as in this new cut-off which was almost finished. He pulled a blade of grass, split it thoughtfully down the center as he asked questions of his cousins. Finally he said: "I need to think more about this. If I decide on this job I'll ride over."

Before his cousins were out of sight down the canyon Chee was walking toward the fields, a bold plan shaping in his mind. As the plan began to flourish, wild and hardy as young tumbleweed,

Chee added his own voice softly to the song his father was singing: ". . . In the middle of the wide field . . . Yellow Corn Boy . . . I wish to put in."

Chee walked slowly around the field, the rich red earth yielding to his footsteps. His plan depended upon this land and upon the things he remembered most about his wife's people.

Through planting time Chee worked zealously and tirelessly. He spoke little of the large new field he was planting because he felt so strongly that just now this was something between himself and the land. The first days he was ever stooping, piercing the ground with the pointed stick, placing the corn kernels there, walking around the field and through it, singing, ". . . His track leads into the ground . . . Yellow Corn Boy . . . his track leads into the ground." After that, each day Chee walked through his field watching for the tips of green to break through; first a few spikes in the center and then more and more until the corn in all parts of the field was above ground. Surely, Chee thought, if he sang the proper songs, if he cared for this land faithfully, it would not forsake him now, even though through the lonely days of winter he had betrayed the goodness of the earth in his thoughts.

Through the summer Chee worked long days, the sun hot upon his back, pulling weeds from around young corn plants; he planted squash and pumpkin; he terraced a small piece of land near his mother's hogan and planted carrots and onions and the moisture-loving chili. He was increasingly restless. Finally he told his family what he hoped the harvest from this land would bring him. Then the whole family waited with him, watching the corn: the slender graceful plants that waved green arms and bent to embrace each other as young winds wandered through the field, the maturing plants flaunting their pollen-laden tassels in the sun, the tall and sturdy parent corn with new-formed ears and a froth of purple, red and yellow corn-beards against the dusty emerald of broad leaves.

Summer was almost over when Chee slung the bulging packs across two pack ponies. His mother helped him tie the heavy rolled pack behind the saddle of the buckskin. Chee knotted the new yellow kerchief about his neck a little tighter, gave the broad black hat brim an extra tug, but these were only gestures of assurance and he knew it. The land had not failed him. That part was done. But this he was riding into? Who could tell?

When Chee arrived at Red Sands, it was as he had expected to find it—no cars on the highway. His cousins had told him that even the Pueblo farmers were using the new cut-off to town. The barren gravel around the Red Sands Trading Post was deserted. A sign banged against the dismantled gas pumps *Closed until further notice.*

Old Man Fat came from the crude summer shelter built beside the log hogan from a few branches of scrub cedar and the sides of wooden crates. He seemed almost friendly when he saw Chee.

"Get down, my son," he said, eyeing the bulging packs. There was no bluster in his voice today and his face sagged, looking somewhat saddened; perhaps because his cheeks were no longer quite full enough to push his eyes upward at the corners. "You are going on a journey?"

Chee shook his head. "Our fields gave us so much this year, I thought to sell or trade this to the trader. I didn't know he was no longer here."

Old Man Fat sighed, his voice dropping to an injured tone. "He says he and his wife are going to rest this winter; then after that he'll build a place up on the new highway."

Chee moved as though to be traveling on, then jerked his head toward the pack ponies. "Anything you need?"

"I'll ask my wife," Old Man Fat said as he led the way to the shelter. "Maybe she has a little money. Things have not been too good with us since the trader closed. Only a few tourists come this way." He shrugged his shoulders. "And with the trader gone—no credit."

Chee was not deceived by his father-in-law's unexpected confidences. He recognized them as a hopeful bid for sympathy and, if possible, something for nothing. Chee made no answer. He was thinking that so far he had been right about his wife's parents: their thriftlessness had left them with no resources to last until Old Man Fat found another easy way of making a living.

Old Man Fat's Wife was in the shelter working at her loom. She turned rather wearily when her husband asked with noticeable deference if she would give him money to buy supplies. Chee surmised that the only income here was from his mother-in-law's weaving.

She peered around the corner of the shelter at the laden ponies, and then she looked at Chee, "What do you have there, my son?"

Chee smiled to himself as he turned to pull the pack from one of the ponies, dragged it to the shelter where he untied the ropes. Pumpkins and hard-shelled squash tumbled out, and the ears of corn—pale yellow husks fitting firmly over plump ripe kernels, blue corn, red corn, yellow corn, many-colored corn, ears and ears of it—tumbled into every corner of the shelter.

"Yooooh," Old Man Fat's Wife exclaimed as she took some of the ears in her hands. Then she glanced up at her son-in-law. "But we have no money for all this. We have sold almost everything we own—even the brass bed that stood in the hogan."

Old Man Fat's brass bed. Chee concealed his amusement as he started back for another pack. That must have been a hard parting. Then he stopped, for, coming from the cool darkness of the hogan was the Little One, rubbing her eyes as though she had been asleep. She stood for a moment in the doorway and Chee saw that she was dirty, barefoot, her hair uncombed, her little blouse shorn of all its silver buttons. Then she ran toward Chee, her arms outstretched. Heedless of Old Man Fat and his wife, her father caught her in his arms, her hair falling in a dark cloud across his face, the sweetness of her laughter warm against his shoulder.

It was the haste within him to get this slow waiting game played through to the finish that made Chee speak unwisely. It was the desire to swing her before him in the saddle and ride fast to Little Canyon that prompted his words. "The money doesn't matter. You still have something. . . ."

Chee knew immediately that he had overspoken. The old woman looked from him to the corn spread before her. Unfriendliness began to harden in his father-in-law's face. All the old arguments between himself and his wife's people came pushing and crowding in between them now.

Old Man Fat began kicking the ears of corn back onto the canvas as he eyed Chee angrily. "And you rode all the way over here thinking that for a little food we would give up our daughter's daughter?"

Chee did not wait for the old man to reach for the Little One. He walked dazedly to the shelter, rubbing his cheek against her soft dark hair and put her gently into her grandmother's lap. Then he turned back to the horses. He had failed. By his own haste he had failed. He swung into the saddle, his hand touching the roll behind it. Should he ride on into town?

Then he dismounted, scarcely glancing at Old Man Fat, who stood uncertainly at the corner of the shelter, listening to his wife. "Give me a hand with this other pack of corn, Grandfather," Chee said, carefully keeping the small bit of hope from his voice.

Puzzled, but willing, Old Man Fat helped carry the other pack to the shelter, opening it to find more corn as well as carrots and round pale yellow onions. Chee went back for the roll behind the buckskin's saddle and carried it to the entrance of the shelter where he cut the ropes and gave the canvas a nudge with his toe. Tins of coffee rolled out, small plump cloth bags; jerked meat from several butcherings spilled from a flour sack, and bright red chilis splashed like flames against the dust.

"I will leave all this anyhow," Chee told them. "I would not want my daughter nor even you old people to go hungry."

Old Man Fat picked up a shiny tin of coffee, then put it down. With trembling hands he began to untie one of the cloth bags—dried sweet peaches.

The Little One had wriggled from her grandmother's lap, unheeded, and was on her knees, digging her hands into the jerked meat.

"There is almost enough food here to last all winter," Old Man Fat's Wife sought the eyes of her husband.

Chee said, "I meant it to be enough. But that was when I thought you might send the Little One back with me." He looked down at his daughter noisily sucking jerky. Her mouth, both fists were full of it. "I am sorry that you feel you cannot bear to part with her."

Old Man Fat's Wife brushed a straggly wisp of gray hair from her forehead as she turned to look at the Little One. Old Man Fat was looking too. And it was not a thing to see. For in that moment the Little One ceased to be their daughter's daughter and became just another mouth to feed.

"And why not?" the old woman asked wearily.

Chee was settled in the saddle, the barefooted Little One before him. He urged the buckskin faster, and his daughter clutched his shirtfront. The purpling mesas fling back the echo: ". . . My corn embrace each other. In the middle of the wide field . . . Yellow Corn Boy embrace each other."

Discuss

1. Which statement best describes the importance of the land in the life of Chee and his family?

  a. The land provides for nearly all the physical needs of Chee and his family.

  b. Their dependence on the land makes it impossible for Chee and his family to gain any real political power in their community.

  c. The land provides not only food and shelter for the family, but also spiritual belief in a oneness with nature.

2. How do the families of Chee and his wife differ in their cultural values? What, in those differences, provides hope for Chee that his wife's family will return his daughter?

3. What causes Chee to doubt the wisdom he learned from his father? What alternatives does he consider? How does he think schooling might have improved his lot?

Explore

1. What device do the authors use to create suspense in this story? How are you let into Chee's plan? How does this device affect your involvement in the story?

2. There are allusions to songs—in particular to "Yellow Corn Boy"—throughout the story. What role do songs play in the life of the Navaho? When does Chee sing "Yellow Corn Boy" and what is its significance in the story?

3. The story includes details about the land and its products. How does this coverage influence your response to Chee's culture and beliefs?

4. Which of the characters seem most realistic and complex to you? Which ones seem more like types? How does such a character analysis affect your response to the people and events in the story?

5. How convincing do you find the last scene of the story? Why do you think Chee's father-in-law first rejects the idea and then agrees to return the Little One?

For Your Journal

1. Are Chee's cultural conflicts resolved at the end of the story? Do you think he will have further conflicts or confusions? Why or why not?

2. Write about an experience in which you felt caught between two cultures. What was the conflict? Did you resolve it? How?

3. Imagine the Little One's future. What sort of decisions do you think she might have to make about customs and traditions as she grows? In what ways might those decisions be difficult?

Freedom and Justice

The following selections provide an insight into the struggles of people to lead a life in which they may make decisions free of political and economic oppression, free of cultural expectations and traditional roles.

The Man with the Hoe

Edwin Markham

In this poem, a nameless person provides a symbol for all workers
who are exploited by those in power.

Bowed by the weight of centuries he leans
Upon his hoe and gazes on the ground,
The emptiness of ages in his face,
And on his back the burden of the world.
Who made him dead to rapture and despair,
A thing that grieves not and that never hopes,
Stolid and stunned, a brother to the ox?
Who loosened and let down this brutal jaw?
Whose was the hand that slanted back this brow?
Whose breath blew out the light within this brain?

Is this the Thing the Lord God made and gave
To have dominion over sea and land;
To trace the stars and search the heavens for power;
To feel the passion of Eternity?
Is this the dream He dreamed who shaped the suns
And marked their ways upon the ancient deep?
Down all the caverns of Hell to their last gulf
There is no shape more terrible than this—
More tongued with censure of the world's blind greed—
More filled with signs and portents for the soul—
More packt with danger to the universe.

(continued)

What gulfs between him and the seraphim![1]
Slave of the wheel of labor, what to him
Are Plato[2] and the swing of Pleiades?[3]
What the long reaches of the peaks of song,
The rift of dawn, the reddening of the rose?
Through this dread shape the suffering ages look;
Time's tragedy is in that aching stoop;
Through this dread shape humanity betrayed,
Plundered, profaned, and disinherited,
Cries protest to the Judges of the World,
A protest that is also prophecy.

O masters, lords and rulers in all lands,
Is this the handiwork you give to God,
This monstrous thing distorted and soul-quenched?
How will you ever straighten up this shape;
Touch it again with immortality;
Give back the upward looking and the light;
Rebuild in it the music and the dream;
Make right the immemorial infamies,
Perfidious[4] wrongs, immedicable[5] woes?

O masters, lords and rulers in all lands,
How will the Future reckon with this man?
How answer his brute question in that hour
When whirlwinds of rebellion shake all shores?
How will it be with kingdoms and with kings—
With those who shaped him to the thing he is—
When this dumb terror shall rise to judge the world,
After the silence of the centuries?

[1]**seraphim:** angels of the highest order in Isaiah's vision in the Old Testament.
[2]**Plato:** ancient Greek philosopher, writer, and teacher, whose most famous pupil was Aristotle.
[3]**Pleiades:** group of stars named for the daughters of Atlas in Greek mythology.
[4]**perfidious:** treacherous or deceitful.
[5]**immedicable:** incurable.

Discuss

1. Which statement best matches the poet's view of the man with the hoe?

a. The man is a noble creature who has maintained his humanity despite oppression.

b. The man has been reduced to little more than a beast of the field.

c. Although he is weak and tired, the man has hope that the afterlife will bring him happiness.

2. Which statement best pinpoints the blame for the oppression of the man with the hoe, according to the poet?

a. Greedy masters are responsible because they have put their own desires ahead of the well-being of humankind.

b. The workers are responsible because they should have formed unions to protect themselves from exploitation.

c. God is responsible, because he has created the human race and has the power to protect and defend it.

3. What is the poet's hope for the man? What is his idea of a restored humanity?

Explore

1. Although he titles this poem "The Man with the Hoe," the poet is clearly describing more than one man. Who does the man with the hoe represent? Why do you suppose he chose the man with the hoe as a symbol? What other symbols might he have chosen?

2. Describe the injustices that the poet believes workers have suffered. How have those injustices dehumanized the workers? What is missing in their lives?

3. The poet alludes to Plato and Pleiades. How do those allusions relate to the meaning of the poem?

4. Allusions to God, Eternity, and Hell are also important in this poem. How do these images reinforce the message of the poem?

5. Describe the tone of the poem. Is it mocking? Reverent? Excited? Calm? Angry? What other words might you use to describe it? How do language, rhyme, and form contribute to the tone?

For Your Journal

1. The poet alludes to future rebellion. Based on what he says in the last stanza, what do you think his vision of the future is? Write a description of what might happen when "this dumb terror shall rise to judge the world."

2. This poem is abstract and formal. In your own words, describe some present-day instances of the kind of oppression that the poet describes.

3. Write a letter to the poet responding to the concerns he expresses in this poem.

4. Markham's poem was inspired by a painting of the same title by the French artist Jean-François Millet. Examine a copy of the painting and write a few paragraphs giving your own response to what you see. How close is Millet's portrayal to what you pictured from the poem?

The Time Factor

Gloria Steinem

Gloria Steinem, a leader in the women's rights movement, tells of some of the traditions in male and female roles that have limited people's options and made a whole, balanced life difficult.

PLANNING AHEAD is a measure of class. The rich and even the middle class plan for future generations, but the poor can plan ahead only a few weeks or days.

I remember finding this calm insight in some sociological text and feeling instant recognition. Yes, of course, our sense of time was partly a function of power, or the lack of it. It rang true even in the entirely economic sense the writer had in mind. "The guys who own the factories hand them down to their sons and great-grandsons," I remember a boy in my high school saying bitterly. "On this side of town, we just plan for Saturday night."

But it also seemed equally true of most of the women I knew—including myself—regardless of the class we supposedly belonged to. Though I had left my factory-working neighborhood, gone to college, become a journalist, and thus was middle class, I still felt that I couldn't plan ahead. I had to be flexible—first, so that I could be ready to get on a plane for any writing assignment (even though the male writers I knew launched into books and other long-term projects on their own), and then so that I could adapt to the career and priorities of an eventual husband and children (even though I was leading a rewarding life without either). Among the results of this uncertainty were a stunning lack of career planning and such smaller penalties as no savings, no insurance, and an apartment that lacked basic pieces of furniture.

On the other hand, I had friends who were married to men whose longer-term career plans were compatible with their own, yet they still lived their lives in day-to-day response to any possible needs of their husbands and children. Moreover,

the one male colleague who shared or even understood this sense of powerlessness was a successful black journalist and literary critic who admitted that even after twenty years he planned only one assignment at a time. He couldn't forget his dependence on the approval of white editors.

Clearly there is more to this fear of the future than a conventional definition of class could explain. There is also caste: the unchangeable marks of sex and race that bring a whole constellation of cultural injunctions against power, even the limited power of controlling one's own life.

We haven't yet examined time-sense and future planning as functions of discrimination, but we have begun to struggle with them, consciously or not. As a movement, women have become painfully conscious of too much reaction and living from one emergency to the next, with too little initiative and planned action of our own; hence many of our losses to a much smaller but more entrenched and consistent right wing.

Though the cultural habit of living in the present and glazing over the future goes deep, we've begun to challenge the cultural punishment awaiting the "pushy" and "selfish" women (and the "uppity" minority men) who try to break through it and control their own lives.

Even so, feminist writers and theorists tend to avoid the future by lavishing all our analytical abilities on what's wrong with the present, or on revisions of history and critiques of the influential male thinkers of the past. The big, original, and certainly courageous books of this wave of feminism have been more diagnostic than prescriptive. We need pragmatic planners and visionary futurists, but can we think of even one feminist five-year-plan? Perhaps the closest we have come is visionary architecture or feminist science fiction, but they generally avoid the practical steps of how to get from here to there.

Obviously, many of us need to extend our time-sense—to have the courage to plan for the future, even while most of us are struggling to keep our heads above water in the present. But this does not mean a flat-out imitation of the culturally masculine habit of planning ahead, living in the future, and thus living a deferred life. It doesn't mean the traditional sacrifice of spontaneous action, or a sensitive awareness of the present, that comes from long years of career education with little intrusion of reality, from corporate pressure to work now for the sake of a reward after retirement, or, least logical of all, from patriarchal religions that expect obedience now in return for a reward after death.

In fact, the ability to live in the present, to tolerate uncertainty, and to remain open, spontaneous, and flexible are all culturally female qualities that many men need and have been denied. As usual, both halves of the polarized masculine-feminine division need to learn from each other's experiences. If men spent more time raising small children, for instance, they would be forced to develop more patience and flexibility. If women had more power in the planning of natural resources and other long-term processes—or even in the planning of our own careers and reproductive lives—we would have to develop more sense of the future and of cause and effect.

An obsession with reacting to the present, feminine-style, or on controlling and living in the future, masculine-style, are both wasteful of time.

And time is all there is.

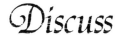Discuss

1. Which statement describes Steinem's view of what people need to do about time?

    a. Both men and women need to become more spontaneous in their behavior and avoid the disappointments that occur when plans fail.

    b. Both men and women need to develop strategies that will help them use time more profitably.

    c. Women need to develop the planning strategies of men, so that they can eliminate the spontaneous acts which cause inefficiency.

2. What does Steinem see as the cause of women's failure to plan ahead?

3. What do women and poor people appear to have in common? Why?

Explore

1. What failures does Steinem see in the women's movement? What does she think ought to be done?

2. What does she see as wrong with the way men plan their lives and careers? How does too much planning lead to living a "deferred life"? What do you suppose she means with that term?

3. Does Steinem see anything positive about women's sense of time? If so, what is it?

For Your Journal

1. Steinem believes that the labeling of many qualities as masculine or feminine stems from cultural values. What instances do you see of qualities that are considered female or male? Would you like to see those cultural expectations change? If so, in what ways?

2. Observe the behaviors of men and women you know. Do you see any instances of the uses of time Steinem describes in her essay?

3. Analyze your own uses of time—your spontaneity and your planning. Write a description of those uses.

The Perfidy[1] of Maatland

Alan Paton

In this story of a university in South Africa, you share the frustration not only of the oppressed, but also of those in power.

THE TWENTY-ONE STUDENTS rose when the Principal entered their common-room, and sat when he was seated. Some looked at him and some looked at the walls and the floor. Their looks told him nothing. They were neither hostile nor friendly. But he sensed that they were fully aware of him, and would hear every word and catch every meaning. They were as vigilant as he, and he, clad in the robes of authority, was conscious of the power of their impotence.

"I have called you together," he said, "to ask your help and advice. You are all leading students, and you will understand that a Principal cannot allow a repetition of last night's events. I have no wish to punish. I wish only to find out why you paint such slogans on the walls, so that I may try, in so far as I am able, to make it unnecessary for you to paint them again. Speak freely, for only I am here, and what you say to me is for my ears alone."

But no one spoke, no one offered to help and advise him. They sat looking at whatever they had looked at before, without noise or shuffling, making the meeting more silent than any other he had ever spoken to.

"Will no one speak?" he asked.

But no one spoke.

"May I ask why you will not speak?"

A young man rose, dark and slender.

"Principal, you asked twenty of us to meet you here. But there are twenty-one. I am the twenty-first. I am not on your list, and I must leave if you order me to do so. If I were on your list, I would not speak either. Why do we not speak? Because the last one of us who rose to speak when he was

invited, and told the truth as he was asked to do, sits now in a small village many miles from here, and he may not leave it. He was our cleverest student, and was about to take his degree, but it would appear that there will never be a degree for him. However, if you wish me to speak, I shall do so."

"Will no one else speak?" asked the Principal. But no one answered.

"If none of you will speak, then I shall ask this young man to speak for you, but you must understand that I assume you wish him to do so."

"Principal," said the young man, "that is what they wish."

"Then you may speak."

"Principal, you must not be offended by me. I do not come here to offend you. But you will no doubt wish to ask me questions. Are you willing that I should question you also?"

The Principal smiled. "You may do so, but I may not always answer you. Nor would I expect you always to answer me."

"Then let me ask you, Principal, why is it these twenty who are asked to meet you? You have been here only a week. How do you know which students to ask? We have no Students' Council. It is too dangerous to be a member of the Students' Council. Who told you that these were the twenty to ask?"

A hard question indeed, the kind to make outraged authority rear up and strike. No one had ever asked him such a question in his life. His own students at Maatland would never have done so. They would have asked, *Professor, what does the professor think about this?* At public meetings people said, *Thank you, professor, for your message,* or even, *Pro-*

[1]**perfidy:** betrayal, treachery, or deceit.

fessor, you are God's gift to our people. Then of his own doing he had left it all behind to come to this troubled and tempestuous place. *We've had too much trouble there,* the minister had said. *It doesn't do us any good. That's why I want you to go there. What we need is a man from Maatland.* So he had left the town of the oaks and the mountains and the historic houses, where the Minister and he had been young men together, and he had come to this dry and barren place. And at his installation, a bare twenty-four hours ago, he had promised that in ten years' time they would take all courses, in the Arts and the Sciences, in Theology and in Medicine, in their own language. Then to be called at four in the morning by his Disciplinary Officer, who was also his Vice-Principal, to see the mocking slogan VERNACULAR[2] DEGREES—HA! HA!, and the insulting one MAASDORP, HUISTCE! painted above his own office.

He smiled at the young man. "I am not willing to tell you who told me that these are the twenty leading students. Just as I would not expect you to tell me who painted the slogans."

"Principal, we think we know who told you. Is it important to you to know what we think?"

Was it important? Or was this the time to say, *No, I wish only to find out why you paint such slogans on the wall?* He had always taught his students to fear no knowledge. How could he say, *No, it is not important?*

"Yes, I wish to know."

"You see, Principal, we have no Students' Council. Whenever anything went wrong here, it was the members of the Students' Council who suffered. This clever student of whom I told you was not insolent. He was brought up to be mannerly and respectful, but he was also taught to respect himself and to speak the truth about all matters on which he was asked to speak or on which he felt a duty to speak. I should know this, for the parents who taught him these things were the ones who taught me also." The young man's voice rose a little, as though he felt suddenly some little pain.

"There is nothing in our village, Principal, no money, no work, no great property, no rich people, only people like my parents, whose one desire is to see their children educated. Do you understand how they feel, Principal, when their clever son must humble himself and plough the fields, and

---

[2]**vernacular**: native or ordinary, instead of learned or literary.

may not move from the valley where they live, because when he was invited he stood up and spoke the truth?"

"Everyone in that valley knows, Principal, even the most unlearned, that this young man was sent home, not because he did not work, not because he stole or murdered or raped, but because he stood up and spoke things that all of them know to be true. That gives great pain, Principal, to know that one of your young men is punished, and so heavily punished, because he speaks what he thinks to be true."

He said with some pride, "He was the best speaker of us all, not humble, not arrogant, but clear and beautiful in thought, with words simple when they needed to be simple, and not so simple when they needed to be otherwise, and every word true."

Maasdorp sat impassively, but inwardly strange emotions were stirring in him, strange and embarrassingly powerful, because they were compounded with some element that could cause the voice to tremble if one did not master it. He was experiencing something hitherto unknown to him, a pride in a young man who though of his own country, was not of his own race or color.

He said slowly and carefully, "You speak well also."

The young man answered him proudly. "We inherited it from my father. When he spoke in council, no one could take his eyes from that face or his ears from that sound." And then again the irony, "He spoke in the vernacular, Principal, not being able to speak in any other language."

Yet though the young man was ironic, he was clearly in some kind of distress, so that Maasdorp said to him quietly, "You were going to tell me something."

"I was going to tell you, Principal, that we believe that the list of twenty names was supplied to you by the Disciplinary Officer, and that this list was given to him by the security police, or compiled by him together with them. Over each of these twenty students hangs the sword that struck off my brother's head. I tell you these things because you are new. We do not know who runs this place, you the Principal, or your Disciplinary Officer and the police. But so long as we think it is your Disciplinary Officer and the police, we shall not speak, and some of us will paint words on the walls, because only in that way can we communicate at all."

The young man sat down, and the twenty-one students sat and looked at the walls and the floor, or at a Principal who, of his own will and choice, had torn down a barrier that no one had breached before. Again he controlled his voice carefully, and said to them, "Are you against university education in your own language?"

The slender young man rose again. "None of us here takes responsibility for the slogan on vernacular education. Another twenty must be found for that. But we are totally opposed to vernacular education. We want to equip ourselves and our people to enter the modern world. We believe that we shall never do so through the medium of our own language. Your people did it through Afrikaans, with the help of English where necessary, but Afrikaans is a western language, and it could be made a language of science and technology. But our language cannot be. Do not think we despise it, Principal. It speaks to us of our land and our people and our aspirations. It will make our literature and our songs, and our deepest thoughts will always be spoken in it, but we cannot make it a language of science and technology."

He looked at the Principal very directly. "I see that you do not believe me, or that you do not want to believe me, but if we had time and could all speak freely, we would give you good reasons for our conviction."

"The Russians entered this modern world through Russian," said Massdorp patiently, "and the Chinese are now doing it through Chinese. What do you say to that?"

"We say nothing, Principal. It is not considered safe by us to discuss anything that happens in those two countries."

He sat down again, and the silence now contained a sharp note of mockery. Maasdorp was not a man to believe that all things could be done by an edict of authority, and he was glad of it, for he was now realizing the strange power of these young men and women who could endure these things in this inscrutable silence. He was aware too that within seven days of his arrival he had made a speech that had deeply antagonized his students. Must he renounce it? The Minister's own wish? *I want to see more and more own-language education in these universities. I don't think ten years too short a time for it. And I want you there because of your own knowledge of the language and the people. You are, if I may say so, a major prophet of own-sort development.*

"I am your Principal, and I cannot bow to threats. You would not respect me if I did. My goal is own-language education, and if I fail to reach it, then I must think again."

He could not tell from their silence whether they were outraged or despairing or did not care. He said to them very deliberately, "This university will be administered by me, and not by any external authority. But I shall not allow insubordination."

They turned their eyes to him, as though he had suddenly said something worthy of direct notice. The mockery of their silence was palpable.[3] They were waiting to hear how he would deal with their insubordination. And again he felt the power of their impotence.

"I shall post notices immediately to say that these acts of last night will be condoned, but that any further act will bring severe punishment. And I appeal to you. You are students of authority. Will you use it to see that no further acts are committed?"

He looked at the slender young man. "Will you answer?"

"How can we answer, Principal? If further acts are committed, will we then be held responsible? We are not students of authority. We are only twenty names on the list of the police, and therefore we cannot be expected to act responsibly. You cannot appoint us as a Students' Council. Only the students can do that, and they refuse to do it, because it is their representatives who are always sent home. Therefore, Principal, we cannot accept any authority."

Maasdorp was angry, but he concealed it. He said tonelessly, "Then I can only express the hope that these acts will cease, and that some or all of you will use your influence to prevent them. Students, good-day."

He rose, and they rose too, and stood in impeccable silence while he walked out. As he walked to his office, he passed many students going to and from their lectures. They walked past him with all correctness, opening their ranks to give him passage, but giving him neither look nor word. He could hear the voice of Van Riet, his Vice-Principal and Disciplinary Officer, saying, *Firmness is the only thing they understand, Principal, swift, firm, strong action—and they like it, because they know where they are.*

[3]**palpable:** obvious, or capable of being felt.

Back in his office Van Riet said to him, "In other words you're offering them a second chance. It won't work, Principal. I know these students. They broke Martens because he gave them a second chance. Now he shuts himself up in his house down there in Riversdale and won't show himself in the street."

When the Principal did not answer, Van Riet said to him, almost angrily, "They don't want a second chance. They want to break *you*, that's all. And it's my duty, to you and the college and to our people, to see that you're not broken."

"I know you are a man of duty," said Maasdorp. "But I am a man of duty too, and in the end it is my duty that I must do."

"Naturally," said Van Riet, if not with contempt, then with impatience for a man who could utter truisms when a nation was fighting for its life. "Principal, Captain Smith is in my office and wishes to meet you."

"Send him in," said Maasdorp, "in ten minutes."

He had heard of Smith, a hated, feared, admired policeman. He was correct with superiors and equals, and ruthless to all enemies of authority, whether they plotted secretly or opposed openly. Unmarried, he lived alone in a house whose garden was always ablaze, so that people in passing would say, *A man who loves flowers can't be a bad man.* Without vices, he knew all the vices of others, and it was said that he knew the thoughts and intentions of all of the thousand students of Mount Jerboa. And they in their turn supposed him to be the true head of the university. The Minister had said, *The head of the security police, Captain Smith, is an extraordinary man, and you will find his help invaluable.* Then after a pause he said, *I know what is in your mind, Professor. But this is no ordinary job you are undertaking. It is my considered opinion that it can't be done without the police.*

What sort of a job was this, that could not be done without the police? This university, that was preparing a nation for its independence, why must it depend for its being on the police. Had he come here merely to teach, and to leave discipline in the hands of others? He did not delude himself. His predecessors had all worked closely with the police. But Martens, the poor creature who shut himself up in his Riversdale house, had not been able to endure it any longer. It was not only the students that had broken him, it was the police also. In their battle Martens had been the main casualty.

"Principal," said Smith, "firstly I am here to meet you. Your writings and speeches are well known to us, and I am glad to welcome you to Mount Jerboa."

"Thank you, Captain. I hope our relations will be good."

"I hope so also. Principal, my superiors take this matter of the slogans very seriously. I understand you have decided to take no action on this occasion."

"That is so, Captain."

"It could be argued that you are not empowered in law to do so, but I am not going to raise the matter. However, if the offense is repeated, then the police must take action. But it would be better for all concerned if we took it together."

"You know as well as I do," said Maasdorp, "that I am trying a new approach. I admit I am trying to do what my predecessors were unable to do. I am trying to administer this university without threats, particularly the threat of expulsion. I want to administer it without any help from the police, except of course when a criminal offense is committed. I have nothing against the police, Captain, but just as you would not want me in your police offices, just so do I not want you in my university."

"The painting of slogans is a criminal offense, Principal. Let me make it clear to you. I do not have to be called in. I can come in, not only when an offense has been committed, but when I believe that an offense may be committed."

"I understand you well, Captain. But let me make one thing clear to you also. You reported the painting of the slogans to Dr. Van Riet at four in the morning. In future you will make such reports to me. Dr. Van Riet is the Disciplinary Officer, and his task is to recommend what action should be taken against offending students. He is not an administrative officer."

"I shall do that, Principal. I was merely following your predecessor's arrangements. He did not like the police either, but his solution was different from yours. You want to see them yourself, he did not want to see them at all."

"I must ask you not to say I do not like the police. I don't want them to help me to administer the university, that's all."

"I beg your pardon, Principal. May I say one last thing to you?"

"Certainly."

"I was also at a university, Principal, and I know what you are talking about. But this is not Maatland, it is Mount Jerboa. Neither you nor anyone else could run this place without the police. These students don't trust you, and in the end you won't trust them."

No sooner had the captain gone than the telegram arrived. STRONGLY DISAPPROVE YOUR ACTION IN THE MATTER OF SLOGANS. KINDLY CALL EMERGENCY COUNCIL FOR SATURDAY. VAN ONSELEN, CHAIRMAN.

So the Chairman of the University Council, who lived two hundred miles away, had already heard of his private meeting. Though he had known a lot about Mount Jerboa before he came, he had not been prepared for the web of intelligence that was spun about himself. It was his first experience of such a world. Who could have done it but Van Riet? He suddenly felt sick at heart. His great aim had been to gain the confidence of his students, but how would he ever do it under the surveillance of Van Riet? His Vice-Principal's reputation was well known, as a merciless and humorless ruler of young men and women. He had been the punitive officer of the last three principals, and he had resolved the endemic[4] crises of Mount Jerboa with firm decision, resulting in the expulsion of the best and brightest and most vital students, who would never again find entrance to any other institution.

With sudden clarity Maasdorp realized that such actions were unforgivable whatever the provocation. He remembered with pain the young man punished for life for speaking the truth. His despondency left him. He would call the emergency council, and tell them that he would never consent to any diminution of his authority.

"You'll be appointed without question," said the Minister. "Own-language education in ten

years, and absolute co-operation with the security police. Professor, I wish you luck," he said with emotion. "Our people have always been like that. When one fails, there is always another to make it good. The West is lost, Professor. But one day when it wants to find itself, it will come to us, to you, Professor, and to Mount Jerboa, to learn the way."

Something was troubling the Minister. All was not well with him. He had what is known as *a nail in the soul.* Behind the glow there was anger and pain.

"Do you know, Professor, that Maatland has taken Maasdorp back? Yes, you're right, it *is* a scandal. It's a slap in the face of the nation."

The Minister sat brooding, the professor forgotten. In the Minister's eyes was a look blended of frustration and pain.

"Do you see what I mean about Mount Jerboa? Maatland has failed us, but Mount Jerboa has come to our aid. Professor, you must make it a shining example of our civilizing mission. Don't think nothing will be done, Professor. Notice will be taken. I am discussing it with my colleagues. You are not to repeat this, but some of them think Maatland is too big to touch. But it will be touched, Professor."

The Minister sat there, lost in angry thoughts. "Be assured, Minister," said the professor soothingly, "we shall not fail you at Mount Jerboa. You are a busy man, and I must go."

He rose, and the Minister rose. They shook hands, and the Minister brought himself to attention. He said, "We shall be watching you with approbation."[5]

At the door of the enormous room the professor turned to smile, but the Minister had already retreated into his angry thoughts. The Principal put down the telegram with satisfaction. STRONGLY APPROVE YOUR FIRM ACTION. VAN ONSELEN, CHAIRMAN.

It was a good beginning.

---

[4]**endemic:** peculiar to a particular society or region.

[5]**approbation:** approval or commendation.

Discuss

1. Which phrase best describes the manner in which the twenty-first student addresses Maasdorp?

    a. respectful but direct

    b. pompous and rebellious

    c. mocking and sarcastic

2. How does Maasdorp's attitude and approach differ from that of those in authority at Mount Jerboa? To what do you attribute that difference of opinion?

3. Why did the Minister send Maasdorp to Mount Jerboa?

Explore

1. Why do the Minister and those in authority want own-language education? Why do the students want education in English? Whose position do you see as more substantial, and why?

2. What is the significance of the title of the story? In what way might the title be ambiguous? Who is being betrayed?

3. Why does an extra student come to speak for the twenty on the list invited by Maasdorp? Why is that list important to the students?

4. What do you think are the motives of those in authority regarding the education of the students? Do you think there is a difference between the stated goals of the authorities and their true goals? Explain.

5. Why is the Minister feeling anger and pain at the end of the story?

6. Describe the narrative voice in this story. What is the effect of using a third-person narrator?

For Your Journal

1. What do you think will happen at Mount Jerboa with the new principal? What do you think will happen at Maatland with the return of Maasdorp? On what do you base your guesses?

2. With whom do you sympathize in this story, and why?

3. In this story the students employ a kind of civil obedience—that is, they defy the law to seek what they consider justice. What value do you see in this course of action, if any? Under what circumstances might you engage in civil disobedience?

Equal in Paris

James Baldwin

In this essay, taken from his collection *Notes of a Native Son*, Baldwin tells of going to Paris, seeking alternative ways of living and behaving, but finds a new set of problems in a culture that he doesn't understand.

ON THE 19TH OF DECEMBER in 1949, when I had been living in Paris for a little over a year, I was arrested as a receiver of stolen goods and spent eight days in prison. My arrest came about through an American tourist whom I had met twice in New York, who had been given my name and address and told to look me up. I was then living on the top floor of a ludicrously grim hotel on the rue du Bac, one of those enormous dark, cold, and hideous establishments in which Paris abounds that seem to breathe forth, in their airless, humid, stone-cold halls, the weak light, scurrying chambermaids, and creaking stairs, an odor of gentility long long dead. The place was run by an ancient Frenchman dressed in an elegant black suit which was green with age, who cannot properly be described as bewildered or even as being in a state of shock, since he had really stopped breathing around 1910. There he sat at his desk in the weirdly lit, fantastically furnished lobby, day in and day out, greeting each one of his extremely impoverished and *louche*[1] lodgers with a stately inclination of the head that he had no doubt been taught in some impossibly remote time was the proper way for a *propriétaire*[2] to greet his guests. If it had not been for his daughter, an extremely hardheaded *tricoteuse*[3]—the inclination of *her* head was chilling and abrupt, like the downbeat of an ax—the hotel would certainly have gone bankrupt long before. It was said that this old man had not gone farther than the door of his hotel for thirty years, which was not at all difficult to believe. He looked as though the daylight would have killed him.

I did not, of course, spend much of my time in this palace. The moment I began living in French hotels I understood the necessity of French cafés. This made it rather difficult to look me up, for as soon as I was out of bed I hopefully took notebook and fountain pen off to the upstairs room of the Flore, where I consumed rather a lot of coffee and, as evening approached, rather a lot of alcohol, but did not get much writing done. But one night, in one of the cafés of St. Germain des Près, I was discovered by this New Yorker and only because we found ourselves in Paris we immediately established the illusion that we had been fast friends back in the good old U.S.A. This illusion proved itself too thin to support an evening's drinking, but by that time it was too late. I had committed myself to getting him a room in my hotel the next day, for he was living in one of the nest of hotels near the Gare St. Lazare, where, he said, the *propriétaire* was a thief, his wife a repressed nymphomaniac, the chambermaids "pigs," and the rent a crime. Americans are always talking this way about the French and so it did not occur to me that he meant what he said or that he would take into his own hands the means of avenging himself on the French Republic. It did not occur to me, either, that the means which he *did* take could possibly have brought about such dire results, results which were not less dire for being also comic-opera.

It came as the last of a series of disasters which had perhaps been made inevitable by the fact that I had come to Paris originally with a little over forty dollars in my pockets, nothing in the bank, and no grasp whatever of the French language. It developed, shortly, that I had no grasp of the French

[1] *louche: Fr.*, shifty-eyed, shady.
[2] *propriétaire: Fr.*, landlord or owner.
[3] *tricoteuse: Fr.*, woman who knits.

character either. I considered the French an ancient, intelligent, and cultured race, which indeed
they are. I did not know, however, that ancient
glories imply, at least in the middle of the present
century, present fatigue and, quite probably, para-
noia; that there is a limit to the role of the intelligence in human affairs; and that no people come
into possession of a culture without having paid a
heavy price for it. This price they cannot, of
course, assess, but it is revealed in their personalities and in their institutions. The very word "institutions," from my side of the ocean, where, it
seemed to me, we suffered so cruelly from the lack
of them, had a pleasant ring, as of safety and order
and common sense; one had to come into contact
with these institutions in order to understand that
they were also outmoded, exasperating, completely
impersonal, and very often cruel. Similarly, the
personality which had seemed from a distance to be
so large and free had to be dealt with before one
could see that, if it was large, it was also inflexible
and, for the foreigner, full of strange, high, dusty
rooms which could not be inhabited. One had, in
short, to come into contact with an alien culture
in order to understand that a culture was not a
community basket-weaving project, nor yet an act
of God; was something neither desirable nor unde-
sirable in itself, being inevitable, being nothing
more or less than the recorded and visible effects
on a body of people of the vicissitudes[4] with which
they had been forced to deal. And their great men
are revealed as simply another of these vicissitudes,
even if, quite against their will, the brief battle of
their great men with them has left them richer.

When my American friend left his hotel to
move to mine, he took with him, out of pique,[5] a
bedsheet belonging to the hotel and put it in his
suitcase. When he arrived at my hotel I borrowed
the sheet, since my own were filthy and the chambermaid showed no sign of bringing me any clean
ones, and put it on my bed. The sheets belonging
to *my* hotel I put out in the hall, congratulating
myself on having thus forced on the attention of
the Grand Hôtel du Bac the unpleasant state of its
linen. Thereafter, since, as it turned out, we kept
very different hours—I got up at noon, when, as I
gathered by meeting him on the stairs one day, he
was only just getting in—my new-found friend and
I saw very little of each other.

On the evening of the 19th I was sitting thinking melancholy thoughts about Christmas and staring at the walls of my room. I imagine that I had
sold something or that someone had sent me a
Christmas present, for I remember that I had a little money. In those days in Paris, though I floated,
so to speak, on a sea of acquaintances, I knew almost no one. Many people were eliminated from
my orbit by virtue of the fact that they had more
money than I did, which placed me, in my own
eyes, in the humiliating role of a free-loader; and
other people were eliminated by virtue of the fact
that they enjoyed their poverty, shrilly insisting
that this wretched round of hotel rooms, bad food,
humiliating concierges, and unpaid bills was the
Great Adventure. It couldn't, however, for me, end
soon enough, this Great Adventure; there was a
real question in my mind as to which would end
soonest, the Great Adventure or me. This meant,
however, that there were many evenings when I sat
in my room, knowing that I couldn't work there,
and not knowing what to do, or whom to see. On
this particular evening I went down and knocked
on the American's door.

There were two Frenchmen standing in the
room, who immediately introduced themselves to
me as policemen; which did not worry me. I had
got used to policemen in Paris bobbing up at the
most improbable times and places, asking to see
one's *carte d'identité*.[6] These policemen, however,
showed very little interest in my papers. They were
looking for something else. I could not imagine
what this would be and, since I knew I certainly
didn't have it, I scarcely followed the conversation
they were having with my friend. I gathered that
they were looking for some kind of gangster and
since I wasn't a gangster and knew that gangsterism
was not, insofar as he had one, my friend's style, I
was sure that the two policemen would presently
bow and say *Merci, messieurs*,[7] and leave. For by
this time, I remember very clearly, I was dying to
have a drink and go to dinner.

I did not have a drink or go to dinner for many
days after this, and when I did my outraged stomach promptly heaved everything up again. For now
one of the policemen began to exhibit the most
vivid interest in me and asked, very politely, if he
might see my room. To which we mounted, making, I remember, the most civilized small talk on
the way and even continuing it for some moments

---

[4]**vicissitudes:** changes.
[5]**pique:** irritation or resentment.

[6]**carte d'identité:** *Fr.*, identification card.
[7]**Merci, messieurs:** Thank you, sirs.

after we were in the room in which there was certainly nothing to be seen but the familiar poverty and disorder of that precarious group of people of whatever age, race, country, calling, or intention which Paris recognizes as *les étudiants*[8] and sometimes, more ironically and precisely, as *les nonconformistes*. Then he moved to my bed, and in a terrible flash, not quite an instant before he lifted the bedspread, I understood what he was looking for. We looked at the sheet, on which I read, for the first time, lettered in the most brilliant scarlet I have ever seen, the name of the hotel from which it had been stolen. It was the first time the word *stolen* entered my mind. I had certainly seen the hotel monogram the day I put the sheet on the bed. It had simply meant nothing to me. In New York I had seen hotel monograms on everything from silver to soap and towels. Taking things from New York hotels was practically a custom, though, I suddenly realized, I had never known anyone to take a *sheet*. Sadly, and without a word to me, the inspector took the sheet from the bed, folded it under his arm, and we started back downstairs. I understood that I was under arrest.

And so we passed through the lobby, four of us, two of us very clearly criminal, under the eyes of the old man and his daughter, neither of whom said a word, into the streets where a light rain was falling. And I asked, in French, "But is this very serious?"

For I was thinking, it is, after all, only a sheet, not even new.

"No," said one of them. "It's not serious."

"It's nothing at all," said the other.

I took this to mean that we would receive a reprimand at the police station and be allowed to go to dinner. Later on I concluded that they were not being hypocritical or even trying to comfort us. They meant exactly what they said. It was only that they spoke another language.

In Paris everything is very slow. Also, when dealing with the bureaucracy, the man you are talking to is never the man you have to see. The man you have to see has just gone off to Belgium, or is busy with his family, or has just discovered that he is a cuckold; he will be in next Tuesday at three o'clock, or sometime in the course of the afternoon, or possibly tomorrow, or, possibly, in the next five minutes. But if he is coming in the next five minutes he will be far too busy to be able to see you today. So that I suppose I was not really

astonished to learn at the commissariat[9] that nothing could possibly be done about us before The Man arrived in the morning. But no, we could not go off and have dinner and come back in the morning. Of course he knew that we *would* come back—that was not the question. Indeed, there was no question: we would simply have to stay there for the night. We were placed in a cell which rather resembled a chicken coop. It was now about seven in the evening and I relinquished the thought of dinner and began to think of lunch.

I discouraged the chatter of my New York friend and this left me alone with my thoughts. I was beginning to be frightened and I bent all my energies, therefore, to keeping my panic under control. I began to realize that I was in a country I knew nothing about, in the hands of a people I did not understand at all. In a similar situation in New York I would have had some idea of what to do because I would have had some idea of what to expect. I am not speaking now of legality which, like most of the poor, I had never for an instant trusted, but of the temperament of the people with whom I had to deal. I had become very accomplished in New York at guessing and, therefore, to a limited extent manipulating to my advantage the reactions of the white world. But this was not New York. None of my old weapons could serve me here. I did not know what they saw when they looked at me. I knew very well what Americans saw when they looked at me and this allowed me to play endless and sinister variations on the role which they had assigned me; since I knew that it was, for them, of the utmost importance that they never be confronted with what, in their own personalities, made this role so necessary and gratifying to them, I knew that they could never call my hand or, indeed, afford to know what I was doing; so that I moved into every crucial situation with the deadly and rather desperate advantages of bitterly accumulated perception, of pride and contempt. This is an awful sword and shield to carry through the world, and the discovery that, in the game I was playing, I did myself a violence of which the world, at its most ferocious, would scarcely have been capable, was what had driven me out of New York. It was a strange feeling, in this situation, after a year in Paris, to discover that my weapons would never again serve me as they had.

---

[8]**les étudiants:** *Fr.*, students.

[9]**commissariat:** police headquarters.

It was quite clear to me that the Frenchmen in whose hands I found myself were no better or worse than their American counterparts. Certainly their uniforms frightened me quite as much, and their impersonality, and the threat, always very keenly felt by the poor, of violence, was as present in that commissariat as it had ever been for me in any police station. And I had seen, for example, what Paris policemen could do to Arab peanut vendors. The only difference here was that I did not understand these people, did not know what techniques their cruelty took, did not know enough about their personalities to see danger coming, to ward it off, did not know on what ground to meet it. That evening in the commissariat I was not a despised black man. They would simply have laughed at me if I had behaved like one. For them, I was an American. And here it was they who had the advantage, for that word, *Américain*, gave them some idea, far from inaccurate, of what to expect from me. In order to corroborate none of their ironical expectations I said nothing and did nothing— which was not the way any Frenchman, white or black, would have reacted. The question thrusting up from the bottom of my mind was not *what* I was, but *who*. And this question, since a *what* can get by with skill but a *who* demands resources, was my first real intimation of what humility must mean.

In the morning it was still raining. Between nine and ten o'clock a black Citroën took us off to the Ile de la Cité, to the great, gray Préfecture. I realize now that the questions I put to the various policemen who escorted us were always answered in such a way as to corroborate what I wished to hear. This was not out of politeness, but simply out of indifference—or, possibly, an ironical pity—since each of the policemen knew very well that nothing would speed or halt the machine in which I had become entangled. They knew I did not know this and there was certainly no point in their telling me. In one way or another I would certainly come out at the other side—for they also knew that being found with a stolen bedsheet in one's possession was not a crime punishable by the guillotine. (They had the advantage over me there, too, for there were certainly moments later on when I was not so sure.) If I did *not* come out at the other side—well, that was just too bad. So, to my question, put while we were in the Citroën—"Will it be over today?"—I received a "*Oui, bien sûr.*"[10] He was not lying. As it turned out, the *procès-verbal* was over

that day. Trying to be realistic, I dismissed, in the Citroën, all thoughts of lunch and pushed my mind ahead to dinner.

At the Préfecture we were first placed in a tiny cell, in which it was almost impossible either to sit or to lie down. After a couple of hours of this we were taken down to an office, where, for the first time, I encountered the owner of the bedsheet and where the *procès-verbal* took place. This was simply an interrogation, quite chillingly clipped and efficient (so that there was, shortly, no doubt in one's own mind that one *should* be treated as a criminal), which was recorded by a secretary. When it was over, this report was given to us to sign. One had, of course, no choice but to sign it, even though my mastery of written French was very far from certain. We were being held, according to the law in France, incommunicado, and all my angry demands to be allowed to speak to my embassy or to see a lawyer met with a stony "*Oui, oui. Plus tard.*"[11] The *procès-verbal* over, we were taken back to the cell, before which, shortly, passed the owner of the bedsheet. He said he hoped we had slept well, gave a vindictive wink, and disappeared.

By this time there was only one thing clear: that we had no way of controlling the sequence of events and could not possibly guess what this sequence would be. It seemed to me, since what I regarded as the high point—the *procès-verbal*—had been passed and since the hotel-keeper was once again in possession of his sheet, that we might reasonably expect to be released from police custody in a matter of hours. We had been detained now for what would soon be twenty-four hours, during which time I had learned only that the official charge against me was *receleur*.[12] My mental shifting, between lunch and dinner, to say nothing of the physical lack of either of these delights, was beginning to make me dizzy. The steady chatter of my friend from New York, who was determined to keep my spirits up, made me feel murderous; I was praying that some power would release us from this freezing pile of stone before the impulse became the act. And I was beginning to wonder what was happening in that beautiful city, Paris, which lived outside these walls. I wondered how long it would take before anyone casually asked, "But where's Jimmy? He hasn't been around"—and realized, knowing the people I knew, that it would take several days.

[10]**Oui, bien sûr:** Yes, certainly.

[11]**Plus tard:** later.
[12]**receleur:** *Fr.*, receiver of stolen goods.

Quite late in the afternoon we were taken from our cells; handcuffed, each to a separate officer; led through a maze of steps and corridors to the top of the building; fingerprinted; photographed. As in movies I had seen, I was placed against a wall, facing an old-fashioned camera, behind which stood one of the most completely cruel and indifferent faces I had ever seen, while someone next to me and, therefore, just outside my line of vision, read off in a voice from which all human feeling, even feeling of the most base description, had long since fled, what must be called my public characteristics—which, at that time and in that place, seemed anything but that. He might have been roaring to the hostile world secrets which I could barely, in the privacy of midnight, utter to myself. But he was only reading off my height, my features, my approximate weight, my color—that color which, in the United States, had often, odd as it may sound, been my salvation—the color of my hair, my age, my nationality. A light then flashed, the photographer and I staring at each other as though there was murder in our hearts, and then it was over. Handcuffed again, I was led downstairs to their bottom of the building, into a great enclosed shed in which had been gathered the very scrapings off the Paris streets. Old, old men, so ruined and old that life in them seemed really to prove the miracle of the quickening power of the Holy Ghost—for clearly their life was no longer their affair, it was no longer even their burden, they were simply the clay which had once been touched. And men not so old, with faces the color of lead and the consistency of oatmeal, eyes that made me think of stale *café-au-lait*[13] spiked with arsenic, bodies which could take in food and water—any food and water—and pass it out, but which could not do anything more, except possibly, at midnight, along the riverbank where rats scurried, rape. And young men, harder and crueler than the Paris stones, older by far than I, their chronological senior by some five to seven years. And North Africans, old and young, who seemed the only living people in this place because they yet retained the grace to be bewildered. But they were not bewildered by being in this shed: they were simply bewildered because they were no longer in North Africa. There was a great hole in the center of this shed which was the common toilet. Near it, though it was impossible to get very far from it, stood an old man with white hair, eating a piece of

camembert.[14] It was at this point, probably, that thought, for me, stopped, that physiology, if one may say so, took over. I found myself incapable of saying a word, not because I was afraid I would cry but because I was afraid I would vomit. And I did not think any longer of the city of Paris but my mind flew back to that home from which I had fled. I was sure that I would never see it any more. And it must have seemed to me that my flight from home was the cruelest trick I had ever played on myself, since it had led me here, down to a lower point than any I could ever in my life have imagined—lower, far, than anything I had seen in that Harlem which I had so hated and so loved, the escape from which had soon become the greatest direction of my life. After we had been here an hour or so a functionary came and opened the door and called out our names. And I was sure that *this* was my release. But I was handcuffed again and led out of the Préfecture into the streets—it was dark now, it was still raining—and before the steps of the Préfecture stood the great police wagon, doors facing me, wide open. The handcuffs were taken off, I entered the wagon, which was peculiarly constructed. It was divided by a narrow aisle, and on each side of the aisle was a series of narrow doors. These doors opened on a narrow cubicle, beyond which was a door which opened onto another narrow cubicle: three or four cubicles, each private, with a locking door. I was placed in one of them; I remember there was a small vent just above my head which let in a little light. The door of my cubicle was locked from the outside. I had no idea where this wagon was taking me and, as it began to move, I began to cry. I suppose I cried all the way to prison, the prison called Fresnes, which is twelve kilometers outside of Paris.

For reasons I have no way at all of understanding, prisoners whose last initial is A, B, or C are always sent to Fresnes; everybody else is sent to a prison called, rather cynically it seems to me, La Santé.[15] I will, obviously, never be allowed to enter La Santé, but I was told by people who certainly seemed to know that it was infinitely more unbearable than Fresnes. This arouses in me, until today, a positive storm of curiosity concerning what I promptly began to think of as The Other Prison. My colleague in crime, occurring lower in the alphabet, had been sent there and I confess that the minute he was gone I missed him. I missed him

---

[13]**café-au-lait:** coffee-and-milk beverage.

[14]**camembert:** a type of cheese.
[15]**La Santé:** Fr., Health.

because he was not French and because he was the only person in the world who knew that the story I told was true.

For, once locked in, divested of shoelaces, belt, watch, money, papers, nailfile, in a freezing cell in which both the window and the toilet were broken, with six other adventurers, the story I told of *l'affaire du drap de lit*[16] elicited only the wildest amusement or the most suspicious disbelief. Among the people who shared my cell the first three days no one, it is true, had been arrested for anything much more serious—or, at least, not serious in my eyes. I remember that there was a boy who had stolen a knitted sweater from a *monoprix*,[17] who would probably, it was agreed, receive a six-month sentence. There was an older man there who had been arrested for some kind of petty larceny. There were two North Africans, vivid, brutish, and beautiful, who alternated between gaiety and fury, not at the fact of their arrest but at the state of the cell. None poured as much emotional energy into the fact of their arrest as I did; they took it, as I would have liked to take it, as simply another unlucky happening in a very dirty world. For, though I had grown accustomed to thinking of myself as looking upon the world with a hard, penetrating eye, the truth was that they were far more realistic about the world than I, and more nearly right about it. The gap between us, which only a gesture I made could have bridged, grew steadily, during thirty-six hours, wider. I could not make any gesture simply because they frightened me. I was unable to accept my imprisonment as a fact, even as a temporary fact. I could not, even for a moment, accept my present companions as *my* companions. And they, of course, felt this and put it down, with perfect justice, to the fact that I was an American.

There was nothing to do all day long. It appeared that we would one day come to trial but no one knew when. We were awakened at seven-thirty by a rapping on what I believe is called the Judas, that small opening in the door of the cell which allows the guards to survey the prisoners. At this rapping we rose from the floor—we slept on straw pallets and each of us was covered with one thin blanket—and moved to the door of the cell. We peered through the opening into the center of the prison, which was, as I remember, three tiers high, all gray stone and gunmetal steel, precisely that

prison I had seen in movies, except that, in the movies, I had not known that it was cold in prison. I had not known that when one's shoelaces and belt have been removed one is, in the strangest way, demoralized. The necessity of shuffling and the necessity of holding up one's trousers with one hand turn one into a rag doll. And the movies fail, of course, to give one any idea of what prison food is like. Along the corridor, at seven-thirty, came three men, each pushing before him a great garbage can, mounted on wheels. In the garbage can of the first was the bread—this was passed to one through the small opening in the door. In the can of the second was the coffee. In the can of the third was what was always called *la soupe*, a pallid paste of potatoes which had certainly been bubbling on the back of the prison stove long before that first, so momentous revolution. Naturally, it was cold by this time and, starving as I was, I could not eat it. I drank the coffee—which was not coffee—because it was hot, and spent the rest of the day, huddled in my blanket, munching on the bread. It was not the French bread one bought in bakeries. In the evening the same procession returned. At ten-thirty the lights went out. I had a recurring dream, each night, a nightmare which always involved my mother's fried chicken. At the moment I was about to eat it came the rapping at the door. Silence is really all I remember of those first three days, silence and the color gray.

I am not sure now whether it was on the third or the fourth day that I was taken to trial for the first time. The days had nothing, obviously, to distinguish them from one another. I remember that I was very much aware that Christmas Day was approaching and I wondered if I was really going to spend Christmas Day in prison. And I remember that the first trial came the day before Christmas Eve.

On the morning of the first trial I was awakened by hearing my name called. I was told, hanging in a kind of void between my mother's fried chicken and the cold prison floor, "*Vous préparez. Vous êtes extrait*"[18]—which simply terrified me, since I did not know what interpretation to put on the word "*extrait*," and since my cellmates had been amusing themselves with me by telling terrible stories about the inefficiency of French prisons, an inefficiency so extreme that it had often happened that someone who was supposed to be taken out

[16]**l'affaire du drap de lit:** *Fr.*, the business of the bed-sheet.

[17]**monoprix:** *Fr.*, one-price shop.

[18]**Vous préparez. Vous êtes extrait:** Get ready. You've been released.

and tried found himself on the wrong line and was guillotined instead. The best way of putting my reaction to this is to say that, though I knew they were teasing me, it was simply not possible for me to totally *dis*-believe them. As far as I was concerned, once in the hands of the law in France, anything could happen. I shuffled along with the others who were *extrait* to the center of the prison, trying, rather, to linger in the office, which seemed the only warm spot in the whole world, and found myself again in that dreadful wagon, and was carried again to the Ile de la Cité, this time to the Palais de Justice. The entire day, except for ten minutes, was spent in one of the cells, first waiting to be tried, then waiting to be taken back to prison.

For I was *not* tried that day. By and by I was handcuffed and led through the halls, upstairs to the courtroom where I found my New York friend. We were placed together, both stage-whisperingly certain that this was the end of our ordeal. Nevertheless, while I waited for our case to be called, my eyes searched the courtroom, looking for a face I knew, hoping, anyway, that there was someone there who knew *me*, who would carry to someone outside the news that I was in trouble. But there was no one I knew there and I had had time to realize that there was probably only one man in Paris who could help me, an American patent attorney for whom I had worked as an office boy. He could have helped me because he had a quite solid position and some prestige and would have testified that, while working for him, I had handled large sums of money regularly, which made it rather unlikely that I would stoop to trafficking in bedsheets. However, he was somewhere in Paris, probably at this very moment enjoying a snack and a glass of wine and as far as the possibility of reaching him was concerned, he might as well have been on Mars. I tried to watch the proceedings and to make my mind a blank. But the proceedings were not reassuring. The boy, for example, who had stolen the sweater *did* receive a six-month sentence. It seemed to me that all the sentences meted out that day were excessive; though, again, it seemed that all the people who were sentenced that day had made, or clearly were going to make, crime their career. This seemed to be the opinion of the judge, who scarcely looked at the prisoners or listened to them; it seemed to be the opinion of the prisoners, who scarcely bothered to speak in their own behalf; it seemed to be the opinion of the lawyers, state lawyers for the most part, who were defending them. The great impulse of the courtroom seemed to be to put these people where they could not be seen— and not because they were offended at the crimes, unless, indeed, they were offended that the crimes were so petty, but because they did not wish to know that their society could be counted on to produce, probably in greater and greater numbers, a whole body of people for whom crime was the only possible career. Any society inevitably produces its criminals, but a society at once rigid and unstable can do nothing whatever to alleviate the poverty of its lowest members, cannot present to the hypothetical young man at the crucial moment that so-well-advertised right path. And the fact, perhaps, that the French are the earth's least sentimental people and must also be numbered among the most proud aggravates the plight of their lowest, youngest, and unluckiest members, for it means that the idea of rehabilitation is scarcely real to them. I confess that this attitude on their part raises in me sentiments of exasperation, admiration, and despair, revealing as it does, in both the best and the worst sense, their renowned and spectacular hardheadedness.

Finally our case was called and we rose. We gave our names. At the point that it developed that we were American the proceedings ceased, a hurried consultation took place between the judge and what I took to be several lawyers. Someone called out for an interpreter. The arresting officer had forgotten to mention our nationalities and there was, therefore, no interpreter in the court. Even if our French had been better than it was we would not have been allowed to stand trial without an interpreter. Before I clearly understood what was happening, I was handcuffed again and led out of the courtroom. The trial had been set back for the 27th of December.

I have sometimes wondered if I would *ever* have got out of prison if it had not been for the older man who had been arrested for the mysterious petty larceny. He was acquitted that day and when he returned to the cell—for he could not be released until morning—he found me sitting numbly on the floor, having just been prevented, by the sight of a man, all blood, being carried back to *his* cell on a stretcher, from seizing the bars and screaming until they let me out. The sight of the man on the stretcher proved, however, that screaming would not do much for me. The petty-larceny man went around asking if he could do anything in the world outside for those he was leaving behind. When he came to me I, at first, responded, "No, nothing"—for I suppose I had by now retreated into the attitude, the earliest I remember, that of my father, which was simply (since I had lost his God) that nothing could help me. And I suppose I will remember with gratitude until I die the fact that the man now insisted: "*Mais, êtes-vous sûr?*"[19] Then it swept over me that he was going *outside* and he instantly became my first contact since the Lord alone knew how long with the outside world. At the same time, I remember, I did not really believe that he would help me. There was no reason why he should. But I gave him the phone number of my attorney friend and my own name.

So, in the middle of the next day, Christmas Eve, I shuffled downstairs again, to meet my visitor. He looked extremely well fed and sane and clean. He told me I had nothing to worry about any more. Only not even he could do anything to make the mill of justice grind any faster. He would, however, send me a lawyer of his acquaintance who would defend me on the 27th, and he would himself, along with several other people, appear as a character witness. He gave me a package of Lucky Strikes (which the turnkey took from me on the way upstairs) and said that, though it was doubtful that there would be any celebration in the prison, he would see to it that I got a fine Christmas dinner when I got out. And this, somehow, seemed very funny. I remember being astonished at the discovery that I was actually laughing. I was, too, I imagine, also rather disappointed that my hair had not turned white, that my face was clearly not going to bear any marks of tragedy, disappointed at bottom, no doubt, to realize, facing him in that room, that far worse things had happened to most

[19]**Mais, êtes-vous sûr?:** But, are you sure?

people and that, indeed, to paraphrase my mother, if this was the worst thing that ever happened to me I could consider myself among the luckiest people ever to be born. He injected—my visitor—into my solitary nightmare common sense, the world, and the hint of blacker things to come.

The next day, Christmas, unable to endure my cell, and feeling that, after all, the day demanded a gesture, I asked to be allowed to go to Mass, hoping to hear some music. But I found myself, for a freezing hour and a half, locked in exactly the same kind of cubicle as in the wagon which had first brought me to prison, peering through a slot placed at the level of the eye at an old Frenchman, hatted, overcoated, muffled, and gloved, preaching in this language which I did not understand, to this row of wooden boxes, the story of Jesus Christ's love for men.

The next day, the 26th, I spent learning a peculiar kind of game, played with match-sticks, with my cell-mates. For, since I no longer felt that I would stay in this cell forever, I was beginning to be able to make peace with it for a time. On the 27th I went again to trial and, as had been predicted, the case against us was dismissed. The story of the *drap de lit*, finally told, caused great merriment in the courtroom, whereupon my friend decided that the French were "great." I was chilled by their merriment, even though it was meant to warm me. It could only remind me of the laughter I had often heard at home, laughter which I had sometimes deliberately elicited. This laughter is the laughter of those who consider themselves to be at a safe remove from all the wretched, for whom the pain of the living is not real. I had heard it so often in my native land that I had resolved to find a place where I would never hear it any more. In some deep, black, stony, and liberating way, my life, in my own eyes, began during that first year in Paris, when it was borne in on me that this laughter is universal and never can be stilled.

Discuss

1. Which statement best describes Baldwin's view of French culture after his brush with the law?

a. French institutions are outdated and inefficient.

b. The French are prejudiced against blacks and don't give them a fair deal.

c. The French are more lenient with Americans than with French.

2. The fact that Baldwin is black appears to affect his ability to cope. What were the "old weapons" that he could have used in a similar situation in New York? Why wouldn't they work in Paris?

3. What did Baldwin feel was his greatest disadvantage while struggling with his problem in Paris?

a. He did not know enough about French people and institutions to know what to expect and to prepare a response.

b. He didn't know enough French to be able to tell someone what had actually happened.

c. He didn't know anyone in Paris that he felt had enough influence to get him out of the situation.

Explore

1. What does the essay's title mean? In what ways might it be ironic? Who or what is equal?

2. The color of Baldwin's skin has a different meaning in Paris than it does in the United States. What is the difference, and how does it affect him?

3. Baldwin describes his living conditions both in and out of prison. What is the effect of that description and how does it relate to the meaning of the essay?

4. Baldwin also describes a number of his fellow inmates. On whom does he focus, and why?

5. What is Baldwin's insight at the end of the experience?

For Your Journal

1. Imagine yourself in Baldwin's situation. Write a daily diary for the period of the experience. Describe your perceptions and reactions.

2. What is your reaction to Baldwin's experience in Paris, especially before he was jailed? Do you think you would have considered it a great adventure? Why might his reaction differ from that of his friends?

3. Have you ever been in a situation in which cultural differences made it difficult for you to understand or be understood? If so, describe it.

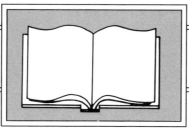

UNIT TWO

Passages

Section A
Discoveries

Section B
Remembrances

Section C
Youth and Age

Discoveries

*Life is discovering. Whether or not
you are aware of it, you are
constantly discovering things about
yourself, other people, and the world
around you. In this section you will
read and think about what in some cases
a writer discovered and what in other
cases a character in a story or
poem discovered. In each case you
will be discovering things, too.
Your discussions and responses in class
will reveal not only what you
discovered, but what other
readers discovered as well.
Their discoveries may parallel yours,
or they may not. It really doesn't
matter. What does matter is
that your involvement in the
discovery process will make what
you read more real and enjoyable.*

Incident

Countee Cullen

It is surprising how an unexpected statement or look can affect the way someone feels about a place for years afterward. The following poem captures the effect of one word on an eight-year-old boy.

Once riding in old Baltimore,
    Heart-filled, head-filled with glee,
I saw a Baltimorean
    Keep looking straight at me.

Now I was eight and very small,
    And he was no whit[1] bigger,
And so I smiled, but he poked out
    His tongue, and called me, "Nigger."

I saw the whole of Baltimore
    From May until December;
Of all the things that happened there
    That's all that I remember.

---

[1]**whit:** bit or particle.

Discuss

1. In the first stanza you learn that the speaker of the poem is feeling happy. Which line tells you of this feeling?

2. In stanza two, which word changes the feeling expressed in stanza one? As a result of this word, what do you know is different about the two boys?

3. How does your knowledge of the difference between the two help you understand why one boy keeps "looking straight at" the other?

4. How does the speaker's glee change after the other boy calls to him? How do you know?

5. It is not only the word that affects the boy but also that the word is an unfriendly response. What action in the poem calls forth this unfriendly response?

6. One negative encounter shapes all the speaker's experiences in Baltimore. Can you sum up how he probably regarded all his other experiences in that city?

7. What discovery has the young speaker made? Do you think that discovery was necessary? Why or why not?

8. Why is Baltimore an important setting for the poem?

9. When do you think the episode in the poem took place? What region of the United States do you think the black boy came from?

Explore

1. Poets often use rhyme to impart a musical quality and tie a stanza or stanzas together. What are the rhyming words in this poem?

2. Notice that skin color is not mentioned in the poem. How does the poet manage to make it obvious that one boy is white and the other black?

3. Without stating the effect on the black boy, the poet has made you aware of that effect. Why does the last stanza reveal the impact of the incident?

For Your Journal

1. Can you recall ever being made to feel ashamed? If so, write about the situation. Explain what you discovered about yourself or other people from that experience.

2. Write about prejudice, focusing on how you think it starts, and what you think needs to be done to eliminate it.

Charles

Shirley Jackson

When Laurie starts kindergarten, he comes home full of stories about Charles. By the third week, Charles seems like part of the family....

THE DAY MY SON LAURIE started kindergarten he re-nounced corduroy overalls with bibs and began wearing blue jeans with a belt; I watched him go off the first morning with the older girl next door, seeing clearly that an era of my life was ended, my sweet-voiced nursery-school tot replaced by a long-trousered, swaggering character who forgot to stop at the corner and wave good-bye to me.

He came home the same way, the front door slamming open, his cap on the floor, and the voice suddenly become raucous shouting, "Isn't anybody *here?*"

At lunch he spoke insolently to his father, spilled his baby sister's milk, and remarked that his teacher said we were not to take the name of the Lord in vain.

"How *was* school today?" I asked, elaborately casual.

"All right," he said.

"Did you learn anything?" his father asked.

Laurie regarded his father coldly. "I didn't learn nothing," he said.

"Anything," I said. "Didn't learn anything."

"The teacher spanked a boy, though," Laurie said, addressing his bread and butter. "For being fresh," he added, with his mouth full.

"What did he do?" I asked. "Who was it?"

Laurie thought. "It was Charles," he said. "He was fresh. The teacher spanked him and made him stand in a corner. He was awfully fresh."

"What did he do?" I asked again, but Laurie slid off his chair, took a cookie, and left, while his father was still saying, "See here, young man."

The next day Laurie remarked at lunch, as soon as he sat down, "Well, Charles was bad again today." He grinned enormously and said, "Today Charles hit the teacher."

"Good heavens," I said, mindful of the Lord's name, "I suppose he got spanked again?"

"He sure did," Laurie said. "Look up," he said to his father.

"What?" his father said, looking up.

"Look down," Laurie said. "Look at my thumb. Gee, you're dumb." He began to laugh insanely.

"Why did Charles hit the teacher?" I asked quickly.

"Because she tried to make him color with red crayons," Laurie said, "Charles wanted to color with green crayons so he hit the teacher and she spanked him and said nobody play with Charles but everybody did."

The third day—it was Wednesday of the first week—Charles bounced a see-saw on to the head of a little girl and made her bleed, and the teacher made him stay inside all during recess. Thursday Charles had to stand in a corner during story-time because he kept pounding his feet on the floor. Friday Charles was deprived of blackboard privileges because he threw chalk.

On Saturday I remarked to my husband, "Do you think kindergarten is too unsettling for Laurie? All this toughness, and bad grammar, and this Charles boy sounds like such a bad influence."

"It'll be all right," my husband said reassuringly. "Bound to be people like Charles in the world. Might as well meet them now as later."

On Monday Laurie came home late, full of news. "Charles," he shouted as he came up the hill; I was waiting anxiously on the front steps. "Charles," Laurie yelled all the way up the hill, "Charles was bad again."

"Come right in," I said, as soon as he came close enough. "Lunch is waiting."

"You know what Charles did?" he demanded, following me through the door. "Charles yelled so in school they sent a boy in from first grade to tell the teacher she had to make Charles keep quiet, and so Charles had to stay after school. And so all the children stayed to watch him."

"What did he do?" I asked.

"He just sat there," Laurie said, climbing into his chair at the table. "Hi, Pop, y'old dust mop."

"Charles had to stay after school today," I told my husband. "Everyone stayed with him."

"What does this Charles look like?" my husband asked Laurie. "What's his other name?"

"He's bigger than me," Laurie said. "And he doesn't have any rubbers and he doesn't ever wear a jacket."

Monday night was the first Parent-Teachers meeting, and only the fact that the baby had a cold kept me from going; I wanted passionately to meet Charles's mother. On Tuesday Laurie remarked suddenly, "Our teacher had a friend come to see her in school today."

"Charles's mother?" my husband and I asked simultaneously.

"Naaah," Laurie said scornfully. "It was a man who came and made us do exercises, we had to touch our toes. Look." He climbed down from his chair and squatted down and touched his toes. "Like this," he said. He got solemnly back into his chair and said, picking up his fork, "Charles didn't even *do* exercises."

"That's fine," I said heartily. "Didn't Charles want to do exercises?"

"Naaah," Laurie said. "Charles was so fresh to the teacher's friend he wasn't *let* do exercises."

"Fresh again?" I said.

"He kicked the teacher's friend," Laurie said. "The teacher's friend told Charles to touch his toes like I just did and Charles kicked him."

"What are they going to do about Charles, do you suppose?" Laurie's father asked him.

Laurie shrugged elaborately. "Throw him out of school, I guess," he said.

Wednesday and Thursday were routine; Charles yelled during story hour and hit a boy in the stomach and made him cry. On Friday Charles stayed after school again and so did all the other children.

With the third week of kindergarten Charles was an institution in our family; the baby was being a Charles when she cried all afternoon; Laurie did a Charles when he filled his wagon full of mud and pulled it through the kitchen; even my husband,

when he caught his elbow in the telephone cord and pulled telephone, ashtray, and a bowl of flowers off the table, said, after the first minute, "Looks like Charles."

During the third and fourth weeks it looked like a reformation in Charles; Laurie reported grimly at lunch on Thursday of the third week, "Charles was so good today the teacher gave him an apple."

"What?" I said, and my husband added warily, "You mean Charles?"

"Charles," Laurie said. "He gave the crayons around and he picked up the books afterward and the teacher said he was her helper."

"What happened?" I asked incredulously.

"He was her helper, that's all," Laurie said, and shrugged.

"Can this be true, about Charles?" I asked my husband that night. "Can something like this happen?"

"Wait and see," my husband said cynically. "When you've got a Charles to deal with, this may mean he's only plotting."

He seemed to be wrong. For over a week Charles was the teacher's helper; each day he handed things out and he picked things up; no one had to stay after school.

"The P.T.A meeting's next week again," I told my husband one evening. "I'm going to find Charles's mother there."

"Ask her what happened to Charles," my husband said. "I'd like to know."

"I'd like to know myself," I said.

On Friday of that week things were back to normal. "You know what Charles did today?" Laurie demanded at the lunch table, in a voice slightly awed. "He told a little girl to say a word and she said it and the teacher washed her mouth out with soap and Charles laughed."

"What word?" his father asked unwisely, and Laurie said, "I'll have to whisper it to you, it's so bad." He got down off his chair and went around to his father. His father bent his head down and Laurie whispered joyfully. His father's eyes widened.

"Did Charles tell the little girl to say *that*?" he asked respectfully.

"She said it *twice*," Laurie said, "Charles told her to say it *twice*."

"What happened to Charles?" my husband asked.

"Nothing," Laurie said. "He was passing out the crayons."

Monday morning Charles abandoned the little girl and said the evil word himself three or four times, getting his mouth washed out with soap each time. He also threw chalk.

My husband came to the door with me that evening as I set out for the P.T.A. meeting. "Invite her over for a cup of tea after the meeting," he said. "I want to get a look at her."

"If only she's there," I said prayerfully.

"She'll be there," my husband said. "I don't see how they could hold a P.T.A. meeting without Charles's mother."

At the meeting I sat restlessly, scanning each comfortable matronly face, trying to determine which one hid the secret of Charles. None of them looked to me haggard enough. No one stood up in the meeting and apologized for the way her son had been acting. No one mentioned Charles.

After the meeting I identified and sought out Laurie's kindergarten teacher. She had a plate with a cup of tea and a piece of chocolate cake; I had a plate with a cup of tea and a piece of marshmallow cake. We maneuvered up to one another cautiously, and smiled.

"I've been so anxious to meet you, " I said "I'm Laurie's mother."

"We're all so interested in Laurie," she said.

"Well, he certainly likes kindergarten," I said. "He talks about it all the time."

"We had a little trouble adjusting, the first week or so," she said primly, "but now he's a fine little helper. With occasional lapses, of course."

"Laurie usually adjusts very quickly," I said. "I suppose this time it's Charles's influence."

"Charles?"

"Yes," I said, laughing, "you must have your hands full in that kindergarten, with Charles."

"Charles?" she said. "We don't have any Charles in the kindergarten."

 *Discuss*

1. Which of the following statements best describes Laurie's feelings about the first day of school? How do you know?

    a. Laurie is sad and fearful.

    b. Laurie is eager to start.

    c. Laurie is resentful.

2. More than once Laurie tells his mother that the whole class stayed after school to watch Charles. Why does he say this? What does this tell you about Laurie?

3. Which statement comes closest to summarizing this story? Explain your choice.

    a. Parents never know when their children are lying.

    b. Little boys behave worse than little girls.

    c. Children often adjust to new situations in surprising ways.

Explore

1. This story is told from the point of view of Laurie's mother. Read the entries in the Glossary of Key Literary Terms on point of view and third person. Why didn't Jackson tell this story from Laurie's point of view or from that of Laurie's teacher?

2. How does the title of this story affect how you read it and react to the ending? Why didn't Jackson title the story "Laurie" or "Starting School"?

3. Why do you think Laurie invents Charles?

4. This story has a surprise ending. To be effective, a surprise ending should not come as a total surprise. The writer needs to prepare for it by planting clues early in the story. What is the earliest clue you can find? How far into the story were you when you first began to suspect Charles's identity?

5. Knowing when to end a story is important. Suppose the author had continued this story and had Laurie's mother explain the situation to his teacher. Suppose the mother then returned home and explained the situation to her husband. The story would be more nearly complete, but would it be better? Is it sometimes better not to tell the whole story? Why or why not?

For Your Journal

1. Laurie's teacher tells his mother that he "had a little trouble adjusting, the first week or so." Think about a time when you found yourself in a new situation and had trouble adjusting. Write about how you felt and what you did. Did you react as strongly as Laurie did? How do you feel about the situation now? Have your feelings changed? Explain.

2. Suppose Laurie were a real person. What would he be like as a high-school student? Write a brief sketch of Laurie as a teenager. Would he be a good student? Would he be involved in extracurricular activities? Would he have a job?

3. Do you think Jackson's story is funny, serious, or both? In a few paragraphs, explain your opinion.

Sucker

Carson McCullers

Have you ever discovered too late that you have sacrificed a worthwhile relationship with one person in order to achieve a relationship with another? The sacrifice can be doubly troubling if you find that the new relationship is a flimsy one, an infatuation, or a fad. In this story characters make painful and important discoveries about themselves and about friendship.

It was always like I had a room to myself. Sucker slept in my bed with me but that didn't interfere with anything. The room was mine and I used it as I wanted to. Once I remember sawing a trap door in the floor. Last year when I was a sophomore in high school I tacked on my wall some pictures of girls from magazines and one of them was just in her underwear. My mother never bothered me because she had the younger kids to look after. And Sucker thought anything I did was always swell.

Whenever I would bring any of my friends back to my room all I had to do was just glance once at Sucker and he would get up from whatever he was busy with and maybe half smile at me, and leave without saying a word. He never brought kids back there. He's twelve, four years younger than I am, and he always knew without me even telling him that I didn't want kids that age meddling with my things.

Half the time I used to forget that Sucker isn't my brother. He's my first cousin but practically ever since I remember he's been in our family. You see his folks were killed in a wreck when he was a baby. To me and my kid sisters he was like our brother.

Sucker used to always remember and believe every word I said. That's how he got his nickname. Once a couple of years ago I told him that if he'd jump off our garage with an umbrella it would act as a parachute and he wouldn't fall hard. He did it and busted his knee. That's just one instance. And the funny thing was that no matter

now many times he got fooled he would still believe me. Not that he was dumb in other ways—it was just the way he acted with me. He would look at everything I did and quietly take it in.

There is one thing I have learned, but it makes me feel guilty and is hard to figure out. If a person admires you a lot you despise him and don't care—and it is the person who doesn't notice you that you are apt to admire. This is not easy to realize. Maybelle Watts, this senior at school, acted like she was the Queen of Sheba[1] and even humiliated me. Yet at this same time I would have done anything in the world to get her attentions. All I could think about day and night was Maybelle until I was nearly crazy. When Sucker was a little kid and on up until the time he was twelve I guess I treated him as bad as Maybelle did me.

Now that Sucker has changed so much it is a little hard to remember him as he used to be. I never imagined anything would suddenly happen that would make us both very different. I never knew that in order to get what has happened straight in my mind I would want to think back on him as he used to be and compare and try to get things settled. If I could have seen ahead maybe I would have acted different.

I never noticed him much or thought about him and when you consider how long we have had the same room together it is funny the few things I remember. He used to talk to himself a lot when

[1] **Queen of Sheba:** Biblical Queen who visited King Solomon of Israel to test his wisdom.

he'd think he was alone—all about him fighting gangsters and being on ranches and that sort of kids' stuff. He'd get in the bathroom and stay as long as an hour and sometimes his voice would go up high and excited and you could hear him all over the house. Usually, though, he was very quiet. He didn't have many boys in the neighborhood to buddy with and his face had the look of a kid who is watching a game and waiting to be asked to play. He didn't mind wearing the sweaters and coats that I outgrew, even if the sleeves did flop down too big and make his wrists look as thin and white as a little girl's. That is how I remember him—getting a little bigger every year but still being the same. That was Sucker up until a few months ago when all this trouble began.

Maybelle was somehow mixed up in what happened so I guess I ought to start with her. Until I knew her I hadn't given much time to girls. Last fall she sat next to me in General Science class and that was when I first began to notice her. Her hair is the brightest yellow I ever saw and occasionally she will wear it set into curls with some sort of gluey stuff. Her fingernails are pointed and manicured and painted a shiny red. All during class I used to watch Maybelle, nearly all the time except when I thought she was going to look my way or when the teacher called on me. I couldn't keep my eyes off her hands, for one thing. They are very little and white except for that red stuff, and when she would turn the pages of her book she always licked her thumb and held out her little finger and turned very slowly. It is impossible to describe Maybelle. All the boys are crazy about her but she didn't even notice me. For one thing she's almost two years older than I am. Between periods I used to try and pass very close to her in the halls but she would hardly ever smile at me. All I could do was sit and look at her in class—and sometimes it was like the whole room could hear my heart beating and I wanted to holler or light out and run for Hell.

At night, in bed, I would imagine about Maybelle. Often this would keep me from sleeping until as late as one or two o'clock. Sometimes Sucker would wake up and ask me why I couldn't get settled and I'd tell him to hush his mouth. I suppose I was mean to him lots of times. I guess I wanted to ignore somebody like Maybelle did me. You could always tell by Sucker's face when his feelings were hurt. I don't remember all the ugly remarks I must

have made because even when I was saying them my mind was on Maybelle.

That went on for nearly three months and then somehow she began to change. In the halls she would speak to me and every morning she copied my homework. At lunch time once I danced with her in the gym. One afternoon I got up nerve and went around to her house with a carton of cigarettes. I knew she smoked in the girls' basement and sometimes outside of school—and I didn't want to take her candy because I think that's been run into the ground. She was very nice and it seemed to me everything was going to change.

It was that night when this trouble really started. I had come into my room late and Sucker was already asleep. I felt too happy and keyed up to get in a comfortable position and I was awake thinking about Maybelle a long time. Then I dreamed about her and it seemed I kissed her. It was a surprise to wake up and see the dark. I lay still and a little while passed before I could come to and understand where I was. The house was quiet and it was a very dark night.

Sucker's voice was a shock to me. "Pete? . . . "

I didn't answer anything or even move.

"You do like me as much as if I was your own brother, don't you Pete?"

I couldn't get over the surprise of everything and it was like this was the real dream instead of the other.

"You have liked me all the time like I was your own brother, haven't you?"

"Sure," I said.

Then I got up for a few minutes. It was cold and I was glad to come back to bed. Sucker hung on to my back. He felt little and warm and I could feel his warm breathing on my shoulder.

"No matter what you did I always knew you liked me."

I was wide awake and my mind seemed mixed up in a strange way. There was this happiness about Maybelle and all that—but at the same time something about Sucker and his voice when he said these things made me take notice. Anyway I guess you understand people better when you are happy than when something is worrying you. It was like I had never really thought about Sucker until then. I felt I had always been mean to him. One night a few weeks before I had heard him crying in the dark. He said he had lost a boy's beebee gun and was scared to let anybody know. He wanted me to tell him what to do. I was sleepy and tried to make him hush and when he wouldn't I kicked at him. That was just one of the things I remembered. It seemed to me he had always been a lonesome kid. I felt bad.

There is something about a dark cold night that makes you feel close to someone you're sleeping with. When you talk together it is like you are the only people awake in the town.

"You're a swell kid, Sucker," I said.

It seemed to me suddenly that I did like him more than anybody else I knew—more than any other boy, more than my sisters, more in a certain way even than Maybelle. I felt good all over and it was like when they play sad music in the movies. I wanted to show Sucker how much I really thought of him and make up for the way I had always treated him.

We talked for a good while that night. His voice was fast and it was like he had been saving up these things to tell me for a long time. He mentioned that he was going to try to build a canoe and that the kids down the block wouldn't let him in on their football team and I don't know what all. I talked some too and it was a good feeling to think of him taking in everything I said so seriously. I even spoke of Maybelle a little, only I made out like it was her who had been running after me all this time. He asked questions about high school and so forth. His voice was excited and he kept on talking fast like he could never get the words out in time. When I went to sleep he was still talking and I could still feel his breathing on my shoulder, warm and close.

During the next couple of weeks I saw a lot of Maybelle. She acted as though she really cared for me a little. Half the time I felt so good I hardly knew what to do with myself.

But I didn't forget about Sucker. There were a lot of old things in my bureau drawer I'd been saving—boxing gloves and Tom Swift books[2] and second rate fishing tackle. All this I turned over to him. We had some more talks together and it was really like I was knowing him for the first time. When there was a long cut on his cheek I knew he had been monkeying around with this new first razor set of mine, but I didn't say anything. His face seemed different now. He used to look timid and sort of like he was afraid of a whack over the head. That expression was gone. His face, with those

[2]**Tom Swift books:** a series of adventure books in which the central character is a boy, Tom Swift, who invents things and solves problems

wide-open eyes and his ears sticking out and his mouth never quite shut, had the look of a person who is surprised and expecting something swell.

Once I started to point him out to Maybelle and tell her he was my kid brother. It was an afternoon when a murder mystery was on at the movie. I had earned a dollar working for my Dad and I gave Sucker a quarter to go and get candy and so forth. With the rest I took Maybelle. We were sitting near the back and I saw Sucker come in. He began to stare at the screen the minute he stepped past the ticket man and he stumbled down the aisle without noticing where he was going. I started to punch Maybelle but couldn't quite make up my mind. Sucker looked a little silly—walking like a drunk with his eyes glued to the movie. He was wiping his reading glasses on his shirt tail and his knickers flopped down. He went on until he got to the first few rows where the kids usually sit. I never did punch Maybelle. But I got to thinking it was good to have both of them at the movie with the money I earned.

I guess things went on like this for about a month or six weeks. I felt so good I couldn't settle down to study or put my mind on anything. I wanted to be friendly with everybody. There were times when I just had to talk to some person. And usually that would be Sucker. He felt as good as I did. Once he said: "Pete, I am gladder that you are like my brother than anything else in the world."

Then something happened between Maybelle and me. I never figured out just what it was. Girls like her are hard to understand. She began to act different toward me. At first I wouldn't let myself believe this and tried to think it was just my imagination. She didn't act glad to see me any more. Often she went out riding with this fellow on the football team who owns this yellow roadster. The car was the color of her hair and after school she would ride off with him, laughing and looking into his face. I couldn't think of anything to do about it and she was on my mind all day and night. When I did get a chance to go out with her she was snippy and didn't seem to notice me. This made me feel like something was the matter—I would worry about my shoes clopping too loud on the floor, or the fly of my pants, or the bumps on my chin. Sometimes when Maybelle was around, a devil would get into me and I'd hold my face stiff and call grown men by their last names without the Mister and say rough things. In the night I would wonder what made me do all this until I was too tired for sleep.

At first I was so worried I just forgot about Sucker. Then later he began to get on my nerves. He was always hanging around until I would get back from high school, always looking like he had something to say to me or wanted me to tell him. He made me a magazine rack in his Manual Training class and one week he saved his lunch money and bought me three packs of cigarettes. He couldn't seem to take it in that I had things on my mind and didn't want to fool with him. Every afternoon it would be the same—him in my room with this waiting expression on his face. Then I wouldn't say anything or I'd maybe answer him rough-like and he would finally go on out.

I can't divide that time up and say this happened one day and that the next. For one thing I was so mixed up the weeks just slid along into each other and I felt like Hell and didn't care. Nothing definite was said or done. Maybelle still rode around with this fellow in his yellow roadster and sometimes she would smile at me and sometimes not. Every afternoon I went from one place to another where I thought she would be. Either she would act almost nice and I would begin thinking how things would finally clear up and she would care for me—or else she'd behave so that if she hadn't been a girl I'd have wanted to grab her by that white little neck and choke her. The more ashamed I felt for making a fool of myself the more I ran after her.

Sucker kept getting on my nerves more and more. He would look at me as though he sort of blamed me for something, but at the same time knew that it wouldn't last long. He was growing fast and for some reason began to stutter when he talked. Sometimes he had nightmares or would throw up his breakfast. Mom got him a bottle of cod liver oil.[3]

Then the finish came between Maybelle and me. I met her going to the drug store and asked for a date. When she said no I remarked something sarcastic. She told me she was sick and tired of my being around and that she had never cared a rap about me. She said all that. I just stood there and didn't answer anything. I walked home very slowly.

For several afternoons I stayed in my room by myself. I didn't want to go anywhere or talk to anyone. When Sucker would come in and look at me

[3] **cod liver oil:** a fish extract rich in vitamins A and D, given to children to strengthen their bones.

sort of funny I'd yell at him to get out. I didn't want to think of Maybelle and I sat at my desk reading *Popular Mechanics* or whittling at a toothbrush rack I was making. It seemed to me I was putting that girl out of my mind pretty well.

But you can't help what happens to you at night. That is what made things how they are now.

You see a few nights after Maybelle said those words to me I dreamed about her again. It was like that first time and I was squeezing Sucker's arm so tight I woke him up. He reached for my hand.

"Pete, what's the matter with you?"

All of a sudden I felt so mad my throat choked—at myself and the dream and Maybelle and Sucker and every single person I knew. I remembered all the times Maybelle had humiliated me and everything bad that had ever happened. It seemed to me for a second that nobody would ever like me but a sap like Sucker.

"Why is it we aren't buddies like we were before? Why—?"

"Shut your damn trap!" I threw off the cover and got up and turned on the light. He sat in the middle of the bed, his eyes blinking and scared.

There was something in me and I couldn't help myself. I don't think anybody ever gets that mad but once. Words came without me knowing what they would be. It was only afterward that I could remember each thing I said and see it all in a clear way.

"Why aren't we buddies? Because you're the dumbest slob I ever saw! Nobody cares anything about you! And just because I felt sorry for you sometimes and tried to act decent don't think I give a damn about a dumb-bunny like you!"

If I'd talked loud or hit him it wouldn't have been so bad. But my voice was slow and like I was very calm. Sucker's mouth was part way open and he looked as though he'd knocked his funny bone. His face was white and sweat came out on his forehead. He wiped it away with the back of his hand and for a minute his arm stayed raised that way as though he was holding something away from him.

"Don't you know a single thing? Haven't you ever been around at all? Why don't you get a girl friend instead of me? What kind of sissy do you want to grow up to be anyway?"

I didn't know what was coming next. I couldn't help myself or think.

Sucker didn't move. He had on one of my pajama jackets and his neck stuck out skinny and small. His hair was damp on his forehead.

"Why do you always hang around me? Don't you know when you're not wanted?"

Afterward I could remember the change in Sucker's face. Slowly that blank look went away and he closed his mouth. His eyes got narrow and his fists shut. There had never been such a look on him before. It was like every second he was getting older. There was a hard look to his eyes you don't see usually in a kid. A drop of sweat rolled down his chin and he didn't notice. He just sat there with those eyes on me and he didn't speak and his face was hard and didn't move.

"No you don't know when you're not wanted. You're too dumb. Just like your name—a dumb Sucker."

It was like something had busted inside me. I turned off the light and sat down in the chair by the window. My legs were shaking and I was so tired I could have bawled. The room was cold and dark. I sat there for a long time and smoked a squashed cigarette I had saved. Outside the yard was black and quiet. After a while I heard Sucker lie down.

I wasn't mad any more, only tired. It seemed awful to me that I had talked like that to a kid only twelve. I couldn't take it all in. I told myself I would go over to him and try to make it up. But I just sat there in the cold until a long time had passed. I planned how I could straighten it out in the morning. Then, trying not to squeak the springs, I got back in bed.

Sucker was gone when I woke up the next day. And later when I wanted to apologize as I had planned he looked at me in this new hard way so that I couldn't say a word.

All of that was two or three months ago. Since then Sucker has grown faster than any boy I ever saw. He's almost as tall as I am and his bones have gotten heavier and bigger. He won't wear any of my old clothes any more and has bought his first pair of long pants—with some leather suspenders to hold them up. Those are just the changes that are easy to see and put into words.

Our room isn't mine at all any more. He's gotten up this gang of kids and they have a club. When they aren't digging trenches in some vacant lot and fighting they are always in my room. On the door there is some foolishness written in Mercurochrome saying "Woe to the Outsider who Enters" and signed with crossed bones and their secret initials. They have rigged up a radio and every afternoon it blares out music. Once as I was coming in I heard a boy telling something in a low voice about what he saw in the back of his big brother's automobile. I could guess what I didn't hear. *That's what her and my brother do. It's the truth—parked in the car.* For a minute Sucker looked surprised and his face was almost like it used to be. Then he got hard and tough again. "Sure, dumbbell. We know all that." They didn't notice me. Sucker began telling them how in two years he was planning to be a trapper in Alaska.

But most of the time Sucker stays by himself. It is worse when we are alone together in the room. He sprawls across the bed in those long corduroy pants with the suspenders and just stares at me with that hard, half sneering look. I fiddle around my desk and can't get settled because of those eyes of his. And the thing is I just have to study because I've gotten three bad cards this term already. If I flunk English I can't graduate next year. I don't want to be a bum and I just have to get my mind on it. I don't care a flip for Maybelle or any particular girl any more and it's only this thing between Sucker and me that is the trouble now. We never speak except when we have to before the family. I don't even want to call him Sucker any more and unless I forget I call him by his real name, Richard. At night I can't study with him in the room and I have to hang around the drug store, smoking and doing nothing, with the fellows who loaf there.

More than anything I want to be easy in my mind again. And I miss the way Sucker and I were for a while in a funny, sad way that before this I never would have believed. But everything is so different that there seems to be nothing I can do to get it right. I've sometimes thought if we could have it out in a big fight that would help. But I can't fight him because he's four years younger. And another thing—sometimes this look in his eyes makes me almost believe that if Sucker could he would kill me.

Discuss

1. Who is Sucker, and how did he get his name?

2. Who is Maybelle? What effect has she had on Pete?

3. Maybelle begins to notice Pete. He says, "every morning she copied my homework." What does this comment suggest about Maybelle's motives?

4. Why does Sucker, who is twelve, want Pete to like him and be like a brother?

5. What happens that makes Pete suddenly become more friendly with Sucker and even confide in him? What does this change tell you about Pete?

6. Why does Sucker eventually begin to get on Pete's nerves?

7. What change occurs in Sucker? What produces this change?

8. Pete says that the "look in his eyes makes me almost believe that if Sucker could he would kill me." Does Sucker really want to kill him? What would make Pete think this of Sucker?

9. Who is the sucker in this story, and why?

10. Both boys in this story grow up by discovering something. What is it that each discovers?

Explore

1. How does the point of view in this story compare to that in the story "Charles"? What is the advantage of having this story presented from this point of view?

2. Foreshadowing is a literary device in which an author gives you a hint of what to expect later in the story. Pick out a statement that foreshadows the outcome of the story.

For Your Journal

1. Suppose Pete came to you for advice about regaining his relationship with Sucker. What would you advise him to do?

2. Have you ever had an experience that parallels Pete's? For instance, have you ever abandoned, or at least disregarded, an old friend in favor of a new one? Describe what happened. How did you treat each other? How was everything resolved?

Fifteen

William Stafford

Mobility and freedom are closely linked in the minds of most Americans, especially young ones. A motorcycle seems very attractive, offering speed, maneuverability, and the roar of power. Think of the temptation for a fifteen-year-old boy to take a ride if he found a motorcycle just lying there, seemingly abandoned and with its motor running.

South of the Bridge on Seventeenth
I found back of the willows one summer
day a motorcycle with engine running
as it lay on its side, ticking over
slowly in the high grass. I was fifteen.

I admired all the pulsing gleam, the
shiny flanks, the demure headlights
fringed where it lay; I led it gently
to the road and stood with that
companion, ready and friendly, I was fifteen.

We could find the end of a road, meet
the sky on out Seventeenth. I thought about
hills, and patting the handle got back a
confident opinion. On the bridge we indulged
a forward feeling, a tremble. I was fifteen.

Thinking, back farther in the grass I found
the owner, just coming to, where he had flipped
over the rail. He had blood on his hand, was pale—
I helped him walk to his machine. He ran his hand
over it, called me good man, roared away.

I stood there, fifteen.

Discuss

1. Notice that the speaker does something different as the stanzas change. What does he do in each stanza?

2. There are three discoveries in this poem. What are they?

3. Why is the boy's age repeated in the statement "I was fifteen"?

Explore

1. The speaker says, "On the bridge we indulged a forward feeling, a tremble." To what does the "we" refer? The poet is using personification, giving human qualities to inhuman things. What feeling does the motorcycle have in common with the boy in this poem?

2. What does the poet do to create a sense of drama or suspense in this poem?

3. How do you think the boy felt when the rider called him "good man" and roared away?

4. Look at stanzas two and three. What suggests that the boy's imagination is running away with him?

For Your Journal

1. Write an essay telling why you think owning a car or motorcycle is important. If you happen to think it is not important, then explain why.

2. What are some places in the world where the freedom to travel is curtailed? How is freedom limited for young people in those places? Explain why as a person approaches adulthood, the desire to travel may become more acute. How is having a ready means of transportation like a car or motorcycle related to the freedom to travel?

On First Looking into Chapman's Homer

John Keats

John Keats is classified as a Romantic poet along with William Wordsworth, Percy Bysshe Shelley, Samuel Taylor Coleridge, and Lord Byron. The Romantics delighted in the past and in the wonders of undisturbed nature. As you read this famous poem, see if you can detect the Romantic flavor of it.

Much have I traveled in the realms of gold,
　　And many goodly states and kingdoms seen:
　　Round many western islands have I been
Which bards[1] in fealty[2] to Apollo[3] hold.
Oft of one wide expanse had I been told
　　That deep-browed Homer[4] ruled as his demesne;[5]
　　Yet did I never breathe its pure serene
Till I heard Chapman[6] speak out loud and bold.
Then felt I like some watcher of the skies
　　When a new planet swims into his ken;[7]
Or like stout Cortez[8] when with eagle eyes
　　He stared at the Pacific—and all his men
Looked at each other with a wild surmise—
　　Silent upon a peak in Darien.[9]

[1]**bards:** singers and poets who recited the heroic deeds of people.
[2]**fealty:** loyalty.
[3]**Apollo:** Greek and Roman god of music, poetry, healing, and manly beauty.
[4]**Homer:** ancient Greek poet believed to have created the *Iliad* and the *Odyssey*, two epic poems.
[5]**demesne** (di mēń): domain.
[6]**Chapman:** George Chapman, an English translator of the *Iliad* and the *Odyssey*.
[7]**ken:** view or range of vision.
[8]**Cortez:** Spanish conqueror of Mexico, but not the first European to see the Pacific; Balboa was the first.
[9]**Darien:** eastern Panama.

Discuss

1. What actual object has the speaker discovered that affects him so deeply?

2. What, as a result of discovering the object, does the poet discover about himself?

3. What does he discover about humankind?

Explore

1. A fourteen-line poem is called a sonnet. Most sonnets have particular rhyme schemes. For a definition of rhyme scheme refer to the Glossary of Key Literary Terms. What is the rhyme scheme of this sonnet?

2. The rhyme scheme divides this poem into eight lines (an octave) and six lines (a sestet). Within its fourteen lines, a sonnet manages to convey a great deal. This kind, called a Petrarchan or Italian sonnet, makes a statement or divulges a thought or observation in the first eight lines, and in the last six lines it adds to the thought, or somehow gives it a twist, perhaps a more penetrating vision or idea. In this poem the sestet seems to elevate Keats's feeling to an insight or sudden revelation. What is the statement in the first eight lines? What is the revelation of the last six lines?

3. With the words, "Much have I traveled in the realms of gold/And many goodly states and kingdoms seen," you know that the poet is speaking figuratively, not literally. Literally would mean that he actually went to those places. He is using the word "traveled" as a figure of speech, a word that gives the image of something that is real, but is not itself real. In what way has he "traveled"?

4. Why does the poet refer to ancient Greece as "the realms of gold"?

For Your Journal

1. In this poem the speaker discovers that words hold the power to influence his mind. Have you ever made a similar discovery with something you read? Read the poem again and see if you can understand the poet's feelings about the words of another person. Put in your own words those feelings.

2. Think about this poem and the poem "Fifteen" and about how each affected you. Which poem produced a greater emotional response in you? In other words, after you reread the two poems, which one did you find yourself most touched by, or interested in? Searching for expressive words or images, explain why one poem seemed more moving or enjoyable.

The Red Wheelbarrow

William Carlos Williams

If you read this poem several times, you might be able to imagine that the words act as a snapshot, as they briefly reveal a picture your camera might take.

so much depends
upon

a red wheel
barrow

glazed with rain
water

beside the white
chickens

Discuss

1. List the objects mentioned in the poem. What do these few details imply about the meaning of the poem?

2. Describe the images presented in the poem.

3. What effect does the word "glazed" produce?

4. Does this picture, which excludes so many images, tell you enough to figure out what prompted the poet to create this poem? Why or why not?

Explore

1. Return to the opening two lines. Why does so much depend upon what follows in the poem?

2. What is the significance of the words "so much"?

For Your Journal

1. In this section you have made some discoveries about poetry. Write out whatever you think are important features of a poem.

2. In this poem you have discovered to some extent what the poet discovered and attempted to convey. Explain what he discovered and whether you feel in touch with his discovery.

3. Reading this poem may have led you to discover something unique in yourself. It could relate to nature, farms, or your personal abilities and goals. If you feel like writing about such a discovery, do so; or write a poem expressing those feelings.

Remembrances

*Remembrances deal with events and
experiences that have passed.
They are closely related to discoveries.
After all, what you often remember,
at least enough to write and
talk about, is an experience
that showed you something
about yourself, other people,
or the world around you. The poems,
the novel excerpt, and the essay in this
section will give you chances to
rethink some of your experiences
and evaluate those of others.*

The Centaur

May Swenson

Remember when, as a young child, you created battleships out of rocks, swords out of sticks, and people out of dolls and stuffed toys? Draw upon that imagination again as you read the following poem about a centaur. You will need to be resourceful, because a centaur itself is an imaginary creature with the head, arms, and upper body of a human being, and the lower body of a horse.

The summer that I was ten—
Can it be there was only one
summer that I was ten? It must

have been a long one then—
each day I'd go out to choose
a fresh horse from from my stable

which was a willow grove
down by the old canal.
I'd go on my two bare feet.

But when, with my brother's jack-knife,
I had cut me a long limber horse
with a good thick knob for a head,

and peeled him slick and clean
except a few leaves for the tail,
and cinched my brother's belt

around his head for a rein,
I'd straddle and canter him fast
up the grass bank to the path,

trot along in the lovely dust
that talcumed over his hoofs,
hiding my toes, and turning

(continued)

his feet to swift half-moons.
The willow knob with the strap
jouncing between my thighs

was the pommel and yet the poll
of my nickering pony's head.
My head and my neck were mine,

yet they were shaped like a horse.
My hair flopped to the side
like the mane of a horse in the wind.

My forelock swung in my eyes,
my neck arched and I snorted.
I shied and skittered and reared,

stopped and raised my knees,
pawed at the ground and quivered.
My teeth bared as we wheeled

and swished through the dust again.
I was the horse and the rider,
And the leather I slapped to his rump

spanked my own behind.
Doubled, my two hoofs beat
a gallop along the bank,

the wind twanged in my mane,
my mouth squared to the bit.
And yet I sat on my steed

quiet, negligent riding,
my toes standing the stirrups,
my thighs hugging his ribs.

At a walk we drew up to the porch.
I tethered him to a paling.
Dismounting, I smoothed my skirt

and entered the dusky hall.
My feet on the clean linoleum
left ghostly toes in the hall.

Where have you been? said my mother.
Been riding, I said from the sink,
and filled me a glass of water.

What's that in your pocket? she said.
Just my knife. It weighted my pocket
and stretched my dress awry.

Go tie back your hair, said my mother,
and *Why is your mouth all green?*
*Rob Roy, he pulled some clover
as we crossed the field,* I told her.

Discuss

1. Who in the poem is the centaur?

2. What is the "long limber horse"?

3. What is humorous about the use of the word "stable"?

4. How do you know that the rider, who is also the horse, is a girl?

5. Who is Rob Roy?

6. What role is this young rider playing, and how is it revealed in the way she speaks?

7. Answer the mother's question of why the girl's mouth is green.

Explore

1. What, if anything, about this girl sets her apart from ten-year old girls you know or have known? Would this difference be a significant point of the poem? If so, how?

2. The conversation between the mother and the daughter suggests a contrast between adulthood and childhood. What is the contrast?

3. A centaur is a creature of Greek and Roman mythology. How do mythology and childhood seem related in this poem?

For Your Journal

1. In remembering, the poet expresses nostalgia, regret over lost innocence. Can you recall a similar type of feeling from your own past, a feeling of regret over some activity you once enjoyed, but can no longer do because of your age? If so, describe that feeling in a short essay, story, or poem.

2. Pretend to create something with a simple object, the way the speaker of this poem created the centaur out of a stick and herself. Write about the imagined experience freely, with the spirit of a child.

Naming the State Bird

Keith Gunderson

You are about to read a prose poem. Notice that on the page it looks more like a paragraph than any other poems you read in this book. It is classified as a poem because it has a rolling rhythm to it and, instead of details and explanations, it gives you a series of impressions: the classroom scene, different types of students, and their responses to the teacher.

AND BECAUSE we lived in a democracy all the school kids got to vote for some bird to be The State Bird and in fact any kid in any class in any grade except kindergarten could nominate a candidate for The State Bird and after the voting the results would be sent to the guys who had been elected to run The State of Minnesota and they would figure out democratically which bird was the lucky winner and I guess the woodduck was or the loon but no one who was in our class which was 8th Grade Room 205 at Jefferson Junior High had ever even heard or thought about those birds so they didn't get considered and there were six or seven of us who were boys who played a lot of ball together and got in trouble for fun so the bird we nominated our class to nominate was THE CHICKEN and anyone in favor of a particular class nomination could give a speech on behalf of that bird so we all gave speeches on behalf of THE CHICKEN and talked about eggs and eating chicken on Sunday and what other bird did so much for everyone and one of us questioned a guy who'd come out for THE CARDINAL about what a cardinal could be used for and all he could think to say was that they were red and pretty and a baseball team was named after them[1] so we booed and hissed at the cardinal until the teacher said no booing or hissing allowed and then the teacher remembered that although she wasn't permitted to vote THE ORIOLE was her favorite bird and probably quite a few people liked THE ORIOLE and they build such interesting nests so about two seconds later at least five kids really liked THE ORIOLE and nominated it even though one of them thought it was green but we kept talking up the usefulness of THE CHICKEN and when the votes were counted THE CHICKEN squeaked in the winner with THE ORIOLE second so we laughed and clapped until the teacher reminded us that laughers and clappers could stay after school and that democracy was a serious business and there'd be no more nonsense about messy chickens and since THE ORIOLE came in second and was the only SERIOUS candidate of the two it would be the nomination of Room 205 and one that we could all be proud of.

[1] **baseball team named after them:** St. Louis Cardinals

Discuss

1. What are the students supposed to be learning in Room 205 at Jefferson Junior High?

2. Why do some students take the procedure as a joke? What action of theirs tells you that they are joking?

3. Why is it funny when one boy nominates the cardinal?

4. Who nominates the oriole? Which bird wins the most votes?

5. How does the election work out? What are its results?

Explore

1. Do you think the original intention to learn about democratic procedures is helped, harmed, or kept neutral by what has happened in Room 205? Why?

2. The poet captures in his phrasing the attitude he remembers having toward this event. You can sense his underlying amusement. Why is he amused?

For Your Journal

1. Most people can remember an attempt to foil authority, whether it was at school, camp, or home. Describe a prank that you and others planned, witnessed, or heard about. Was its goal to embarrass someone or prevent something for working out as intended? Did the prank work?

2. Write a prose poem and introduce it in your journal. In the introduction try to explain why you think the poem is more effective as prose than in any other form.

Black Boy

Richard Wright

In his autobiographical novel *Black Boy,* from which the following excerpt is taken, author Richard Wright recalls his youth and his mistreatment by white people.

THE NEXT DAY at school I inquired among the students about jobs and was given the name of a white family who wanted a boy to do chores. That afternoon, as soon as school had let out, I went to the address. A tall, dour white woman talked to me. Yes, she needed a boy, an honest boy. Two dollars a week. Mornings, evenings, and all day Saturdays. Washing dishes. Chopping wood. Scrubbing floors. Cleaning the yard. I would get my breakfast and dinner. As I asked timid questions, my eyes darted about. What kind of food would I get? Was the place as shabby as the kitchen indicated?

"Do you want this job?" the woman asked.

"Yes, ma'am," I said, afraid to trust my own judgment.

"Now, boy, I want to ask you one question and I want you to tell me the truth," she said.

"Yes, ma'am," I said, all attention.

"Do you steal?" she asked me seriously.

I burst into a laugh, then checked myself.

"What's so damn funny about that?" she asked.

"Lady, if I was a thief, I'd never tell anybody."

"What do you mean?" she blazed with a red face.

I had made a mistake during my first five minutes in the white world. I hung my head.

"No ma'am," I mumbled. "I don't steal."

She stared at me, trying to make up her mind.

"Now, look, we don't want a sassy nigger around here," she said.

"No, ma'am," I assured her. "I'm not sassy."

Promising to report the next morning at six o'clock I walked home and pondered on what could possibly have been in the woman's mind to have made her ask me point-blank if I stole. Then I recalled hearing that white people looked upon Negroes as a variety of children, and it was only in the light of that that her question made any sense. If I had been planning to murder her, I certainly would not have told her and, rationally, she no doubt realized it. Yet habit had overcome her rationality and had made her ask me: "Boy, do you steal?" Only an idiot would have answered: "Yes, ma'am. I steal."

What would happen now that I would be among white people for hours at a stretch? Would they hit me? Curse me? If they did, I would leave at once. In all my wishing for a job I had not thought of how I would be treated, and now it loomed important, decisive, sweeping down beneath every other consideration. I would be polite, humble, saying yes sir and no sir, yes ma'am and no ma'am, but I would draw a line over which they must not step. Oh, maybe I'm just thinking up trouble, I told myself. They might like me . . .

The next morning I chopped wood for the cook stove, lugged in scuttles of coal for the grates, washed the front porch and swept the back porch, swept the kitchen, helped wait on the table, and washed the dishes. I was sweating. I swept the front walk and ran to the store to shop. When I returned the woman said:

"Your breakfast is in the kitchen."

"Thank you, ma'am."

I saw a plate of thick, black molasses and a hunk of white bread on the table. Would I get no more than white bread on the table. Would I get no more than this? They had had eggs, bacon, coffee . . . I picked up the bread and tried to break it; it was stale and hard. Well, I would drink the molasses. I lifted the plate and brought it to my lips and saw floating on the surface of the black liquid green and white bits of mold. Goddamn . . . I can't eat this, I told myself. The food was not even clean. The woman came into the kitchen as I was putting on my coat.

"You didn't eat," she said.

"No, ma'am," I said. "I'm not hungry."

"You'll eat at home?" she asked hopefully.

"Well, I just wasn't hungry this morning, ma'am." I lied.

"You don't like molasses and bread," she said dramatically.

"Oh, yes, ma'am, I do," I defended myself quickly, not wanting her to think that I dared criticize what she had given me.

"I don't know what's happening to you niggers nowadays," she sighed, wagging her head. She looked closely at the molasses. "It's a sin to throw out molasses like that. I'll put it up for you this evening."

"Yes, ma'am," I said heartily.

Neatly she covered the plate of molasses with another plate, then felt the bread and dumped it into the garbage. She turned to me, her face lit with an idea.

"What grade are you in school?"

"Seventh, ma'am."

"Then why are you going to school?" she asked in surprise.

"Well, I want to be a writer," I mumbled, unsure of myself; I had not planned to tell her that, but she had made me feel so utterly wrong and of no account that I needed to bolster myself.

"A what?" she demanded.

"A writer," I mumbled.

"For what?"

"To write stories," I mumbled defensively.

"You'll never be a writer," she said. "Who on earth put such ideas into your nigger head?"

"Nobody," I said.

"I didn't think anybody ever would," she declared indignantly.

As I walked around her house to the street, I knew that I would not go back. The woman had assaulted my ego; she had assumed that she knew my place in life, what I felt, what I ought to be, and I resented it with all my heart. Perhaps she was right; perhaps I would never be a writer; but I did not want her to say so.

Had I kept the job I would have learned quickly just how white people acted toward Negroes, but I was too naive to think that there were many white people like that. I told myself that there were good white people, people with money and sensitive feelings. As a whole, I felt that they were bad, but I would be lucky enough to find the exceptions.

Fearing that my family might think I was finicky, I lied to them, telling them that the white woman had already hired a boy. At school I continued to ask about jobs and was directed to another address. As soon as school was out I made for the house. Yes, the woman said that she wanted a boy who could milk a cow, feed chickens, gather vegetables, help serve breakfast and dinner.

"But I can't milk a cow, ma'am," I said.

"Where are you from?" she asked incredulously.

"Here in Jackson," I said.[1]

"You mean to stand there, nigger, and tell me that you live in Jackson and don't know how to milk a cow?" she demanded in surprise.

I said nothing, but I was quickly learning the reality—a Negro's reality—of the white world. One woman had assumed that I would tell her if I stole, and now this woman was amazed that I could not milk a cow, I, a nigger who dared live in Jackson . . . They were all turning out to be alike, differing only in detail. I faced a wall in the woman's mind, a wall that she did not know was there.

"I just never learned," I said finally.

"I'll show you how to milk," she said, . . .

SUMMER. Bright hot days. Hunger still a vital part of my consciousness. Passing relatives in the hallways of the crowded home and not speaking. Eating in silence at a table where prayers are said. My mother recovering slowly, but now definitely crippled for life. Will I be able to enter school in September? Loneliness. Reading. Job hunting. Vague hopes of going north. But what would become of my mother if I left her in this queer house? And how would I fare in a strange city? Doubt. Fear. My friends are buying long-pants suits that cost from seventeen to twenty dollars, a sum as huge to me as the Alps! This was my reality in 1924.

Word came that a near-by brickyard was hiring and I went to investigate. I was frail, not weighing a hundred pounds. At noon I sneaked into the yard and walked among the aisles of damp, clean-

[1]Jackson: the city of Jackson, Mississippi.

smelling clay and came to a barrow full of wet bricks just taken from the machine that shaped them. I caught hold of the handles of the barrow and was barely able to lift it; it weighed perhaps four times as much as I did. If I were only stronger and heavier!

Later I asked questions and found that the water boy was missing; I ran to the office and was hired. I walked in the hot sun lugging a big zinc pail from one laboring gang of black men to another for a dollar a day; a man would lift the tin dipper to his lips, take a swallow, rinse out his mouth, spit, and then drink in long, slow gulps as sweat dripped into the dipper. And off again I would go, chanting:

"Water!"

And somebody would yell:

"Here, boy!"

Deep into wet pits of clay, into sticky ditches, up slippery slopes I would struggle with the pail. I stuck it out, reeling at times from hunger, pausing to get my breath before clambering up a hill. At the end of the week the money sank into the endless expenses at home. Later I got a job in the yard that paid a dollar and a half a day, that of bat boy. I went between the walls of clay and picked up bricks that had cracked open; when my barrow was full, I would wheel it out onto a wooden scaffold and dump it into a pond.

I had but one fear here: a dog. He was owned by the boss of the brickyard and he haunted the clay aisles, snapping, growling. The dog had been wounded many times, for the black workers were always hurling bricks at it. Whenever I saw the animal, I would take a brick from my load and toss it at him; he would slink away, only to appear again, showing his teeth. Several of the Negroes had been bitten and had been ill; the boss had been asked to leash the dog, but he had refused. One afternoon I was wheeling my barrow toward the pond when something sharp sank into my thigh. I whirled; the dog crouched a few feet away, snarling. I had been bitten. I drove the dog away and opened my trousers; teeth marks showed deep and red.

I did not mind the stinging hurt, but I was afraid of an infection. When I went to the office to report that the boss's dog had bitten me, I was met by a tall blonde white girl.

"What do you want?" she asked.

"I want to see the boss, ma'am."

"For what?"

"His dog bit me, ma'am, and I'm afraid I might get an infection."

"Where did he bite you?"

"On my leg," I lied, shying from telling her where the bite was.

"Let's see," she said. "No ma'am. Can't I see the boss?"

"He isn't here now," she said, and went back to her typing.

I returned to work, stopping occasionally to examine the teeth marks; they were swelling. Later in the afternoon a tall white man wearing a cool white suit, a Panama hat, and white shoes came toward me.

"Is this the nigger?" he asked a black boy as he pointed at me.

"Yes, sir," the black boy answered.

"Come here, nigger," he called me.

I went to him.

"They tell me my dog bit you," he said.

"Yes, sir."

I pulled down my trousers and he looked.

"Humnnn," he grunted, then laughed, "A dog bite can't hurt a nigger."

"It's swelling and it hurts," I said.

"If it bothers you, let me know," he said. "But I never saw a dog yet that could really hurt a nigger."

He turned and walked away and the black boys gathered to watch his tall form disappear down the aisles of wet bricks.

Discuss

1. How old is the narrator in this story?

2. What would he earn, in his first job, for working mornings, evenings, and all day Saturdays?

3. Why does he quit his first job?

4. What is his job during the summer? When he is bitten by the boss's dog, what is his boss's reaction?

5. What word do both the narrator's employers use to refer to him? Why does the author include this offensive label?

Explore

1. The author is describing attitudes and treatment of black people that he encountered in which year? What has changed for black people since then?

2. What hasn't changed?

3. Wright became very critical of the United States, and even left it to live in France for many years. How do you think he would feel about conditions for black people in this country if he were alive today?

For Your Journal

Reviewing what you have read from *Black Boy,* select the episode that bothered you the most and tell why it disturbed you.

My Last Duchess
Robert Browning

The following poem is a dramatic monologue. Monologue simply means that one person is speaking. The monologue is dramatic because the speaker reveals to a silent listener what could be considered a tragic situation. See if you can detect the underlying tragedy by examining what the speaker says and how he says it.

That's my last Duchess painted on the wall,
Looking as if she were alive. I call
That piece a wonder, now: Frà Pandolf's hands[1]
Worked busily a day, and there she stands.
Will't please you sit and look at her? I said
"Frà Pandolf" by design, for never read
Strangers like you that pictured countenance,
The depth and passion of its earnest glance,
But to myself they turned (since none puts by
The curtain I have drawn for you, but I)
And seemed as they would ask me, if they durst,
How such a glance came there; so, not the first
Are you to turn and ask thus. Sir, 't was not
Her husband's presence only, called that spot
Of joy into the Duchess' cheek: perhaps
Frà Pandolf chanced to say "Her mantle laps
Over my lady's wrist too much," or "Paint
Must never hope to reproduce the faint
Half-flush that dies along her throat:" such stuff
Was courtesy, she thought, and cause enough
For calling up that spot of joy. She had
A heart—how shall I say?—too soon made glad,
Too easily impressed; she liked whate'er
She looked on, and her looks went everywhere.
Sir, 't was all one! My favor at her breast,
The dropping of the daylight in the West,

---

[1]**Frà Pandolf:** a painter.

(continued)

The bough of cherries some officious fool
Broke in the orchard for her, the white mule
She rode with round the terrace—all and each
Would draw from her alike the approving speech,
Or blush, at least. She thanked men,—good! but thanked
Somehow—I know not how—as if she ranked
My gift of nine-hundred-years-old name
With anybody's gift. Who'd stoop to blame
This sort of trifling? Even had you skill
In speech—(which I have not)—to make your will
Quite clear to such an one, and say, "Just this
Or that in you disgusts me; here you miss,
Or there exceed the mark"—and if she let
Herself be lessoned so, nor plainly set
Her wits to yours, forsooth, and made excuse,
—E'en then would be some stooping; and I choose
Never to stoop. Oh sir, she smiled, no doubt,
When'er I passed her; but who passed without
Much the same smile? This grew; I gave commands;
Then all smiles stopped together. There she stands
As if alive. Will 't please you rise? We'll meet
The company below, then. I repeat,
The Count your master's known munificence[2]
Is ample warrant that no just pretence
Of mine for dowry[3] will be disallowed;
Though his fair daughter's self, as I avowed
At starting, is my object. Nay, we'll go
Together down, sir. Notice Neptune,[4] though,
Taming a sea-horse, thought a rarity,
Which Claus of Innsbruck[5] cast in bronze for me!

[2]**munificence:** display of generosity.
[3]**dowry:** sum of money given by a bride's parents to her husband.
[4]**Neptune:** Roman god of the sea.
[5]**Claus of Innsbruck:** a sculptor.

Discuss

1. What is the speaker doing in this poem?

2. What is a Duchess? What is the speaker's title?

3. From what the speaker says about his wife, what sort of person do you conclude she was? How does he feel about her as a person?

4. To whom and for what purpose is the speaker showing the painting?

5. What became of the Duchess, and why do you think it happened?

6. How does the speaker seem to feel about what happened to his wife?

Explore

1. As a monologue, this poem provides an interesting probe into a person's mind. Write a brief personality profile of the speaker.

2. Is the speaker implying anything evil or sinister by opening his monologue with reference to "my last Duchess"? If so, explain.

3. What are two statements that reveal the speaker's snobbery?

4. What is the effect of having the speaker end his monologue on the painting of his last Duchess with "Notice Neptune . . . Which Claus of Innsbruck cast in bronze for me"?

For Your Journal

Imagine that you are a movie director assigned to shoot a film version of this poem. The first thing you need to do is develop a story board. A story board is a picture outline of the sequences of the movie (not necessarily the order in which the sequences will be shot). Decide what background information you need for the Duke and Duchess. For example, how did the couple meet? Why did they decide to get married? Was the marriage arranged by others, or did the two fall in love? How do you picture the Duke? The Duchess? What are their ages? Their looks? After the marriage what scenes would you show to illustrate the marital problems?

Roommates

Max Apple

Do you think you could live with a roommate sixty-four years older than you? This essay by fiction writer Max Apple describes just such a roommate.

I CAME RATHER LATE to understanding myself in the cycle of life. Until three years ago, I was a boy in relation to my grandfather. He lived to 107 and remained mentally and physically capable until the end of his life. A generation after the last of his friends died, he could still mow the lawn on a hot summer afternoon, and he insisted on doing so. I usually wrestled the mower from his grip, but his extraordinary energy I took for granted. I had seen it all my life; he was my roommate.

At my birth he was 64, middle age to him, and he was not a gentle old soul. He argued with the men in the synagogue, screamed at his fellows in the bakery where he worked until his mid-80's. He was a lover of strife, even at a distance. For war news he turned up the volume on the television.

We never had to take care of each other, but as I learned to read, I voluntarily became his teacher. My grandfather came to the United States from Lithuania[1] before World War I. He went to night school, could read and write English. Still, I, the emissary of elementary school, considered it my duty to inform him about subtle things like electricity as he got ready for bed after a 12-hour work-day.

He was not too interested in my lectures. Within minutes, he fell into a deep sleep. His characteristic snoring pattern was a muted whistle that ended in a great puff of breath. But even asleep there was nothing gentle about this man. He specialized in hating his enemies, even those long dead. As he talked in his sleep, he exploded in anger. From his dreams I learned the curse words of English and Yiddish. Cushioned by his puffs of

[1]**Lithuania:** at present an ethnic entity of the Soviet Union.

breath, visions of destruction crowded our room. Boils sprouted on the intestines of his enemies. Cholera[2] depopulated their villages. The deep background of his life as it escaped through his lips became the chorus of my nights. I heard him the way you hear static through a radio. My young ears didn't want to listen to the uncorked anger, didn't know what to make of feelings that could stretch back 70 years. But now, I recall those staccato outbursts as music.

When I went to college, I switched to roommates my age. Then, in graduate school, I had my own apartment, and my old roommate joined me. All his friends were dead, and he had lived long enough to become, once again, a stranger in the community he had inhabited for more than half a century. It was clear to both of us that in spite of a 60-year age gap I was his most congenial companion.

So he joined me in the late 1960's at the University of Michigan. He made new friends, took care of himself, and did most of the housework. In Ann Arbor he found plenty of allies in hating Republicans, but it was even better than that. Ideologically it was the best of times. He could enjoy both the war and the anti-war movement.

He was usually asleep when I brought a girl-friend home. By then, Richard Nixon[3] had replaced the men in the bakery at the top of my grandfather's hate list. The girls, accustomed in those days to hallucinatory experience, did not question my explanation of the snoring and the

[2]**cholera:** a disease, often fatal, that occurs under unsanitary conditions.
[3]**Richard Nixon:** U.S. president involved in Watergate, a major political scandal; resigned under threat of impeachment in 1974.

anti-Nixon ejaculations in the next room. I was just "far out."

Our only serious problem was what he called my laziness. I was studying for Ph.D. preliminary exams. My work consisted of lying on the couch with a book in my lap. Sometimes I dozed off, now and then I highlighted a significant passage. He would pick up a pencil and mockingly mark the newspaper to imitate what I was doing. I could not convince him that it was work.

But I did convince others. I finished my studies, married, fathered a daughter and a son and settled in Texas. Though reluctant to move once again, my grandfather joined us in Houston. He was exactly 100 years older than my son.

Now that I was established, a man with a career, a family, a job, I intended to help my grandfather in the last years of his life. But in the crazy irony of things, it turned out that I was the one who would need help. My solid life cracked in a matter of months, when my wife was stricken with a terrible neurologic disease. The life of the family became the life of the hospital. I lost touch with my friends, my work, even my children. I could not scream out my anger as my grandfather did in his sleep. Instead, I turned it against myself, and it settled in my bones as depression. I returned to the couch where I had studied for my Ph.D. exams, but I no longer saw anything glorious to underline.

At 103 and 104, my grandfather began to take an active role in helping me care for my children. He did not understand what had happened to my wife and had no sympathy for my depression. But he saw the work of daily life in front of him and, as always, he did it. Although by then he must have been wearing the shadow of death as an undershirt, the aroma of life stayed in his nostrils. He listened to the news, he read the paper, he took out the garbage, he played with my children, he mowed the lawn. He never offered me advice or understanding, he just kept doing things. After about two years of melancholy, I joined him, started to see how much there was to do.

Now I get up early and I stay busy. There's a lot of garbage to take out, and in Texas there's always a lawn to mow. I don't talk in my sleep yet, but even if I start, nobody will hear me. Roommates like him only come along about one a century.

Discuss

1. Apple grew up more or less with his grandfather. According to the description, do you think he considers the experience good or bad?

2. The relationship between Apple and his grandfather was an unusual one. Why?

3. To what age did the grandfather live? How did he help his grandson most?

Explore

1. Describe the grandfather's background. Where did he come from?

2. What does Apple say his grandfather specialized in?

3. How can you account for, given his background, the grandfather's specialization?

For Your Journal

1. Do you know some remarkable elderly people? If you do, interview one or more of them. Prepare your questions carefully, deciding in particular upon your focus. Do you want to know where your subjects came from and why? Are you interested in specific deeds they performed? Did they live through the Great Depression of the 1930s? Did they serve during a war? What do they think of the current generation? What do they think of the problems in today's society? Either tape the interview or take notes, and then write the interview up.

2. Perhaps there is or was an elderly person in your family about whom you would prefer to reminisce. Write about that person in a reflective essay similar to "Roommates."

Youth and Age

*So far in this unit you have thought about
discoveries—how they are made
both in everyday life and in the world
of literature as it deals with life—
and remembrances, especially of those
experiences that mark an important
moment in life. Through the minds of
writers expressing their discoveries
and remembrances, you discover and
remember, too. In this section you will
be reading about the passage called
maturation or growing up. What is
remarkable is that the growing-up
process never ends. Each passage of life
requires adjustments, new understandings
of yourself and others, and interesting
perspectives on where you have been and
where you are thinking of going. In all
this growth there is some humor,
some sadness, and much courage.*

old age sticks
E. E. Cummings

You have already read several different kinds of poems, ranging from a formal sonnet to an informal one-sentence poem. Now you will read a poem in which the poet suggests his ideas by lines, by running words together or separating them, and by funny combinations of spellings, sounds, and symbols. Many of his poems seem like puzzles at first. However, by just reading them aloud you can gain an immediate sense of what he's saying.

old age sticks
up Keep
Off
signs)&

youth yanks them
down(old
age
cries No

Tres)&(pas)
youth laughs
(sing
old age

scolds Forbid
den Stop
Must
n't Don't

&)youth goes
right on
gr
owing old

Discuss

1. What does old age do?

2. What does youth do?

3. What does the contrast between youth and old age suggest?

4. What is meant by "youth goes right on growing old"?

Explore

1. Notice the opening line of the poem: "old age sticks." If you take that line by itself, what meaning can you give to it?

2. If you see old age as an accumulation of something valuable, then the word "sticks" takes on an interesting connotation. What actually sticks as part of aging?

3. The poet definitely adds new meaning to "sticks" by starting the next line with the word "up." Now you read "old age sticks up." How does this phrase support the poem's meaning? What does old age stick up?

For Your Journal

1. Jot down some advice older people have given you about what not to do.

2. Think of an experience in which you went against the advice of an older person. Tell what happened and what you learned.

3. Can you see how you have gone right on growing old? Think of some escapade or prank you indulged in when you were younger. Explain why you would not do something like that now.

Those Winter Sundays

Robert Hayden

Do young people realize and appreciate what older people do for
them? Don't they take things for granted that only in later years are
revealed to them from the hidden depths of their memories?

Sundays too my father got up early
and put his clothes on in the blueblack cold,
then with cracked hands that ached
from labor in the weekday weather made
banked fires blaze. No one ever thanked him.

I'd wake and hear the cold splintering, breaking.
When the rooms were warm, he'd call,
and slowly I would rise and dress,
fearing the chronic angers of that house,

Speaking indifferently to him,
who had driven out the cold
and polished my good shoes as well.
What did I know, what did I know
of love's austere[1] and lonely offices?[2]

---

[1]**austere:** severe, plain, or self-denying.
[2]**offices:** duties or obligations.

Discuss

1. Why is what the speaker's father did on Sundays so memorable?

2. What can you conclude about the speaker's living conditions?

Explore

1. Why are the first two words of the poem important?

2. What are "the chronic angers of that house"?

3. Two key words, austere and offices, occur in the last line. How do they sum up what the narrator did not know then, but knows now?

4. Once you understand "austere" and "offices," the words "love" and "lonely" take on special meanings. Explain those meanings.

5. Should children be expected to understand and appreciate what parents or caring guardians do for them? Why or why not?

For Your Journal

1. What kind of person is this father? On the basis of what the poem says, write a profile of this person as you imagine him.

2. Think about your own childhood. Are there things that adults (parents, guardians, relatives, or friends) have done for you that you have taken for granted? Describe such a deed that you now, upon reflection, cherish.

Flight

Doris Lessing

The problem of aging is a problem of loss of power or control. It also may be a sense of loss as people die or depart to other places and other lives. It usually happens that those who die are old, but those who depart are young. The departure of young people can be very upsetting to old people who are left behind. Often, surprisingly, the young departers feel upset, too, torn by the need to separate and the longing to preserve what has always been.

ABOVE THE OLD MAN'S HEAD was the dovecote, a tall wire-netted shelf on stilts, full of strutting, preening birds. The sunlight broke on their gray breasts into small rainbows. His ears were lulled by their crooning; his hands stretched up toward his favorite, a homing pigeon, a young plump-bodied bird, which stood still when it saw him and cocked a shrewd bright eye.

"Pretty, pretty, pretty," he said, as he grasped the bird and drew it down, feeling the cold coral claws tighten around his finger. Content, he rested the bird lightly on his chest and leaned against a tree, gazing out beyond the dovecote into the landscape of a late afternoon. In folds and hollows of sunlight and shade, the dark red soil, which was broken into great dusty clods, stretched wide to a tall horizon. Trees marked the course of the valley; a stream of rich green grass the road.

His eyes traveled homeward along this road until he saw his granddaughter swinging on the gate underneath a frangipani tree.[1] Her hair fell down her back in a wave of sunlight; and her long bare legs repeated the angles of the frangipani stems, bare, shining brown stems among patterns of pale blossoms.

She was gazing past the pink flowers, past the railway cottage where they lived, along the road to the village.

His mood shifted. He deliberately held out his wrist for the bird to take flight, and caught it again

at the moment it spread its wings. He felt the plump shape strive and strain under his fingers; and, in a sudden access of troubled spite, shut the bird into a small box and fastened the bolt. "Now you stay there," he muttered and turned his back on the shelf of birds. He moved warily along the hedge, stalking his granddaughter, who was now looped over the gate, her head loose on her arms, singing. The light happy sound mingled with the crooning of the birds, and his anger mounted.

"Hey!" he shouted, and saw her jump, look back, and abandon the gate. Her eyes veiled themselves, and she said in a pert, neutral voice, "Hullo, Grandad." Politely she moved toward him, after a lingering backward glance at the road.

"Waiting for Steven, hey?" he said, his fingers curling like claws into his palms.

"Any objection?" she asked lightly, refusing to look at him.

He confronted her, his eyes narrowed, shoulders hunched, tight in a hard knot of pain that included the preening birds, the sunlight, the flowers, herself. He said, "Think you're old enough to go courting, hey?"

The girl tossed her head at the old-fashioned phrase and sulked. "Oh, Grandad!"

"Think you want to leave home, hey? Think you can go running around the field at night?"

Her smile made him see her, as he had every evening of this warm end-of-summer month, swinging hand in hand along the road to the village with that red-handed, red-throated, violent-

[1]**frangipani tree:** a flowering tree that grows in tropical regions.

bodied youth, the son of the postmaster. Misery went to his head and he shouted angrily: "I'll tell your mother!"

"Tell away!" she said, laughing, and went back to the gate.

He heard her singing, for him to hear:

"I've got you under my skin,
I've got you deep in the heart of . . ."

"Rubbish," he shouted. "Rubbish. Impudent little bit of rubbish!"

Growling under his breath, he turned toward the dovecote, which was his refuge from the house he shared with his daughter and her husband and their children. But now the house would be empty. Gone all the young girls with their laughter and their squabbling and their teasing. He would be left, uncherished and alone, with that square-fronted, clam-eyed woman, his daughter.

He stooped, muttering, before the dovecote, resenting the absorbed, cooing birds.

From the gate the girl shouted: "Go and tell! Go on, what are you waiting for?"

Obstinately he made his way to the house, with quick pathetic, persistent glances of appeal back at her. But she never looked around. Her defiant but anxious young body stung him into love and repentance. He stopped. "But I never meant . . ." he muttered, waiting for her to turn and run to him. "I didn't mean . . ."

She did not turn. She had forgotten him. Along the road came the young man Steven, with something in his hand. A present for her? The old man stiffened as he watched the gate swing back and the couple embrace. In the brittle shadows of the frangipani tree his granddaughter, his darling, lay in the arms of the postmaster's son, and her hair flowed back over his shoulder.

"I see you!" shouted the old man spitefully. They did not move. He stumped into the little whitewashed house, hearing the wooden veranda creak angrily under his feet. His daughter was sewing in the front room, threading a needle held to the light.

He stopped again, looking back into the garden. The couple were now sauntering among the bushes, laughing. As he watched he saw the girl escape from the youth with a sudden mischievous movement and run off through the flowers with him in pursuit. He heard shouts, laughter, a scream, silence.

"But it's not like that at all," he muttered miserably. "It's not like that. Why can't you see? Running and giggling, and kissing and kissing. You'll come to something quite different."

He looked at his daughter with sardonic hatred, hating himself. They were caught and finished, both of them, but the girl was still running free.

"Can't you *see?*" he demanded of his invisible granddaughter, who was at that moment lying in the thick green grass with the postmaster's son.

His daughter looked at him and her eyebrows went up in tired forbearance.

"Put your birds to bed?" she asked, humoring him.

"Lucy," he said urgently. "Lucy. . . ."

"Well, what is it now?"

"She's in the garden with Steven."

"Now you just sit down and have your tea."

He stumped his feet alternately, thump, thump, on the hollow wooden floor and shouted: "She'll marry him. I'm telling you, she'll be marrying him next!"

His daughter rose swiftly, brought him a cup, set him a plate.

"I don't want any tea. I don't want it, I tell you."

"Now, now," she crooned. "What's wrong with it? Why not?"

"She's eighteen. Eighteen!"

"I was married at seventeen, and I never regretted it."

"Liar," he said. "Liar. Then you should regret it. Why do you make your girls marry? It's you who do it. What do you do it for? Why?"

"The other three have done fine. They've three fine husbands. Why not Alice?"

"She's the last," he mourned. "Can't we keep her a bit longer?"

"Come, now, Dad. She'll be down the road, that's all. She'll be here every day to see you."

"But it's not the same." He thought of the other three girls, transformed inside a few months from charming, petulant, spoiled children into serious young matrons.

"You never did like it when we married." she said. "Why not? Every time, it's the same. When I got married you made me feel like it was something wrong. And my girls the same. You get them all crying and miserable the way you go on. Leave Alice alone. She's happy." She sighed, letting her eyes linger on the sunlit garden. "She'll marry next month. There's no reason to wait."

"You've said they can marry?" he said incredulously.

"Yes, Dad. Why not?" she said coldly and took up her sewing.

His eyes stung, and he went out on to the veranda. Wet spread down over his chin, and he took out a handkerchief and mopped his whole face. The garden was empty.

From around the corner came the young couple; but their faces were no longer set against him. On the wrist of the postmaster's son balanced a young pigeon, the light gleaming on its breast.

"For me?" said the old man, letting the drops shake off his chin. "For me?"

"Do you like it?" The girl grabbed his hand and swung on it. "It's for you, Grandad. Steven brought it for you." They hung about him, affectionate, concerned, trying to charm away his wet eyes and his misery. They took his arms and directed him to the shelf of birds, one on each side, enclosing him, petting him, saying wordlessly that nothing would be changed, nothing could change, and that they would be with him always. The bird was proof of it, they said, from their lying happy eyes, as they thrust it on him. "There, Grandad, it's yours. It's for you."

They watched him as he held it on his wrist, stroking its soft, sun-warmed back, watching the wings lift and balance.

"You must shut it up for a bit," said the girl intimately, "until it knows this is its home."

"Teach your grandmother to suck eggs," growled the old man.

Released by his half-deliberate anger, they fell back, laughing at him. "We're glad you like it." They moved off, now serious and full of purpose, to the gate, where they hung, backs to him, talking quietly. More than anything could, their grown-up seriousness shut him out, making him alone; also, it quietened him, took the sting out of their tumbling like puppies on the grass. They had forgotten him again. Well, so they should, the old man reassured himself, feeling his throat clotted with tears, his lips trembling. He held the new bird to his face, for the caress of its silken feathers. Then he shut it in a box and took out his favorite.

"*Now* you can go," he said aloud. He held it poised, ready for flight, while he looked down the garden toward the boy and the girl. Then, clenched in the pain of loss, he lifted the bird on his wrist and watched it soar. A whirr and a spatter of wings, and a cloud of birds rose into the evening from the dovecote.

At the gate Alice and Steven forgot their talk and watched the birds.

On the veranda, that woman, his daughter, stood gazing, her eyes shaded with a hand that still held her sewing.

It seemed to the old man that the whole afternoon had stilled to watch his gesture of self-command, that even the leaves of the trees had stopped shaking.

Dry-eyed and calm, he let his hands fall to his sides and stood erect, staring up into the sky.

The cloud of shining silver birds flew up and up, with a shrill cleaving of wings, over the dark ploughed land and the darker belts of trees and the bright folds of grass, until they floated high in the sunlight, like a cloud of motes of dust.

They wheeled in a wide circle, tilting their wings so there was flash after flash of light, and one after another they dropped from the sunshine of the upper sky to shadow, one after another, returning to the shadowed earth over trees and grass and field, returning to the valley and the shelter of night.

The garden was all a fluster and a flurry of returning birds. Then silence, and the sky was empty.

The old man turned, slowly, taking his time; he lifted his eyes to smile proudly down the garden at his granddaughter. She was staring at him. She did not smile. She was wide-eyed and pale in the cold shadow, and he saw the tears run shivering off her face.

Discuss

1. What is happening in this story?

2. Why does the grandfather, at the beginning of the story, imprison the dove that seeks to fly?

3. In the conversation that follows, how does Alice treat her grandfather?

4. How old is Alice? How old was her mother when she got married? What do you think about getting married at that age?

5. Getting married at the age that the mother did and at the age the granddaughter considers tells you something about the time, the society, and the role of women. What does it tell you?

6. Why is the story titled "Flight"? Is it an ironic title? Why or why not?

Explore

1. The setting of the story, a rural and traditional one, reaches you in a subtle way through the mention of the dark red soil and the frangipani stems. What else can you guess about the setting from the word "frangipani"?

2. What is symbolic about the gift of the pigeon that Steven gives to Alice's grandfather?

3. What does the grandfather realize toward the end of the story?

4. This story has a sense of the cyclical nature of life. What is that cycle?

5. Why does the grandfather release his favorite bird, and why does he stand erect as all the birds fly aloft?

6. Why does the grandfather lift his eyes to smile proudly at his granddaughter? Why does she, staring at him, cry?

For Your Journal

Do you foresee a flight of your own? How do you see it taking place? What effect will it have on people you know? Pick one person in particular and describe what that effect might be.

Ulysses[1]

Alfred Tennyson

Have you witnessed the courage of people who were nearing the end of life and regretted the ebb of physical power but refused to give up enjoying the world around them? This poem portrays such an attitude toward life through the mind of an aged epic hero.

It little profits that an idle king,
By this still hearth, among these barren crags,
Match'd with an aged wife, I mete and dole
Unequal laws unto a savage race,
That hoard, and sleep, and feed, and know not me.

I cannot rest from travel: I will drink
Life to the lees:[2] all times I have enjoy'd
Greatly, have suffer'd greatly, both with those
That loved me, and alone; on shore, and when
Thro' scudding drifts the rainy Hyades[3]
Vext the dim sea: I am become a name;
For always roaming with a hungry heart
Much have I seen and known; cities of men
And manners, climates, councils, governments,
Myself not least, but honour'd of them all;
And drunk delight of battle with my peers,
Far on the ringing plains of windy Troy.[4]
I am a part of all that I have met;
Yet all experience is an arch wherethro'
Gleams that untravell'd world, whose margin fades
For ever and for ever when I move.
How dull it is to pause, to make an end,
To rust unburnish'd, not to shine in use!
As tho' to breathe were life. Life piled on life
Were all too little, and of one to me
Little remains: but every hour is saved
From that eternal silence, something more,
A bringer of new things; and vile it were

(continued)

[1]**Ulysses:** Latin name of the Greek hero who spent years tying to return home after the Trojan War. The tale of his adventurous homecoming is told in the *Odyssey,* an ancient epic poem thought to have been created by Homer.
[2]**lees:** particles or dregs that settle from a liquid, especially wine.
[3]**Hyades:** group of stars viewed by ancient Greeks to predict the approach of rain.
[4]**Troy:** city-state besieged by the Greeks in the ten-year Trojan War.

For some three suns to store and hoard myself,
And this gray spirit yearning in desire
To follow knowledge like a sinking star,
Beyond the utmost bound of human thought.
    This is my son, mine own Telemachus,
To whom I leave the sceptre and the isle—
Well-loved of me, discerning to fulfil
This labour, by slow prudence to make mild
A rugged people, and thro' soft degrees
Subdue them to the useful and the good.
Most blameless is he, centred in the sphere
Of common duties, decent not to fail
In offices of tenderness, and pay
Meet adoration to my household gods,
When I am gone. He works his work, I mine.

    There lies the port; the vessel puffs her sail:
There gloom the dark broad seas. My mariners,
Souls that have toil'd, and wrought, and thought with
        me—
That ever with a frolic welcome took
The thunder and the sunshine, and opposed
Free hearts, free foreheads—you and I are old;
Old age hath yet his honour and his toil;
Death closes all: but something ere the end,
Some work of noble note, may yet be done,
Not unbecoming men that strove with Gods.
The lights begin to twinkle from the rocks:
The long day wanes: the slow moon climbs: the deep
Moans round with many voices. Come, my friends,
'Tis not too late to seek a newer world.
Push off, and sitting well in order smite
The sounding furrows; for my purpose holds
To sail beyond the sunset, and the baths
Of all the western stars, until I die.
It may be that the gulfs will wash us down:
It may be we shall touch the Happy Isles,[5]
And see the great Achilles,[6] whom we knew.

Tho' much is taken, much abides; and tho'
We are not now that strength which in old days
Moved earth and heaven; that which we are, we are;
One equal-temper of heroic hearts,
Made weak by time and fate, but strong in will
To strive, to seek, to find, and not to yield.

[5]**Happy Isles:** another name for Elysium, in Greek mythology the abode of souls of deceased virtuous people.
[6]**Achilles:** famous Greek warrior killed in the Trojan War.

Discuss

1. How does Ulysses feel now that he is safe at home?

2. What does it mean to say, "I will drink life to the lees"?

3. Ulysses says, "I am part of all that I have met." What does this mean in other words?

4. As a result of how Ulysses feels, what does he do?

5. To whom is Ulysses speaking at the end of the poem?

6. Ulysses says, "Old age hath yet his honour and his toil." What is he suggesting?

Explore

1. This poem is told through the voice of one man. What is the name of this literary device? Through this voice the poet is able to capture an attitude, a way of looking at life. What is that attitude?

2. What are one or two lines in the poem, other than those you've already discussed, that reveal Ulysses' attitude?

3. Neither you nor the poet knows whether Ulysses actually spoke these words or thought these thoughts. So the poet has constructed this monologue for a purpose. What do you believe was that purpose?

4. The Ulysses of this poem can be seen as a symbol. What do you think he symbolizes?

For Your Journal

1. Write a brief essay telling which characteristic you most admire in people. Does a person have to be a certain age to have that quality? Explain.

2. Anticipate your own old age. Tell what kind of person you would like to be. What kinds of things would you want to be able to do?

3. Look up one or two famous people who lived very long lives and who, to the very end, stayed involved in life around them. Such people include George Bernard Shaw, Oliver Wendell Holmes, Bertrand Russell, Jane Addams, and Jeanette Rankin. What information can you find in their deeds, writings, or other accomplishments about their attitudes toward life? Write a few paragraphs describing what impressed you most.

Warning

Jenny Joseph

Does age, which some societies consider fearsome and repelling, have some redeeming qualities? Is it possible to anticipate old age as a freeing from obligations and restraints? The poem that follows suggests some positive aspects of old age.

When I am an old woman I shall wear purple
With a red hat which doesn't go, and doesn't suit me,
And I shall spend my pension on brandy and summer gloves
And satin sandals, and say we've no money for butter.
I shall sit down on the pavement when I'm tired
And gobble up samples in shops and press alarm bells
And run my stick along the public railings
And make up for the sobriety of my youth.
I shall go out in my slippers in the rain
And pick the flowers in other people's gardens
And learn to spit.

You can wear terrible shirts and grow more fat
And eat three pounds of sausages at a go
Or only bread and pickle for a week
And hoard pens and pencils and beermats and things in
    boxes.

But now we must have clothes that keep us dry
And pay our rent and not swear in the street
And set a good example for the children.
We will have friends to dinner and read the papers.
But maybe I ought to practise a little now?
So people who know me are not too shocked and surprised
When suddenly I am old and start to wear purple.

Discuss

1. What sort of person does the speaker want to become in her old age?

2. Why does the speaker say she should start practicing now for old age?

3. How do you think you would react to the type of old person described in the poem? Explain why.

Explore

1. Why is the poem titled "Warning"?

2. Is it possible that the speaker protests too much in her present way of life? In other words, is she truthfully anticipating the privileges of old age?

3. Do you agree or disagree with the speaker's view of old age? Why or why not?

For Your Journal

1. When you are old, do you see yourself enjoying certain advantages that you do not have now? Perhaps you can also see disadvantages. In a paragraph describe those advantages and disadvantages.

2. Picture yourself as old. What will you be wearing? What will you be doing? How do you envision your family?

3. Write a letter of warning to a friend or imaginary companion about the change that will occur when you become old.

Do not go gentle into that good night
Dylan Thomas

When you say good night, you are usually wishing someone a gentle, peaceful sleep. But when Horatio, at the of Shakespeare's play *Hamlet,* says, "Good night, sweet prince," he is wishing Hamlet peaceful, permanent sleep. The word night often becomes a euphemism for something else, as the following poem suggests.

Do not go gentle into that good night,
Old age should burn and rave at close of day;
Rage, rage against the dying of the light.

Though wise men at their end know dark is right,
Because their words had forked no lightning they
Do not go gentle into that good night.

Good men, the last wave by, crying how bright
Their frail deeds might have danced in a green bay,
Rage, rage against the dying of the light.

Wild men who caught and sang the sun in flight,
And learn, too late, they grieved it on its way,
Do not go gentle into that good night.

Grave men, near death, who see with blinding sight
Blind eyes could blaze like meteors and be gay,
Rage, rage against the dying of the light.

And you, my father, there on the sad height,
Curse, bless, me now with your fierce tears, I pray.
Do not go gentle into that good night.
Rage, rage against the dying of the light.

Discuss

1. What is the figurative meaning of "good night" in this poem? Who is the speaker beseeching to "not go gentle"?

2. Why does the speaker not want the person to whom he is speaking to go gently into that good night?

3. There is irony in the sense with which "good night" is used in this poem. What is the irony?

4. The word "rage" is powerful and important in this poem. Who is raging and why?

Explore

1. This poem can be classified as a villanelle, as defined in The Glossary of Key Literary Terms. Study the poem's structure. Notice the number of stanzas, the number of lines in each stanza, the repetition of lines, and the rhyme scheme.

2. Notice the first lines of stanzas two, three, four, and five. Each refers to a certain type of person. Why does the speaker do this?

3. Why should "old age . . . burn and rave at close of day"?

For Your Journal

1. Many people have said that, until they became aware of their own mortality and the shortness of life, they did not truly appreciate living. Once they attained that awareness, life took on new meaning and new purpose. What sort of experience do you think brings people to this level of awareness? Describe the influence that an awareness of your own mortality might have on how you choose to live.

2. Is dying sufficient cause for rage? Identify the circumstances under which you would rage and those under which you would not rage.

THREE

Visionaries and Dreamers

Section A
Utopias and
Dystopias

Section B
Other Worlds

Section C
The Mysterious

Utopias and Dystopias

*People's visions of an ideal world—
a utopia—depend on their experiences,
their values, and their hopes and dreams.
Similarly, people have
different visions of dystopia,
a life that seems utterly hopeless
and wretched. You can tell what writers
care about by reading about
their utopias and dystopias.
In this section you will encounter
different views of the best
and the worst ways to live.*

The Big Rock Candy Mountains
Anonymous

The following poem by an unknown author represents one view of an ideal life—life lived in ease, and, at least, relative comfort. However, the view of comfort presented in this poem may not be your idea of comfort.

One evenin' as the sun went down
And the jungle fire was burnin'
Down the track came a hobo hikin'
And he said: "Boys, I'm not turnin',
I'm headed fer a land that's far away
Beside the crystal fountains,
So come with me, we'll all go see
The Big Rock Candy Mountains."

In the Big Rock Candy Mountains,
There's a land that's fair and bright,
Where the handouts grow on bushes,
And you sleep out every night.
Where the boxcars are all empty,
And the sun shines every day
On the birds and the bees and the cigarette trees,
And the lemonade springs where the bluebird sings,
In the Big Rock Candy Mountains.

In the Big Rock Candy Mountains,
All the cops have wooden legs,
The bulldogs all have rubber teeth,
And the hens lay soft-boiled eggs.
The farmers' trees are full of fruit,
And the barns are full of hay.
Oh, I'm bound to go where there ain't no snow,
Where the rain don't pour, the wind don't blow,
In the Big Rock Candy Mountains.

(continued)

In the Big Rock Candy Mountains,
You never change your socks,
And the little streams of alcohol
Come tricklin' down the rocks.
There the brakemen have to tip their hats
And the railroad bulls are blind.
There's a lake of stew and of whisky too,
You can paddle all around 'em in a big canoe,
In the Big Rock Candy Mountains.

In the Big Rock Candy Mountains,
All the jails are made of tin,
And you can bust right out again
As soon as you are in.
There ain't no short-handled shovels,
No axes, saws or picks.
I'm going to stay where you sleep all day,
Where they hung the Turk that invented work,
In the Big Rock Candy Mountains.

Discuss

1. Who is telling this story? Whom does the speaker encourage to seek the Big Rock Candy Mountains?

2. What is the setting of this poem? What is the jungle fire? Why is the setting important to the meaning of the poem?

3. Which statement best summarizes the speaker's view of the perfect place?

> a. The perfect place would be nothing like the world in which the hobo presently lives.
>
> b. The hobo would keep everything the way it is, because his present way of life offers challenge and opportunity.
>
> c. The hobo would make the uncomfortable aspects of his life comfortable.

Explore

1. What concerns felt by the hobos do you see in this description of an ideal world?

2. How does the diction, the choice of words in the poem, reflect the character of the speaker?

3. How does the speaker feel toward authority? How can you tell?

4. How would you describe the tone of this poem? Is it hostile? Serious? Playful? Mocking? Which aspects of rhythm and rhyme contribute to the poem?

For Your Journal

1. On the basis of what the hobo wishes his life were like, write a description titled "A Day in the Life of a Hobo."

2. Write a poem or essay describing your own Big Rock Candy Mountains. What food would be in them? How would you spend your time? What would the scenery be like? What other people would be there and how would they behave?

Where I Lived, and What I Lived For

Henry David Thoreau

Do authors actually attempt to create utopias for themselves? This essay by Henry David Thoreau, who lived in the 1800s, is an excerpt from his book *Walden,* an account of the two years he lived in the woods near Walden Pond in Massachusetts.

I WENT TO THE WOODS because I wished to live deliberately, to front only the essential facts of life, and see if I could not learn what it had to teach, and not, when I came to die, discover that I had not lived. I did not wish to live what was not life, living is so dear; nor did I wish to practise resignation, unless it was quite necessary. I wanted to live deep and suck out all the marrow of life, to live so sturdily and Spartan-like[1] as to put to rout all that was not life, to cut a broad swath and shave close, to drive life into a corner, and reduce it to its lowest terms, and, if it proved to be mean, why then to get the whole and genuine meanness of it, and publish its meanness to the world; or if it were sublime, to know it by experience, and be able to give a true account of it in my next excursion. For most men, it appears to me, are in a strange uncertainty about it, whether it is of the devil or of God, and have *somewhat hastily* concluded that it is the chief end of man here to "glorify God and enjoy him forever."

Still we live meanly, like ants; though the fable tells us that we were long ago changed into men; like pygmies[2] we fight with cranes; it is error upon error, and clout upon clout, and our best virtue has for its occasion a superfluous and evitable wretchedness. Our life is frittered away by detail. An honest man has hardly need to count more than his ten fingers, or in extreme cases he may add his ten toes, and lump the rest. Simplicity, simplicity, simplicity! I say, let your affairs be as two or three, and not a hundred or a thousand; instead of a million count half a dozen, and keep your accounts on your thumb-nail. In the midst of this chopping sea of civilized life, such are the clouds and storms and quicksands and thousand-and-one items to be allowed for, that a man has to live, if he would not founder and go to the bottom and not make his port at all, by dead reckoning, and he must be a great calculator indeed who succeeds. Simplify, simplify. Instead of three meals a day, if it be necessary eat but one; instead of a hundred dishes, five; and reduce other things in proportion. Our life is like a German Confederacy, made up of petty states, with its boundary forever fluctuating, so that even a German cannot tell you how it is bounded at any moment. The nation itself, with all its so-called internal improvements, which, by the way, are all external and superficial, is just such an unwieldy and overgrown establishment, cluttered with furniture and tripped up by its own traps, ruined by luxury and heedless expense, by want of calculation and a worthy aim, as the million households in the land; and the only cure for it, as for them, is in a rigid economy, a stern and more than Spartan simplicity of life and elevation of purpose. It lives too fast. Men think that it is essential that the *Nation* have commerce, and export ice, and talk through a telegraph, and ride thirty miles an hour, without a doubt, whether *they* do or not; but whether we should live like baboons or like men, is a little uncertain. If we do not get

[1]**Spartan-like:** resembling the people of Sparta, an ancient Greek city-state; they thrived on discipline and abstinence from luxury.
[2]**pygmies:** a term used commonly to mean people short in physical height or lacking some mental or moral quality.

out sleepers, and forge rails, and devote days and nights to the work, but go to tinkering upon our *lives* to improve *them*, who will build railroads? And if railroads are not built, how shall we get to Heaven in season? But if we stay at home and mind our business, who will want railroads? We do not ride on the railroad; it rides upon us. Did you ever think what those sleepers are that underlie the railroad? Each one is a man, an Irishman, or a Yankee man. The rails are laid on them, and they are covered with sand, and the cars run smoothly over them. They are sound sleepers, I assure you. And every few years a new lot is laid down and run over; so that, if some have the pleasure of riding on a rail, others have the misfortune to be ridden upon. And when they run over a man that is walking in his sleep, a supernumerary[3] sleeper in the wrong position, and wake him up, they suddenly stop the cars, and make a hue and cry about it, as if this were an exception. I am glad to know that it takes a gang of men for every five miles to keep the sleepers down and level in their beds as it is, for this is a sign that they may sometime get up again. . . .

Let us spend one day as deliberately as Nature, and not be thrown off the track by every nutshell and mosquito's wing that falls on the rails. Let us rise early and fast, or break fast, gently and without perturbation; let company come and let company go, let the bells ring and the children cry—determined to make a day of it. Why should we knock under and go with the stream? Let us not be upset and overwhelmed in that terrible rapid and whirlpool called a dinner, situated in the meridian shallows. Weather this danger and you are safe, for the rest of the way is down hill. With unrelaxed nerves, with morning vigor, sail by it, looking another way, tied to the mast like Ulysses.[4] If the engine whistles, let it whistle till it is hoarse for its pains. If the bell rings, why should we run? We will consider what kind of music they are like. Let us settle ourselves, and work and wedge our feet downward through the mud and slush of opinion, and prejudice, and tradition, and delusion, and appearance, that alluvion[5] which covers the globe, through Paris and London, through New York and Boston and Concord, through Church and State, through poetry and philosophy and religion, till we come to a hard bottom and rocks in place, which we can call *reality*, and say, This is, and no mistake; and then begin, having a *point d'appui*,[6] below freshet[7] and frost and fire, a place where you might found a wall or a state, or set a lamp-post safely, or perhaps a gauge, not a Nilometer, but a Realometer, that future ages might know how deep a freshet of shams and appearances had gathered from time to time. If you stand right fronting and face to face to a fact, you will see the sun glimmer on both its surfaces, as if it were a cimeter,[8] and feel its sweet edge dividing you through the heart and marrow, and so you will happily conclude your mortal career. Be it life or death, we crave only reality. If we are really dying, let us hear the rattle in our throats and feel cold in the extremities; if we are alive, let us go about our business.

[4]**Ulysses:** Latin name of the hero of the ancient Greek epic, the *Odyssey*. At one point during his ten-year voyage home, he had himself tied to his ship's mast in order to resist mythical nymphs said to seduce sailors to their death.
[5]**alluvion:** flood.
[6]**point d'appui:** *Fr.* foundation or base.
[7]**freshet:** huge rise or overflowing of a stream.
[8]**cimeter:** another spelling of scimitar, a sword with a broad, curved blade.

[3]**supernumerary:** One who is unnecessary.

Discuss

1. Which of the following might make a better title for this essay?

   a. Who Will Build the Railroads?

   b. Learning Self-Reliance

   c. Living Off the Land

2. When Thoreau advises, "keep your accounts on your thumb-nail," what does he mean?

3. What does Thoreau mean when he says, "We do not ride on the railroad; it rides upon us"?

Explore

1. What does Thoreau mean when he says that he wished to live deliberately?

2. Do you agree with Thoreau's view of activity and goals of the Nation? Why or why not? Do you see any parallels between his view of government in the 1800s and your view of government in the late 1900s? If so, what are they?

3. What metaphors and similes does Thoreau use to illustrate his notion that people's lives are overly complex and ruled by the direction of others?

4. Thoreau alludes to Paris and London, New York and Boston and Concord, and Church and State in emphasizing the need to come to a "hard bottom and rocks in place." Why?

5. What are the effects of Thoreau's uses of "we," and "I," and "you" when he discusses the errors people have made in living?

For Your Journal

1. On the basis of what you have read in this essay, published in 1854, what sorts of reactions do you suppose Thoreau would have to U.S. culture in the second half of the 1900s? Write an essay from his point of view describing his reaction to one aspect of this culture—for example, television, advertising, air travel, or surrogate motherhood.

2. Even the most committedly modern people would sometimes like to free themselves of what is often called a rat race. If you were to simplify your life, what would you change and how would you change it?

3. Write an imaginary letter to Thoreau challenging his values and arguments with which you disagree.

The Unknown Citizen

W. H. Auden

In the following poem you will read about the life of an ideal citizen in dystopia, a society robbed of individuality.

He was found by the Bureau of Statistics to be
One against whom there was no official complaint,
And all the reports on his conduct agree
That, in the modern sense of an old-fashioned word he was a
    saint,
For in everything he did he served the Greater Community.
Except for the War till the day he retired
He worked in a factory and never got fired,
But satisfied his employers, Fudge Motors Inc.
Yet he wasn't a scab[1] or odd in his views
For his Union reports that he paid his dues,
(Our report on his Union shows it was sound)
And our Social Psychology workers found
That he was popular with his mates and liked a drink.
The Press are convinced that he bought a paper every day
And that his reactions to advertisements were normal
    in every way.
Policies taken out in his name prove that he was fully insured,
And his Health-card shows he was once in hospital
    but left it cured.
Both Producers Research and High-Grade Living declare
He was fully sensible to the advantages of the Installment Plan
And had everything necessary to the Modern Man,
A phonograph, radio, a car and a frigidaire.
Our researchers into Public Opinion are content
That he held the proper opinions for the time of year;
When there was peace, he was for peace; when there
    was war, he went.
He was married and added five children
    to the population,
Which our Eugenist[2] says was the right number
    for a parent of his generation,
And our teachers report that he never interfered
    with their education.
Was he free? Was he happy? The question is absurd:
Had anything been wrong, we should certainly have heard.

---

[1]**scab:** worker who refuses to join a labor union or strike with one, or works in place of striking workers.
[2]**Eugenist:** one who is concerned with the quality of offspring.

Discuss

1. Which statement best describes the Unknown Citizen?

    a. The Unknown Citizen was happy because he followed the rules.
    b. The Unknown Citizen put freedom above all other values.
    c. The Unknown Citizen was conventional in his behavior.

2. How do you learn about the Unknown Citizen's life? Who has provided the information about him?

3. For what purpose is the poem written? Where is it supposed to appear?

Explore

1. Do you believe that this poem presents a dystopia, rather than a utopia? Why or why not?

2. Note the capitalization of certain words in the poem at the beginning of lines. Why do you suppose those words are capitalized? What effect does the capitalization have on your view of the world that is indirectly being described?

3. Who are the "we" of the last line? What irony, if any, do you see in that line? Do you accept the truth of the last line? Why or why not?

4. Do you think the Unknown Citizen was happy and free? Why or why not? What evidence can you find in the poem to support your view?

For Your Journal

1. Some critics believe this view of the Unknown Citizen summarizes the fate of the modern person in society. Do you agree or disagree? Explain.

2. Describe the Unknown Citizen from the point of view of his wife or one of his children.

Caliban in the Coal Mines

Louis Untermeyer

The society depicted in the following poem is not as "civilized" as that depicted in "The Unknown Citizen." Instead, it is an underground world. Caliban, a character in Shakespeare's play *The Tempest,* is a deformed slave who wishes for freedom. In this poem, the speaker describes a dark, dreary, depressing world.

God, we don't like to complain
   We know that the mine is no lark.
But—there's the pools from the rain;
   But—there's the cold and the dark.

God, You don't know what it is—
   You, in Your well-lighted sky—
Watching the meteors whizz;
   Warm, with a sun always by.

God, if You had but the moon
   Stuck in Your cap for a lamp,
Even You'd tire of it soon,
   Down in the dark and the damp.

Nothing but blackness above
   And nothing that moves but the cars . . .
God, if You wish for our love,
   Fling us a handful of stars!

Discuss

1. Who are the "we" of the poem?

2. What bargain does the speaker of the poem strike with God? Why?

3. In stanza three, what does "the moon/Stuck in Your cap for a lamp" mean?

Explore

1. What effect does the name Caliban in the title have on your response to the poem? Would you have responded differently if the name were George or Harold?

2. How do the images of the miners differ from God's images? What are these images, and how do they affect your response to the poem?

3. What manner of speaking does the miner use to address God? Based on this monologue, how would you describe his relationship with God?

For Your Journal

1. Write an imaginary letter to someone you feel has power over the quality of your life. Like the miner, ask that person to take steps to improve your lot in life.

2. This poem and the previous one, "The Unknown Citizen," have provided two versions of a dystopian world. Write your own description of a dystopia.

Other Worlds

*In this section you will read
literature in which things
are not always as they appear
and characters seek worlds
better than their own.
These stories and poems also reveal
that different people have different
perspectives. People's values,
experiences, and expectations
influence their ideas of reality,
so that, in fact, they may not
even see the same world.*

A Room Full of Leaves

Joan Aiken

Wil lives with relatives whose values are alien to those of a little boy trying
to grow up. Fortunately, Wil finds someone who shares his views.

ONCE THERE WAS a poor little boy who lived with a
lot of his relatives in an enormous house called
Troy. The relatives were rich, but they were so
nasty that they might just as well have been poor,
for all the good their money did them. The worst
of them all was Aunt Agatha, who was thin and
sharp, and the next worst was Uncle Umbert, who
was stout and prosperous. We shall return to them
later. There was also a fierce old nurse called
Squabb, and a tutor, Mr. Buckle, who helped to
make the little boy's life a burden. His name was
Wilfred, which was a family name, but he was so
tired of hearing them all say: "You must live up to
your name, child," that in his own mind he called
himself Wil. It had to be in his mind, for he had
no playmates—other children were declared to be
common, and probably dangerous and infectious
too.

One rainy Saturday afternoon Wil sat in his
schoolroom finishing some Latin parsing for Mr.
Buckle before being taken for his walk, which was
always in one of two directions. If Squabb took him
they went downtown "to look at the shops" in a
suburb of London which was sprawling out its claws
toward the big house; but the shops were never the
ones Wil would have chosen to look at. If he went
with Mr. Buckle they crossed the Common diago-
nally (avoiding the pond where rude little boys
sailed their boats) and came back along the white-
railed ride[1] while Mr. Buckle talked about plant
life.

So Wil was not looking forward with great enthusiasm to his walk, and when Squabb came in
and told him that it was too wet to go out and he
must amuse himself quietly with his transfers, he

[1]**ride:** path suitable for riding.

was delighted. He sat gazing dreamily at the transfers for a while, not getting on with them, while
Squabb did some ironing. It was nearly dark, although the time was only three. Squabb switched
on the light and picked a fresh heap of ironing off
the fender.

All of a sudden there was a blue flash and a
report from the iron; a strong smell of burnt rubber
filled the room and all the lights went out.

"Now I suppose the perishing thing's fused all
this floor," exclaimed Squabb, and she hurried out
of the room, muttering something under her breath
about new-fangled gadgets.

Wil did not waste a second. Before the door
had closed after her he was tiptoeing across the
room and out of the other door. In the darkness
and confusion no one would miss him for quite a
considerable time, and he would have a rare opportunity to be on his own for a bit.

The house in which he lived was very huge.
Nobody knew exactly how many rooms there
were—but there was one for each day of the year
and plenty left over. Innumerable little courtyards,
each with its own patch of green velvet grass, had
passages leading away in all directions to different
blocks and wings. Toward the back of the house
there were fewer courtyards; it drew itself together
into a solid mass which touched the forest behind.
The most important rooms were open to the public
on four days a week; Mr. Buckle and a skinny lady
from the town showed visitors round, and all the
relics and heirlooms were carefully locked up inside
glass cases where they could be gazed at—the silver
washbasin used by James II, a dirty old exercise
book belonging to the poet Pope, the little pot of
neat's foot ointment left by Henry VIII, and all the

other tiny bits of history. Even in those days visitors were careless about leaving things behind.

Wil was indifferent to the public rooms, though his relatives were not. They spent their lives polishing and furbishing and when everything was polished they went on endless grubbing searches through the unused rooms looking for more relics which could be cleaned up and sold to the British Museum.

Wil stood outside the schoolroom door listening. Down below he could hear the murmur of voices. Saturday was cheap visiting day—only two and six instead of five shillings—so there were twice as many people, and both Mr. Buckle and the skinny lady were at work escorting their little groups. Wil nodded to himself and slipped away, softly as a mouse, toward the back of the house where the tourists were never taken. Here it became darker and dustier, the windows were small, heavily leaded and never cleaned. Little passages, unexpected stairways and landings, wound about past innumerable doors, many of which had not been opened since Anne Boleyn[2] popped her head around to say good-bye to some bedridden old retainer[3] before taking horse to London. Tapestries hung thick with velvet dust—had Wil touched them they would have crumbled to pieces but he slid past them like a shadow.

He was already lost, but he meant to be; he stood listening to the old house creaking and rustling around him like a forest. He had a fancy that if he penetrated far enough he would find himself in the forest without having noticed the transition. He was following a particularly crooked and winding passage, leading to a kind of crossroads or cross-passages from which other alleys led away, mostly dark, some with a faint gleam from a rain-streaked window far away down their length, and all lined with doors.

He paused, wondering which to choose, and then heard something which might have been the faintest of whispers—but it was enough to decide him on taking the passage directly fronting him. He went slowly to a door some twelve feet along it, rather a low, small door on his right.

After pushing he discovered that it opened outward toward him. He pulled it back, stepped around, and gazed in bewilderment at what he saw.

[2]**Anne Boleyn:** second wife of King Henry VIII of England and mother of Queen Elizabeth I; ordered beheaded by Henry VIII in 1536.
[3]**retainer:** servant.

It was like a curtain, of a silvery, faded brown, which hung across the doorway. Then looking closer he saw that it was really *leaves*—piled high and drifted one on another, lying so heaped up that the entrance was filled with them, and if the door had swung inward he could never have pushed it open. Wil felt them with his hand; they were not brittle like dead beech-leaves, but soft and supple, making only the faintest rustle when he touched them. He took one and looked at it in the palm of his hand. It was almost a skeleton, covered with faint silvery marks like letters. As he stood looking at it he heard a little voice whisper from inside the room:

"Well, boy, aren't you coming in?"

Much excited, he stared once more at the apparently impenetrable wall of leaves in front of him, and said softly:

"How do I get through?"

"Burrow, of course," whispered the voice impatiently.

He obeyed, and stooping a little plunged his head and arms among the leaves and began working his way into them like a mole. When he was entirely inside the doorway he wriggled around and pulled the door shut behind him. The leaves made hardly any noise as he inched through them. There was just enough air to breathe, and a dryish aromatic scent. His progress was slow, and it seemed to take about ten minutes before the leaves began to thin out, and striking upward like a diver he finally came to the surface.

He was in a room, or so he supposed, having come into it through an ordinary door in a corridor, but the walls could not be seen at all on account of the rampart[4] of leaves piled up all round him. Toward the center there was a clear space on the ground, and in this grew a mighty trunk, as large round as a table, covered with roughish silver bark, all protrusions and knobs. The branches began above his head, thrusting out laterally like those of an oak or beech, but very little could be seen of them on account of the leaves which grew everywhere in thick clusters, and the upper reaches of the tree were not visible at all. The growing leaves were yellow—not the faded yellow of autumn but a brilliant gold which illuminated the room. At least there was no other source of light, and it was not dark.

There appeared to be no one else under the tree and Wil wondered who had spoken to him and where they could be.

[4]**rampart:** wall-like ridge.

As if in answer to his thoughts the voice spoke again:

"Can't you climb up?"

"Yes, of course I can," he said, annoyed with himself for not thinking of this, and he began setting his feet on the rough ledges of bark and pulling himself up. Soon he could not see the floor below, and was in a cage of leaves which fluttered all round him, dazzling his eyes. The scent in the tree was like thyme on the downs on a hot summer's day.

"Where are you?" he asked in bewilderment.

He heard a giggle.

"I'm here," said the voice, and he saw an agitation among the leaves at the end of a branch, and worked his way out to it. He found a little girl—a rather plain little girl with freckles and reddish hair hidden under some kind of cap. She wore a long green velvet dress and a ruff, and she was seated comfortably swinging herself up and down in a natural hammock of small branches.

"Really I thought you'd *never* find your way here," she said, giving him a derisive welcoming grin.

"I'm not used to climbing trees," he excused himself.

"I know, poor wretch. Never mind, this one's easy enough. What's your name? Mine's Em."

"Mine's Wil. Do you live here?"

"Of course. This isn't really my branch—some of them are very severe about staying on their own branches—look at *him.*" She indicated a very Puritanical-looking gentleman in black knee-breeches who appeared for a moment and then vanished again as a cluster of leaves swayed. "I go where I like, though. My branch isn't respectable—we were on the wrong side in every war from Matilda and Stephen on. As soon as the colonies were invented they shipped a lot of us out there, but it was no use, they left a lot behind. They always hope that we'll die out, but of course we don't. Shall I show you some of the tree?"

"Yes, please."

"Come along then. Don't be frightened, you can hold my hand a lot of the time. It's almost as easy as stairs."

When she began leading him about he realized that the tree was much more enormous than he had supposed; in fact he did not understand how it could be growing in a room inside a house. The branches curved about making platforms, caves, spiral staircases, seats, cupboards and cages. Em led

him through the maze, which she seemed to know by heart, pushing past the clusters of yellow leaves. She showed him how to swing from one branch to another, how to slide down the slopes and wriggle through the crevices, and how to lie back in a network of boughs and rest his head on a thick pillow of leaves.

They made quite a lot of noise and several disapproving old faces peered at them from the ends of branches, though one crusader smiled faintly and his dog wagged its tail.

"Have you anything to eat?" asked Em presently, mopping her brow with her kerchief.

"Yes, I've got some biscuits I didn't eat at break this morning. I'm not allowed to keep them of course, they'd be cross if they knew."

"Of course," nodded Em, taking a biscuit. "Thanks. Dryish, your comfits, aren't they—but welcome. Wait a minute and I'll bring you a drink." She disappeared among the boughs and came back in a few moments with two little greenish crystal cups full of a golden liquid.

"It's sap," she said, passing one over. "It has a sort of forest taste, hasn't it; makes you think of horns. Now I'll give you a present."

She took the cups away and he heard her rummaging somewhere down by the trunk of the tree.

"There's all sorts of odds and ends down there. This is the first thing I could find. Do you like it?"

"Yes, very much," he said, handling the slender silver thing with interest. "What is it?"

She looked at it critically. "I think it's the shoehorn that Queen Elizabeth used (she always had trouble with wearing too tight shoes). She must have left it behind here sometime. You can have it anyway—you might find a use for it. You'd better be going now or you'll be in trouble and then it won't be so easy for you to come here another time."

"How shall I ever find my way back here?"

"You must stand quite still and listen. You'll hear me whisper, and the leaves rustling. Goodbye." She suddenly put a skinny little arm around his neck and gave him a hug. "It's nice having someone to play with; I've been a bit bored sometimes."

Wil squirmed out through the leaves again and shut the door, turning to look at it as he did so. There was nothing in the least unusual about its appearance.

When he arrived back in the schoolroom (after some false turnings) he found his Aunt Agatha waiting for him. Squabb and Buckle were hovering on the threshold, but she dismissed them with a wave of her hand. The occasion was too serious for underlings.

"Wilfred," she said, in a very awful tone.

"Yes, Aunt Agatha."

"Where have you been?"

"Playing in the back part of the house."

"*Playing!* A child of your standing and responsibilities playing? Instead of getting on with your transfers? What is that?" She pounced on him and dragged out the shoehorn which was protruding from his pocket.

"Concealment! I suppose you found this and intended to creep out and sell it to some museum. You are an exceedingly wicked, disobedient boy, and as punishment for running away and hiding in this manner you will go to bed as soon as I have finished with you, you will have nothing to eat but toast-gruel, and you will have to take off your clothes *yourself*, and feed *yourself*, like a common child."

"Yes, Aunt."

"You know that you are the Heir to this noble house (when your great-uncle Winthrop dies)?"

"Yes, Aunt."

"Do you know anything about your parents?"

"No."

"It is as well. Look at this." She pulled out a little case, containing two miniatures of perfectly ordinary people. Wil studied them.

"That is your father—our brother. He disgraced the family—he sullied the scutcheon[5]—by becoming—*a writer*, and worse—he married a *female writer*, your mother. Mercifully for the family reputation they were both drowned in the *Oranjeboot* disaster, before anything worse could happen. You were rescued, floating in a pickle barrel. *Now* do you see why we all take such pains with your education? It is to save you from the taint of your unfortunate parentage."

Wil was still digesting this when there came a knock at the door and Mr. Buckle put his head round.

"There is a Mr. Slockenheimer demanding to see you, Lady Agatha," he said. "Apparently he will not take No for an answer. Shall I continue with the reprimand?"

"No, Buckle—you presume," said Aunt Agatha coldly. "I have finished."

[5]**scutcheon:** family shield.

Wil put himself to bed, watched minutely by Buckle to see that he did not omit to brush his teeth with the silver brush or comb his eyebrows with King Alfred's comb in the manner befitting an heir of Troy. The toast and water was brought in a gold porringer.[6] Wil ate it absently; it was very nasty, but he was so overcome by the luck of not having been found out, and wondering how he could get back to see Em another time, that he hardly noticed it.

Next morning at breakfast (which he had with his relatives) he expected to be in disgrace, but curiously enough they paid no attention to him. They were all talking about Mr. Slockenheimer.

"Such a piece of luck," said Cousin Cedric. "Just as the tourist season is ending."

"Who is this man?" creaked Great-Aunt Gertrude.

"He is a film director, from Hollywood," explained Aunt Agatha, loudly and patiently. "He is making a film about Robin Hood and he has asked permission to shoot some of the indoor scenes in Troy—for which we shall all be handsomely paid, naturally."

"Naturally, naturally," croaked the old ravens, all round the table.

Wil pricked up his ears, and then an anxious thought struck him. Supposing Mr. Slockenheimer's people discovered the room with the tree?

"They are coming today," Uncle Umbert was shrieking into Great-Uncle Ulric's ear trumpet.

Mr. Slockenheimer's outfit arrived after breakfast while Wil was doing his daily run—a hundred times round the triangle of grass in front of the house, while Mr. Buckle timed him with a stop watch.

A lovely lady shot out of a huge green motor car, shrieked:

"Oh, you cute darling! Now you must tell me the way to the nearest milk bar," and whisked him back into the car with her. Out of the corner of his eye he saw that Mr. Buckle had been commandeered to show somebody the spiral staircase.

Wil ate his raspberry sundae in a daze. He had never been in the milk bar before, never eaten ice cream, never ridden in a car. To have it all following on his discovery of the day before was almost too much for him.

"Gracious!" exclaimed his new friend, looking at her wristwatch. "I must be on the set! I'm Maid

[6]**porringer:** dish or cup for porridge, soup, or similar food.

Marian, you know. Tarzan, I mean Robin, has to rescue me from the wicked baron at eleven in the Great Hall."

"I'll show you where it is," said Wil.

He expected more trouble when he reached home, but the whole household was disorganized; Mr. Buckle was showing Robin Hood how to put on the Black Prince's casque[7] (which was too big) and Aunt Agatha was having a long business conversation with Mr. Slockenheimer, so his arrival passed unnoticed.

He was relieved to find that the film was only going to be shot in the main public rooms, so there did not seem to be much risk of the tree being discovered.

After lunch Mr. Buckle was called on again to demonstrate the firing of the ninth Earl's crossbow (he shot an extra) and Wil was able to escape once more and reach in safety the regions at the back.

He stood on a dark landing for what seemed like hours, listening to the patter of his own heart. Then, tickling his ear like a thread of cobweb he heard Em's whisper:

"Wil! Here I am! This way!" and below it he heard the rustle of the tree, as if it, too, were whispering: "Here I am."

It did not take him long to find the room, but his progress through the leaves was slightly impeded by the things he was carrying. When he emerged at the foot of the tree he found Em waiting there. The hug she gave him nearly throttled him.

"I've been thinking of some more places to show you. And all sorts of games to play!"

"I've brought you a present," he said, emptying his pockets.

"Oh! What's in those little tubs?"

"Ice cream. The chief electrician gave them to me."

"What a strange confection," she said, tasting it. "It is smooth and sweet but it makes my teeth chatter."

"And here's your present." It was a gold Mickey Mouse with ruby eyes which Maid Marian had given him. Em handled it with respect and presently stored it away in one of her hidey holes in the trunk. Then they played follow-my-leader until they were so tired that they had to lie back on thick beds of leaves and rest.

"I did not expect to see you again so soon," said Em as they lay picking the aromatic leaves and

chewing them, while a prim Jacobean lady shook her head at them.

Wil explained about the invasion of the film company and she listened with interest.

"A sort of strolling players," she commented. "My father was one—flat contrary to the family's commands, of course. I saw many pieces performed before I was rescued from the life by my respected grandmother to be brought up as befitted one of our name." She sighed.

For the next two months Wil found many opportunities to slip off and visit Em, for Mr. Buckle became greatly in demand as an adviser on matters of costume, and even Squabb was pressed into service ironing doublets and mending hose.

But one day Wil saw his relatives at breakfast with long faces, and he learned that the company had finished shooting the inside scenes and were about to move to Florida to take the Sherwood Forest sequences. The handsome additional income which the family had been making was about to cease, and Wil realized with dismay that the old life would begin again.

Later when he was starting off to visit Em he found a little group, consisting of Aunt Agatha, Uncle Umbert, Mr. Slockenheimer, and his secretary, Mr. Jakes, on one of the back landings. Wil shrank into the shadows and listened to their conversation with alarm.

"One million," Mr. Slockenheimer was saying. "Yes, sir, one million's my last word. But I'll ship the house over to Hollywood myself, as carefully as if it was a new-laid egg. You may be sure of that, ma'am, I appreciate your feelings, and you and all your family may go on living in it for the rest of your days. Every brick will be numbered and every floorboard will be lettered so that they'll go back in their exact places. This house certainly will be a gold mine to me—it'll save its value twice over in a year as sets for different films. There's Tudor, Gothic, Norman, Saxon, Georgian, Decorated, all under one roof."

"But we shall have to have salaries, too, mind," said Uncle Umbert greedily. "We can't be expected to uproot ourselves like this and move to Hollywood all for nothing."

Mr. Slockenheimer raised his eyebrows at this, but said agreeably:

"Okay, I'll sign you on as extras." He pulled out a fistful of forms, scribbled his signature on them, and handed them to Aunt Agatha. "There you are, ma'am, twenty-year contracts for the whole bunch."

[7]**casque**: armor for the head

"Dirt cheap at the price, even so," Wil heard him whisper to the secretary.

"Now as we've finished shooting I'll have the masons in tomorrow and start chipping the old place to bits. Hangings and furniture will be crated separately. It'll take quite a time, of course; shouldn't think we'll get it done under three weeks." He looked with respect over his shoulder at a vista of dark corridor which stretched away for half a mile.

Wil stole away with his heart thudding. Were they actually proposing to pull down the house, *this* house, and ship it to Hollywood for film sets? What about the tree? Would they hack it down, or dig it up and transport it, leaves and all?

"What's the matter, boy?" asked Em, her cheek bulging with the giant humbug he had brought her.

"The film company's moving away; and they're going to take Troy with them for using as backgrounds for films."

"The whole house?"

"Yes."

"Oh," said Em, and became very thoughtful.

"Em."

"Yes?"

"What—I mean, what would happen to you if they found this room and cut the tree down, or dug it up?"

"I'm not sure," she said, pondering. "I shouldn't go *on* after that—none of us would in here—but as to exactly *what* would happen—; I don't expect it would be bad. Perhaps we should just go out like lamps."

"Well, then, it must be stopped," said Wil so firmly that he surprised himself.

"Can you forbid it? You're the Heir, aren't you?"

"Not till old Uncle Winthrop dies. We'll have to think of some other plan."

"I have an idea," said Em, wrinkling her brow with effort. "In my days, producers would do much for a well-written new play, one that had never been seen before. Is it still like that nowadays?"

"Yes I think so, but we don't know anyone who writes plays," Wil pointed out.

"I have a play laid by somewhere," she explained. "The writer was a friend of my father—he asked my father to take it up to London to have it printed. My father bade me take care of it and I put it in my bundle of clothes. It was on that journey, as we were passing through Oxford, that I was

seen and carried off by my respected grandmother, and I never saw my father or Mr. Shakespeere again, so the poor man lost his play."

"Mr. Shakespeere, did you say?" asked Wil, stuttering slightly. "What was the name of the play?"

"I forget. I have it here somewhere." She began delving about in a cranny between two branches and presently drew out a dirty old manuscript. Wil stared at it with popping eyes.

The Tragicall Historie of Robin Hoode
A play by Wm. Shakespeere
Act 1, Scene I. Sherwood Forest. Enter John Lackland, De Bracy, Sheriff of Nottingham, Knights, Lackeys and attendants.

JOHN L. Good sirs, the occasion of our coming hither
Is, since our worthy brother Coeur de Lion
Far from our isle now wars on Paynim soil,
The apprehension of that recreant knave
Most caitiff outlaw who is known by some
As Robin Locksley; by others Robin Hood;
More, since our coffers gape with idle locks
The forfeiture of his ill-gotten gains.
Thus Locksley's stocks will stock our locks enow
While he treads air beneath the forest bough.

"Golly," said Wil, "Shakespeere's *Robin Hood*. I wonder what Mr. Slockenheimer would say to this?"

"Well, don't wait. *Go and ask him.* It's yours—I'll make you a present of it."

He wriggled back through the leaves with frantic speed, slammed the door, and raced down the passage toward the Great Hall. Mr. Slockenheimer was there superintending the packing of some expensive and elaborate apparatus.

"Hello, Junior. Haven't seen you in days. Well, how d'you like the thought of moving to Hollywood, eh?"

"Not very much," said Wil frankly. "You see, I'm used to it here, and—and the house is too; I don't think the move would be good for it."

"Think the dry air would crumble it, mebbe? Well, there's something to what you say. I'll put in air-conditioning apparatus the other end. I'm sorry you don't take to the idea, though. Hollywood's a swell place."

"Mr. Slockenheimer," said Wil. "I've got something here which is rather valuable. It's mine—somebody gave it to me. And it's genuine. I was wondering if I could do a sort of swap—exchange it for the house, you know."

"It would have to be mighty valuable," replied Mr. Slockenheimer cautiously. "Think it's worth a million, son? What is it?"

"It's a play by Mr. Shakespeere—a new play that no one's seen before."

"Eh?"

"I'll show you," said Wil confidently, pulling out the ms.

"The Tragicall Historie of Robin Hoode," read Mr. Slockenheimer slowly. "By Wm. Shakespeere. Well, I'll be gosh darned. Just when I'd finished the indoor scenes. Isn't that just my luck. Hey, Junior—are you sure this is genuine?—Well, Jakes will know, he knows everything; hey," he called to his secretary, "come and have a look at this."

The dry Mr. Jakes let out a whistle when he saw the signature.

"That's genuine all right," he said. "It's quite something you've got there. First production of the original Shakespeare play by Q. P. Slockenheimer."

"Well, will you swap?" asked Wil once more.

"I'll say I will," exclaimed Mr. Slockenheimer slapping him thunderously on the back. "You can keep your moldering old barracks. I'll send you twenty stalls for the premiere. *Robin Hoode by Wm. Shakespeere.* Well, what do you know!"

"There's just one thing," said Wil pausing.

"Yes, Bud?"

"These contracts you gave my uncle and aunt and the others. Are they still binding?"

"Not if you don't want."

"Oh, but I do—I'd much rather they went to Hollywood."

Mr. Slockenheimer burst out laughing.

"Oh, I get the drift. Okay, Junior, I daresay they won't bother me as much as they do you. I'll hold them to those contracts as tight as glue. Twenty years, eh? You'll be of age by then, I guess? Your Uncle Umbert can be the Sheriff of Nottingham, he's about the build for the part. And we'll fit your Aunt Aggie in somewhere."

"And Buckle and Squabb?"

"Yes, yes," said Mr. Slockenheimer, much tickled. "Though what you'll do here all on your own—however, that's your affair. Right, boys, pack up those cameras next."

Three days later the whole outfit was gone, and with them, swept away among the flash bulbs, cameras, extras, crates, props and costumes, went Squabb, Buckle, Aunt Agatha, Uncle Umbert, Cousin Cedric, and all the rest.

Empty and peaceful the old house dreamed, with sunlight shifting from room to room and no sound to break the silence, save in one place, where the voices of children could be heard faintly above the rustling of a tree.

Discuss

1. In what ways does Wil differ from his relatives? How do you know?

2. What parallels do you see between Wil and Em?

3. What circumstances allow Wil to find the room full of leaves and later return to it?

4. Why does Slockenheimer want the house?

Explore

1. How does the author create a transition between the world of the house and the room full of leaves? What foreshadowing does she provide to prepare you for what Wil is to find?

2. How do Wil's relatives change from the beginning to the end of the story? Why does this change occur? In what ways does it seem inconsistent with what has been established about them? In what ways is the change desirable?

3. Account for the change in Mr. Slockenheimer's plans. Do you find it believable? Why or why not?

For Your Journal

1. If you could escape from reality, where would you go? What would your new world look like? How would you spend your time there?

2. Wil's fantasy world might be described as a creation of a world in rebellion against his relatives. Write a description of some other ways that children try to create alternatives to their families' expectations and demands.

Sand Hill Road

Morton Grosser

In this poem the poet creates a new, different world suggested by
the real world.

The landscape here is Africa
in California, scattered stands
of flattened Eucalyptus spread
their shallow horizontal hands
and make a spotted shade for leopards
or giraffes. I look for leopards
under every tree, for lions
in the grass; the passage signs
are not the tracks of elephants
but panting yellow tractors, stamping
down the bushes, trampling on
the slender trees, like elephants.

But still, the river draws a belt
of green across the brown, the veldt[1]
is still a perfect veldt. I know
that if at dusk I climb a tree
and if the moon is bright, I could
be watching when the cautious,
softly snorting herd of bulldozers
comes watering at night.

[1]**veldt:** grassland scattered with shrubs, especially in Africa.

Discuss

1. What is the setting of the poem?

    a. Africa

    b. Any grassy plain

    c. California

2. What sort of landscape do you picture from this poem? Which words and images paint that picture for you?

Explore

1. How do the speaker's expectations of what he will see differ from what he actually finds?

2. How would you describe the speaker's attitude toward what he sees? Is he angry? Disappointed? Intrigued? Matter-of-fact? Why do you think so?

3. What comparisons does the speaker use? What effect do they have on your response?

4. What contrast do you think the speaker is making between the two stanzas with the word "but'?

For Your Journal

1. Write a description in which you turn a familiar world—such as your bedroom, a park in winter, or a construction site—into a remote world—like a disaster area, glaciers in Antarctica, or a bombing zone. Use specific images and comparisons to call upon that other world.

2. Many writers use animals as a basis for comparison to describe such traits as motion, strength, age, and size. In this poem, for example, tractors stamp like elephants. Create some animal comparisons to provide pictures of familiar objects in your environment.

The Subliminal Man

J. G. Ballard

Descriptions of future worlds can help you focus on your own world more clearly. That appears to be the intent in this science fiction story. The word "subliminal" means below the threshold of consciousness. Does the society in this story seem familar to you?

"THE SIGNS, DOCTOR! Have you seen the signs?"

Frowning with annoyance, Dr. Franklin quickened his pace and hurried down the hospital steps toward the line of parked cars. Over his shoulder he caught a glimpse of a man in ragged sandals and lime-stained jeans waving to him from the far side of the drive, then break into a run when he saw Franklin try to evade him.

"Dr. Franklin! The signs!"

Head down, Franklin swerved around an elderly couple approaching the out-patients department. His car was over a hundred yards away. Too tired to start running himself, he waited for the young man to catch him up.

"All right, Hathaway, what is it this time?" he snapped irritably. "I'm getting sick of you hanging around here all day."

Hathaway lurched to a halt in front of him, uncut black hair like an awning over his eyes. He brushed it back with a claw-like hand and turned on a wild smile, obviously glad to see Franklin and oblivious of the latter's hostility.

"I've been trying to reach you at night, Doctor, but your wife always puts the phone down on me," he explained without a hint of rancor, as if well-used to this kind of snub. "And I didn't want to look for you inside the Clinic." They were standing by a privet[1] hedge that shielded them from the lower windows of the main administration block, but Franklin's regular rendezvous with Hathaway and his strange messianic cries had already been the subject of amused comment.

[1]**privet:** a European evergreen shrub used for hedges.

Franklin began to say: "I appreciate that—" but Hathaway brushed this aside. "Forget it, Doctor, there are more important things happening now. They've started to build the first big signs! Over a hundred feet high, on the traffic islands just outside town. They'll soon have all the approach roads covered. When they do we might as well stop thinking."

"Your trouble is that you're thinking too much," Franklin told him. "You've been rambling about these signs for weeks now. Tell me, have you actually seen one signalling?"

Hathaway tore a handful of leaves from the hedge, exasperated by this irrelevancy. "Of course I haven't, that's the whole point, Doctor." He dropped his voice as a group of nurses walked past, watching him uneasily out of the corners of their eyes. "The construction gangs were out again last night, laying huge power cables. You'll see them on the way home. Everything's nearly ready now."

"They're traffic signs," Franklin explained patiently. "The flyover has just been completed. Hathaway, for God's sake relax. Try to think of Dora and the child."

"I *am* thinking of them!" Hathaway's voice rose to a controlled scream. "Those cables were 40,000-volt lines, Doctor, with terrific switch-gear. The trucks were loaded with enormous metal scaffolds. Tomorrow they'll start lifting them up all over the city, they'll block off half the sky! What do you think Dora will be like after six months of that? We've got to stop them, Doctor, they're trying to transistorize our brains!"

Embarrassed by Hathaway's high-pitched shouting, Franklin had momentarily lost his sense of direction and helplessly searched the sea of cars for his own. "Hathaway, I can't waste any more time talking to you. Believe me, you need skilled help, these obsessions are beginning to master you."

Hathaway started to protest, and Franklin raised his right hand firmly. "Listen. For the last time, if you can show me one of these new signs, and prove that it's transmitting subliminal commands, I'll go to the police with you. But you haven't got a shred of evidence, and you know it. Subliminal advertising was banned thirty years ago, and the laws have never been repealed. Anyway, the technique was unsatisfactory; any success it had was marginal. Your idea of a huge conspiracy with all these thousands of giant signs everywhere is preposterous."

"All right, Doctor." Hathaway leaned against the bonnet of one of the cars. His moods seemed to switch abruptly from one level to the next. He watched Franklin amiably. "What's the matter—lost your car?"

"All your damned shouting has confused me." Franklin pulled out his ignition key and read the number off the tag: "NYN 299–566–367–21—can you see it?"

Hathaway leaned around lazily, one sandal up on the bonnet,[2] surveying the square of a thousand or so cars facing them. "Difficult, isn't it, when they're all identical, even the same color? Thirty years ago there were about ten different makes, each in a dozen colors."

Franklin spotted his car, began to walk toward it. "Sixty years ago there were a hundred makes. What of it? The economies of standardization are obviously bought at a price."

Hathaway drummed his palm lightly on the roofs. "But these cars aren't all that cheap, Doctor. In fact, comparing them on an average income basis with those of thirty years ago they're about forty percent more expensive. With only one make being produced you'd expect a substantial reduction in price, not an increase."

"Maybe," Franklin said, opening his door. "But mechanically the cars of today are far more sophisticated. They're lighter, more durable, safer to drive."

Hathaway shook his head sceptically. "They *bore* me. The same model, same styling, same color, year after year. It's a sort of communism." He rubbed a greasy finger over the windshield. "This is

[2]**bonnet:** British term for the hood of a car.

a new one again, isn't it, Doctor? Where's the old one—you only had it for three months?"

"I traded it in," Franklin told him, starting the engine. "If you ever had any money you'd realize that it's the most economical way of owning a car. You don't keep driving the same one until it falls apart. It's the same with everything else—television sets, washing machines, refrigerators. But you aren't faced with the problem—you haven't got any."

Hathaway ignored the gibe and leaned his elbow on Franklin's window. "Not a bad idea, either, Doctor. It gives me time to think. I'm not working a twelve-hour day to pay for a lot of things I'm too busy to use before they're obsolete."

He waved as Franklin reversed the car out of its line, then shouted into the wake of exhaust: "Drive with your eyes closed, Doctor!"

On the way home Franklin kept carefully to the slowest of the four-speed lanes. As usual after his discussions with Hathaway he felt vaguely depressed. He realized that unconsciously he envied Hathaway's foot-loose existence. Despite the grimy cold-water apartment in the shadow and roar of the flyover, despite his nagging wife and their sick child, and the endless altercations with the landlord and the supermarket credit manager, Hathaway still retained his freedom intact. Spared any responsibilities, he could resist the smallest encroachment upon him by the rest of society, if only by generating obsessive fantasies, such as his latest one about subliminal advertising.

The ability to react to stimuli, even irrationally, was a valid criterion of freedom. By contrast, what freedom Franklin possessed was peripheral, sharply demarked by the manifold responsibilities in the center of his life—the three mortgages on his home, the mandatory rounds of cocktail and TV parties, the private consultancy occupying most of Saturday which paid the instalments on the multitude of household gadgets, clothes and past holidays. About the only time he had to himself was driving to and from work.

But at least the roads were magnificent. Whatever other criticisms might be leveled at the present society, it certainly knew how to build roads. Eight-, ten- and twelve-lane expressways interlaced across the continent, plunging from overhead causeways into the giant car parks in the center of the cities, or dividing into the great suburban arteries with their multiacre parking aprons around the marketing centers. Together the roadways and car parks covered more than a third of the country's entire area, and in the neighborhood of the cities the proportion was higher. The old cities were surrounded by the vast, dazzling abstract sculptures of the clover-leaves and flyovers, but even so the congestion was unremitting.

The ten-mile journey to his home in fact covered over twenty-five miles and took him twice as long as it had done before the construction of the expressway, the additional miles contained within the three giant clover-leaves. New cities were springing from the motels, cafés and car marts around the highways. At the slightest hint of an intersection a shanty town of shacks and filling stations sprawled away among the forest of electric signs and route indicators, many of them substantial cities.

All around him cars bulleted along, streaming toward the suburbs. Relaxed by the smooth motion of the car, Franklin edged outward into the next-speed lane. As he accelerated from 40 to 50 mph a strident ear-jarring noise drummed out from his tires, shaking the chassis of the car. Ostensibly an aid to lane discipline, the surface of the road was covered with a mesh of small rubber studs, spaced progressively further apart in each of the lanes so that the tire hum resonated exactly on 40, 50, 60, and 70 mph. Driving at an intermediate speed for more than a few seconds became physiologically painful, and soon resulted in damage to the car and tires.

When the studs wore out they were replaced by slightly different patterns, matching those on the latest tires, so that regular tire changes were necessary, increasing the safety and efficiency of the expressway. It also increased the revenues of the car and tire manufacturers, for most cars over six months old soon fell to pieces under the steady battering, but this was regarded as a desirable end, the greater turnover reducing the unit price and making necessary more frequent model changes, as well as ridding the roads of dangerous vehicles.

A quarter of a mile ahead, at the approach to the first of the clover-leaves, the traffic stream was slowing, huge police signs signaling "Lanes Closed Ahead" and "Drop Speed by 10 mph." Franklin tried to return to the previous lane, but the cars were jammed bumper to bumper. As the chassis began to shudder and vibrate, jarring his spine, he clamped his teeth and tried to restrain himself from sounding the horn. Other drivers were less self-controlled, and everywhere engines were plunging and snarling, horns blaring. Road taxes were now so high, up to 30 percent of income (by contrast, income taxes were a bare 2 percent) that any delay on the expressways called for an immediate government inquiry, and the major departments of state were concerned with the administration of the road systems.

Nearer the clover-leaf the lanes had been closed to allow a gang of construction workers to erect a massive metal sign on one of the traffic islands. The palisaded area swarmed with engineers and surveyors and Franklin assumed that this was the sign Hathaway had seen unloaded the previous night. His apartment was in one of the gimcrack buildings in the settlement that straggled away around a nearby flyover, a low-rent area inhabited by service station personnel, waitresses and other migrant labor.

The sign was enormous, at least a hundred feet high, fitted with heavy concave grilles similar to radar bowls. Rooted in a series of concrete caissons, it reared high into the air above the approach roads, visible for miles. Franklin craned up at the grilles, tracing the power cables from the transformers up into the intricate mesh of metal coils that covered their surface. A line of red aircraft-warning beacons was already alight along the top strut, and Franklin assumed that the sign was part of the ground approach system of the city airport ten miles to the east.

Three minutes later, as he accelerated down the two-mile link of straight highway to the next clover-leaf, he saw the second of the giant signs looming up into the sky before him.

Changing down into the 40 mph lane, Franklin uneasily watched the great bulk of the second sign recede in his rearview mirror. Although there were no graphic symbols among the wire coils covering the grilles, Hathaway's warnings still sounded in his ears. Without knowing why, he felt sure that the signs were not part of the airport approach system. Neither of them was in line with the principal airlanes. To justify the expense of siting them in the center of the expressway—the second sign required elaborate angled buttresses to support it on the narrow island—obviously meant that their role related in some way to the traffic streams.

Two hundred yards away was a roadside auto-mart and Franklin abruptly remembered that he needed some cigarettes. Swinging the car down the entrance ramp, he joined the queue slowly passing the self-service dispenser at the far end of the rank. The auto-mart was packed with cars, each of the five purchasing ranks lined with tired-looking men hunched over their wheels.

Inserting his coins (paper money was no longer in circulation, unmanageable by the automats) he took a carton from the dispenser. This was the only brand of cigarettes available—in fact there was only one brand of everything—though giant economy packs were an alternative. Moving off, he opened the dashboard locker.

Inside, still sealed in their wrappers, were three other cartons.

A strong fish-like smell pervaded the house when he reached home, steaming out from the oven in the kitchen. Sniffing it uneagerly, Franklin took off his coat and hat, and found his wife crouched over the TV set in the lounge. An announcer was dictating a stream of numbers, and Judith scribbled them down on a pad, occasionally cursing under her breath. "What a muddle!" she snapped finally. "He was talking so quickly I took only a few things down."

"Probably deliberate," Franklin commented. "New panel game?"

Judith kissed him on the cheek, discreetly hiding the ashtray loaded with cigarette butts and chocolate wrappings. "Hullo, darling, sorry not to have a drink ready for you. They've started this series of Spot Bargains. They give you a selection of things on which you get a ninety percent trade-in discount at the local stores, if you're in the right area and have the right serial numbers. It's all terribly complicated."

"Sounds good, though. What have you got?"

Judith peered at her checklist. "Well, as far as I can see the only thing is the infra-red barbecue spit. But we have to be there before eight o'clock tonight. It's seven-thirty already."

"Then that's out. I'm tired, angel, I need something to eat." When Judith started to protest he added firmly: "Look, I don't want a new infra-red barbecue spit; we've only had this one for two months. Damn it, it's not even a different model."

"But, darling, don't you see, it makes it cheaper if you keep buying new ones. We'll have to trade ours in at the end of the year anyway, we signed the contract, and this way we save at least twenty dollars. These Spot Bargains aren't just a gimmick, you know. I've been glued to that set all

day." A note of irritation had crept into her voice, but Franklin sat his ground, doggedly ignoring the clock.

"Right, we lose twenty dollars. It's worth it." Before she could remonstrate he said, "Judith, please, you probably took the wrong number down anyway." As she shrugged and went over to the bar he called, "Make it a stiff one. I see we have health foods on the menu."

"They're good for you, darling. You know you can't live on ordinary foods all the time. They don't contain any proteins or vitamins. You're always saying we ought to be like people in the old days and eat nothing but health foods."

"I would, but they smell so awful." Franklin lay back, nose in the glass of whiskey, gazing at the darkened skyline outside.

A quarter of a mile away, gleaming out above the roof of the neighborhood supermarket, were the five red beacon lights. Now and then, as the headlamps of the Spot Bargainers swung up across the face of the building, he could see the square massive bulk of the giant sign clearly silhouetted against the evening sky.

"Judith!" He went into the kitchen and took her over to the window. "That sign, just behind the supermarket. When did they put it up?"

"I don't know." Judith peered at him curiously. "Why are you so worried, Robert? Isn't it something to do with the airport?"

Franklin stared thoughtfully at the dark hull of the sign. "So everyone probably thinks."

Carefully he poured his whiskey into the sink.

After parking his car on the supermarket apron at seven o'clock the next morning, Franklin carefully emptied his pockets and stacked the coins in the dashboard locker. The supermarket was already busy with early morning shoppers and the line of thirty turnstiles clicked and slammed. Since the introduction of the "twenty-four-hour spending day" the shopping complex was never closed. The bulk of the shoppers were discount buyers, housewives contracted to make huge volume purchases of food, clothing and appliances against substantial overall price cuts, and forced to drive around all day from supermarket to supermarket, frantically trying to keep pace with their purchase schedules and grappling with the added incentives inserted to keep the schemes alive.

Many of the women had teamed up, and as Franklin walked over to the entrance a pack of them charged toward their cars, stuffing their pay slips into their bags and gesticulating at each other. A moment later their cars roared off in a convoy to the next marketing zone.

A large neon sign over the entrance listed the latest discount—a mere 5 percent—calculated on the volume of turnover. The highest discounts, sometimes up to 25 percent, were earned in the housing estates where junior white-collar workers lived. There, spending had a strong social incentive, and the desire to be the highest spender in the neighborhood was given moral reinforcement by the system of listing all the names and their accumulating cash totals on a huge electric sign in the supermarket foyers. The higher the spender, the greater his contribution to the discounts enjoyed by others. The lowest spenders were regarded as social criminals, free-riding on the backs of others.

Luckily this system had yet to be adopted in Franklin's neighborhood. Not because the professional men and their wives were able to exercise more discretion, but because their higher incomes allowed them to contract into more expensive discount schemes operated by the big department stores in the city.

Ten yards from the entrance Franklin paused, looking up at the huge metal sign mounted in an enclosure at the edge of the car park. Unlike the other signs and hoardings that proliferated everywhere, no attempt had been made to decorate it, or disguise the gaunt bare rectangle of riveted steel mesh. Power lines wound down its sides, and the concrete surface of the car park was crossed by a long scar where a cable had been sunk.

Franklin strolled along, then fifty feet from the sign stopped and turned, realizing that he would be late for the hospital and needed a new carton of cigarettes. A dim but powerful humming emanated from the transformers below the sign, fading as he retraced his steps to the supermarket.

Going over to the automats in the foyer, he felt for his change, then whistled sharply when he remembered why he had deliberately emptied his pockets.

"The cunning thing!" he said, loud enough for two shoppers to stare at him. Reluctant to look directly at the sign, he watched its reflection in one of the glass doorpanes, so that any subliminal message would be reversed.

Almost certainly he had received two distinct signals—"Keep Away" and "Buy Cigarettes." The

people who normally parked their cars along the perimeter of the apron were avoiding the area under the enclosure, the cars describing a loose semi-circle fifty feet around it.

He turned to the janitor sweeping out the foyer. "What's that sign for?"

The man leaned on his broom, gazing dully at the sign. "Dunno," he said, "must be something to do with the airport." He had an almost fresh cigarette in his mouth, but his right hand reached unconsciously to his hip pocket and pulled out a pack. He drummed the second cigarette absently on his thumbnail as Franklin walked away.

Everyone entering the supermarket was buying cigarettes.

Cruising quietly along the 40 mph lane, Franklin began to take a closer interest in the landscape around him. Usually he was either too tired or too preoccupied to do more than think about his driving, but now he examined the expressway methodically, scanning the roadside cafés for any smaller versions of the new signs. A host of neon displays covered the doorways and windows, but most of them seemed innocuous, and he turned his attention to the larger billboards erected along the open stretches of the expressway. Many of these were as high as four-story houses, elaborate three-dimensional devices in which giant glossy-skinned housewives with electric eyes and teeth jerked and postured around their ideal kitchens, neon flashes exploding from their smiles.

The areas on either side of the expressway were wasteland, continuous junkyards filled with cars and trucks, washing machines and refrigerators, all perfectly workable but jettisoned by the economic pressure of the succeeding waves of discount models. Their intact chrome hardly tarnished, the mounds of metal shells and cabinets glittered in the sunlight. Nearer the city the billboards were sufficiently close together to hide them, but now and then, as he slowed to approach one of the flyovers, Franklin caught a glimpse of the huge pyramids of metal, gleaming silently like the refuse grounds of some forgotten El Dorado.

That evening Hathaway was waiting for him as he came down the hospital steps. Franklin waved him across the court, then led the way quickly to his car.

"What's the matter, Doctor?" Hathaway asked as Franklin wound up the windows and glanced around the lines of parked cars. "Is someone after you?"

Franklin laughed somberly. "I don't know. I hope not, but if what you say is right, I suppose there is."

Hathaway leaned back with a chuckle, propping one knee up on the dashboard. "So you've seen something, Doctor, after all."

"Well, I'm not sure yet, but there's just a chance you may be right. This morning at the Fairlawne supermarket—" He broke off, uneasily remembering the huge blank sign and the abrupt way in which he had turned back to the supermarket as he approached it, then described his encounter.

Hathaway nodded slowly. "I've seen the sign there. It's big, but not as big as some that are going up. They're building them everywhere now. All over the city. What are you going to do, Doctor?"

Franklin gripped the wheel tightly. Hathaway's thinly veiled amusement irritated him. "Nothing, of course. Damn it, it may be just auto-suggestion, you've probably got me imagining—"

Hathaway sat up with a jerk, his face mottled and savage. "Don't be absurd, Doctor! If you can't believe your own senses what chance have you left? They're invading your brain; if you don't defend yourself they'll take it over completely! We've got to act now, before we're all paralyzed."

Wearily, Franklin raised one hand to restrain him. "Just a minute. Assuming that these signs *are* going up everywhere, what would be their object? Apart from wasting the enormous amount of capital invested in all the other millions of signs and billboards, the amounts of discretionary spending power still available must be infinitesimal. Some of the present mortgage and discount schemes reach half a century ahead, so there can't be much slack left to take up. A big trade war would be disastrous."

"Quite right, Doctor," Hathaway rejoined evenly, "but you're forgetting one thing. What would supply that extra spending power? A big increase in production. Already they've started to raise the working day from twelve hours to fourteen. In some of the appliance plants around the city Sunday working is being introduced as a norm. Can you visualize it, Doctor—a seven-day week, everyone with at least three jobs."

Franklin shook his head. "People won't stand for it."

"They will. Within the last twenty-five years the gross national product has risen by fifty percent, but so have the average hours worked. Ultimately we'll all be working and spending twenty-four hours a day, seven days a week. No one will dare refuse. Think what a slump would mean—millions of lay-offs, people with time on their hands and nothing to spend it on. Real leisure, not just time spent buying things." He seized Franklin by the shoulder. "Well, Doctor, are you going to join me?"

Franklin freed himself. Half a mile away, partly hidden by the four-story bulk of the Pathology Department, was the upper half of one of the giant signs, workmen still crawling across its girders. The airlines over the city had deliberately been routed away from the hospital, and the sign obviously had no connection with approaching aircraft.

"Isn't there a prohibition on subliminal living? How can the unions accept it?"

"The fear of a slump. You know the new economic dogmas. Unless output rises by a steady inflationary 5 percent the economy is stagnating. Ten years ago increased efficiency alone would raise output, but the advantages there are minimal now and only one thing is left. More work. Increased consumption and subliminal advertising will provide the spur."

"What are you planning to do?"

"I can't tell you, Doctor, unless you accept equal responsibility for it."

"Sounds rather Quixotic,"[3] Franklin commented. "Tilting at windmills. You won't be able to chop those things down with an axe."

"I won't try." Hathaway suddenly gave up and opened the door. "Don't wait too long to make up your mind, Doctor. By then it may not be yours to make up." With a wave he was gone.

On the way home Franklin's scepticism returned. The idea of the conspiracy was preposterous, and the economic arguments were too plausible. As usual, though, there had been a hook in the soft bait Hathaway dangled before him—Sunday working. His own consultancy had been extended into Sunday morning with his appointment as visiting factory doctor to one of the automobile plants that had started Sunday shifts. But instead of resenting this incursion into his already meager hours of leisure he had been glad. For one frightening reason—he needed the extra income.

---

[3]**Quixotic:** foolishly extravagant or impractical; the term comes from *Don Quixote de la Mancha*, Miguel de Cervantes' novel whose chivalrous hero fought for lofty ideals.

Looking out over the lines of scurrying cars, he noticed that at least a dozen of the great signs had been erected along the expressway. As Hathaway had said, more were going up everywhere, rearing over the supermarkets in the housing developments like rusty metal sails.

Judith was in the kitchen when he reached home, watching the TV program on the hand-set over the cooker. Franklin climbed past a big card-board carton, its seals still unbroken, which blocked the doorway, and kissed her on the cheek as she scribbled numbers down on her pad. The pleasant odor of pot-roast chicken—or, rather, a gelatine dummy of a chicken fully flavored and free of any toxic or nutritional properties—molified his irritation at finding her still playing the Spot Bargains.

He tapped the carton with his foot. "What's this?"

"No idea, darling, something's always coming these days, I can't keep up with it all." She peered through the glass door at the chicken—an economy twelve-pounder, the size of a turkey, with stylized legs and wings and an enormous breast, most of which would be discarded at the end of the meal (there were no dogs or cats these days, the crumbs from the rich man's table saw to that) and then glanced at him pointedly.

"You look rather worried, Robert. Bad day?"

Franklin murmured noncommittally. The hours spent trying to detect false clues in the faces of the Spot Bargain announcers had sharpened Judith's perceptions, and he felt a pang of sympathy for the legion of husbands similarly outmatched.

"Have you been talking to that crazy beatnik again?"

"Hathaway? As a matter of fact I have. He's not all that crazy." He stepped backward into the carton, almost spilling his drink. "Well, what is this thing? As I'll be working for the next fifty Sundays to pay for it I'd like to find out."

He searched the sides, finally located the label, "A *TV set?* Judith, do we need another one? We've already got three. Lounge, dining room and the hand-set. What's the fourth for?"

"The guest room, dear, don't get so excited. We can't leave a hand-set in the guest room, it's rude. I'm trying to economize, but four TV sets is the bare minimum. All the magazines say so."

"*And* three radios?" Franklin stared irritably at the carton. "If we do invite a guest here how much time is he going to spend alone in his room watching television? Judith, we've got to call a halt. It's not as if these things were free, or even cheap. Anyway, television is a total waste of time. There's only one program. It's ridiculous to have four sets."

"Robert, there are *four* channels."

"But only the commercials are different." Before Judith could reply the telephone rang. Franklin lifted the kitchen receiver, listened to the gabble of noise that poured from it. At first he wondered whether this was some off-beat prestige commercial, then realized it was Hathaway in a manic swing.

"Hathaway!" he shouted back. "Relax, man! What's the matter now?"

"—Doctor, you'll have to believe me this time. I tell you I got on to one of the islands with a stroboscope; they've got hundreds of high-speed shutters blasting away like machine-guns straight into people's faces and they can't see a thing, it's fantastic! The next big campaign's going to be cars and TV sets, they're trying to swing a two-month model change—can you imagine it, Doctor, a new car every two months? God Almighty, it's just—"

Franklin waited impatiently as the five-second commercial break cut in (all telephone calls were free, the length of the commercial extending with range—for long-distance calls the ratio of commercial to conversation was as high as 10:1, the participants desperately trying to get a word in edgeways between the interminable interruptions), but just before it ended he abruptly put the telephone down, then removed the receiver from the cradle.

Judith came over and took his arm. "Robert, what's the matter? You look terribly strained."

Franklin picked up his drink and walked through into the lounge. "It's just Hathaway. As you say, I'm getting a little too involved with him. He's starting to prey on my mind."

He looked at the dark outline of the sign over the supermarket, its red warning lights glowing in the night sky. Blank and nameless, like an area forever closed-off in an insane mind, what frightened him was its total anonymity.

"Yet I'm not sure," he muttered. "So much of what Hathaway says makes sense. These subliminal techniques are the sort of last-ditch attempt you'd expect from an overcapitalized industrial system."

He waited for Judith to reply, then looked at her. She stood in the center of the carpet, hands folded limply, her sharp, intelligent face curiously dull and blunted. He followed her gaze out over the rooftops, then with an effort turned his head and quickly switched on the TV set.

"Come on," he said grimly. "Let's watch television. God, we're going to need that fourth set."

A week later Franklin began to compile his inventory. He saw nothing more of Hathaway; as he left the hospital in the evening the familiar scruffy figure was absent. When the first of the explosions sounded dimly around the city and he read of the attempts to sabotage the giant signs he automatically assumed that Hathaway was responsible, but later he heard on a newscast that the detonations had been set off by construction workers excavating foundations.

More of the signs appeared over the rooftops, isolated on the palisaded islands near the suburban shopping centers. Already there were over thirty on the ten-mile route from the hospital, standing shoulder to shoulder over the speeding cars like giant dominoes. Franklin had given up his attempt to avoid looking at them, but the slim possibility that the explosions might be Hathaway's counterattack kept his suspicions alive.

He began his inventory after hearing the newscast, discovered that in the previous fortnight he and Judith had traded in their

> Car (previous model 2 months old)
> 2 TV sets (4 months)
> Power mower (7 months)
> Electric cooker (5 months)
> Hair dryer (4 months)
> Refrigerator (3 months)
> 2 radios (7 months)
> Record player (5 months)
> Cocktail bar (8 months)

Half these purchases had been made by himself, but exactly when he could never recall realizing at the time. The car, for example, he had left in the garage near the hospital to be greased; that evening he had signed for the new model as he sat at its wheel, accepting the salesman's assurance that the depreciation on the two-month trade-in was virtually less than the cost of the grease-job. Ten minutes later, as he sped along the expressway, he suddenly realized that he had bought a new car. Similarly, the TV sets had been replaced by identical models after developing the same irritating interference pattern (curiously, the new sets also

displayed the pattern, but as the salesman assured them, this promptly vanished two days later).

Not once had he actually decided of his own volition that he wanted something and then gone out to a store and bought it!

He carried the inventory around with him, adding to it as necessary, quietly and without protest analyzing these new sales techniques, wondering whether total capitulation might be the only way of defeating them. As long as he kept up even a token resistance, the inflationary growth curve would show a controlled annual 10 percent climb. With that resistance removed, however, it would begin to rocket upward out of control. . . .

Then driving home from the hospital two months later, he saw one of the signs for the first time.

He was in the 40 mph lane, unable to keep up with the flood of new cars, had just passed the second of the three clover-leaves when the traffic half a mile away began to slow down. Hundreds of cars had driven up on to the grass verge, and a large crowd was gathering around one of the signs. Two small black figures were climbing up the metal face, and a series of huge grid-like patterns of light flashed on and off, illuminating the evening air. The patterns were random and broken, as if the sign was being tested for the first time.

Relieved that Hathaway's suspicions had been completely groundless, Franklin turned off onto the soft shoulder, then walked forward through the spectators as the lights blinked and stuttered in their faces. Below, behind the steel palisades around the island, was a large group of police and engineers, craning up at the men scaling the sign a hundred feet over their heads.

Suddenly Franklin stopped, the sense of relief fading instantly. With a jolt he saw that several of the police on the ground were armed with shotguns, and that the two policemen climbing the sign carried submachine-guns slung over their shoulders. They were converging on a third figure, crouched by a switchbox on the penultimate tier, a ragged bearded man in a grimy shirt, a bare knee poking through his jeans.

Hathaway!

Franklin hurried toward the island, the sign hissing and sputtering, fuses blowing by the dozen.

Then the flicker of lights cleared and steadied, blazing out continuously, and together the crowd looked up at the decks of brilliant letters. The phrases and every combination of them possible, were entirely familiar, and Franklin knew that he had been reading them unconsciously in his mind for weeks as he passed up and down the expressway.

BUY NOW BUY NOW BUY NOW BUY NOW BUY NOW NEW CAR NOW NEW CAR NOW NEW CAR NOW YES YES YES YES YES YES YES YES YES YES YES

Sirens blaring, two patrol cars swung up onto the verge through the crowd and plunged across the damp grass. Police spilled from its doors, batons in their hands, and quickly began to force back the crowd. Franklin held his ground as they approached, started to say: "Officer, I know the man—" but the policeman punched him in the chest with the flat of his hand. Winded, he stumbled back among the cars, leaned helplessly against a fender as the police began to break the windshields, the hapless drivers protesting angrily, those further back rushing for their vehicles.

The noise fell away abruptly when one of the submachine-guns fired a brief roaring burst, then rose in a massive gasp of horror as Hathaway, arms outstretched, let out a cry of triumph and pain, and jumped.

"But, Robert, what does it really matter?" Judith asked as Franklin sat inertly in the lounge the next morning. "I know it's tragic for his wife and daughter, but Hathaway was in the grip of an obsession. If he hated advertising signs so much why didn't he dynamite those we *can* see, instead of worrying so much about those we can't?"

Franklin stared at the TV screen, hoping the program would distract him.

"Hathaway was *right*," he said simply.

"Was he? Advertising is here to stay. We've no real freedom of choice, anyway. We can't spend more than we can afford, the finance companies soon clamp down."

"You accept that?" Franklin went over to the window. A quarter of a mile away, in the center of the estate, another of the signs was being erected. It was due east from them, and in the early morning light the shadows of its rectangular superstructure fell across the garden, reaching almost to the steps of the French windows at his feet. As a concession to the neighborhood, and perhaps to allay any suspicions while it was being erected by an appeal to petty snobbery the lower sections had been encased in mock-Tudor paneling.

Franklin stared at it numbly, counting the half-dozen police lounging by their patrol cars as the construction gang unloaded prefabricated grilles from a couple of trucks. Then he looked at the sign by the supermarket, trying to repress his memories of Hathaway and the pathetic attempts the man had made to convince Franklin and gain his help.

He was still standing there an hour later when Judith came in, putting on her hat and coat, ready to visit the supermarket.

Franklin followed her to the door: "I'll drive you down there, Judith," he said in a flat dead voice. "I have to see about booking a new car. The next models are coming out at the end of the month. With luck we'll get one of the early deliveries."

They walked out into the trim drive, the shadows of the great signs swinging across the quiet neighborhood as the day progressed, sweeping over the heads of the people on their way to the supermarket like the dark blades of enormous scythes.

Discuss

1. Which statement best describes Dr. Franklin's attitude toward Hathaway at the beginning of the story, and why?

    a. Franklin thinks Hathaway is mentally ill and in need of a psychiatrist.

    b. Franklin knows that what Hathaway says is true, but he doesn't want to admit it for fear of being different.

    c. Franklin cannot identify with Hathaway's determination to remain independent.

2. Complete this statement with the best choice: Subliminal advertising

    a. encourages people to buy new cars.

    b. commands people to buy, without their being aware of it.

    c. succeeds only with people who have minimal intelligence.

3. What does Franklin think is the obvious reason why people have identical cars? Why doesn't Hathaway accept it as the real reason? What do you think is the real reason?

4. At which point in the story does Franklin begin to believe Hathaway? Trace Franklin's growing suspicion of the signs.

Explore

1. Why does Hathaway tell Franklin to drive with his eyes closed? How might this command have more than one meaning?

2. What irony do you see in Franklin's observation that the roads are magnificent?

3. What is the significance of the road taxes being 30 percent and the income tax being only 2 percent?

4. What is Hathaway's interpretation of the reason for subliminal advertising? Why is Franklin inclined to agree?

5. What is the difference in the way Franklin and his wife respond to Hathaway's final act? Why do you suppose they differ?

6. Do you see any parallels between the society described in this story and the society in which you live? Explain.

For Your Journal

1. Look at some aspects of the society in which you live. Which do you find most objectionable? Write an explanation of your objections or a letter to a government official expressing your complaints.

2. Write a brief science fiction story about a new other world in which you exaggerate problems of modern life.

Museums

Louis MacNeice

Sometimes people find ways of creating their own worlds and living in them, at least for a time.

Museums offer us, running from among the 'buses,
A centrally heated refuge, parquet floors and sarcophaguses,[1]
Into whose tall fake porches we hurry without a sound
Like a beetle under a brick that lies, useless on the ground.
Warmed and cajoled by the silence, the cowed[2] cipher[3] revives,
Mirrors himself in the cases of pots, paces himself by marble lives,
Makes believe it was he that was the glory that was Rome,
Soft on his cheek the nimbus of other people's martyrdom,
And then returns to the street, his mind an arena where sprawls
Any number of consumptive[4] Keatses and dying Gauls.[5]

---

[1] **sarcophaguses:** coffins.
[2] **cowed:** frightened or overawed.
[3] **cipher:** one who has little weight or influence.
[4] **consumptive:** ill with a progressive wasting away of the body, especially from tuberculosis, a disease that killed author John Keats at the age of twenty-five.
[5] **Gauls:** residents of Gaul, a region of ancient origin (now part of Western Europe).

Discuss

1. Which statement best summarizes the message of this poem?

    a. Museums are places in which visitors can relive the lives of others.

    b. Museums provide an escape from the hustle and bustle of daily life.

    c. Only people who feel lives are useless can find pleasure in a museum.

2. What image do you have of the visitor described in the poem? Why is he called a "cowed cipher"?

3. What does the visitor do in the museum?

Explore

1. How is the visitor different when he leaves the museum from when he comes in? What imagery shows this difference?

2. What is the effect of the shift from "we" and "us" in the first four lines to "he" and "himself" in the rest of the poem?

3. What is the nature of the fantasy the museum visitor creates? Do you believe it is positive, negative, or both? What does his make-believe world say about him?

For Your Journal

1. When you visit museums—in any field, including art, science, history, and natural history—do you ever fantasize about what life might have been like during the period you see depicted? If so, describe the daydreams such displays have inspired in you.

2. Perhaps you like reading about other worlds in historical novels, science fiction, or fantasy stories. What is the attraction of those other worlds? Do they make you wish you could live in another time or place? Explain.

The Mysterious

*In this section, ingenious characters
draw on observation and intuition
to solve mysteries created by
magic, human nature, and science.
As you read the stories and essay,
look for clues that will allow
you to detect the secrets as
they unfold during the
mysterious events described.*

Dr. Heidegger's Experiment

Nathaniel Hawthorne

The mad scientist, whose experiments do not aim for the betterment of humankind but fulfill his own curiosity and perverse pleasure, provides the action in this strange tale by Nathaniel Hawthorne.

THAT VERY singular man, old Dr. Heidegger, once invited four venerable[1] friends to meet him in his study. There were three white-bearded gentlemen, Mr. Medbourne, Colonel Killigrew, and Mr. Gascoigne, and a withered gentlewoman, whose name was the Widow Wycherly. They were all melancholy old creatures, who had been unfortunate in life, and whose greatest misfortune it was that they were not long ago in their graves. Mr. Medbourne, in the vigor of his age, had been a prosperous merchant, but had lost his all by a frantic speculation, and was now little better than a mendicant.[2] Colonel Killigrew had wasted his best years, and his health and substance, in the pursuit of sinful pleasures, which had given birth to a brood of pains, such as the gout,[3] and divers other torments of soul and body. Mr. Gascoigne was a ruined politician, a man of evil fame, or at least had been so till time had buried him from the knowledge of the present generation, and made him obscure instead of infamous. As for the Widow Wycherly, tradition tells us that she was a great beauty in her day; but, for a long while past, she had lived in deep seclusion, on account of certain scandalous stories which had prejudiced the gentry of the town against her. It is a circumstance worth mentioning that each of these three old gentlemen, Mr. Medbourne, Colonel Killigrew, and Mr. Gascoigne, were early lovers of the Widow Wycherly, and had once been on the point of cutting each other's throats for her sake. And, before proceeding further, I will merely hint

[1]**venerable:** respected because of great age.
[2]**mendicant:** beggar.
[3]**gout:** tender condition of the joints, mainly in the feet or hands.

that Dr. Heidegger and all his four guests were sometimes thought to be a little beside themselves,—as is not unfrequently the case with old people, when worried either by present troubles or woeful recollections.

"My dear old friends," said Dr. Heidegger, motioning them to be seated, "I am desirous of your assistance in one of those little experiments with which I amuse myself here in my study."

If all stories were true, Dr. Heidegger's study must have been a very curious place. It was a dim, old-fashioned chamber, festooned with cobwebs, and besprinkled with antique dust. Around the walls stood several oaken bookcases, the lower shelves of which were filled with rows of gigantic folios and black-letter quartos, and the upper with little parchment-covered duodecimos. Over the central bookcase was a bronze bust of Hippocrates,[4] with which, according to some authorities, Dr. Heidegger was accustomed to hold consultations in all difficult cases of his practice. In the obscurest corner of the room stood a tall and narrow oaken closet, with its door ajar, within which doubtfully appeared a skeleton. Between two of the bookcases hung a looking-glass, presenting its high and dusty plate within a tarnished gilt frame. Among many wonderful stories related of this mirror, it was fabled that the spirits of all the doctor's deceased patients dwelt within its verge, and would stare him in the face whenever he looked thitherward. The opposite side of the chamber was ornamented with the full-length portrait of a young lady, arrayed in the faded magnificence of silk, satin, and

[4]**Hippocrates:** ancient Greek physician, known as the father of modern medicine.

brocade, and with a visage [5] as faded as her dress. Above half a century ago, Dr. Heidegger had been on the point of marriage with this young lady; but, being affected with some slight disorder, she had swallowed one of her lover's prescriptions, and died on the bridal evening. The greatest curiosity of the study remains to be mentioned; it was a ponderous folio volume, bound in black leather, with massive silver clasps. There were no letters on the back, and nobody could tell the title of the book. But it was well known to be a book of magic; and once, when a chambermaid had lifted it, merely to brush away the dust, the skeleton had rattled in its closet, the picture of the young lady had stepped one foot upon the floor, and several ghastly faces had peeped forth from the mirror; while the brazen head of Hippocrates frowned, and said,—"Forbear!"

Such was Dr. Heidegger's study. On the summer afternoon of our tale a small round table, as black as ebony, stood in the centre of the room, sustaining a cut-glass vase of beautiful form and elaborate workmanship. The sunshine came through the window between the heavy festoons of two faded damask curtains, and fell directly across this vase; so that a mild splendor was reflected from it on the ashen visages of the five old people who sat around. Four champagne glasses were also on the table.

"My dear old friends," repeated Dr. Heidegger, "may I reckon on your aid in performing an exceedingly curious experiment?"

Now Dr. Heidegger was a very strange old gentleman, whose eccentricity had become the nucleus for a thousand fantastic stories. Some of these fables, to my shame be it spoken, might possibly be traced back to my own veracious[6] self; and if any passages of the present tale should startle the reader's faith, I must be content to bear the stigma of a fiction monger.

When the doctor's four guests heard him talk of his proposed experiment, they anticipated nothing more wonderful than the murder of a mouse in an air pump, or the examination of a cobweb by the microscope, or some similar nonsense, with which he was constantly in the habit of pestering his intimates. But without waiting for a reply, Dr. Heidegger hobbled across the chamber, and returned with the same ponderous folio, bound in black leather, which common report affirmed to be a book of magic. Undoing the silver clasps, he

[5] **visage:** face.
[6] **veracious:** truthful.

opened the volume, and took from among its black-letter pages a rose, or what was once a rose, though now the green leaves and crimson petals had assumed one brownish hue, and the ancient flower seemed ready to crumble to dust in the doctor's hands.

"This rose," said Dr. Heidegger, with a sigh, "this same withered and crumbling flower, blossomed five and fifty years ago. It was given me by Sylvia Ward, whose portrait hangs yonder; and I meant to wear it in my bosom at our wedding. Five and fifty years it has been treasured between the leaves of this old volume. Now, would you deem it possible that this rose of half a century could ever bloom again?"

"Nonsense!" said the Widow Wycherly, with a peevish toss of her head. "You might as well ask whether an old woman's wrinkled face could ever bloom again."

"See!" answered Dr. Heidegger.

He uncovered the vase, and threw the faded rose into the water which it contained. At first, it lay lightly on the surface of the fluid, appearing to imbibe none of its moisture. Soon, however, a singular change began to be visible. The crushed and dried petals stirred, and assumed a deepening tinge of crimson, as if the flower were reviving from a deathlike slumber; the slender stalk and twigs of foliage became green; and there was the rose of half a century, looking as fresh as when Sylvia Ward had first given it to her lover. It was scarcely full blown; for some of its delicate red leaves curled modestly around its moist bosom, within which two or three dewdrops were sparkling.

"That is certainly a very pretty deception," said the doctor's friends; carelessly, however, for they had witnessed greater miracles at a conjurer's show; "pray how was it effected?"

"Did you never hear of the 'Fountain of Youth?' " asked Dr. Heidegger, "which Ponce De Leon, the Spanish adventurer, went in search of two or three centuries ago?"

"But did Ponce De Leon ever find it?" said the Widow Wycherly.

"No," answered Dr. Heidegger, "for he never sought it in the right place. The famous Fountain of Youth, if I am rightly informed, is situated in the southern part of the Floridian peninsula, not far from Lake Macaco. Its source is overshadowed by several gigantic magnolias, which, though numberless centuries old, have been kept as fresh as violets by the virtues of this wonderful water. An acquaintance of mine, knowing my curiosity in such matters, has sent me what you see in the vase."

"Ahem!" said Colonel Killigrew, who believed not a word of the doctor's story: "and what may be the effect of this fluid on the human frame?"

"You shall judge for yourself, my dear colonel," replied Dr. Heidegger; "and all of you, my respected friends, are welcome to so much of this admirable fluid as may restore to you the bloom of youth. For my own part, having had much trouble in growing old, I am in no hurry to grow young again. With your permission, therefore, I will merely watch the progress of the experiment."

While he spoke, Dr. Heidegger had been filling the four champagne glasses with the water of the Fountain of Youth. It was apparently impregnated with an effervescent gas, for little bubbles were continually ascending from the depths of the glasses, and bursting in silvery spray at the surface. As the liquor diffused a pleasant perfume, the old people doubted not that it possessed cordial and comfortable properties; and though utter sceptics as to its rejuvenescent power, they were inclined to swallow it at once. But Dr. Heidegger besought them to stay a moment.

"Before you drink, my respectable old friends," said he, "it would be well that, with the experience of a lifetime to direct you, you should draw up a few general rules for your guidance, in passing a second time through the perils of youth. Think what a sin and shame it would be, if, with your peculiar advantages, you should not become patterns of virtue and wisdom to all the young people of the age!"

The doctor's four venerable friends made him no answer, except by a feeble and tremulous laugh; so very ridiculous was the idea that, knowing how closely repentance treads behind the steps of error, they should ever go astray again.

"Drink, then," said the doctor, bowing: "I rejoice that I have so well selected the subjects of my experiment."

With palsied hands, they raised the glasses to their lips. The liquor, if it really possessed such virtues as Dr. Heidegger imputed to it, could not have been bestowed on four human beings who needed it more woefully. They looked as if they had never known what youth or pleasure was, but had been the offspring of Nature's dotage, and always the

gray, decrepit, sapless, miserable creatures, who now sat stooping round the doctor's table, without life enough in their souls or bodies to be animated even by the prospect of growing young again. They drank off the water, and replaced their glasses on the table.

Assuredly there was an almost immediate improvement in the aspect of the party, not unlike what might have been produced by a glass of generous wine, together with a sudden glow of cheerful sunshine brightening over all their visages at once. There was a healthful suffusion on their cheeks, instead of the ashen hue that had made them look so corpse-like. They gazed at one another, and fancied that some magic power had really begun to smooth away the deep and sad inscriptions which Father Time had been so long engraving on their brows. The Widow Wycherly adjusted her cap, for she felt almost like a woman again.

"Give us more of this wondrous water!" cried they, eagerly. "We are younger—but we are still too old! Quick—give us more!"

"Patience, patience!" quoth Dr. Heidegger, who sat watching the experiment with philosophic coolness. "You have been a long time growing old. Surely, you might be content to grow young in half an hour! But the water is at your service."

Again he filled their glasses with the liquor of youth, enough of which still remained in the vase to turn half the old people in the city to the age of their own grandchildren. While the bubbles were yet sparkling on the brim, the doctor's four guests snatched their glasses from the table, and swallowed the contents at a single gulp. Was it delusion? Even while the draught was passing down their throats, it seemed to have wrought a change on their whole systems. Their eyes grew clear and bright; a dark shade deepened among their silvery locks, they sat around the table, three gentlemen of middle age, and a woman, hardly beyond her buxom prime.

"My dear widow, you are charming!" cried Colonel Killigrew, whose eyes had been fixed upon her face, while the shadows of age were flitting from it like darkness from the crimson daybreak.

The fair widow knew, of old, that Colonel Killigrew's compliments were not always measured by sober truth; so she started up and ran to the mirror, still dreading that the ugly visage of an old woman would meet her gaze. Meanwhile, the three gentlemen behaved in such a manner as proved that the water of the Fountain of Youth possessed some intoxicating qualities; unless, indeed, their exhilaration of spirits were merely a lightsome dizziness caused by the sudden removal of the weight of years. Mr. Gascoigne's mind seemed to run on political topics, but whether relating to the past, present, or future, could not easily be determined, since the same ideas and phrases have been in vogue these fifty years. Now he rattled forth full-throated sentences about patriotism, national glory, and the people's right; now he muttered some perilous stuff or other, in a sly and doubtful whisper, so cautiously that even his own conscience could scarcely catch the secret; and now, again, he spoke in measured accents, and a deeply deferential tone, as if a royal ear were listening to his well-turned periods. Colonel Killigrew all this time had been trolling forth a jolly bottle song, and ringing his glass in symphony with the chorus, while his eyes wandered toward the buxom figure of the Widow Wycherly. On the other side of the table, Mr. Medbourne was involved in a calculation of dollars and cents, with which was strangely intermingled a project for supplying the East Indies with ice, by harnessing a team of whales to the polar icebergs.

As for the Widow Wycherly, she stood before the mirror courtesying and simpering to her own image, and greeting it as the friend whom she loved better than all the world beside. She thrust her face close to the glass, to see whether some long-remembered wrinkle or crow's foot had indeed vanished. She examined whether the snow had so entirely melted from her hair that the venerable cap could be safely thrown aside. At last, turning briskly away, she came with a sort of dancing step to the table.

"My dear old doctor," cried she, "pray favor me with another glass!"

"Certainly, my dear madam, certainly!" replied the complaisant doctor; "see! I have already filled the glasses."

There, in fact, stood the four glasses, brimful of this wonderful water, the delicate spray of which, as it effervesced from the surface, resembled the tremulous glitter of diamonds. It was now so nearly sunset that the chamber had grown duskier than ever; but a mild and moonlike splendor gleamed from within the vase, and rested alike on the four guests and on the doctor's venerable figure. He sat in a high-backed, elaborately-carved, oaken arm-chair, with a gray dignity of aspect that might have well befitted that very Father Time, whose power had

never been disputed, save by this fortunate company. Even while quaffing the third draught of the Fountain of Youth, they were almost awed by the expression of his mysterious visage.

But, the next moment, the exhilarating gush of young life shot through their veins. They were now in the happy prime of youth. Age, with its miserable train of cares and sorrows and diseases, was remembered only as the trouble of a dream, from which they had joyously awoke. The fresh gloss of the soul, so early lost, and without which the world's successive scenes had been but a gallery of faded pictures, again threw its enchantment over all their prospects. They felt like new-created beings in a new-created universe.

"We are young! We are young!" they cried exultingly.

Youth, like the extremity of age, had effaced the strongly-marked characteristics of middle life, and mutually assimilated them all. They were a group of merry youngsters, almost maddened with the exuberant frolicsomeness of their years. The most singular effect of their gayety was an impulse to mock the infirmity and decrepitude of which they had so lately been the victims. They laughed loudly at their old-fashioned attire, the wide-skirted coats and flapped waistcoats of the young men, and the ancient cap and gown of the blooming girl. One limped across the floor like a gouty grandfather; one set a pair of spectacles astride of his nose, and pretended to pour over the black-letter pages of the book of magic; a third seated himself in an arm-chair, and strove to imitate the venerable dignity of Dr. Heidegger. Then all shouted mirthfully, and leaped about the room. The Widow Wycherly—if so fresh a damsel could be called a widow—tripped up to the doctor's chair, with a mischievous merriment in her rosy face.

"Doctor, you dear old soul," cried she, "get up and dance with me!" And then the four young people laughed louder than ever, to think what a queer figure the poor old doctor would cut.

"Pray excuse me," answered the doctor quietly. "I am old and rheumatic, and my dancing days were over long ago. But either of these gay young gentlemen will be glad of so pretty a partner."

"Dance with me, Clara!" cried Colonel Killigrew.

"No, no, I will be her partner!" shouted Mr. Gascoigne.

"She promised me her hand, fifty years ago!" exclaimed Mr. Medbourne.

They all gathered round her. One caught both her hands in his passionate grasp—another threw his arm about her waist—the third buried his hand among the glossy curls that clustered beneath the widow's cap. Blushing, panting, struggling, chiding, laughing, her warm breath fanning each of their faces by turns, she strove to disengage herself, yet still remained in their triple embrace. Never was there a livelier picture of youthful rivalship, with bewitching beauty for the prize. Yet, by a strange deception, owing to the duskiness of the chamber, and the antique dresses which they still wore, the tall mirror is said to have reflected the figures of the three old, gray, withered grandsires, ridiculously contending for the skinny ugliness of a shrivelled grandam.

But they were young: their burning passions proved them so. Inflamed to madness by the coquetry of the girl-widow, who neither granted nor quite withheld her favors, the three rivals began to interchange threatening glances. Still keeping hold of the fair prize, they grappled fiercely at one another's throats. As they struggled to and fro, the table was overturned, and the vase dashed into a thousand fragments. The precious Water of Youth flowed in a bright stream across the floor, moistening the wings of a butterfly, which, grown old in the decline of summer, had alighted there to die. The insect fluttered lightly through the chamber, and settled on the snowy head of Dr. Heidegger.

"Come, come, gentlemen!—come, Madam Wycherly," exclaimed the doctor, " I really must protest against this riot."

They stood still and shivered; for it seemed as if gray Time were calling them back from their sunny youth, far down into the chill and darksome vale of years. They looked at old Dr. Heidegger, who sat in his carved arm-chair, holding the rose of half a century, which he had rescued from among the fragments of the shattered vase. At the motion of his hand, the four rioters resumed their seats; the

more readily, because their violent exertions had wearied them, youthful though they were.

"My poor Sylvia's rose!" ejaculated Dr. Heidegger, holding it in the light of the sunset clouds; "it appears to be fading again."

And so it was. Even while the party were looking at it, the flower continued to shrivel up, till it became as dry and fragile as when the doctor had first thrown it into the vase. He shook off the few drops of moisture which clung to its petals.

"I love it as well thus as in its dewy freshness," observed he, pressing the withered rose to his withered lips. While he spoke, the butterfly fluttered down from the doctor's snowy head, and fell upon the floor.

His guests shivered again. A strange chillness, whether of the body or spirit they could not tell, was creeping gradually over them all. They gazed at one another, and fancied that each fleeting moment snatched away a charm, and left a deepening furrow where none had been before. Was it an illusion? Had the changes of a lifetime been crowded into so brief a space, and were they now four aged people, sitting with their old friend, Dr. Heidegger?

"Are we grown old again, so soon?" cried they, dolefully.

In truth they had. The Water of Youth possessed merely a virtue more transient than that of wine. The delirium which it created had effervesced away. Yes! they were old again. With a shuddering impulse, that showed her a woman still, the widow clasped her skinny hands before her face, and wished that the coffin lid were over it, since it could be no longer beautiful.

"Yes, friends, ye are old again," said Dr. Heidegger, "and lo! the Water of Youth is all lavished on the ground. Well—I bemoan it not; for if the fountain gushed at my very doorstep, I would not stoop to bathe my lips in it—no, though its delirium were for years instead of moments. Such is the lesson ye have taught me!"

But the doctor's four friends had taught no such lesson to themselves. They resolved forthwith to make a pilgrimage to Florida, and quaff at morning, noon and night, from the Fountain of Youth.

Discuss

1. What do you learn about Dr. Heidegger through the description of his study room?

2. What advice does Dr. Heidegger give his friends before they take the drink? Do they agree? Why or why not? Do they act as they say they will?

3. What changes are most evident in the old people who drink the water?

4. Which statement best summarizes the meaning of this story? Why?

   a. People would rather be young than old.

   b. Even when given an opportunity to correct mistakes, people will take the path that they have already set for themselves.

   c. Through age people learn wisdom.

Explore

1. Why do you suppose Dr. Heidegger performs this experiment?

2. Why doesn't Dr. Heidegger want to take part in the experiment along with the four participants? Why do they respond differently?

3. Who is the narrator of this story? What does he know about the characaters and their situations and how has he gained his knowledge? How and why does he interrupt the story?

4. Hawthorne lived more than one hundred years ago, and the diction he uses in this story reflects that period. What words and phrases did you find unusual or used in ways to which you are unaccustomed?

For Your Journal

1. If you could drink from the Fountain of Youth and stay young forever, would you? Why or why not?

2. What do you think would happen if there really were a way that people could stay their same age or reverse the process of aging? Would people try to stay young or become younger? Explain your response.

3. Write a short story or description involving a world that has discovered the Fountain of Youth.

The Red-headed League

Arthur Conan Doyle

The most famous detective in English literature, Sherlock Holmes, uses deductive reasoning to discover what's behind the Red-headed League and solve a major crime.

I HAD CALLED UPON MY FRIEND, Mr. Sherlock Holmes, one day in the autumn of last year, and found him in deep conversation with a very stout, florid-faced elderly gentleman, with fiery red hair. With an apology for my intrusion, I was about to withdraw, when Holmes pulled me abruptly into the room and closed the door behind me.

"You could not possibly have come at a better time, my dear Watson," he said, cordially.

"I was afraid that you were engaged."

"So I am. Very much so."

"Then I can wait in the next room."

"Not at all. This gentleman, Mr. Wilson, has been my partner and helper in many of my most successful cases, and I have no doubt that he will be of the utmost use to me in yours also."

The stout gentleman half rose from his chair and gave a bob of greeting, with a quick little questioning glance from his small, fat-encircled eyes.

"Try the settee," said Holmes, relapsing into his armchair, and putting his finger-tips together, as was his custom when in judicial moods. "I know, my dear Watson, that you share my love of all that is bizarre and outside the conventions and humdrum routine of everyday life. You have shown your relish for it by the enthusiasm which has prompted you to chronicle, and, if you will excuse my saying so, somewhat to embellish so many of my own little adventures."

"Your cases have indeed been of the greatest interest to me," I observed.

"You will remember that I remarked the other day, just before we went into the very simple problem presented by Miss Mary Sutherland, that for strange effects and extraordinary combinations we must go to life itself, which is always far more daring than any effort of the imagination."

"A proposition which I took the liberty of doubting."

"You did, doctor, but none the less you must come round to my view, for otherwise I shall keep on piling fact upon fact on you, until your reason breaks down under them and acknowledges me to be right. Now, Mr. Jabez Wilson here has been good enough to call upon me this morning, and to begin a narrative which promises to be one of the most singular which I have listened to for some time. You have heard me remark that the strangest and most unique things are very often connected not with the larger but with the smaller crimes, and occasionally, indeed, where there is room for doubt whether any positive crime has been committed. As far as I have heard, it is impossible for me to say whether the present case is an instance of crime or not, but the course of events is certainly among the most singular that I have ever listened to. Perhaps, Mr. Wilson, you would have the great kindness to recommence your narrative. I ask you, not merely because my friend, Dr. Watson, has not heard the opening part, but also because the peculiar nature of the story makes me anxious to have every possible detail from your lips. As a rule, when I have heard some slight indication of the course of events I am able to guide myself by the thousands of other similar cases which occur to my memory. In the present instance I am forced to admit that the facts are, to the best of my belief, unique."

The portly client puffed out his chest with an appearance of some little pride, and pulled a dirty and wrinkled newspaper from the inside pocket of his greatcoat. As he glanced down the advertisement column, with his head thrust forward, and the paper flattened out upon his knee, I took a good look at the man, and endeavored, after the fashion of my companion, to read the indications which might be presented by his dress or appearance.

I did not gain very much, however, by my inspection. Our visitor bore every mark of being an average commonplace British tradesman, obese, pompous, and slow. He wore rather baggy gray shepherd's check trousers, a not over-clean black frock-coat, unbuttoned in the front, and a drab waistcoat with a heavy brassy Albert chain, and a square pierced bit of metal dangling down as an ornament. A frayed top hat and a faded brown overcoat with a wrinkled velvet collar lay upon a chair beside him. Altogether, look as I would, there was nothing remarkable about the man save his blazing red head and the expression of extreme chagrin and discontent upon his features.

Sherlock Holmes' quick eye took in my occupation, and he shook his head with a smile as he noticed my questioning glances. "Beyond the obvious facts that he has at some time done manual labor, that he takes snuff, that he is a Freemason, that he has been in China, and that he has done a considerable amount of writing lately, I can deduce nothing else."

Mr. Jabez Wilson started up in his chair, with his forefinger upon the paper, but his eyes upon my companion.

"How, in the name of good fortune, did you know all that, Mr. Holmes?" he asked. "How did you know, for example, that I did manual labor? It's as true as gospel, for I began as a ship's carpenter."

"Your hands, my dear sir. Your right hand is quite a size larger than your left. You have worked with it and the muscles are more developed."

"Well, the snuff, then, and the Freemasonry?"

"I won't insult your intelligence by telling you how I read that, especially as, rather against the strict rules of your order, you use an arc and compass breastpin."

"Ah, of course, I forgot that. But the writing?"

"What else can be indicated by that right cuff so very shiny for five inches, and the left one with the smooth patch near the elbow where you rest it upon the desk."

"Well, but China?"

"The fish which you have tattooed immediately above your wrist could only have been done in China. I have made a small study of tattoo marks, and have even contributed to the literature of the subject. That trick of staining the fishes' scales of a delicate pink is quite peculiar to China. When, in addition, I see a Chinese coin hanging from your watch-chain, the matter becomes even more simple."

Mr. Jabez Wilson laughed heavily. "Well, I never!" said he. "I thought at first that you had done something clever, but I see that there was nothing in it after all."

"I begin to think, Watson," said Holmes, "that I make a mistake in explaining. 'Omne ignotum pro magnifico,'[1] you know, and my poor little reputation, such as it is, will suffer shipwreck if I am so candid. Can you not find the advertisement, Mr. Wilson?"

"Yes, I have got it now," he answered, with his thick, red finger planted half-way down the column. "Here it is. This is what began it all. You just read it for yourself, sir."

I took the paper from him and read as follows:

"To the Red-headed League: On account of the bequest of the late Ezekiah Hopkins, of Lebanon, Pa., U. S. A., there is now another vacancy open which entitles a member of the League to a salary of four pounds a week for purely nominal services. All red-headed men who are sound in body and mind and above the age of twenty-one years are eligible. Apply in person on Monday, at eleven o'clock, to Duncan Ross, at the offices of the League, 7 Pope's Court, Fleet Street."

"What on earth does this mean?" I ejaculated, after I had twice read over the extraordinary announcement.

Holmes chuckled and wriggled in his chair, as was his habit when in high spirits. "It is a little off the beaten track, isn't it?" said he. "And now, Mr. Wilson, off you go at scratch, and tell us all about yourself, your household, and the effect which this advertisement had upon your fortunes. You will first make a note, doctor, of the paper and the date."

"It is *The Morning Chronicle* of April 27, 1890. Just two months ago."

"Very good. Now, Mr. Wilson."

---

[1] *Omne ignotum pro magnifico: Lat.*, That about which little is known is assumed to be wonderful.

"Well, it is just as I have been telling you, Mr. Sherlock Holmes," said Jabez Wilson, mopping his forehead, "I have a small pawnbroker's business at Coburg Square, near the City. It's not a very large affair, and of late years it has not done more than just give me a living. I used to be able to keep two assistants, but now I only keep one; and I would have a job to pay him but that he is willing to come for half wages, so as to learn the business."

"What is the name of this obliging youth?" asked Sherlock Holmes.

"His name is Vincent Spaulding, and he's not such a youth either. It's hard to say his age. I should not wish a smarter assistant, Mr. Holmes; and I know very well that he could better himself, and earn twice what I am able to give him. But, after all, if he is satisfied, why should I put ideas in his head?"

"Why, indeed? You seem most fortunate in having an employee who comes under the full market price. It is not a common experience among employers in this age. I don't know that your assistant is not as remarkable as your advertisement."

"Oh, he has his faults, too," said Mr. Wilson. "Never was such a fellow for photography. Snapping away with a camera when he ought to be improving his mind, and then diving down into the cellar like a rabbit into its hole to develop his pictures. That is his main fault; but, on the whole, he's a good worker. There's no vice in him."

"He is still with you, I presume?"

"Yes, sir. He and a girl of fourteen, who does a bit of simple cooking, and keeps the place clean— that's all I have in the house, for I am a widower, and never had any family. We live very quietly, sir, the three of us; and we keep a roof over our heads, and pay our debts, if we do nothing more.

"The first thing that put us out was that advertisement. Spaulding, he came down into the office just this day eight weeks, with this very paper in his hand, and he says:

" 'I wish to the Lord, Mr. Wilson, that I was a red-headed man.'

" 'Why that?' I asks.

" 'Why,' says he, 'here's another vacancy on the League of the Red-headed Men. It's worth quite a little fortune to any man who gets it, and I understand that there are more vacancies than there are men, so that the trustees are at their wits' end what to do with the money. If my hair would only change color here's a nice little crib all ready for me to step into.'

" 'Why, what is it, then?' I asked. You see, Mr. Holmes, I am a very stay-at-home man, and, as my business came to me instead of my having to go to it, I was often weeks on end without putting my foot over the door-mat. In that way I didn't know much of what was going on outside, and I was always glad of a bit of news.

" 'Have you never heard of the League of the Red-headed Men?' he asked, with his eyes open.

" 'Never.'

" 'Why, I wonder at that, for you are eligible yourself for one of the vacancies.'

" 'And what are they worth?' I asked.

" 'Oh, merely a couple of hundred a year, but the work is slight, and it need not interfere very much with one's other occupations.'

"Well, you can easily think that that made me prick up my ears, for the business has not been over good for some years, and an extra couple of hundred would have been very handy.

" 'Tell me all about it,' said I.

" 'Well,' said he, showing me the advertisement, 'you can see for yourself that the League has a vacancy, and there is the address where you should apply for particulars. As far as I can make out, the League was founded by an American millionaire, Ezekiah Hopkins, who was very peculiar in his ways. He was himself red-headed, and he had a great sympathy for all red-headed men; so, when he died, it was found that he had left his enormous fortune in the hands of trustees, with instructions to apply the interest to the providing of easy berths to men whose hair is of that color. From all I hear it is splendid pay, and very little to do.'

" 'But,' said I, 'there would be millions of red-headed men who would apply.'

" 'Not so many as you might think,' he answered. 'You see it is really confined to Londoners, and to grown men. This American had started from London when he was young, and he wanted to do the old town a good turn. Then, again, I have heard it is no use your applying if your hair is light red, or dark red, or anything but real, bright, blazing, fiery red. Now, if you cared to apply, Mr. Wilson, you would just walk in; but perhaps it would hardly be worth your while to put yourself out of the way for the sake of a few hundred pounds.'

"Now it is a fact, gentlemen, as you may see for yourselves, that my hair is of a very full and rich tint, so that it seemed to me that, if there was to be any competition in the matter, I stood as good a chance as any man that I had ever met. Vincent Spaulding seemed to know so much about it that I thought he might prove useful, so I just ordered him to put up the shutters for the day, and to come right away with me. He was very willing to have a holiday, so we shut the business up, and started off for the address that was given us in the advertisement.

"I never hope to see such a sight as that again, Mr. Holmes. From north, south, east, and west every man who had a shade of red in his hair had tramped into the City to answer the advertisement. Fleet Street was choked with red-headed folk, and Pope's Court looked like a coster's orange barrow. I should not have thought there were so many in the whole country as were brought together by that single advertisement. Every shade of color they were—straw, lemon, orange, brick, Irish-setter, liver, clay; but, as Spaulding said, there were not many who had the real vivid flame-colored tint. When I saw how many were waiting, I would have given it up in despair; but Spaulding would not hear of it. How he did it I could not imagine, but he pushed and pulled and butted until he got me through the crowd, and right up to the steps which led to the office. There was a double stream upon the stair, some going up in hope, and some coming back dejected; but we wedged in as well as we could and soon found ourselves in the office."

"Your experience has been a most entertaining one," remarked Holmes, as his client paused and refreshed his memory with a huge pinch of snuff. "Pray continue your very interesting statement."

"There was nothing in the office but a couple of wooden chairs and a deal table, behind which sat a small man, with a head that was even redder than mine. He said a few words to each candidate as he came up, and then he always managed to find some fault in them which would disqualify them. Getting a vacancy did not seem to be such a very easy matter after all. However, when our turn came, the little man was much more favorable to me than to any of the others, and he closed the door as we entered, so that he might have a private word with us.

" 'This is Mr. Jabez Wilson,' said my assistant, 'and he is willing to fill a vacancy in the League.'

" 'And he is admirably suited for it,' the other answered. 'He has every requirement. I cannot recall when I have seen anything so fine.' He took a step backward, cocked his head on one side, and gazed at my hair until I felt quite bashful. Then suddenly he plunged forward, wrung my hand, and congratulated me warmly on my success.

" 'It would be injustice to hesitate,' said he. 'You will, however, I am sure, excuse me for taking an obvious precaution.' With that he seized my hair in both his hands, and tugged until I yelled with the pain. 'There is water in your eyes,' said he, as he released me. 'I perceive that all is as it should be. But we have to be careful, for we have twice been deceived by wigs and once by paint. I could tell you tales of cobbler's wax which would disgust you with human nature.' He stepped over to the window and shouted through it at the top of his voice that the vacancy was filled. A groan of disappointment came up from below, and the folk all trooped away in different directions, until there was not a red head to be seen except my own and that of the manager.

" 'My name,' said he, 'is Mr. Duncan Ross, and I am myself one of the pensioners upon the fund left by our noble benefactor. Are you a married man, Mr. Wilson? Have you a family?'

"I answered that I had not.

"His face fell immediately.

" 'Dear me!' he said gravely, 'that is very serious indeed! I am sorry to hear you say that. The fund was of course, for the propagation and spread of the redheads as well as for their maintenance. It is exceedingly unfortunate that you should be a bachelor.'

"My face lengthened at this, Mr. Holmes, for I thought that I was not to have the vacancy after all; but, after thinking it over for a few minutes, he said that it would be all right.

" 'In the case of another,' said he, 'the objection might be fatal, but we must stretch a point in favor of a man with such a head of hair as yours. When shall you be able to enter upon your new duties?'

" 'Well, it is a little awkward, for I have a business already,' said I.

" 'Oh, never mind about that, Mr. Wilson!' said Vincent Spaulding. 'I shall be able to look after that for you.'

" 'What would be the hours?" I asked.

" 'Ten to two.'

"Now a pawnbroker's business is mostly done of an evening, Mr. Holmes, especially Thursday and Friday evenings, which is just before pay-day; so it would suit me very well to earn a little in the mornings. Besides, I knew that my assistant was a good man, and that he would see to anything that turned up.

" 'That would suit me very well,' said I. 'And the pay?'

" 'Is four pounds a week.'

" 'And the work?'

" 'Is purely nominal.'

" 'What do you call purely nominal?'

" 'Well, you have to be in the office, or at least in the building, the whole time. If you leave, you forfeit your whole position forever. The will is very clear upon that point. You don't comply with the conditions if you budge from the office during that time.'

" 'It's only four hours a day, and I should not think of leaving,' said I.

" 'No excuse will avail,' said Mr. Duncan Ross, 'neither sickness, nor business, nor anthing else. There you must stay, or you lose your billet.'

" 'And the work?'

" 'Is to copy out the "Encyclopædia Britannica." There is the first volume of it in that press. You must find your own ink, pens, and blotting-paper, but we provide this table and chair. Will you be ready to-morrow?'

" 'Certainly,' I answered.

" 'Then, good-by, Mr. Jabez Wilson, and let me congratulate you once more on the important position which you have been fortunate enough to gain.' He bowed me out of the room, and I went home with my assistant hardly kowing what to say or do, I was so pleased at my own good fortune.

"Well, I thought over the matter all day, and by evening I was in low spirits again; for I had quite persuaded myself that the whole affair must be some great hoax or fraud, though what its object might be I could not imagine. It seemed altogether past belief that anyone could make such a will, or that they would pay such a sum for doing anything so simple as copying out the 'Encyclopædia Brittanica.' Vincent Spaulding did what he could to cheer me up, but by bed-time I had reasoned myself out of the whole thing. However, in the morning I determined to have a look at it anyhow, so I bought a penny bottle of ink, and with a quill pen and seven sheets of foolscap paper I started off for Pope's Court.

"Well, to my surprise and delight everything was as right as possible. The table was set out ready for me, and Mr. Duncan Ross was there to see that I got fairly to work. He started me off upon the letter A, and then he left me; but he would drop in from time to time to see that all was right with me. At two o'clock he bade me good-day, complimented me upon the amount that I had written, and locked the door of the office after me.

"This went on day after day, Mr. Holmes, and on Saturday the manager came in and planked down four golden sovereigns for my week's work. It was the same the next week, and the same the week after. Every morning I was there at ten, and every afternoon I left at two. By degrees Mr. Duncan Ross took to coming in only once of a morning, and then, after a time, he did not come in at all. Still, of course, I never dared to leave the room for an instant, for I was not sure when he might come, and the billet was such a good one, and suited me so well, that I would not risk the loss of it.

"Eight weeks passed away like this, and I had written about Abbots, and Archery, and Armor, and Architecture, and Attica, and hoped with diligence that I might get on to the Bs before very long. It cost me something in foolscap, and I had pretty nearly filled a shelf with my writings. And then suddenly the whole business came to an end."

"To an end?"

"Yes, sir. And no later than this morning. I went to my work as usual at ten o'clock, but the door was shut and locked, with a little square of cardboard hammered onto the middle of the panel with a tack. Here it is, and you can read for yourself."

He held up a piece of white cardboard, about the size of a sheet of note-paper. It read in this fashion:

"The Red-headed League is Dissolved.
Oct. 9, 1890."

Sherlock Holmes and I surveyed this curt announcement and the rueful face behind it, until the comical side of the affair so completely overtopped every consideration that we both burst out into a roar of laughter.

"I cannot see that there is anything very funny," cried our client, flushing up to the roots of his flaming head. "If you can do nothing better than laugh at me, I can go elsewhere."

"No, no," cried Holmes, shoving him back into the chair from which he had half risen. "I really wouldn't miss your case for the world. It is most refreshingly unusual. But there is, if you will excuse my saying so, something just a little funny about it. Pray what steps did you take when you found the card upon the door?"

"I was staggered, sir. I did not know what to do. Then I called at the offices round, but none of them seemed to know anything about it. Finally, I went to the landlord, who is an accountant living on the ground floor, and I asked him if he could tell me what had become of the Red-headed League. He said that he had never heard of any such body. Then I asked him who Mr. Duncan Ross was. He answered that the name was new to him.

" 'Well,' said I, 'the gentlemen at No. 4.'

" 'What, the red-headed man?'

" 'Yes.'

" 'Oh,' said he, 'his name was William Morris. He was a solicitor, and was using my room as a temporary convenience until his new premises were ready. He moved out yesterday.'

" 'Where could I find him?'

" 'Oh, at his new offices. He did tell me the address. Yes, 17 King Edward Street, near St. Paul's.'

"I started off, Mr. Holmes, but when I got to that address it was a manufactory of artifical knee-caps, and no one in it had ever heard of either Mr. William Morris, or Mr. Duncan Ross."

"And what did you do then?" asked Holmes.

"I went home to Saxe-Coburg Square, and I took the advice of my assistant. But he could not help me in any way. He could only say that if I waited I should hear by post. But that was not quite good enough, Mr. Holmes. I did not wish to lose such a place without a struggle, so, as I had heard that you were good enough to give advice to poor folk who were in need of it, I came right away to you."

"And you did very wisely," said Holmes. "Your case is an exceedingly remarkable one, and I shall be happy to look into it. From what you have told me I think that it is possible that graver issues hang from it than might at first sight appear."

"Grave enough!" said Mr. Jabez Wilson. "Why, I have lost four pound a week."

"As far as you are personally concerned," remarked Holmes, "I do not see that you have any grievance against this extraordinary league. On the contrary, you are, as I understand, richer by some thirty pounds, to say nothing of the minute knowledge which you have gained on every subject which comes under the letter A. You have lost nothing by them."

"No, sir. But I want to find out about them, and who they are, and what their object was in playing this prank—if it was a prank—upon me. It was a pretty expensive joke for them, for it cost them two-and-thirty pounds."

"We shall endeavor to clear up these points for you. And, first, one or two questions, Mr. Wilson. This assistant of yours who first called your attention to the advertisement—how long had he been with you?"

"About a month then."

"How did he come?"

"In answer to an advertisement."

"Was he the only applicant?"

"No, I had a dozen."

"Why did you pick him?"

"Because he was handy and would come cheap."

"At half wages, in fact."

"Yes."

"What is he like, this Vincent Spaulding?"

"Small, stout-built, very quick in his ways, no hair on his face, though he's not short of thirty. Has a white splash of acid upon his forehead."

Holmes sat up in his chair in considerable excitement. "I thought as much," said he. "Have you ever observed that his ears are pierced for earrings?"

"Yes, sir. He told me that a gypsy had done it for him when he was a lad."

"Hum!" said Holmes, sinking back in deep thought. "He is still with you?"

"Oh, yes, sir; I have only just left him."

"And has your business been attended to in your absence?"

"Nothing to complain of, sir. There's never very much to do of a morning."

"That will do, Mr. Wilson. I shall be happy to give you an opinion upon the subject in the course of a day or two. To-day is Saturday, and I hope that by Monday we may come to a conclusion.

"Well, Watson," said Holmes, when our visitor had left us, "what do you make of it all?"

"I make nothing of it," I answered, frankly. "It is a most mysterious business."

"As a rule," said Holmes, "the more bizarre a thing is the less mysterious it proves to be. It is your commonplace, featureless crimes which are really puzzling, just as a commonplace face is the most difficult to identify. But I must be prompt over this matter."

"What are you going to do, then?" I asked.

"To smoke," he answered. "It is quite a three-pipe problem, and I beg that you won't speak to me for fifty minutes." He curled himself up in his chair, with his thin knees drawn up to his hawk-like nose, and there he sat with his eyes closed and his black clay pipe thrusting out like the bill of some strange bird. I had come to the conclusion that he had dropped asleep, and indeed was nodding myself, when he suddenly sprang out of his chair with the gesture of a man who has made up his mind, and put his pipe down upon the mantelpiece.

"Sarasate plays at St. James's Hall this afternoon," he remarked. "What do you think Watson? Could your patients spare you for a few hours?"

"I have nothing to do to-day. My practice is never very absorbing."

"Then put on your hat and come. I am going through the City first, and we can have some lunch on the way. I observe that there is a good deal of German music on the programme, which is rather more to my taste than Italian or French. It is introspective, and I want to introspect. Come along!"

We traveled by the Underground as far as Aldersgate; and a short walk took us to Saxe-Coburg Square, the scene of the singular story which we had listened to in the morning. It was a poky, little, shabby-genteel place, where four lines of dingy, two-storied brick houses looked out into a small railed-in inclosure, where a lawn of weedy grass, and a few clumps of faded laurel bushes made a hard fight against a smoke-laden and uncongenial atmosphere. Three gilt balls and a brown board with JABEZ WILSON in white letters, upon a corner house, announced the place where our red-headed client carried on his business. Sherlock Holmes stopped in front of it with his head on one side, and looked it all over, with his eyes shining brightly between puckered lids. Then he walked slowly up the street, and then down again to the corner, still looking keenly at the houses. Finally he returned to the pawnbroker's and, having thumped viorously upon the pavement with his stick two or three times, he went up to the door and knocked. It was instantly opened by a bright-looking, clean-shaven young fellow, who asked him to step in.

"Thank you," said Holmes, "I only wished to ask you how you would go from here to the Strand."

"Third right, fourth left," answered the assistant, promptly, closing the door.

"Smart fellow, that," observed Holmes as we walked away. "He is, in my judgment, the fourth smartest man in London, and for daring I am not sure that he has not a claim to be third. I have known something of him before."

"Evidently," said I, "Mr. Wilson's assistant counts for a good deal in this mystery of the Red-headed League. I am sure that you inquired your way merely in order that you might see him."

"Not him."

"What then?"

"The knees of his trousers."

"And what did you see?"

"What I expected to see."

"Why did you beat the pavement?"

"My dear doctor, this is a time for observation, not for talk. We are spies in an enemy's country. We know something of Saxe-Coburg Square. Let us now explore the parts which lie behind it."

The road in which we found ourselves as we turned round the corner from the retired Saxe-Coburg Square presented as great a contrast to it as the front of a picture does to the back. It was one of the main arteries which convey the traffic of the City to the north and west. The roadway was blocked with the immense stream of commerce flowing in a double tide inward and outward, while the footpaths were black with the hurrying swarm of pedestrians. It was difficult to realize, as we looked at the line of fine shops and stately business premises, that they really abutted on the other side upon the faded and stagnant square which we had just quitted.

"Let me see," said Holmes, standing at the corner, and glancing along the line, "I should like just to remember the order of the houses here. It is a hobby of mine to have an exact knowledge of London. There is Mortimer's, the tobacconist; the little newspaper shop, the Coburg branch of the City and Suburban Bank, the Vegetarian Restaurant, and McFarlane's carriage-building depot. That carries us right on to the other block. And now, doctor, we've done our work, so it's time we had some play. A sandwich and a cup of coffee, and then off to violin-land, where all is sweetness, and delicacy, and harmony, and there are no red-headed clients to vex us with their conundrums."[2]

My friend was an enthusiastic musician, being himself not only a very capable performer, but a composer of no ordinary merit. All the afternoon he sat in the stalls wrapped in the most perfect happiness, gently waving his long thin fingers in time to the music, while his gently smiling face and his languid, dreamy eyes were as unlike those of Holmes the sleuth-hound, Holmes the relentless, keen-witted, ready-handed criminal agent, as it was possible to conceive. In his singular character the dual nature alternately asserted itself, and his extreme exactness and astuteness represented, as I have often thought, the reaction against the poetic and contemplative mood which occasionally predominated in him. The swing of his nature took him from extreme languor to devouring energy; and, as I knew well, he was never so truly formidable as when, for days on end, he had been lounging in his armchair amid his improvisations and his black-letter editions. Then it was that the lust of the chase would suddenly come upon him, and that his brilliant reasoning power would rise to the level of intuition, until those who were unacquainted with his methods would look askance at him as on a man whose knowledge was not that of other mortals. When I saw him that afternoon so enwrapped in the music at St. James's Hall, I felt that an evil time might be coming upon those whom he had set himself to hunt down.

"You want to go home, no doubt, doctor," he remarked, as we emerged.

"Yes, it would be as well."

"And I have some business to do which will take some hours. This business at Coburg Square is serious."

"Why serious?"

"A considerable crime is in contemplation. I have every reason to believe that we shall be in time to stop it. But to-day being Saturday rather complicates matters. I shall want your help tonight."

"At what time?"

"Ten will be early enough."

"I shall be at Baker Street at ten."

[2]**conundrums:** intricate, puzzling problems.

"Very well. And, I say, doctor! there may be some little danger, so kindly put your army revolver in your pocket." He waved his hand, turned on his heel, and disappeared in an instant among the crowd.

I trust that I am not more dense than my neighbors, but I was always oppressed with a sense of my own stupidity in my dealings with Sherlock Holmes. Here I had heard what he had heard, I had seen what he had seen, and yet from his words it was evident that he saw clearly not only what had happened, but what was about to happen, while to me the whole business was still confused and grotesque. As I drove home to my house in Kensington I thought over it all, from the extraordinary story of the red-headed copier of the "Encyclopædia" down to the visit to Saxe-Coburg Square, and the ominous words with which he had parted from me. What was this nocturnal expedition, and why should I go armed? Where were we going, and what were we to do? I had the hint from Holmes that this smooth-faced pawnbroker's assistant was a formidable man—a man who might play a deep game. I tried to puzzle it out, but gave up in despair, and set the matter aside until night should bring an explanation.

It was quarter-past nine when I started from home and made my way across the Park, and so through Oxford Street to Baker Street. Two hansoms[3] were standing at the door, and as I entered the passage, I heard the sound of voices from above. On entering his room, I found Holmes in animated conversation with two men, one of whom I recognized as Peter Jones, the official police agent; while the other was a long, thin, sad-faced man, with a very shiny hat and oppressively respectable frock-coat.

"Ha! our party is complete," said Holmes, buttoning up his pea-jacket, and taking his heavy hunting crop from the rack. "Watson, I think you know Mr. Jones, of Scotland Yard? Let me introduce you to Mr. Merryweather, who is to be our companion in to-night's adventure."

"We're hunting in couples again, doctor, you see," said Jones, in his consequential way. "Our friend here is a wonderful man for starting a chase. All he wants is an old dog to help him do the running down."

[3]**hansoms:** two-wheeled horse-drawn vehicles used as cabs.

"I hope a wild goose may not prove to be the end of our chase," observed Mr. Merryweather, gloomily.

"You may place considerable confidence in Mr. Holmes, sir," said the police agent loftily. "He has his own little methods, which are, if he won't mind my saying so, just a little too theoretical and fantastic, but he has the making of a detective in him. It is not too much to say that once or twice, as in that business of the Sholto murder and the Agra treasure, he has been more nearly correct than the official force."

"Oh, if you say so, Mr. Jones, it is all right!" said the stranger, with deference. "Still, I confess that I miss my rubber. It is the first Saturday night for seven-and-twenty years that I have not had my rubber."[4]

"I think you will find," said Sherlock Holmes, "that you will play for a higher stake to-night than you have ever done yet, and that the play will be more exciting. For you, Mr. Merryweather, the stake will be some thirty thousand pounds; and for you, Jones, it will be the man upon whom you wish to lay your hands."

"John Clay, the murderer, thief, smasher, and forger. He's a young man, Mr. Merryweather, but he is at the head of his profession, and I would rather have my bracelets on him than on any criminal in London. He's a remarkable man, is young John Clay. His grandfather was a Royal Duke, and he himself has been to Eton and Oxford. His brain is as cunning as his fingers, and though we meet signs of him at every turn, we never know where to find the man himself. He'll crack a crib in Scotland one week, and be raising money to build an orphanage in Cornwall the next. I've been on his track for years, and I have never set eyes on him yet."

"I hope that I may have the pleasure of introducing you to-night. I've had one or two little turns also with Mr. John Clay, and I agree with you that he is at the head of his profession. It is past ten, however, and quite time that we started. If you two will take the first hansom, Watson and I will follow in the second."

Sherlock Holmes was not very communicative during the long drive, and lay back in the cab humming the tunes which he had heard in the afternoon. We rattled through an endless labyrinth of gas-lit streets until we emerged into Farringdon Street.

[4]**rubber:** a round of the card game bridge.

"We are close there now," my friend remarked. "This fellow Merryweather is a bank director and personally interested in the matter. I thought it as well to have Jones with us also. He is not a bad fellow, though an absolute imbecile in his profession. He has one positive virtue. He is as brave as a bulldog, and as tenacious as a lobster if he gets his claws upon anyone. Here we are, and they are waiting for us."

We had reached the same crowded thoroughfare in which we had found ourselves in the morning. Our cabs were dismissed, and following the guidance of Mr. Merryweather, we passed down a narrow passage, and through a side door which he opened for us. Within there was a small corridor, which ended in a very massive iron gate. This also was opened, and led down a flight of winding stone steps, which terminated at another formidable gate. Mr. Merryweather stopped to light a lantern, and then conducted us down a dark, earth-smelling passage, and so, after opening a third door, into a huge vault or cellar, which was piled all round with crates and massive boxes.

"You are not very vulnerable from above," Holmes remarked, as he held up the lantern and gazed about him.

"Nor from below," said Mr. Merryweather, striking his stick upon the flags which lined the floor. "Why, dear me, it sounds quite hollow!" he remarked, looking up in surprise.

"I must really ask you to be a little more quiet," said Holmes, severely. "You have already imperiled the whole success of our expedition. Might I beg that you would have the goodness to sit down upon one of those boxes, and not to interfere?"

The solemn Mr. Merryweather perched himself upon a crate, with a very injured expression upon his face, while Holmes fell upon his knees upon the floor, and, with the lantern and a magnifying lens, began to examine minutely the cracks between the stones. A few seconds sufficed to satisfy him, for he sprang to his feet again, and put his glass in his pocket.

"We have at least an hour before us," he remarked, "for they can hardly take any steps until the good pawnbroker is safely in bed. Then they will not lose a minute, for the sooner they do their work the longer time they will have for their escape. We are at present, doctor—as no doubt you have divined—in the cellar of the City branch of one of the principal London banks. Mr. Merryweather is the chairman of directors, and he will explain to you that there are reasons why the more daring criminals of London should take a considerable interest in this cellar at present."

"It is our French gold," whispered the director. "We have had several warnings that an attempt might be made upon it."

"Your French gold?"

"Yes. We had occasion some months ago to strengthen our resources, and borrowed, for that purpose, thirty thousand napoleons from the Bank of France. It has become known that we have never had occasion to unpack the money, and that it is still lying in our cellar. The crate upon which I sit contains two thousand napoleons packed between layers of lead foil. Our reserve of bullion is much larger at present than is usually kept in a single branch office, and the directors have had misgivings upon the subject.

"Which were very well justified," observed Holmes. "And now it is time that we arranged our little plans. I expect that within an hour matters will come to a head. In the meantime, Mr. Merryweather, we must put the screen over that dark lantern."

"And sit in the dark?"

"I am afraid so. I had brought a pack of cards in my pocket, and I thought that, as we were a *partie carrée*,[5] you might have your rubber after all. But I see that the enemy's preparations have gone so far that we cannot risk the presence of a light. And, first of all, we must choose our positions. These are daring men, and, though we shall take them at a disadvantage, they may do us some harm, unless we are careful. I shall stand behind this crate, and do you conceal yourself behind those. Then, when I flash a light upon them, close in swiftly. If they fire, Watson, have no compunction about shooting them down."

I placed my revolver, cocked, upon the top of the wooden case behind which I crouched. Holmes shot the slide across the front of his lantern, and left us in pitch darkness—such an absolute darkness as I have never before experienced. The smell of hot metal remained to assure us that the light was still there, ready to flash out at a moment's notice. To me, with my nerves worked up to a pitch of expectancy, there was something depressing and subduing in the sudden gloom, and in the cold, dank air of the vault.

"They have but one retreat," whispered Holmes. "That is back through the house into Saxe-Coburg Square. I hope that you have done what I asked you, Jones?"

"I have an inspector and two officers waiting at the front door."

"Then we have stopped all the holes. And now we must be silent and wait."

What a time it seemed! From comparing notes afterwards, it was but an hour and a quarter, yet it appeared to me that the night must have almost gone, and the dawn be breaking above us. My limbs were weary and stiff, for I feared to change my position, yet my nerves were worked up to the highest pitch of tension, and my hearing was so acute that I could not only hear the gentle breathing of my companions, but I could distinguish the deeper, heavier inbreath of the bulky Jones from the thin, sighing note of the bank director. From my position I could look over the case in the direction of the floor. Suddenly my eyes caught the glint of a light.

At first it was but a lurid spark upon the stone pavement. Then it lengthened out until it became a yellow line, and then, without any warning or sound, a gash seemed to open and a hand appeared, a white, almost womanly hand, which felt about in the center of the little area of light. For a minute or more the hand, with its writhing fingers, protruded out of the floor. Then it was withdrawn as suddenly as it appeared, and all was dark again save the single lurid spark, which marked a chink between the stones.

Its disappearance, however, was but momentary. With a rending, tearing sound, one of the broad white stones turned over upon its side, and left a square, gaping hole, through which streamed the light of a lantern. Over the edge there peeped a clean-cut, boyish face, which looked keenly about it, and then, with a hand on either side of the aperture, drew itself shoulder-high and waist-high, until one knee rested upon the edge. In another instant he stood at the side of the hole, and was hauling after him a companion, lithe and small like himself, with a pale face and a shock of very red hair.

"It's all clear," he whispered. "Have you the chisel and the bags? Great Scott! Jump, Archie, jump, and I'll swing for it!"

Sherlock Holmes had sprung out and seized the intruder by the collar. The other dived down the hole, and I heard the sound of rending cloth as Jones clutched at his skirts. The light flashed upon the barrel of a revolver, but Holmes's hunting crop

[5] **partie carrée:** *Fr.*, party of four: two men and two women.

came down on the man's wrist, and the pistol clinked upon the stone floor.

"It's no use, John Clay," said Holmes, blandly, "you have no chance at all."

"So I see," the other answered, with the utmost coolness. "I fancy that my pal is all right, though I see you have got his coat-tails."

"There are three men waiting for him at the door," said Holmes.

"Oh, indeed. You seem to have done the thing very completely. I must compliment you."

"And I you," Holmes answered. "Your red-headed idea was very new and effective."

"You'll see your pal again presently," said Jones. "He's quicker at climbing down holes than I am. Just hold out while I fix the derbies."

"I beg that you will not touch me with your filthy hands," remarked our prisoner, as the handcuffs clattered upon his wrists. "You may not be aware that I have royal blood in my veins. Have the goodness also, when you address me, always to say 'sir' and 'please.'"

"All right," said Jones, with a stare and a snigger. "Well, would you please, sir, march upstairs where we can get a cab to carry your highness to the police station."

"That is better," said John Clay, serenely. He made a sweeping bow to the three of us, and walked quietly off in the custody of the detective.

"Really, Mr. Holmes," said Mr. Merryweather, as we followed them from the cellar, "I do not know how the bank can thank you or repay you. There is no doubt that you have detected and defeated in the most complete manner one of the most determined attempts at bank robbery that have ever come within my experience."

"I have had one or two little scores of my own to settle with Mr. John Clay," said Holmes. "I have been at some small expense over this matter, which I shall expect the bank to refund, but beyond that I am amply repaid by having had an experience which is in many ways unique, and by hearing the very remarkable narrative of the Red-headed League."

"You see, Watson," he explained, in the early hours of the morning, as we sat over a glass of whisky and soda in Baker Street, "it was perfectly obvious from the first that the only possible object of this rather fantastic business of the advertisements of the League, and the copying of the 'Encyclopædia,' must be to get this not over-bright pawnbroker out of the way for a number of hours every day. It was a curious way of managing it, but really it would be difficult to suggest a better. The method was no doubt suggested to Clay's ingenious mind by the color of his accomplice's hair. The four pounds a week was a lure which must draw him, and what was it to them, who were playing for thousands? They put in the advertisement, one rogue has the temporary office, the other rogue incites the man to apply for it, and together they manage to secure his absence every morning in the week. From the time that I heard of the assistant having come for half wages, it was obvious to me that he had some strong motive for securing the situation."

"But how could you guess what the motive was?"

"Had there been women in the house, I should have suspected a mere vulgar intrigue. That, however, was out of the question. The man's business was a small one, and there was nothing in his house which could account for such elaborate preparations, and such an expenditure as they were at. It must then be something out of the house. What could it be? I thought of the assistant's fondness for photography, and his trick of vanishing into the cellar. The cellar! There was the end of this tangled clew. Then I made inquiries as to this mysterious assistant, and found that I had to deal with one of the coolest and most daring criminals in London. He was doing something in the cellar—something which took many hours a day for months on end. What could it be, once more? I could think of nothing save that he was running a tunnel to some other building.

"So far I had got when we went to visit the scene of action. I surprised you by beating upon the pavement with my stick. I was ascertaining whether the cellar stretched out in front or behind. It was not in front. Then I rang the bell, and, as I hoped, the assistant answered it. We have had some skirmishes, but we had never set eyes upon each other before. I hardly looked at his face. His knees were what I wished to see. You must yourself have remarked how worn, wrinkled, and stained they were. They spoke of those hours of burrowing. The only remaining point was what they were burrowing for. I walked around the corner, saw that the City and Suburban Bank abutted on our friend's premises, and felt that I had solved my problem. When you drove home after the concert I called upon Scotland Yard, and upon the chairman of the bank directors, with the result that you have seen."

"And how could you tell that they would make their attempt to-night?" I asked.

"Well, when they closed their League offices that was a sign that they cared no longer about Mr. Jabez Wilson's presence; in other words, that they had completed their tunnel. But it was essential that they should use it soon, as it might be discovered, or the bullion might be removed. Saturday would suit them better than any other day, as it would give them two days for their escape. For all these reasons I expected them to come to-night."

"You reasoned it out beautifully," I exclaimed, in unfeigned admiration. "It is so long a chain, and yet every link rings true."

"It saved me from ennui,[6]" he answered, yawning. "Alas! I already feel it closing in upon me. My life is spent in one long effort to escape from the commonplaces of existence. These little problems help me to do so."

"And you are a benefactor of the race," said I. He shrugged his shoulders. "Well, perhaps, after all, it is of some little use," he remarked. " 'L'homme c'est rien'—l'œuvre c'est tout,' as Gustave Flaubert wrote to Georg Sand."[7]

[6]**ennui:** boredom.
[7]**L'homme c'est rien—l'œuvre c'est tout:** *Fr.,* Man is nothing—the work is all. Gustave Flaubert and Georg [sic] Sand were French writers who lived during the 1800s.

Discuss

1. Sherlock Holmes relies on his powers of deduction to solve crimes. Which statement best describes that process?

   a. Holmes gathers a lot of information based on his observations and then draws conclusions on the basis of those details.

   b. Holmes has a vivid imagination which he uses to reconstruct crimes in his mind and then fantasize about how they were committed.

   c. Holmes has solved many crimes and depends on his memory of them as a starting point for solving his current case.

2. Why does Mr. Jabez Wilson come to Holmes? What does he hope to gain? What is Holmes' response? How does Holmes change the focus of the mystery?

3. What is Vincent Spaulding's role in the story? When did you begin to become aware of the part he was playing?

4. As you read, what information did you come upon that you thought was a clue to the solution of the mystery? How close did each such discovery bring you to solving the mystery?

5. What are the police's attitudes toward Holmes? How do they differ from Watson's?

6. Why had the police had so much trouble capturing John Clay?

Explore

1. What is Watson's role in the story? What is his relation to Holmes? What role does he serve for the reader?

2. What knowledge did you have of Sherlock Holmes before you read this story? Had you read any other stories by Conan Doyle? Had you seen movies or television shows about Holmes? Compare your preconceptions, if you had any, with what you learned in this story.

3. How do the attitudes of Holmes and Watson differ? What does each find appealing in the other? What is the basis of their relationship?

4. What does Watson mean when he says that Holmes has a dual nature? How does that characteristic serve Holmes as a detective?

5. Compare and contrast Sherlock Holmes with other detectives you have read about or watched on television or in movies.

For Your Journal

1. Write a letter to a movie director telling why a television film should be made from "The Red-headed League." Which of its qualitites especially would make for good television? Which episodes would have to be adapted? Do you have any ideas of who could play the main roles?

2. Create a detective story. What sorts of elements make for a mysterious story? What sorts of characters make the story interesting? What kinds of clues would you provide for the reader? What information would you withhold to keep the reader in suspense?

3. You might like to play detective yourself. Jabez Wilson produces the ad from *The Morning Chronicle,* dated April 27, 1890. He tells Holmes and Watson that he has worked for the Red-headed League for two months. So, today should be June 27. However, the closing notice at the Red-headed League is dated October 9, 1890. See if you can find other discrepancies in the story. You might also look up the days of the week mentioned in the story in a perpetual calendar. Was Conan Doyle accurate? In your journal, make a note of your findings and decide whether—in your opinion—the discrepancies have a negative impact on the story.

Eleven Blue Men

Berton Roueché

Sometimes real-life mysteries provide greater suspense and require more complex problem-solving skills than those dreamed up in the most creative fiction. And the solution of real mysteries can make the difference between life or death. In this nonfiction essay doctors serve as detectives to crack the unusual case of eleven men admitted to a hospital with the same unknown ailment.

AT ABOUT EIGHT O'CLOCK on Monday morning, September 25, 1944, a ragged, aimless old man of eighty-two collapsed on the sidewalk on Dey Street, near the Hudson Terminal. Innumerable people must have noticed him, but he lay there alone for several minutes, dazed, doubled up with abdominal cramps, and in an agony of retching. Then a policeman came along. Until the policeman bent over the old man, he may have supposed that he had just a sick drunk on his hands; wanderers dropped by drink are common in that part of town in the early morning. It was not an opinion that he could have held for long. The old man's nose, lips, ears, and fingers were sky-blue. The policeman went to a telephone and put in an ambulance call to Beekman-Downtown Hospital, half a dozen blocks away. The old man was carried into the emergency room there at eight-thirty. By that time, he was unconscious and the blueness had spread over a large part of his body. The examining physician attributed the old man's morbid color to cyanosis, a condition that usually results from an insufficient supply of oxygen in the blood, and also noted that he was diarrheic and in a severe state of shock. The course of treatment prescribed by the doctor was conventional. It included an instant gastric lavage, heart stimulants, bed rest, and oxygen therapy. Presently the old man recovered an encouraging, if painful, consciousness and demanded, irascibly and in the name of God, to know what had happened to him. It was a question that, at the moment, nobody could answer with much confidence.

For the immediate record, the doctor made a free-hand diagnosis of carbon-monoxide poisoning—from what source, whether an automobile or a gas pipe, it was, of course, pointless even to guess. Then, because an isolated instance of gas poisoning is something of a rarity in a section of the city as crammed with human beings as downtown Manhattan, he and his colleagues in the emergency room braced themselves for at least a couple more victims. Their foresight was promptly and generously rewarded. A second man was rolled in at ten-twenty-five. Forty minutes later, an ambulance drove up with three more men. At eleven-twenty, two others were brought in. An additional two arrived during the next fifteen minutes. Around noon, still another was admitted. All of these nine men were also elderly and dilapidated, all had been in misery for at least an hour, and all were rigid, cyanotic, and in a state of shock. The entire body of one, a bony, seventy-three-year-old consumptive named John Mitchell, was blue. Five of the nine, including Mitchell, had been stricken in the Globe Hotel, a sunless, upstairs flophouse at 190 Park Row, and two in a similar place, called the Star Hotel, at 3 James Street. Another had been found slumped in the doorway of a condemned building on Park Row, not far from City Hall Park, by a policeman. The ninth had keeled over in front of the Eclipse Cafeteria, at 6 Chatham Square. At a quarter to seven that evening, one more aged blue man was brought in. He had been lying, too sick to ask for help, on his cot in a cubicle in the Lion Hotel, another flop-house, at 26 Bowery, since ten o'clock that morn-ing. A clerk had finally looked in and seen him.

By the time this last blue man arrived at the hospital, an investigation of the case by the De-partment of Health, to which all outbreaks of an epidemiological[1] nature must be reported, had been under way for five hours. Its findings thus far had not been illuminating. The investigation was con-ducted by two men. One was the Health Depart-ment's chief epidemiologist, Dr. Morris Greenberg, a small fragile, reflective man of fifty-seven, who is now acting director of the Bureau of Preventable Diseases; the other was Dr. Ottavio Pellitteri, a field epidemiologist, who, since, 1946, has been administrative medical inspector for the Bureau. He is thirty-six years old, pale, and stocky, and has a bristling black mustache. One day, when I was in Dr. Greenberg's office, he and Dr. Pellitteri told me about the case. Their recollection of it is, under-standably, vivid. The derelicts were the victims of a type of poisoning so rare that only ten previous outbreaks of it had been recorded in medical liter-ature. Of these, two were in the United States and two in Germany; the others had been reported in France, England, Switzerland, Algeria, Australia, and India. Up to September 25, 1944, the largest number of people stricken in a single outbreak was four. That was in Algeria, in 1926.

The Beekman-Downtown Hospital telephoned a report of the occurrence to the Health Depart-ment just before noon. As is customary, copies of the report were sent to all the Department's admin-istrative officers. "Mine was on my desk when I got back from lunch," Dr. Greenberg said to me. "It didn't sound like much. Nine persons believed to be suffering from carbon-monoxide poisoning had been admitted during the morning, and all of them said that they had eaten breakfast at the Eclipse Cafeteria, at 6 Chatham Square. Still, it was a job for us. I checked with the clerk who han-dles assignments and found that Pellitteri had gone out on it. That was all I wanted to know. If it amounted to anything, I knew he'd phone me be-fore making a written report. That's an arrange-ment we have here. Well, a couple of hours later I got a call from him. My interest perked right up."

"I was at the hospital," Dr. Pellitteri told me, "and I'd talked to the staff and most of the men.

[1]**epidemiological:** concerning the incidence, distribu-tion, and spread of a disease in a population.

There were ten of them by then, of course. They were sick as dogs, but only one was in really bad shape."

"That was John Mitchell." Dr. Greenberg put in. "He died the next night. I understand his con-dition was hopeless from the start. The others, in-cluding the old boy who came in last, pulled through all right. Excuse me, Ottavio, but I just thought I'd get that out of the way. Go on."

Dr. Pellitteri nodded. "I wasn't at all con-vinced that it was gas poisoning," he continued. "The staff was beginning to doubt it, too. The symptoms weren't quite right. There didn't seem to be any of the headache and general dopiness that you get with gas. What really made me suspicious was this: Only two or three of the men had eaten breakfast in the cafeteria at the same time. They had straggled in all the way from seven o'clock to ten. That meant that place would have had to be full of gas for at least three hours, which is prepos-terous. It also indicated that we ought to have a lot more sick people than we did. Those Chatham Square eating places have a big turnover. Well, to make sure, I checked with Bellevue, Gouverneur, St. Vincent's, and the other downtown hospitals. None of them had seen a trace of cyanosis. Then I talked to the sick men some more. I learned two interesting things. One was that they had all got sick right after eating. Within thirty minutes. The other was that all but one had eaten oatmeal, rolls and coffee. He ate just oatmeal. When ten men eat the same thing in the same place on the same day and then all come down with the same illness . . . I told Greenberg that my hunch was food poisoning."

"I was willing to rule out gas," Dr. Greenberg said. A folder containing data on the case lay on the desk before him. He lifted the cover thought-fully, then let it drop. "And I agreed that the oat-meal sounded pretty suspicious. That was as far as I was willing to go. Common, ordinary, everyday food poisoning—I gathered that was what Pellitteri had in mind—wasn't a very satisfying answer. For one thing, cyanosis is hardly symptomatic of that. On the other hand, diarrhea and severe vomiting are, almost invariably. But they weren't in the clin-ical picture, I found, except in two or three of the cases. Moreover, the incubation periods—the time lapse between eating and illness—were extremely short. As you probably know, most food poisoning is caused by eating something that has been con-taminated by bacteria. The useful offenders are the staphylococci—they're mostly responsible for boils and skin infections and so on—and the salmonella. The latter are related to the typhoid organism. In a staphylococcus case, the first symptoms rarely develop in under two hours. Often, it's closer to five. The incubation period in the other ranges from twelve to thirty-six hours. But here we were with something that hit in thirty minutes or less. Why, one of the men had got only as far as the sidewalk in front of the cafeteria before he was knocked out. Another fact that Pellitteri had dug up struck me as very significant. All of the men told him that the illness had come on with extraordinary suddenness. One minute they were feeling fine, and the next minute they were practically helpless. That was another point against the ordinary food-poisoning theory. Its onset is never that fast. Well, that suddenness began to look like a lead. It led me to suspect that some drug might be to blame. A quick and sudden reaction is characteristic of a great many drugs. So is the combination of cyanosis and shock."

"None of the men were on dope," Dr. Pellitteri said. "I told Greenberg I was sure of that. Their pleasure was booze."

"That was O.K.," Dr. Greenberg said. "They could have got a toxic dose of some drug by accident. In the oatmeal, most likely. I couldn't help thinking that the oatmeal was relevant to our problem. At any rate, the drug idea was very persuasive."

"So was Greenberg," Dr. Pellitteri remarked with a smile. "Actually, it was the only explanation in sight that seemed to account for everything we knew about the clinical and environmental picture."

"All we had to do now was prove it," Dr. Greenberg went on mildly. "I asked Pellitteri to get a blood sample from each of the men before leaving the hospital for a look at the cafeteria. We agreed he would send the specimens to the city toxicologist, Dr. Alexander O. Gettler, for an overnight analysis. I wanted to know if the blood contained methemoglobin. Methemoglobin is a compound that's formed only when any one of several drugs enters the blood. Gettler's report would tell us if we were at least on the right track. That is, it would give us a yes-or-no answer on drugs. If the answer was yes, then we could go on from there to identify the particular drug. How we would go about that would depend on what Pellitteri was about to turn up at the cafeteria. In the meantime, there was nothing for me to do but wait for their reports. I'd theorized myself hoarse."

Dr. Pellitteri, having attended to his bloodletting with reasonable dispatch, reached the Eclipse Cafeteria at around five o'clock. "It was about what I'd expected," he told me. "Strictly a horse market and dirtier than most. The sort of place where you can get a full meal for fifteen cents. There was a grind house on one side, a cigar store on the other, and the 'L' overhead. Incidentally, the Eclipse went out of business a year or so after I was there, but that had nothing to do with us. It was just coincidence. Well, the place looked deserted and the door was locked. I knocked, and a man came out of the back and let me in. He was one of our people, a health inspector for the Bureau of Food and Drugs, named Weinberg. His bureau had stepped into the case as a matter of routine, because of the reference to a restaurant in the notification report. I was glad to see him and to have his help. For one thing, he had put a temporary embargo on everything in the cafeteria. That's why it was closed up. His main job, though, was to check the place for violations of the sanitation code. He was finding plenty."

"Let me read you a few of Weinberg's findings," Dr. Greenberg said, extracting a paper from the folder on his desk. "None of them had any direct bearing on our problem, but I think they'll give you a good idea of what the Eclipse was like—what too many restaurants are like. This copy of his report lists fifteen specific violations. Here they are: 'Premises heavily infested with roaches. Fly infestation throughout premises. Floor defective in rear part of dining room. Kitchen walls and ceiling encrusted with grease and soot. Kitchen floor encrusted with dirt. Refuse under kitchen fixtures. Sterilizing facilities inadequate. Sink defective. Floor and walls at serving tables and coffee urns encrusted with dirt. Kitchen utensils encrusted with dirt and grease. Storage-cellar walls, ceiling, and floor encrusted with dirt. Floor and shelves in cellar covered with refuse and useless material. Cellar ceiling defective. Sewer pipe leaking. Open sewer line in cellar.' Well . . ." He gave me a squeamish smile and stuck the paper back in the folder.

"I can see it now," Dr. Pellitteri said. "And smell it. Especially the kitchen, where I spent most of my time. Weinberg had the proprietor and the cook out there, and I talked to them while he prowled around. They were very cooperative. Naturally. They were scared to death. They knew nothing about gas in the place and there was no sign of any, so I went to work on the food. None of what had been prepared for breakfast that morning was left. That, of course, would have been too much to hope for. But I was able to get together some of the kind of stuff that had gone into the men's breakfast, so that we could make a chemical determination at the Department. What I took was ground coffee, sugar, a mixture of evaporated milk and water that passed for cream, some bakery rolls, a five-pound carton of dry oatmeal, and some salt. The salt had been used in preparing the oatmeal. That morning, like every morning, the cook told me, he had prepared six gallons of oatmeal, enough to serve around a hundred and twenty-five people. To make it, he used five pounds of dry cereal, four gallons of water—regular city water—and a handful of salt. That was his term—a handful. There was an open gallon can of salt standing on the stove. He said the handful he'd put in that morning's oatmeal had come from that. He refilled the can on the stove every morning from a big supply can. He pointed out the big can—it was up on a shelf— and as I was getting it down to take with me, I saw another can, just like it, nearby. I took that one down, too. It was also full of salt, or, rather something that looked like salt. The proprietor said it wasn't salt. He said it was saltpetre—sodium nitrate—that he used in corning beef and in making pastrami. Well, there isn't any harm in saltpetre; it doesn't even act as an antiaphrodisiac, as a lot of people seem to think. But I wrapped it up with the other loot and took it along, just for fun. The fact is, I guess, everything in that damn place looked like poison."

After Dr. Pellitteri had deposited his loot with a Health Department chemist, Andrew J. Pensa, who promised to have a report ready by the following afternoon, he dined hurriedly at a restaurant in which he had confidence and returned to Chatham Square. There he spent the evening making the rounds of the lodging houses in the neighborhood. He had heard at Mr. Pensa's office that an eleventh blue man had been admitted to the hospital, and before going home he wanted to make sure that no other victims had been overlooked. By midnight, having covered all the likely places and having rechecked the downtown hospitals, he was satisfied. He repaired to his office and composed a formal progress report for Dr. Greenberg. Then he went home and to bed.

The next morning, Tuesday, Dr. Pellitteri dropped by the Eclipse, which was still closed but whose proprietor and staff he had told to return for questioning. Dr. Pellitteri had another talk with the proprietor and the cook. He also had a few inconclusive words with the rest of the cafeteria's employees—two dishwashers, a busboy, and a counterman. As he was leaving, the cook, who had apparently passed an uneasy night with his conscience, remarked that it was possible that he had absent-mindedly refilled the salt can on the stove from the one that contained saltpetre. "That was interesting," Dr. Pellitteri told me, "even though such a possibility had already occurred to me, and even though I didn't know whether it was important or not. I assured him that he had nothing to worry about. We had been certain all along that nobody had deliberately poisoned the old men." From the Eclipse, Dr. Pellitteri went on to Dr. Greenberg's office, where Dr. Gettler's report was waiting.

"Gettler's test for methemoglobin was positive." Dr. Greenberg said. "It had to be a drug now. Well, so far so good. Then we heard from Pensa."

"Greenberg almost fell out of his chair when he read Pensa's report," Dr. Pellitteri observed cheerfully.

"That's an exaggeration," Dr. Greenberg said. "I'm not easily dumfounded. We're inured to the incredible around here. Why a few years ago we had a case involving some numskull who stuck a fistful of potassium-thiocyanate crystals, a very nasty poison, in the coils of an office water cooler, just for a practical joke. However, I can't deny that Pensa rather taxed our credulity. What he had found was that the small salt can and the one that was supposed to be full of sodium nitrate both contained sodium *nitrite*. The other food samples, incidentally, were O.K."

"That also taxed my credulity," Dr. Pellitteri said.

Dr. Greenberg smiled. "There's a great deal of difference between nitrate and nitrite," he continued. "Their only similarity, which is an unfortunate one, is that they both look and taste more or less like ordinary table salt. Sodium nitrite isn't the most powerful poison in the world, but a little of it will do a lot of harm. If you remember, I said before that this case was almost without precedent—only ten outbreaks like it on record. Ten is practically none. In fact, sodium-nitrite poisoning is so unusual that some of the standard texts on toxicology don't even mention it. So Pensa's report was pretty startling. But we accepted it, of course, without question or hesitation. Facts are facts. And we were glad to. It seemed to explain everything very nicely. What I've been saying about sodium-nitrite poisoning doesn't mean that sodium nitrite itself is rare. Actually, it's fairly common. It's used in the manufacture of dyes and as a medical drug. We use it in treating certain heart conditions and for high blood pressure. But it also has another important use, one that made its presence at the Eclipse sound plausible. In recent years, and particularly during the war, sodium nitrite has been used as a substitute for sodium nitrate in preserving meat. The government permits it but stipulates that the finished meat must not contain more than one part of sodium nitrite per five thousand parts of meat. Cooking will safely destroy enough of that small quantity of the drug." Dr. Greenberg shrugged. "Well, Pellitteri had had the cook pick up a handful of salt—the same amount, as nearly as possible, as went into the oatmeal—and then had taken this to his office and found that it weighed approximately a hundred grams. So we didn't have to think twice to realize that the proportion of nitrite in that batch of cereal was considerably higher than one to five thousand. Roughly, it must have been around one to about eighty before cooking destroyed part of the nitrite. It certainly looked as though Gettler, Pensa, and the cafeteria cook between them had given us our answer. I called up Gettler and told him what Pensa had discovered and asked him to run a specific test for nitrites on his blood samples. He had, as a matter of course, held some blood back for later examination. His confirmation came through in a couple of hours. I went home that night feeling pretty good."

Dr. Greenberg's serenity was a fugitive one. He awoke on Wednesday morning troubled in mind. A question had occurred to him that he was unable to ignore. "Something like a hundred and twenty-five people ate oatmeal at the Eclipse that morning," he said to me, "but only eleven of them got sick. Why? The undeniable fact that those eleven old men were made sick by the ingestion of a toxic dose of sodium nitrite wasn't enough to rest on. I wanted to know exactly how much sodium nitrite each portion of that cooked oatmeal had contained. With Pensa's help again, I found out. We prepared a batch just like the one the cook had made on Monday. Then Pensa measured out six

ounces, the size of the average portion served at the Eclipse, and analyzed it. It contained two and a half grains of sodium nitrite. That explained why the hundred and fourteen other people did not become ill. The toxic dose of sodium nitrite is three grains. But it didn't explain how each of our eleven old men had received an additional half grain. It seemed extremely unlikely that the extra touch of nitrite had been in the oatmeal when it was served. It had to come in later. Then I began to get a glimmer. Some people sprinkle a little salt, instead of sugar, on hot cereal. Suppose, I thought, that the busboy, or whoever had the job of keeping the table salt shakers filled, had made the same mistake that the cook had. It seemed plausible. Pellitteri was out of the office—I've forgotten where—so I got Food and Drugs to step over to the Eclipse, which was still under embargo, and bring back the shakers for Pensa to work on. There were seventeen of them, all good sized, one for each table. Sixteen contained either pure sodium chloride or just a few inconsequential traces of sodium nitrite mixed in with the real salt, but the other was point thirty-seven percent nitrite. That one was enough. A spoonful of that salt contained a bit more than half a grain."

"I went over to the hospital Thursday morning," Dr. Pellitteri said. "Greenberg wanted me to check the table-salt angle with the men. They could tie the case up neatly for us. I drew a blank. They'd been discharged the night before, and God only knew where they were."

"Naturally," Dr. Greenberg said, "it would have been nice to know for a fact that the old boys all sat at a certain table and that all of them put about a spoonful of salt from that particular shaker on their oatmeal, but it wasn't essential. I was morally certain that they had. There just wasn't any other explanation. There was one other question, however. Why did they use so *much* salt? For my own peace of mind, I wanted to know. All of a sudden, I remembered Pellitteri had said they were all heavy drinkers. Well, several recent clinical studies have demonstrated that there is usually a subnormal concentration of sodium chloride in the blood of alcoholics. Either they don't eat enough to get sufficient salt or they lose it more rapidly than other people do, or both. Whatever the reasons are, the conclusion was all I needed. Any animal, you know, whether a mouse or a man, tends to try to obtain a necessary substance that his body lacks. The final question had been answered."

Discuss

1. Which statement best describes the process by which Doctors Pellitteri and Greenberg discovered what was wrong with the eleven blue men?

   a. They formed hunches that they tested on the basis of the men's symptoms and causes known to be related to those symptoms.

   b. They researched the complete medical backgrounds of the men to see what illnesses they might be susceptible to.

   c. They interviewed the men's friends and families to find out what they might have been exposed to.

2. Why were Pellitteri and Greenberg involved in the case of the eleven blue men? What were their jobs?

3. What was the first guess of the examining physician in diagnosing the condition the men suffered from? What was the basis of that diagnosis? Why was it rejected?

4. Why did Pellitteri suspect food poisoning was the cause of the men's illness? Why didn't Greenberg accept Pellitteri's diagnosis? What cause did Greenberg suspect instead?

5. What is methemoglobin? How did knowledge of it help the doctors?

6. By what process did the doctors discover the presence of sodium nitrite? Why was the sodium nitrite at the restaurant?

7. Why were just eleven men poisioned, when many people at the oatmeal containing sodium nitrite? How did the doctors discover the answer?

8. How did the fact that the men stricken were heavy drinkers complete the puzzle?

Explore

1. How would you characterize Roueché's narration of this incident? Is the description technical? Formal? Casual? Personal? Why do you suppose he uses this style?

2. Why do you suppose Roueché includes information about the appearance of the doctors, the names of other doctors who participate in the solution, and the description of the restaurant provided by the Health Department, details that don't appear strictly related to the solution?

For Your Journal

1. Turn this essay into a murder mystery story using the same problems, but providing a villain who intentionally uses sodium nitrite.

2. Which doctor are you more interested in—Dr. Greenberg or Dr. Pellitteri? Write a character sketch of the doctor. On the basis of what you have learned about how he works, describe his values, beliefs, interests, and concerns.

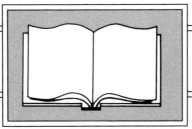

U N I T · F O U R

Challenges

Section A
Creatures Great
and Small

Section B
On Native Grounds

Section C
Hostilities

Creatures Great and Small

The world is made up of variety.
Think how dull it would be if you
lived in an environment with
everything the same color,
the same size, and, even worse,
the same species. Without diversity
life lacks an element of challenge,
appreciation, and possibly survival.
In this section you will read about
people's responses to animals
that often appear human.
You will need to judge whether
you would respond in similar
or different ways.

Thinking Like a Mountain

Aldo Leopold

The title of this excerpt from *A Sand County Almanac: and Sketches from Here and There* should intrigue you. What does it means to think like a mountain? Is such thought possible? After all, a mountain is a huge object— or is it? Aldo Leopold, a renowned naturalist, may surprise you into thinking differently not only about mountains but also about other natural things.

A DEEP CHESTY BAWL echoes from rimrock to rimrock,[1] rolls down the mountain, and fades into the far blackness of the night. It is an outburst of wild defiant sorrow, and of contempt for all the adversities of the world.

Every living thing (and perhaps many a dead one as well) pays heed to that call. To the deer it is a reminder of the way of all flesh, to the pine a forecast of midnight scuffles and of blood upon the snow, to the coyote a promise of gleanings to come, to the cowman a threat of red ink at the bank, to the hunter a challenge of fang against bullet. Yet behind these obvious and immediate hopes and fears there lies a deeper meaning, known only to the mountain itself. Only the mountain has lived long enough to listen objectively to the howl of a wolf.

Those unable to decipher the hidden meaning know nevertheless that it is there, for it is felt in all wolf country, and distinguishes that country from all other land. It tingles in the spine of all who hear wolves by night, or who scan their tracks by day. Even without sight or sound of wolf, it is implicit in a hundred small events: the midnight whinny of a pack horse, the rattle of rolling rocks, the bound of a fleeing deer, the way shadows lie under the spruces. Only the ineducable tyro[1] can fail to sense the presence or absence of wolves, or the fact that mountains have a secret opinion about them.

My own conviction on this score dates from the day I saw a wolf die. We were eating lunch on a high rimrock, at the foot of which a turbulent river elbowed its way. We saw what we thought was a doe fording the torrent, her breast awash in white water. When she climbed the bank toward us and shook out her tail, we realized our error: it was a wolf. A half-dozen others, evidently grown pups, sprang from the willows and all joined in a welcoming mêlée[3] of wagging tails and playful maulings. What was literally a pile of wolves writhed and tumbled in the center of an open flat at the foot of our rimrock.

In those days we had never heard of passing up a chance to kill a wolf. In a second we were pumping lead into the pack, but with more excitement than accuracy: how to aim a steep downhill shot is always confusing. When our rifles were empty, the old wolf was down, and a pup was dragging a leg into impassable slide-rocks.

We reached the old wolf in time to watch a fierce green fire dying in her eyes. I realized then, and have known ever since, that there was something new to me in those eyes—something known only to her and to the mountain. I was young then, and full of trigger-itch; I thought that because fewer wolves meant more deer, that no wolves would mean hunters' paradise. But after seeing the green fire die, I sensed that neither the wolf nor the mountain agreed with such a view.

Since then I have lived to see state after state extirpate its wolves. I have watched the face of

[1]**rimrock:** rock forming the boundary or upper part of a steep slope.
[2]**tyro:** beginner.

[3]**mêlée:** noisy, confusing fight or struggle.

many a newly wolfless mountain, and seen the south-facing slopes wrinkle with a maze of new deer trails. I have seen every edible bush and seedling browsed, first to anaemic desuetude,[4] and then to death. I have seen every edible tree defoliated[5] to the height of a saddlehorn. Such a mountain looks as if someone had given God a new pruning shears, and forbidden Him all other exercise. In the end the starved bones of the hoped-for deer herd, dead of its own too-much, bleach with the bones of the dead sage, or molder under the high-lined junipers.

I now suspect that just as a deer herd lives in mortal fear of its wolves, so does a mountain live in mortal fear of its deer. And perhaps with better cause, for while a buck pulled down by wolves can be replaced in two or three years, a range pulled down by too many deer may fail of replacement in as many decades.

[4]**desuetude:** disuse.
[5]**defoliated:** deprived of leaves.

So also with cows. The cowman who cleans his range of wolves does not realize that he is taking over the wolf's job of trimming the herd to fit the range. He has not learned to think like a mountain. Hence we have dustbowls, and rivers washing the future into the sea.

We all strive for safety, prosperity, comfort, long life, and dullness. The deer strives with his supple legs, the cowman with trap and poison, the statesman with pen, the most of us with machines, votes, and dollars, but it all comes to the same thing: peace in our time. A measure of success in this is all well enough, and perhaps is a requisite to objective thinking, but too much safety seems to yield only danger in the long run. Perhaps this is behind Thoreau's dictum: In wildness is the salvation of the world. Perhaps this is the hidden meaning in the howl of the wolf, long known among mountains, but seldom perceived among men.

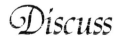

Discuss

1. In the second paragraph the wolf's call means something different to the deer, the pine, the coyote, the cowman, and the hunter. What does that howl mean to each of these living things, and why?

2. In earlier times, what justification did young, trigger-happy Leopold give for killing the mother wolf and her young?

3. What does Leopold learn?

4. What is the mountain's secret opinion of wolves?

Explore

1. How do you know whether Leopold's ecological view of balance between wolves and deer is accurate? What information can you find about wolves in the wild?

2. Leopold was influenced by author Henry David Thoreau who said, "In wildness is the salvation of the earth." Do you agree with this statement? Why or why not?

3. Explain the author's last sentence. How does it help you begin to think like a mountain?

4. What do you believe is Leopold's argument and why does he title his essay "Thinking Like a Mountain"?

For Your Journal

1. Write an essay either supporting or opposing hunting. Be prepared to defend your point of view in a class debate.

2. Describe your reaction to Leopold's account of shooting the wolves.

3. Research an environmental controversy, such as that concerning the destruction of rain forests. Many people worry that the damage to these forests will have serious effects upon climate, air, soil, and other natural things. Others emphasize the less harmful effects. You might want to forage through journals and publications of organizations that seek to protect wildlife. Sum up the issues, including your own opinion.

A Blessing

James Wright

Have you ever experienced a sudden feeling of great pleasure over something very simple? It could have been an unexpected scene, a startling awareness of moment, or just about anything else. Strangely, such a sensation is often accompanied by a subtle sadness, probably because you realize that the pleasure is fleeting. When you read this poem, try to picture a scene: two people driving somewhere stop to rest or enjoy the roadside view. And then something happens.

Just off the highway to Rochester, Minnesota,
Twilight bounds softly forth on the grass.
And the eyes of those two Indian ponies
Darken with kindness.
They have come gladly out of the willows
To welcome my friend and me.
We step over the barbed wire into the pasture
Where they have been grazing all day, alone.
They ripple tensely, they can hardly contain their happiness
That we have come.
They bow shyly as wet swans. They love each other.
There is no loneliness like theirs.
At home once more,
They begin munching the young tufts of spring in the darkness.
I would like to hold the slenderer one in my arms,
For she has walked over to me
And nuzzled my left hand.
She is black and white,
Her mane falls wild on her forehead,
And the light breeze moves me to caress her long ear
That is delicate as the skin over a girl's wrist.
Suddenly I realize
That if I stepped out of my body I would break
Into blossom.

Discuss

1. What hint do you get that the speaker is traveling?

2. The speaker establishes a relationship between the people and the ponies of this poem. It is as if he and his friend are the guests of the horses. What in the poem suggests this sort of relationship?

3. Why does the speaker say, "They love each other," and immediately follow by saying, "There is no loneliness like theirs."

4. The last three lines of the poem express a sudden realization, an insight. Explain what the speaker really means when he says, "if I stepped out of my body I would break / Into blossom."

Explore

1. Which images in this poem are most important?

2. This poem relies heavily on imagery conveyed by similes, comparisons between dissimilar objects using the words *like* or *as*. Pick out the two similes in this poem and give your impressions of their effects.

For Your Journal

Recall a moment in your life when you suddenly felt ecstatic over something, such as a vista in the mountains, the appearance of a spectacular bird, or an evening around a campfire with friends. Put your feelings into words. Set the scene descriptively with images. Try using similes. Does what you have written bring back the feelings you once had? Why or why not?

The Jersey Heifer

Peggy Harding Love

Everyone has a vision of the idyllic life, peaceful and perfect. In this vision, harsh reality doesn't intrude. The story you are about to read presents a conflict between a vision and reality, as the characters try to extend their dream life to their farm animals. When you have finished the story, you will perhaps wonder what is to become of the dream.

IN OCTOBER THE COWS went apple-crazy. The sweet, sun-warmed apple smell drifted down from the orchard, tempting them unbearably; and by afternoon one or the other—the heifer usually, she was the mischief-maker—would have nudged down a rail from the old wooden fence around the pasture. Once, only once, young Phoebe Matthews looked out the kitchen window and caught them in the act, but the picture stayed forever in her mind, an image of transcendent innocence and freedom. Leaping negligently, her hoofs tucked up delicately, the Jersey heifer[1] went over the lower rails like a deer, and close behind, clumsy but with drooling haste, Daisy, the three-year-old Guernsey,[2] stepped clumsily out, one stiff leg at a time, banging her plump udder with shocking heedlessness against the bar.

They trotted eagerly along the quiet dirt lane, turning their wary heads from side to side; and later, near milking time, Phoebe and Joe, her husband, had come upon them drunk with bliss in the long grass of the orchard. Each time they were discovered there, the cows stood perfectly still, their red and tawny coats bright against the blue sky, their soft wide eyes looking out innocently among the apple branches. Long threads of saliva trailed from their velvety muzzles and glistened in the late sunlight, and under their hoofs the crushed and rotting apples gave off a heady fragrance.

Always at the sight of them there Phoebe's heart leaped in delight. She hated to drive them

out; but Joe, slapping lightly at their smooth, hard flanks, would chivvy them back to the pasture with a slow-moving, gentle stubbornness that matched their own. "Apples cut down Daisy's milk," he told Phoebe firmly. "I've got to wire that fence," but he lingered beside her, smiling to see the tipsy heifer prance off down the pasture.

"Let them go," Phoebe pleaded, begging as earnestly as for herself, "let them have a little freedom. I'll bring them back when they get out." "Well," Joe said, musing, "well," and he looked off over the fields that were so newly theirs. "The apples will be picked pretty soon now anyway," he said, and running his thumb lightly down Phoebe's arm, he headed back to where he had left the horses hitched to the spring-tooth harrow.

By the end of October they had picked all the apples on the trees and stored them in barrels in the cellar. They were Baldwins, small, tart and juicy, the best-flavored apples anywhere, Joe insisted; and though the trees were old and shamefully neglected, though curculio[3] and scab had made their inroads and no one bought Baldwins any more, still Joe and Phoebe knelt carefully in the long grass, collecting even the windfalls and hauling them up the wagon ramp into the upper story of the old bank barn for cider-making.

They were pressing cider the afternoon the county agent stopped by for his first visit, and the first thing he told them was that the orchard should be cut down. Those old trees would never show a profit, he said, no matter how they were

[1] **heifer:** young cow that has not borne a calf.
[2] **Guernsey:** a breed of cow.
[3] **curculio:** worm harmful to fruit.

pruned and sprayed. Joe walked around the farm with him with a pocket edition of Thoreau[4] sticking out of his hip pocket—he liked to read it while he was resting the horses or waiting for the cider to drain. Pax, their springer spaniel, raced ahead while Phoebe, trailing behind, listened uneasily to the agent's suggestions. The orchard should go, the horses should be replaced by a tractor and modern equipment, new fences should be built, the chickens not allowed to run; and when Phoebe said in alarm, "But we like horses!" the agent smiled like a wise, indulgent uncle.

"You know, I'm always glad to see city folks coming back to the farm," he said. "A fine young couple like you, not afraid of hard work, and I can see you've done a lot here already, why, there's no reason at all why you shouldn't have a good, solid return on your investment. But you've got to remember, first and last, farming is a business."

"We figured farming was a way of life," Joe said. For a long moment they all were silent, and Phoebe, kneeling suddenly, gave Pax a fierce, quiet hug. After a minute Joe said: "I guess you better not put us down as farmers. We're grateful for your advice and we sure need a lot of it, but maybe we're aiming at two different things. We don't want a business, or an investment either. We just want to live right and do right by our land and animals." Joe's smile was apologetic and a little troubled, but his voice was earnest. "Put us down as shiftless no-accounts or crazy damn fools," he said, "but I guess we'd rather live peaceful than make money."

"No, son, I'll put you down as two romantic dreamers and come around again next spring." The agent got in his car and was starting out the dirt lane when he leaned out the window again, grinning like a paternal old tomcat and pointing to where the pasture fence rail was down again. "Your cows are out," he called. "Who's boss around here, you or bossy?"[5] and, laughing slyly, he jounced away in his dusty sedan.

For a little while Phoebe and Joe stood where he left them, quiet and abstracted in the pale, slanting sunlight. Phoebe's hands were cold and sticky from the apple juice, and she held them up in the sun to warm them. At last she said, "I'd better get the cows." The orchard was stripped

now, completely appleless, so she wouldn't find them there; but the scent of apples still hung everywhere in the air, filling the cows with yearning, and searching restlessly for fulfillment they still broke out of the pasture. Joe looked at Phoebe as if he hadn't heard her. "What if he's right?" he said broodingly. "Maybe it's all an impossible dream." But when Phoebe protested, "No, he's wrong! We've never been so happy," Joe smiled and touched her reassuringly, because of course it was true.

In a minute Joe went back to the barn to finish pressing the last batch of cider, and Phoebe started down the lane. "Co' ba, co' ba," she sang out dreamily, taking comfort from the sound of her voice in the quiet air. It was a call for cows she had read in a book, but of course they never came. Back in the barn she heard Joe snort with laughter, and off behind the orchard great rustlings and upheavals in the underbrush signaled that Pax was on his way. "No, not you, foolish," she cried before he even got there, but he bounded out through the sumac beside the road, grinning and panting, with dirt from his diggings all over his face and tongue and his long, silky ears matted with burrs. She was going to let him greet her before she sent him back, but after a token snuffle at her legs he ignored her utterly. He zigzagged wildly across the lane, nose in the dust, and in a minute he was off again, hot after a recent rabbit.

Phoebe walked on past the fenced-in vegetable garden, nipped now by frost but still green with broccoli and parsley, still orderly and serene; past the cropped-down empty pasture that sloped gently to the stream. The woods beyond flamed with color in the horizontal sunlight, and in the pasture the fierce old pin oak stood all alone in crimson splendor among the hummocks and the browning grass. Up the lane two sets of hoofprints lay guilelessly in the dust—one set large and clumsy, moving ponderously after the smaller, dancing crescents that led the way and among them, steaming faintly in the cooling air, three insolent small cowflops on the rutted road. "They can't have been out long," Phoebe said out loud to herself. "That minx, that little devil," and, smiling ruefully, looking all around, she walked on after them.

Ever since they moved to the farm eight months ago she had started talking to herself. She wasn't lonely—even when Joe was working off in the fields she had the animals for company; but she

---

[4]**Thoreau:** Henry David Thoreau, author of *Walden,* a record of the two years he spent at Walden Pond in Massachusetts in an attempt to live simply and in harmony with nature.

[5]**bossy:** a term commonly applied to cows.

talked to them the way she talked to herself, loving, reassuring and scolding in calm, sensible words that vanquished any wayward feelings of uncertainty, any possible tremor of fear. Yet she wondered sometimes—she wondered now, with an unreasoning, anxious moment of panic as she walked down the lane—why she should ever be uncertain and afraid. After the lost, dismal years when she had followed Joe from one Army camp to another, the farm seemed like a paradise. Joe had been hopelessly miserable in the Army, putting in his whole three years as cook's helper in vast base kitchens in the South. With dogged non-cooperation he stayed a p.f.c.[6] throughout the war, unable to adjust to necessary evils and ridden by a constant sense of guilt, of being party to an infinite wrong.

Phoebe suffered with him in nearby furnished rooms, clerking in five-and-tens or typing in sweltering, alien offices. On weekends they rushed together in joy and despair, and lying in some mildewed, roach-infested haven they talked with helpless longing of the North, of the small New England college where they had met, of the good life they must find away from all this. It seemed to them that love and innocence had been destroyed everywhere, and that all the values of the world they knew had become false and unreal. Without their knowing quite how it happened, the good life of their desperate Sunday longings gradually came to mean a small farm of their own, in a climate with decent, changing seasons, where they could raise their own food, earn just what they needed and no more and live in honesty and freedom. Only there, starting a new life from scratch, did goodness and integrity seem possible. It didn't matter that they were both city-bred: the last few months before Joe got his discharge they pored in fierce absorption over the Strout farm real estate catalogues, and Phoebe took out every book in the public library on vegetable crops, dairy management and poultry-raising for profit.

They bought the farm on a GI loan[7]—ninety rolling north New Jersey acres, a quarter-mile back from the highway and no improvements. There were plenty of reasons why it was cheap—the sagging clapboard house, the long dirt lane that drifted shut in winter and ran with mud in spring, the hand pump at the sink and the dirt floor in the

stable; but Joe and Phoebe looked at the mulberry tree and the maples, the lush curves of the hayfields, the broad shallow stream in the pasture, the thirty acres of well-grown woods so silent you could hear the mushrooms growing. They bought it in November and moved in in February. They had a mortgage Joe felt they could handle and enough money saved up to buy some stock and tide them over the first year.

For Joe the core of the farm was the fields and topsoil and green crops making their intricate, purposeful growth—he had been going to teach botany once; but from the beginning it was the animals Phoebe loved most of all. She saw the whole farm as a combination Eden[8] and Noah's Ark,[9] where she and Joe and Pax and the cows and horses could live together as joint tenants on equal terms in innocence and mutual respect. In her heart she could not believe that God had made her truly different from the animals she loved, born in sin with a heritage of guilt; and she would gladly have traded all her human knowledge and foresight for Pax's trustfulness or the Jersey heifer's wild, free spirit. "There's a serpent in your garden," Joe had teased her one day in May, holding up a wriggling five-foot black snake he had found behind the barn, but Phoebe's faith had not been shaken. She knew black snakes were harmless and ate lots of rats and mice. "Or chickens or eggs," Joe added dubiously; but he had built a fine tight henhouse, and he let the snake writhe peacefully away.

Up by the jog in the road Phoebe found the cows. They were off on the edge of the woods, nosing around in the faded goldenrod and wild asters under two ancient, half-dead crab apple trees. There was nothing there but a few dried-up, worm-hollowed crab apples, and the cows seemed apathetic, sunk in depression. "Don't look at me like that," Phoebe said, "it isn't my fault." The Jersey stared at her with great accusing eyes, her long fringed eyelashes sticking out beneath the gentle curve of her pale, sharp horns. She held her head low, petulantly, the warm black markings on the dainty face shading away to the velvety umbers of her chest and back, her broad saucy nose thrust out

[6]**p.f.c.:** private first class, a low rank in the Army.
[7]**GI loan:** government-issued loan given at a low interest rate to a military veteran for buying a home.

[8]**Eden:** Garden of Eden, the place in the Old Testament where people and animals lived in contentment.
[9]**Noah's Ark:** In the Old Testament Noah, warned by God of a terrible flood designed to wipe out evildoers, assembles in a ship a male and a female of every kind of animal known, so that when the waters recede animal life can be renewed.

and her nostrils working slowly. When Phoebe touched her muzzle, she tossed her head and leaped sharply back.

"All right, if that's the way you feel," Phoebe said. "Come on, Daisy, we'll let her sulk." Phoebe put her arm across Daisy's broad russet-patched rump, and obediently Daisy lumbered back to the dusty road. She plodded slowly back toward the farm, now and then stopping in her tracks and turning her shy, hornless forehead to look around at Phoebe. When Phoebe clapped her on the hip she went on amiably, switching her tail rhythmically behind her in the late chill air.

Before they had gone far, Phoebe heard the Jersey scrambling back onto the road and the quick, light thud of her hoofs coming after them. Phoebe smiled to herself and kept on, purposely not looking back; but in a moment she became aware of a strange, unnerving silence. The quiet struck her suddenly as deeply suspicious, even terrifying, and for a long, disoriented instant she felt herself walking down an endless alien road surrounded by unimaginable hidden dangers. She stopped, whirled quickly and found the heifer so close behind her that her horns could not have been an inch away from the seat of her jeans. "What are you doing?" Phoebe cried sharply. "Go on, you get in front of me." But the Jersey stood her ground stubbornly, head lowered and eyes rolling with audacity. After a moment Phoebe went on, walking stiff and wary, driving Daisy before her and turning her head every minute to look distrustfully behind. "Cut it out now," she ordered fiercely, stopping, turning and going on uneasily; but all the way back to the barn the Jersey followed a hairbreadth behind, the bracketed horns lowered and dark eyes rolling boldly while her hoofs stepped delicately in perfect silence in the soft dust of the road.

"She threatened me, she threatened me all the way," Phoebe told Joe when she got back. She was laughing, but hurt and outraged just the same, and the strange nightmare feeling had not quite worn off. She had fastened Daisy in her stanchion[10] in the stable below, on the ground floor of the barn, brought her hay and grain, jockeyed the heifer out through the stable door into the pasture and replaced—how many times now?—the fallen fence rail. The sun was nearly gone and she was shivering in a sweater when she went up the steep crude stairs from the stable to the upper story, through the narrow trap door where they threw down the

[10]**stanchion:** neck support that keeps a cow in place.

hay. Joe had finished the last batch of cider and was lining up the clear amber jugs beside the door, ready for loading on the Model A tomorrow to take to town. Discarded apples and the pressed-out apple cakes lay in a heap below the haymow, and in the cavernous gloom the autumn smell of apples, sweet and sour, mingled with the summer smell, dusty and sweet, of tender-cut green timothy and clover.

"That heifer thinks she's pretty cute," Joe said, pulling on his leather jacket, getting ready to go. "I think I'll keep Daisy in tonight after milking. Maybe the Jersey won't wander without her." Leaving the wide wagon doors open to the last rays of the sun, they went out of the barn together and up the path to the house. It was time to get the milk pail from the kitchen, time to start the fire for supper. "What are we having?" Joe asked, putting his long arm across Phoebe's shoulders. "What do you think, silly?" Phoebe said wearily, dreamily. "Apple fritters, apple butter, apple pie."

It was late that night, so late it was early morning, that Phoebe woke up suddenly with her heart pounding heavily. She sat up in bed listening tensely and in a moment she heard it, a terrible bawling cry from somewhere outside. "Joe, Joe," she cried, shaking him frantically, "somebody's crying terribly." He struggled up and in the dark bedroom they listened for the sound. At once it came again, a strangling, agonized bawl rising hideous with pain and terror through the cold black night.

"It's the heifer," Joe said, leaping out of bed and searching in the dark for his clothes. "That's not Daisy's voice, it's the heifer, somewhere near the barn." He was pulling on his pants and shoes blindly, fumbling in haste. "Oh, hurry," Phoebe cried, "please hurry," and she scrambled wildly on the cold bare floor trying to find the place where she had dropped her clothes.

"Light the lamp first, Phoebe," Joe said. "No, baby, please, light the lamp first so I can get down there fast. Then you can dress." His voice calmed her a little and in a moment she had found the matches and lit the kerosene lamp that stood on the old pine dresser. Joe's back and arms made great black shadows on the ceiling, flailing into his heavy sweater, and then he picked up the lamp and clattered out, down the narrow boxed-in stairs. Dressing as fast as she could, shivering with cold and fear, she heard Joe downstairs unhooking the big flashlight that hung in the kitchen. His footsteps strode across the kitchen, Pax's claws clicking behind, and both of them rushed out into the night. In a minute she was dressed herself and running for the barn, a lantern in her hand, through the clear, chill blackness.

The bellowing grew closer, more localized, and she headed up the wagon ramp and through the wide door of the barn's upper story. On the other side of the floor Joe's flashlight lay on the rough boards, throwing an arc of light across the shadowy loft. The apple heap was trampled, disarrayed, and the scattered fruit rolled, thumping hollowly, under her stumbling feet. Pax stood stiffly, cautious and curious, and beyond him Joe knelt beside the open trap door, the trap door for forking hay down to the stable. Phoebe saw the opening filled with a grotesque, meaningless shape, and then she saw it was the heifer, hanging head down in the narrow stairwell. All she could see was the slender rump and lower back wedged tight in the aperture, the hind legs caught on the floor boards, kicking feebly, and the long fringed tail thrashing blindly back and forth across the pitiful, terror-soiled buttocks. From below, the gasping cries came up in rhythmic agony, hushed a little but not stopped by Joe's quiet voice talking and talking to her as he crouched at the opening, trying to see how she was caught.

"The apples," Phoebe moaned, flinging herself down beside him, "she smelled the apples and came to find them." But Joe had jumped up, taking the flashlight, and was running out and around to the stable door below. Phoebe ran after, her heart hammering, the lantern swinging insanely from her hand, and Pax eager at her heels. The low, oak-beamed ceiling and thick stone walls of the stable made a warm, cozy cave, and in it the heifer hung crazily upside down, her head and one foreleg wedged at an impossible angle between two treads of the heavy, ladder-like stairs. The wedged foreleg was broken, bone thrusting through the skin, and in her struggles she was slowly strangling herself. In the lantern light her eyes rolled whitely, blindly, and the helpless, rasping cries grew steadily fainter. Beyond the plank partition the horses stomped restlessly in their stalls, and through it all Daisy stood facing the stairwell, shaking her head in her stanchion and shifting ceaselessly in troubled bewilderment on her clean straw bedding. She lowed nervously, swinging her hindquarters from one side to the other while Joe and Phoebe worked desperately with the tortured heifer.

"If we could saw the stair!" Phoebe cried in anguish. "Wouldn't that free her?"

"It's no use," Joe said. "The weight of her fall would snap her neck. Phoebe, you'd better get the gun."

"No, Joe, oh, no! Can't we lift her, can't we try again?" she begged frantically.

Joe's face was drawn and despairing. "It's no use. She's close to six hundred pounds and there's no way to lever her up." The heifer bawled again, a hopeless choking cry, and in the lantern light her free leg kicked futilely in the air. "She's suffering, Phoebe. Get the gun."

Phoebe had turned, blindly, and was rushing out the door when Joe called, "Phoebe, bring a knife too, the sharp knife in the kitchen." For a moment she didn't understand, and then she turned back whimpering in horror. "No, no, we can't. I won't!" Across the shadowy stable Joe's voice rose in furious torment. "Get the knife! You know we can't waste food." He stared at her relentlessly. "We wanted a farm, didn't we? To make our own life, our own food? We've eaten meat all our lives, now we've got to earn it."

Wordlessly Phoebe went out, Joe's voice, soft and exhausted now, calling after her, "Hurry, baby, I don't want to leave her." Running mechanically back to the house, Phoebe kept thinking dully, the gun and the knife, the gun and the knife. The .22 rifle for shooting rats, used only twice even for that, and the long clean knife, the knife for slicing cabbage from the garden, for cutting the fresh-baked bread she was so proud of. With the flashlight she found the gun and the box of cartridges on the parlor mantel, the knife in the kitchen drawer, and not thinking at all, moving in a desperate, mindless agony she ran with them back to the stable. Joe still stood beside the heifer, his arm under the tawny, gasping chest in unavailing support, still comforting the Jersey in a hoarse, gentle voice, while Pax lay quiet in the straw, alert and watching, and Daisy lowed uneasily.

Phoebe laid the knife, the gun and cartridges beside Joe and turned away. She went to Daisy quickly and unfastened her stanchion, turning her toward the door out to the barnyard. With clumsy hands she got the door open and Daisy out, the stiff cow legs hesitating as always before the step over the doorsill. She walked beside her down the slope of the pasture, and they were well away from the stable when Phoebe heard the shot. She stopped then, letting Daisy swing slowly on by herself into the darkness, and for a long moment she stood quiet, shaking in the cold.

She was still standing there when Joe shouted from the stable, "Phoebe, call Pax." Numbly she walked back to the door, and in a fleeting glimpse she saw the heifer hanging limp in the lamplight, a dark stain on the stairs beneath her head, and Joe shoving Pax roughly away from a bucket that stood on the floor. Pax came reluctantly when she called, and holding him wearily, detachedly, without love, she took him with her back to the house.

When Joe came in they sat in the cold kitchen for several minutes before they went to bed. At last Joe said, "I'll try and get Mr. Myers first thing in the morning to help me butcher." He looked at Phoebe sadly in exhaustion. "You know we had to, don't you?" She looked at him hopelessly, nodding slowly. "It was all my fault," she said, "all of it. I wouldn't let you wire the fence. I killed her, I killed our sweet Jersey heifer," and when Joe put his arms around her she finally began to cry. "No, baby, don't say that," Joe said painfully. "It was a crazy accident and no one's fault." But Phoebe shook her head. "I killed her. I laughed when she pushed down the fence rail, I didn't care. I liked her to be saucy. And only when she threatened me," Phoebe sobbed, "only her horns, only her horns made me afraid."

After her tears Phoebe slept, but she woke early, long before milking time. She lay quietly in bed, her body aching, her mind calm but filled with a clear despair. Beside her Joe slept deeply, and for a moment she felt a bitter, shocked wave of resentment that he still slept, escaping so easily; but turning her head stiffly on the pillow, she saw the anxious lines tensing the sleeping eyelids, the jaw clenched tight and grinding faintly in a dream of agonized effort. Looking at his sleeping face, she was washed with shame and wracking love—beside his goodness, his unforced selflessness, she was a monster of childish frailty. Oh, it's easy, it's easy, her mind whispered, to scream and run and cover your eyes, but how much harder to pull the trigger in love, to bleed the dead for the sake of the living. Always, always Joe had had the hard part and she the easy mournings, the easy joys. For a moment in the cold gray light she thought hopefully: It will be different when we have children. Then the hard part will be mine, our life will be fairer; but when she tried to vision it she saw with aching conviction that even then it wouldn't change. After the painful hour of birth all would be as before, and she saw herself a wayward, feckless mother, overemotional, given to reasonless euphorias and panics, unable to provide that calm and certainty that children need.

Just before sunrise Phoebe got up and went down to start the kitchen stove. Pax slept curled tightly in his wicker chair, but when he woke he unwound happily, yawning and stretching down onto the floor, and came up wagging his wavy-haired rear. At first she looked at him with horror, unable to touch him, remembering in a flash his avid interest in the bucket in the stable. He came to her like a friendly, handsome stranger, and even when she knelt, suddenly humble, and stroked his soft liver-and-white coat and burr-brocaded ears, she went on thinking: But how can I ever really know him, know the real meaning of his life?

She went on out for firewood and kindling, and coming back from the woodpile with her arms full she stopped above the pasture, shivering in the still, gray light. Below the pin oak Daisy lay placidly on the drying grass, her head held high in quiet dignity as she chewed faithfully on her cud. The fence rail was still down where the heifer had got out last night, but Daisy ignored it, content by herself in the deserted pasture. Like Pax, she met the morning serene, untouched by tragedy, and for a long time Phoebe stood watching her from another world. Of course they can't care, she thought, watching all alone; it's part of their innocence. She thought of all the innocent ones—the horses and chickens, the black snakes and the rats—and she knew at last that she was hopelessly excluded, forever responsible. The serpent had been there in the garden all the time, a thousand apples joyfully offered and taken. She heard again the county agent's wise, indulgent voice, and already she saw the barbed wire strung along the wooden fence posts. Daisy's next calf born and sent away, flock after flock of chickens in their biennial cycle of birth, production and early, practical death. She turned away, lonely and chilled, but with her armful of firewood she went on resolutely through her own human cycle, up the steps and into the kitchen to kindle once more the comforting fire for breakfast.

Discuss

1. Why do the cows in this story go "apple-crazy"?

2. The heifer acts like a child who enjoys playing pranks. Phoebe indulges in the amusement brought by these pranks. What is the result of this indulgence? What parallel could you draw between the way she treats the heifer and the way some parents treat their children?

3. Why does the heifer have to be destroyed?

4. Explain the contrast between the values of Phoebe and her husband and those of the county agent.

5. Whose point of view, the county agent's or Phoebe and Joe's, do you support?

Explore

1. What insight do you gain when Phoebe says, "Let them go, let them have a little freedom."

2. What is revealed by having Joe walk around with an edition of Thoreau sticking out of his pocket?

3. What was the "infinite wrong" Joe feels he was a party to?

4. At one point Joe holds up a snake and says to Phoebe, "There's a serpent in your garden." What is the significance of this statement at that time and later in the story?

5. The serpent and Phoebe's garden also are metaphors. What do they represent? What things represent Phoebe's innocence?

For Your Journal

1. Do you favor farms run as businesses, or as a special way of life close to animals and nature? Argue your point of view convincingly in an essay.

2. Write a character sketch of Phoebe. Do you see her in a favorable or unfavorable light? What are her strong points? Her weak points?

Grizzly

John McPhee

This essay from *Coming into the Country* offers a realistic portrait of the grizzly bear. Too often, people project human personalities onto animals, sometimes romanticizing them and sometimes brutalizing them. What is your attitude toward grizzlies? When you have read this essay, see if your attitude has changed.

WE PASSED FIRST through stands of fireweed, and then over ground that was wine-red with the leaves of bearberries. There were curlewberries, too, which put a deep-purple stain on the hand. We kicked at some wolf scat,[1] old as winter. It was woolly and white and filled with the hair of a snowshoe hare. Nearby was a rich inventory of caribou pellets and, in increasing quantity as we moved downhill, blueberries—an outspreading acreage of blueberries. Fedeler stopped walking. He touched my arm. He had in an instant become even more alert than he usually was, and obviously apprehensive. His gaze followed straight on down our intended course. What he saw there I saw now. It appeared to me to be a hill of fur. "Big boar[2] grizzly," Fedeler said in a near-whisper. The bear was about a hundred steps away, in the blueberries, grazing. The head was down, the hump high. The immensity of muscle seemed to vibrate slowly—to expand and contract, with the grazing. Not berries alone but whole bushes were going into the bear. He was big for a barren-ground grizzly. The brown bears of Arctic Alaska (or grizzlies; they are no longer thought to be different) do not grow to the size they will reach on more ample diets elsewhere. The barren-ground grizzly will rarely grow larger than six hundred pounds.

"What if he got too close?" I said.

[1]**wolf scat:** wolf droppings.
[2]**boar:** male.

Fedeler said, "We'd be in real trouble."

"You can't outrun them," Hession said.

A grizzly, no slower than a racing horse, is about half again as fast as the fastest human being. Watching the great mound of weight in the blueberries, with a fifty-five-inch waist and a neck more than thirty inches around, I had difficulty imagining that he could move with such speed, but I believed it, and was without impulse to test the proposition. Fortunately, a slight southerly wind was coming up the Salmon valley. On its way to us, it passed the bear. The wind was relieving, coming into our faces, for had it been moving the other way the bear would not have been placidly grazing. There is an old adage that when a pine needle drops in the forest the eagle will see it fall; the deer will hear it when it hits the ground; the bear will smell it. If the boar grizzly were to catch our scent, he might stand on his hind legs, the better to try to see. Although he could hear well and had an extraordinary sense of smell, his eyesight was not much better than what was required to see a blueberry inches away. For this reason, a grizzly stands and squints, attempting to bring the middle distance into focus, and the gesture is often misunderstood as a sign of anger and forthcoming attack. If the bear were getting ready to attack, he would be on four feet, head low, ears cocked, the hair above his hump muscle standing on end. As if that message were not clear enough, he would also chop his jaws. His teeth would make a sound that would carry like the ringing of an axe.

One could predict, but not with certainty, what a grizzly would do. Odds were very great that one touch of man scent would cause him to stop his activity, pause in a moment of absorbed and alert curiosity, and then move, at a not undignified pace, in a direction other than the one from which the scent was coming. That is what would happen almost every time, but there was, to be sure, no guarantee. The forest Eskimos fear and revere the grizzly. They know that certain individual bears not only will fail to avoid a person who comes into their country but will approach and even stalk the trespasser. It is potentially inaccurate to extrapolate the behavior of any one bear from the behavior of most, since they are both intelligent and independent and will do what they choose to do according to mood, experience, whim. A grizzly that has ever been wounded by a bullet will not forget it, and will probably know that it was a human being who sent the bullet. At sight of a human, such a bear will be likely to charge. Grizzlies hide food sometimes—a caribou calf, say, under a pile of scraped-up moss—and a person the bear might otherwise ignore might suddenly not be ignored if the person were inadvertently to step into the line between the food cache and the bear. A sow[3] grizzly with cubs, of course, will charge anything that suggests danger to the cubs, even if the cubs are nearly as big as she is. They stay with their mother two and a half years.

If a wolf kills a caribou, and a grizzly comes along while the wolf is feeding on the kill, the wolf puts its tail between its legs and hurries away. A black bear will run from a grizzly, too. Grizzlies sometimes kill and eat black bears. The grizzly takes what he happens upon. He is an opportunistic eater. The predominance of the grizzly in his terrain is challenged by nothing but men and ravens. To frustrate ravens from stealing his food, he will lie down and sleep on top of a carcass, occasionally swatting the birds as if they were big black flies. He prefers a vegetable diet. He can pulp a moosehead with a single blow, but he is not lusting always to kill, and when he moves through his country he can be something munificent,[4] going into copses of willow among unfleeing moose and their calves, touching nothing, letting it all breathe as before. He may, though, get the head of a cow moose between his legs and rake her flanks with the five-inch knives that protrude from the ends of his paws. Opportunistic. He removes and eats her entrails. He likes porcupines, too, and when one turns and presents to him a pygal bouquet of quills, he will leap into the air, land on the other side, chuck the fretful porpentine beneath the chin, flip it over, and, with a swift ventral incision, neatly remove its body from its skin, leaving something like a sea urchin behind him on the ground. He is nothing if not athletic. Before he dens, or just after he emerges, if his mountains are covered with snow he will climb to the brink of some impossible schuss,[5] sit down on his butt, and shove off. Thirty-two, sixty-four, ninety-six feet per second, he plummets down the mountainside, spray snow flying to either side, as he approaches collision with boulders and trees. Just short of catastrophe, still going at bonecrushing speed, he flips to his feet and walks sedately onward as if his ride had not occurred.

His population density is thin on the Arctic barren ground. He needs for his forage at least fifty and perhaps a hundred square miles that are all his own—sixty-four thousand acres, his home range. Within it, he will move, typically, eight miles a summer day, doing his travelling through the twilight hours of the dead of night. To scratch his belly he walks over a tree—where forest exists. The tree bends beneath him as he passes. He forages in the morning, generally; and he rests a great deal, particularly after he eats. He rests fourteen hours a day. If he becomes hot in the sun, he lies down in a pool in the river. He sleeps on the tundra[6]—restlessly tossing and turning, forever changing position. What he could be worrying about I cannot imagine.

His fur blends so well into the tundra colors that sometimes it is hard to see him. Fortunately, we could see well enough the one in front of us, or we would have walked right to him. He caused a considerable revision of our travel plans. Not wholly prepared to follow the advice of Andy Russell, I asked Fedeler what one should do if a bear were to charge. He said, "Take off your pack and throw it into the bear's path, then crawl away, and hope the pack will distract the bear. But there is no good thing to do, really. It's just not a situation to be in."

[3]**sow:** female.
[4]**munificent:** greatly generous.

[5]**schuss:** a straight-down ski route.
[6]**tundra:** vast, treeless plains of the Arctic region.

Discuss

1. What are two names for the kind of bear this essay describes? Where would you find this particular bear?

2. How close did McPhee and his friends come to this bear?

3. Why didn't the bear notice the people?

4. If the bear had noticed them and decided to attack, what chance would they have had of outrunning it?

5. Which senses does the bear mainly rely upon? Which is its weakest sense?

6. When a bear is ready to charge, does it rear up on its hind legs, or stand on its four feet?

7. What else indicates that the bear is ready to attack?

8. How long do cubs stay with a sow bear?

9. What happens if a grizzly comes upon a wolf feeding on its kill?

Explore

1. The brown bears of Arctic Alaska grow only to six hundred pounds compared to the larger size of brown bears elsewhere. Why do you think this is the case?

2. What adage, or saying, does McPhee give you to highlight the bear's delicate sense of smell?

3. Which facts indicate the grizzly's strength?

4. Explain why McPhee says that the grizzly is athletic.

5. How large is the grizzly's home range, within which it forages for food? Why does it need such a tremendous range?

6. McPhee must answer the dreaded question of what to do when encountering such a bear. He says, "He [the bear] caused a considerable revision of our travel plans." What did McPhee and the other hikers do?

7. What in this essay suggests that grizzlies are intelligent?

For Your Journal

1. Observe your pet or someone else's. See if you can capture its "personality" by describing some of its behavior—for example: how it sits, walks, or runs; how it eats and drinks; how it stalks its prey; how it plays; expressions it may have.

2. Jot down your opinion about hunting brown bears of Arctic Alaska. Are you in favor or not, and why?

On Native Grounds

How much are people shaped by their surroundings? How much by traits inherited from their parents? These questions have been debated— without resolution—for generations. The stories and poem in this section examine the effect of different environments on the human personality. As you read, imagine yourself in another time and in another place faced with new and unfamiliar challenges. Consider how you would respond. For the moment, try to live within the skin of another person and view the world from his or her perspective.

How to Ride a Water Buffalo

Pira Sudham

Literature is one way to learn about different, remote cultures while exploring familiar themes, too. The story that follows takes place in a rural village of Thailand, probably in the northeastern part of the country. The major crop is rice, and the water buffalo is the most common work animal in the fields. The people's customs probably differ greatly from yours. But this is really a story about family ties, and about bonding among brothers, sisters, and parents.

IN THE YEAR OF THE HORSE, Mrs. Surin gave birth to her fourth child. Then the monsoon[1] came, promising and bountiful. And like most peasants in the village of Napoti the Surins looked hopefully upon the surrounding rice fields, which were now inundated, viable. They were ready to wring out, for another season, their existence from the ancient soil.

Consequently, the birth of the baby boy was associated with the year of a good monsoon. They agreed to call him Prem, which corresponded to their exaltation for a good year.

When the time was suitable, Mr. Surin went to the village headman's house and said: "I've just had another son whom we have named Prem."

The old, august headman,[2] reclining on the wooden floor, half-naked because it was a hot day, coughed somewhat spasmodically to tear himself from the lethargy and the drowsiness in which he had passed the empty afternoon. Time seemed to stand still, while the man re-arranged his loincloth. He sat up, cross-legged spat into the nearby spittoon and ran his gnarled fingers three times through his hair and over his face.

"You're indeed fortunate to have another son," the headman uttered at last. For he had only four daughters, and his wife had passed the age, so to speak.

Mr. Surin was a quiet man. He remained still, preparing to say what he had come for. In the silence the headman regained his dignity. "Will someone bring a tray of betel nuts[3] and my shirt," said the headman, with more authority now.

His wife was kindling the fire in her kitchen. Blinded by smoke and tears, she took time to tighten her sarong[4] and shake herself free of ashes. Finally, she appeared with what had been demanded of her. So the old man nonchalantly adorned himself with a cotton shirt smelling of age and dust. He changed his sitting position and got hold of the humid census book that had been serving as a headrest during his afternoon repose. It also smelled of age.

The old man, whose wizened hands trembled because of the immensity of the book and his own weariness, carefully and slowly thumbed page by page, bending his white head in great concentration so that he could see. "Ah, my eyes fail me," he mumbled. But official duty braced him, and his grim countenance called for solemnity.

"We call the boy Prem," Mr. Surin said cautiously, afraid that it was not time for him to speak as yet.

[1]**monsoon:** heavy, rainy season that causes flooding, necessary for growing rice.
[2]**headman:** leader of the village.

[3]**betel nuts:** nuts and seeds of the betel palm, chewed as a stimulant. The older people in Thai villages customarily have it; among the younger people, the custom seems to be dying out.
[4]**sarong:** skirtlike garment, a strip of cloth draped loosely about the body.

The headman waited, for he had finally reached the page on which the name, the date of birth and the sex of the child could be recorded. So Mr. Surin repeated his words with more assurance, giving the date and time when the boy was born. How articulate he seemed then; in fact, Mr. Surin had spent hours reciting these facts so that they would be registered in his memory, because he could not write or read.

The headman could hold only a few words at a time writing them down slowly and painfully. Mr. Surin had to give him information when required. This the father of the boy did with some pride, as if to prove that he remembered well. He was leaning forward towards the book so that he might see what his son looked like being spelled out into written words.

The headman's wife returned, putting herself down at a suitable distance and submitting to the air of authority which her beloved husband was emanating. Time stood still.

"It's quite a good name for the boy," the old man eventually said. But the two witnesses were drained, choked with dust and their humility. "Being born on Friday of the third month and in a good time of the day, this son of yours will become gentle and obedient," the headman predicted.

Mr. Surin accepted that remark with his usual silence. He fumbled for some coins in his shirt pocket to reward the old man who had performed his official duty. Mr. Surin was a poor man; therefore, he had brought with him a bucketful of cucumbers and melons as well, to make up for the little sum of money he could offer.

"How are Liang and the baby?" the headman's wife asked. Her voice broke and rose as if she had just come to life.

"She is getting well, and so is the baby," Mr. Surin said.

Now there was no doubt of his son's existence in the eye of the law. But Mr. Surin appeared somewhat anxious, for the headman's wife had asked about the baby's health. The father had been rather concerned because since birth his frail little baby had not opened his eyes and made hardly any movement or sound.

Mrs. Surin, who was confined to the fireside and to drinking hot water in order to heal herself after the laborious delivery, knew instinctively that there was nothing wrong with the baby. She had been feeding him with life and warmth that flowed from her body. He would survive, she was convinced. In her placid mind she called to him,

"Prem, Prem, Prem Surin," as if at once she had to stabilize, to mold within that name and so nurture it along with the child.

Kiang Surin, the eldest son, crouching next to the baby, said: "I'll name him Tadpole." Because Kiang, who attended the village primary school, had read in his spelling book about a tadpole. The mother did not acknowledge that name until Kiang had gone and she was drinking hot water that smelt of herbs. She saw the tiny hands stirring the air as if to show that the baby was still alive. "The tadpole, the wriggling little tadpole," murmured Mrs. Surin, to taste the name with her own lips. She smiled.

A long time later, when Prem Surin had become a quiet, timid boy, and the people in Napoti began to refer to him as the Mute, Mrs. Surin neither protested nor showed her resentment. She held that such a deficiency, if it was one, could be the boy's own retribution: that in a past life he could have scolded his parents or committed a verbal sacrilege. However, when she was sometimes annoyed with his recurring silence or when she got no response from him whatsoever, Mrs. Surin would say: "What's the matter, you Mute?"

How the word echoed! How it pierced her heart through. But the boy had learned to accept such names. They had become his identity now.

Only Piang Surin, the older sister, often put up a fight. The Tadpole was not dumb, she said. "Don't you call him the Mute, for he's not," Piang raised her voice.

"Why Piang, he's as dumb as a tree," one girl said.

"Or a buffalo," another added.

"He talks to me sometimes," Piang said, proud of the fact that she understood him.

"Make him talk then," the girl who was covered with heat rash said.

Piang Surin looked at her brother, asking him to speak, begging him to make some sound; but there was only silence.

"He can't talk. He's as mute as the paddy[5] fields," the second girl said.

"He talks to me!" Piang defended.

"He's mute, mute. That's what he is. Ta la la la la la," the third girl sang.

Piang Surin aimed at the eyes of the girl who sang; her nails dug into the flesh. Then she went

[5]**paddy:** rice field.

at the rest, sending them crying all the way to their mothers. Mrs. Surin came, dragged her daughter away from the scene to their hut, and beat her there with what she could get hold of, till the girl cried.

"If you can't play nicely with others, you stay away from them," the mother shouted. She spat red betel nut juice as she climbed back into the house so that she could go on spinning silk, and also because she could not endure what she could see from the corner of her eyes: Prem, who had not spoken, had gone to his sister and was holding her hand, looking up at her with bright, expressive eyes that showed his love and sympathy.

Piang Surin became quiet too, and wiped away tears with the fringe of her sarong. "I know you can speak, Tadpole, but you don't have to talk if you don't want to," Piang said.

Kiang Surin thought himself very lucky to have a brother. He saw the little boy as a partner in strength. For they, as men, would have to take on a great deal of responsibility. They would be working side by side in the fields, one needing the other's help. Sometimes Kiang would look at the quiet boy as if a sudden sickness or some evil spirit would deprive him of his brother. "The quiet one must survive," Kiang told himself. "I'll look after him; the one before him died in infancy, the one after was still-born. The Tadpole must live and be strong." So, when they were alone in an empty paddy, Kiang Surin said to his brother: "I'll teach you how to ride a water buffalo."

Prem Surin stood close to his brother, ready and yet motionless. He had learned to listen and obey.

Kiang brought the animal and made it stand near a bund.[6] "Watch me," said the big brother, and jumped swiftly from the bund on to the buffalo's back. The docile brute showed no annoyance or fright; it went on grazing. "See, you keep your legs apart and press them on the flanks, so you can urge it to walk or gallop by nudging it with your knees or toes. Like this."

Kiang's muscles moved and squirmed. The animal pulled another mouthful of grass, and snorted knowingly. Kiang gave it a gentle whip with a rope. The buffalo jerked its head and moved quickly.

Kiang could also make certain sounds and speak a language the animal understood, so it came to a halt in front of the little boy.

[6]**bund:** embankment.

Kiang slid down and said: "If there is no bund or mound nearby, I can still jump up on its back from the ground." Kiang, at the age of nine, was agile, angular. "But you," he continued, "will have to hold on to its tail, put your toes on its hind knee and push yourself up. So you try now."

The Tadpole looked at the beast's long, sharp horns, at its great size, and became weak and afraid.

"Come on now," Kiang commanded. "Right foot on one of the buffalo's knees, hold on to the tail and push yourself up." The big brother stood aside, making way.

The buffalo grazed on, unperturbed; its black skin and coarse hair smelled of mud and miasma. The boy hung on to its tail, unsure of his strength. The buffalo moved and shook him off. Kiang patted the buffalo and ordered it to be still, and helped the boy up. "There you are. It's quite easy, isn't it?"

The buffalo turned its head as if to question the mastery; its large, protruding eyes rolled. The sweltering sun and the moldering fields looked on. Kiang gave the animal a pat and it walked, shaking its thick head, flapping its hairy ears. But it stopped short, waiting for direction and purpose.

"Make it move on," Kiang said.

Because he had already surrendered, the boy became powerless.

"Go on, get him to walk ahead," Kiang repeated; there was some disappointment in his voice. The buffalo went back to grazing, ignoring its burden.

Kiang Surin got angry now at the mountain of silence, at the face that bore no expression, at the mouth that knew no language. So he slapped the buffalo's haunch with a hand that showed his anger. The surprised beast ran, and, a second later, the Tadpole fell.

The placidity of the open fields passed judgment on Kiang. The manliness in him deterred him from going to soothe the boy's bruises. He went to the buffalo instead, and harnessed it while the boy gathered himself up from the dust.

"Let's go home now," Kiang called from a distance. It was necessary at times to disguise feelings.

And now Kiang carefully helped his brother on to the buffalo's back. Then he, too, mounted, riding with his arms around the boy, who silently endured the tenderness. Together they rode homeward to the village of Napoti.

Discuss

1. What facts do you immediately learn about the Surins and their village in this story?

2. How does Mr. Surin pay the headman?

3. Prem suffers from an affliction. What is it?

4. How do the villagers treat Prem?

5. How does Prem's sister react to the way she and her little brother are treated?

6. Because the water buffalo is so important in their lives, Prem's brother Kiang wants to teach him to ride one. How well does Kiang succeed?

Explore

1. Why do you think having a son is important to this Thai family?

2. Riding a water buffalo can be considered a sign of manliness; thus, Prem's failure disappoints Kiang. How does Kiang treat Prem after the failure?

For Your Journal

Write a short essay about an experience you imagine having with a person who is mute. Give the person a name and pretend that you have been hired to help that person. What would you do? If you have read about Helen Keller, who was blind and deaf from infancy, and Annie Sullivan, her tutor, consider incorporating ideas from the experiences of Keller and Sullivan into your essay.

A Question of Blood

Ernest Haycox

Do you believe that blood distinguishes people from one another? Most people realize that they cannot tell the difference between the actual blood of, for example, a European and a Native American. Often, when the word "blood" is used to refer to differences among people, another word is really meant. That word could be "culture" or "custom." What usually makes people different from one another, aside from hereditary and environmental differences, are inbred ways of thinking, behaving, and looking at the world. These ways are difficult to change, and when people of differing ways come into contact with one another it can lead to conflict. The story you are about to read centers on conflict arising from such cultural differences.

THAT FALL OF 1869 when Frank Isabel settled in the Yellow Hills the nearest town was a four-day ride to the north and his closest white neighbor lived at the newly established Hat ranch, seventy miles over in Two Dance Valley. The Indians were on reservation[1] but it was still risky for a man to be alone in the country.

It made no difference to Isabel. He was young and self-willed and raised in that impoverished and faction-torn part of Missouri where manhood came to a male child almost as soon as he could lift a gun. He had a backwoodsman's lank loose height, his eyes were almost black, and though he kept a smooth-shaven face there was always a clay-blue cast to the long sides of his jaw. The land was free, well grassed and watered and ideal for a poor man who had ambition. This is why he had come.

Yet self-sufficient as he was he had made no calculation for the imperious hungers that soon or late come to a lonely man. And presently, seeing no hope of a white woman in the land for many years, he went down to the reservation and took unto himself a Crow[2] girl, the bargain being sealed by payment to her father of one horse and a quart of whisky.

[1]**reservation:** land the Native American groups were given and restricted to by the U.S. government.
[2]**Crow:** member of a Sioux group that lived in Montana and Wyoming.

She was quick and small and neat, with enormous eyes looking out of a round smooth face. The price paid was small and that hurt her pride for a little while, yet it was a white man who wanted her and the hurt died down and she moved quietly into Frank Isabel's log house and settled down to the long, lonesome days without murmur.

She was more than he had expected in an Indian woman: quick to perceive the way his mind ran, showing him sudden streaks of mischief-making gaiety, and sometimes a flash of affection. Before the boy baby was born he drove her three hundred miles to Cheyenne and married her in the white way.

It was a sense of justice that impelled him to do this rather than any need in her eyes. For he was learning that the horse and bottle of whisky were as binding as any ceremony on earth; and he was also learning that though an Indian woman was a dutiful woman, immemorial custom guided her in a way he could not hope to touch or change. A man's work was a man's; a woman's work was hers and the line was hard and clear. In the beginning he had shocked her by cutting the firewood and by dressing down the game he brought in. It had shamed her for a while that he should descend to those things; and only by angry command had he established the habit of eating at table instead of crosslegged on a floor blanket. She was faithful to the discharge of the duty she owed him, but behind that girlish face was an adamant will. The ways of a thousand generations were ingrained in her.

Often at night, smoking before the fire and watching his boy crawl so awkwardly across the floor, he felt a strangeness at seeing her darkly crouched in a corner, lost in thoughts he could never reach. Sometimes the color and the sound of his early days in Missouri came strongly to him and he wished that she might know what was in his head. But he talked her tongue poorly and she would speak no English; and so silence lay between them.

Meanwhile Two Dance town was born on the empty prairie sixty miles away and the valley below him began to fill up with cattlemen long before he had thought they would come. Looking down from the ramparts of the Yellows he could see houses far off under the sun and dust spiral up along the Two Dance road, signals of a vanishing wilderness. His own people had finally caught up with him. And then he knew he had become a squaw[3] man.

One by one the few trappers who had pioneered the Yellows began to send their squaws and their half-breed children back to the reservation as a shamefaced gesture of a mistake that had to be righted. He said nothing of this to the Crow woman, yet when fear showed its luminous shadow in her eyes he knew she had heard. He said then: "Those men are fools. I am not ashamed of you." And was happy to see the fear die.

This was why he took her to Two Dance. It pleased him to have her be seen in that lively little cattle town for she was a pretty woman with her black hair braided and her clothes neat and colorful under the sun. But he had forgotten her customs and when they walked up the street she followed behind him as a squaw always did, obediently and with her head faintly lowered. He knew how Two Dance would see that and anger colored his talk to her on the way home. "A white man's wife walks beside him, not behind."

He saw that dark fear in her eyes again, and had no way of softening it. Never afterward did she come to town.

He knew then how it was to be. At hay time when he went down to help out on Hat he could

feel that faint line drawn between him and the others; at the roundup fire he sat apart, with the strangeness there—a white man who was yet not quite white. One fall night at town he stepped in to watch the weekly dance and felt all the loose bitterness of his position rise and grow to be a hard lump in his chest. Once he would have had a part in this, but the odor of the blanket was upon him now and those fair, pleasant girls went wheeling by and he saw their eyes touch him and pass on. Over the whisky bottle in Faro Charley's saloon later he understood how fatal his mistake had been; and how everlastingly long its penalty would be.

He went home late that night quite drunk. In the morning the Crow girl was gone with her boy.

He didn't follow, for he knew that either she would return or she wouldn't, and that nothing he did could change her mind. Late in the third day she came back without a word. When he went in to supper that night he sat down to a single plate on the table. Her own plate and the boy's were on a floor blanket in a corner of the room.

It was, he saw, her decision. He had told her nothing of the misery in his mind, but she knew it without need of speech and so had answered him. He was white and might eat at his table. But she was Indian and so was the boy, and the table was not for them.

There was a kindness in Frank Isabel that governed the strongest of his emotions and this was what held him still as the days went on. He was remembering back to the horse and bottle of whisky and to the time when her lips had been warm with humor. In those days the Yellows had been wild and his world had not caught up with him, but he could see the depth and the length of his mistake now. He had committed it and could stand it. Yet it had passed beyond him and touched the Crow girl and the boy who was neither Crow nor white. For himself, Frank Isabel thought, there was no help. For the girl, none. It was the boy he kept weighing in his mind, so slowly and so painfully.

One winter night at meal time Jim Benbow of Hat dropped in for a cup of coffee. There was a little talk of cattle snowed into the timber and afterward Benbow put on his hat and went to the door. As he left his glance crossed to the Crow woman and to the boy crouched in the corner and he said briefly: "Your youngster's growin' up, Frank," and left.

[3]**squaw:** a wife; in some cases, "squaw" seems to have had negative connotations among Native American groups. It usually was a disrespectful term when used by white people.

There was the rush of wind along the cabin eaves and deep silence inside. Isabel sat with his arms idle on the table remembering Benbow's words, which had contained a note of judgment. Presently he rose and brought another chair to the table and went over to where the Crow girl crouched mutely in the corner. He lifted the boy and put him in the chair at the table and stood there a moment, a long man throwing a thin shadow across the room. He said: "Hereafter he eats at the table."

She drew farther and farther back into the corner, like a shadow vanishing. And then, with his face turned suddenly away, he heard her stifled and terrible crying tremble the room's silence.

Discuss

1. Why does Frank Isabel take an Indian wife?

2. What native group does Isabel's wife come from? How does he pay her father for the marriage? What does the author mean in saying they married "in the white way"?

3. What does it mean to be "a squaw man"?

4. What problem occurs when Isabel takes his wife into Two Dance?

5. What incident reveals the sensitivity of his wife?

6. What action of hers at home symbolizes the difference between them?

7. What suddenly occurs to Isabel with regard to his son? Why does he insist that the boy eat at the table?

Explore

1. How would you judge Frank Isabel? Is he a good man or a bad man? Should he have married an Indian woman? Should he have stayed married to her once the society changed? Why or why not?

2. What about his wife? Was she correct to return with the child? Did she too easily give in to Frank's assertiveness? Should she have adopted the white ways immediately? Explain your answer.

3. What attitudes described in the story show the differences in their ways?

4. Why does fear show in her eyes?

5. What is meant by "the odor of the blanket was upon him now"?

6. Isabel keeps thinking that he has made a mistake in marrying an Indian woman. What makes him think he has?

7. What is your opinion of the act that removes the boy from his mother's culture?

8. Where do you think the author's sympathies lie?

For Your Journal

1. The last two paragraphs of the story are crucial. Explain how they together emphasize the sad ending. In your explanation identify your sympathies for the characters.

2. Have you ever associated with someone who differed from you strongly in personal values, social beliefs, religious or political ideas? Perhaps the difference was based upon geographical contrasts. For instance, the person may have been from a rural area while you have always lived in an urban area. If you have had such an experience, describe the differences and tell whether they made your association better or worse.

Girl's-Eye View of Relatives
Phyllis McGinley

Fathers and mothers, and the way children view them, isn't that a serious thing? Can't it also be humorous? Is it different for a girl than for a boy? Do parents set more restrictions for a girl and worry more about her? What do you and your classmates think about this issue? After you have debated it, read the following poem and see whether or not you agree with the speaker.

FIRST LESSON

The thing to remember about fathers is, they're men.
A girl has to keep it in mind.
They are dragon-seekers, bent on improbable rescues.
Scratch any father, you find
Someone chock-full of qualms and romantic terrors,
Believing change is a threat—
Like your first shoes with heels on, like your first bicycle
It took such months to get.

Walk in strange woods, they warn you about the snakes there.
Climb, and they fear you'll fall.
Books, angular boys, or swimming in deep water—
Fathers mistrust them all.
Men are the worriers. It is difficult for them
To learn what they must learn:
How you have a journey to take and very likely,
For a while, will not return.

THE ADVERSARY

A mother's hardest to forgive.
Life is the fruit she longs to hand you,
Ripe on a plate. And while you live,
Relentlessly she understands you.

Discuss

1. What items does the speaker list that threaten fathers?

2. Why do those things threaten fathers? Does it have anything to do with the speaker's observation that they are "dragon-seekers"?

3. The first two stanzas are titled "First Lesson." What is the lesson?

4. Why is the last stanza titled "The Adversary"?

Explore

1. What does the speaker mean when she says, "you have a journey to take and very likely, / For a while, will not return"?

2. Why are mothers hardest to forgive?

For Your Journal

1. Express yourself: If you are a boy, do you think your parents treat you differently from the way they treat or would treat a daughter? Is this situation as it should be? If you are a girl, reverse the first question.

2. Whether you are a girl or a boy what do you think you could do to improve your relationship with your parents or other people who supervise you? Realistically, do you think you will make these changes? How do you see these same relationships five years in the future?

Counterparts

James Joyce

The main character of this story is an office clerk in Dublin, Ireland. His personality is a type that undoubtedly exists in many societies. As you read, think about the unstated reasons for his behavior. You also may have a hard time deciding your sympathies, at least for a while, because in a strange way the author succeeds in making you partially identify with the main character. Is this character a victim of his job and his society? Or, is he the one solely responsible for his lot?

THE BELL RANG furiously and, when Miss Parker went to the tube,[1] a furious voice called out in a piercing North of Ireland accent:

"Send Farrington here!"

Miss Parker returned to her machine, saying to a man who was writing at a desk:

"Mr. Alleyne wants you upstairs."

The man muttered "*Blast* him!" under his breath and pushed back his chair to stand up. When he stood up he was tall and of great bulk. He had a hanging face, dark wine-colored, with fair eyebrows and moustache: his eyes bulged forward slightly and the whites of them were dirty. He lifted up the counter and, passing by the clients, went out of the office with a heavy step.

He went heavily upstairs until he came to the second landing, where a door bore a brass plate with the inscription *Mr. Alleyne*. Here he halted, puffing with labor and vexation, and knocked. The shrill voice cried:

"Come in!"

The man entered Mr. Alleyne's room. Simultaneously Mr. Alleyne, a little man wearing gold-rimmed glasses on a clean-shaven face, shot his head up over a pile of documents. The head itself was so pink and hairless it seemed like a large egg reposing on the papers. Mr. Alleyne did not lose a moment:

"Farrington? What is the meaning of this? Why have I always to complain of you? May I ask

¹**tube:** intercommunication system.

you why you haven't made a copy of that contract between Bodley and Kirwan? I told you it must be ready by four o'clock."

"But Mr. Shelley said, sir—"

"*Mr. Shelley said, sir.* . . . Kindly attend to what I say and not to what *Mr. Shelley says, sir.* You have always some excuse or another for shirking work. Let me tell you that if the contract is not copied before this evening I'll lay the matter before Mr. Crosbie. . . . Do you hear me now?"

"Yes, sir."

"Do you hear me now? . . . Ay and another little matter! I might as well be talking to the wall as talking to you. Understand once for all that you get a half an hour for your lunch and not an hour and a half. How many courses do you want, I'd like to know. . . . Do you mind me now?"

"Yes, sir."

Mr. Alleyne bent his head again upon his pile of papers. The man stared fixedly at the polished skull which directed the affairs of Crosbie & Alleyne, gauging its fragility. A spasm of rage gripped his throat for a few moments and then passed, leaving after it a sharp sensation of thirst. The man recognized the sensation and felt that he must have a good night's drinking. The middle of the month was passed and, if he could get the copy done in time, Mr. Alleyne might give him an order on the cashier. He stood still, gazing fixedly at the head upon the pile of papers. Suddenly Mr. Alleyne began to upset all the papers, searching for something. Then, as if he had been unaware of the man's presence till that moment, he shot up his head again, saying:

"Eh? Are you going to stand there all day? Upon my word, Farrington, you take things easy!"

"I was waiting to see. . . ."

"Very good, you needn't wait to see. Go downstairs and do your work."

The man walked heavily towards the door and, as he went out of the room, he heard Mr. Alleyne cry after him that if the contract was not copied by evening Mr. Crosbie would hear of the matter.

He returned to his desk in the lower office and counted the sheets which remained to be copied. He took up his pen and dipped it in the ink but he continued to stare stupidly at the last words he had written: *In no case shall the said Bernard Bodley be. . . .* The evening was falling and in a few minutes they would be lighting the gas: then he could write. He felt that he must slake the thirst in his throat. He stood up from his desk and, lifting the counter as before, passed out of the office. As he was passing out the chief clerk looked at him inquiringly.

"It's all right, Mr. Shelley," said the man, pointing with his finger to indicate the objective of his journey.

The chief clerk glanced at the hatrack, but, seeing the row complete, offered no remark. As soon as he was on the landing the man pulled a shepherd's plaid cap out of his pocket, put it on his head, and ran quickly down the rickety stairs. From the street door he walked on furtively on the inner side of the path towards the corner and all at once dived into a doorway. He was now safe in the dark snug of O'Neill's shop, and filling up the little window that looked into the bar with his inflamed face, the color of dark wine or dark meat, he called out:

"Here, Pat, give us a g.p., like a good fellow."

The curate[2] brought him a glass of plain porter. The man drank it at a gulp and asked for a caraway seed. He put his penny on the counter and, leaving the curate to grope for it in the gloom, retreated out of the snug as furtively as he had entered it.

Darknesss, accompanied by a thick fog, was gaining upon the dusk of February and the lamps in Eustace Street had been lit. The man went up by the houses until he reached the door of the office, wondering whether he could finish his copy in time. On the stairs a moist pungent odor of per-

[2]**curate:** bartender.

fumes saluted his nose: evidently Miss Delacour had come while he was out in O'Neill's. He crammed his cap back again into his pocket and re-entered the office, assuming an air of absent-mindedness.

"Mr. Alleyne has been calling for you," said the chief clerk severely. "Where were you?"

The man glanced at the two clients who were standing at the counter as if to intimate that their presence prevented him from answering. As the clients were both male the chief clerk allowed himself a laugh.

"I know that game," he said. "Five times in one day is a little bit. . . . Well, you better look sharp and get a copy of our correspondence in the Delacour case for Mr. Alleyne."

This address in the presence of the public, his run upstairs, and the porter he had gulped down so hastily confused the man and, as he sat down at his desk to get what was required, he realized how hopeless was the task of finishing his copy of the contract before half past five. The dark damp night was coming and he longed to spend it in the bars, drinking with his friends amid the glare of gas and the clatter of glasses. He got out the Delacour correspondence and passed out of the office. He hoped Mr. Alleyne would not discover that the last two letters were missing.

The moist pungent perfume lay all the way up to Mr. Alleyne's room. Miss Delacour was a middle-aged woman of Jewish appearance. Mr. Alleyne was said to be sweet on her or on her money. She came to the office often and stayed a long time when she came. She was sitting beside his desk now in an aroma of perfumes, smoothing the handle of her umbrella and nodding the great black feather in her hat. Mr. Alleyne had swiveled his chair round to face her and thrown his right foot jauntily upon his left knee. The man put the correspondence on the desk and bowed respectfully but neither Mr. Alleyne nor Miss Delacour took any notice of his bow. Mr. Alleyne tapped a finger on the correspondence and then flicked it towards him as if to say: *"That's all right: you can go."*

The man returned to the lower office and sat down again at his desk. He stared intently at the incomplete phrase: *In no case shall the said Bernard Bodley be . . .* and thought how strange it was that the last three words began with the same letter. The chief clerk began to hurry Miss Parker, saying she would never have the letters typed in time for post. The man listened to the clicking of the machine for a few minutes and then set to work to finish his copy. But his head was not clear and his mind wandered away to the glare and rattle of the public house.[3] It was a night for hot punches. He struggled on with his copy, but when the clock struck five he had still fourteen pages to write. Blast it! He couldn't finish it in time. He longed to execrate[4] aloud, to bring his fist down on something violently. He was so enraged that he wrote *Bernard Bernard* instead of *Bernard Bodley* and had to begin again on a clean sheet.

He felt strong enough to clear out the whole office singlehanded. His body ached to do something, to rush out and revel in violence. All the indignities of his life enraged him. . . . Could he ask the cashier privately for an advance? No, the cashier was no good, no damn good; he wouldn't give an advance. . . . He knew where he would meet the boys: Leonard and O'Halloran and Nosey Flynn. The barometer of his emotional nature was set for a spell of riot.

His imagination had so abstracted him that his name was called twice before he answered. Mr. Alleyne and Miss Delacour were standing outside the counter and all the clerks had turned round in anticipation of something. The man got up from his desk. Mr. Alleyne began a tirade of abuse, saying that two letters were missing. The man answered that he knew nothing about them, that he had made a faithful copy. The tirade continued: it was so bitter and violent that the man could hardly restrain his fist from descending upon the head of the manikin before him:

"I know nothing about any other two letters," he said stupidly.

"*You—know—nothing.* Of course you know nothing," said Mr. Alleyne. "Tell me," he added, glancing first for approval to the lady beside him, "do you take me for a fool? Do you think me an utter fool?"

The man glanced from the lady's face to the little egg-shaped head and back again; and, almost before he was aware of it, his tongue had found a felicitous moment:

"I don't think, sir," he said, "that that's a fair question to put to me."

There was a pause in the very breathing of the clerks. Everyone was astounded (the author of the witticism no less than his neighbors) and Miss Delacour, who was a stout amiable person, began

to smile broadly. Mr. Alleyne flushed to the hue of a wild rose and his mouth twitched with a dwarf's passion. He shook his fist in the man's face till it seemed to vibrate like the knob of some electric machine:

"You impertinent ruffian! You impertinent ruffian! I'll make short work of you! Wait till you see! You'll apologize to me for your impertinence or you'll quit the office instanter! You'll quit this, I'm telling you, or you'll apologize to me!"

He stood in a doorway opposite the office watching to see if the cashier would come out alone. All the clerks passed out and finally the cashier came out with the chief clerk. It was no use trying to say a word to him when he was with the chief clerk. The man felt that his position was bad enough. He had been obliged to offer an abject apology to Mr. Alleyne for his impertinence but he knew what a hornet's nest the office would be for him. He could remember the way in which Mr. Alleyne had hounded little Peake out of the office in order to make room for his own nephew. He felt savage and thirsty and revengeful, annoyed with himself and with everyone else. Mr. Alleyne would never give him an hour's rest; his life would be a hell to him. He had made a proper fool of himself this time. Could he not keep his tongue in his cheek? But they had never pulled together from the first, he and Mr. Alleyne, ever since the day Mr. Alleyne had overheard him mimicking his North of Ireland accent to amuse Higgins and Miss Parker: that had been the beginning of it. He might have tried Higgins for the money, but sure Higgins never had anything for himself. A man with two establishments to keep up, of course he couldn't. . . .

He felt his great body again aching for the comfort of the public house. The fog had begun to chill him and he wondered could he touch Pat in O'Neill's. He could not touch him for more than a bob[5]—and a bob was no use. Yet he must get money somewhere or other: he had spent his last penny for the g.p. and soon it would be too late for getting money anywhere. Suddenly, as he was fingering his watch chain, he thought of Terry Kelly's pawn-office in Fleet Street. That was the dart! Why didn't he think of it sooner?

He went through the narrow alley of Temple Bar quickly, muttering to himself that they could all go to hell because he was going to have a good

---

[3]**public house:** bar.
[4]**execrate:** curse.

[5]**bob:** British slang meaning one shilling.

night of it. The clerk in Terry Kelly's said *A crown!* but the consignor[6] held out for six shillings; and in the end the six shillings was allowed him literally. He came out of the pawn-office joyfully, making a little cylinder of the coins between his thumb and fingers. In Westmoreland Street the footpaths were crowded with young men and women returning from business and ragged urchins ran here and there yelling out the names of the evening editions. The man passed through the crowd, looking on the spectacle generally with proud satisfaction and staring masterfully at the office girls. His head was full of the noises of tram gongs and swishing trolleys and his nose already sniffed the curling fumes of punch. As he walked on he preconsidered the terms in which he would narrate the incident to the boys:

"So, I just looked at him—coolly, you know, and looked at her. Then I looked back at him again—taking my time, you know. 'I don't think that that's a fair question to put to me,' says I."

Nosey Flynn was sitting up in his usual corner of Davy Byrne's, and when he heard the story, he stood Farrington a half-one, saying it was as smart a thing as ever he heard. Farrington stood a drink in his turn. After a while O'Halloran and Paddy Leonard came in and the story was repeated to them. O'Halloran stood tailors of malt, hot, all round[7] and told the story of the retort he had made to the chief clerk when he was in Callan's of Fownes's Street; but, as the retort was after the manner of the liberal shepherds in the eclogues,[8] he had to admit that it was not as clever as Farrington's retort. At this Farrington told the boys to polish off that and have another.

Just as they were naming their poisons who should come in but Higgins! Of course he had to join in with the others. The men asked him to give his version of it, and he did so with great vivacity for the sight of five small hot whiskies was very exhilarating. Everyone roared laughing when he showed the way in which Mr. Alleyne shook his fist in Farrington's face. Then he imitated Farrington, saying, *"And here was my nabs, as cool as you please,"* while Farrington looked at the company out of his heavy dirty eyes, smiling and at times drawing forth stray drops of liquor from his moustache with the aid of his lower lip.

[6]**consignor:** dispatcher of goods.
[7]**stood tailors of malt, hot, all round:** bought drinks for everyone.
[8]**eclogues:** poems in dialogue form imitating rural banter.

When that round was over there was a pause. O'Halloran had money but neither of the other two seemed to have any; so the whole party left the shop somewhat regretfully. At the corner of Duke Street Higgins and Nosey Flynn beveled off to the left while the other three turned back towards the city. Rain was drizzling down on the cold streets and, when they reached the Ballast Office, Farrington suggested the Scotch House. The bar was full of men and loud with the noise of tongues and glasses. The three men pushed past the whining match sellers at the door and formed a little party at the corner of the counter. They began to exchange stories. Leonard introduced them to a young fellow named Weathers who was performing at the Tivoli as an acrobat and knockabout *artiste*. Farrington stood a drink all round. Weathers said he would take a small Irish and Apollinaris. Farrington, who had definite notions of what was what, asked the boys would they have an Apollinaris too but the boys told Tim to make theirs hot. The talk became theatrical. O'Halloran stood a round and then Farrington stood another round, Weathers protesting that the hospitality was too Irish. He promised to get them in behind the scenes and introduce them to some nice girls. O'Halloran said that he and Leonard would go, but that Farrington wouldn't go because he was a married man; and Farrington's heavy dirty eyes leered at the company in token that he understood he was being chaffed. Weathers made them all have just one little tincture at his expense and promised to meet them later on at Mulligan's in Poolbeg Street.

When the Scotch House closed they went round to Mulligan's. They went into the parlor at the back and O'Halloran ordered small hot specials all round. They were all beginning to feel mellow. Farrington was just standing another round when Weathers came back. Much to Farrington's relief he drank a glass of bitter this time. Funds were getting low but they had enough to keep them going. Presently two young women with big hats and a young man in a check suit came in and sat at a table close by. Weathers saluted them and told the company that they were out of the Tivoli. Farrington's eyes wandered at every moment in the direction of one of the young women. There was something striking in her appearance. An immense scarf of peacock-blue muslin was wound round her hat and knotted in a great bow under her chin; and she wore bright yellow gloves, reaching to the elbow. Farrington gazed admiringly at the plump arm which she moved very often and with much grace; and when, after a little time, she answered his gaze he admired still more her large dark brown eyes. The oblique staring expression in them fascinated him. She glanced at him once or twice and, when the party was leaving the room, she brushed against his chair and said *"O, pardon!"* in a London accent. He watched her leave the room in the hope that she would look back at him, but he was disappointed. He cursed his want of money and cursed all the rounds he had stood, particularly to all the whiskies and Apollinaris which he had stood to Weathers. If there was one thing that he hated it was a sponge. He was so angry that he lost count of the conversation of his friends.

When Paddy Leonard called him he found that they were talking about feats of strength. Weathers was showing his biceps muscle to the company and boasting so much that the other two had called on Farrington to uphold the national honor. Farrington pulled up his sleeve accordingly and showed his biceps muscle to the company. The two arms were examined and compared and finally it was agreed to have a trial of strength. The table was cleared and the two men rested their elbows on it, clasping hands. When Paddy Leonard said *"Go!"* each was to try to bring down the other's hand on to the table. Farrington looked very serious and determined.

The trial began. After about thirty seconds Weathers brought his opponent's hand slowly down on to the table. Farrington's dark wine-colored face flushed darker still with anger and humiliation at having been defeated by such a stripling.

"You're not to put the weight of your body behind it. Play fair," he said.

"Who's not playing fair?" said the other. "Come on again. The two best out of three."

The trial began again. The veins stood out on Farrington's forehead, and the pallor of Weathers' complexion changed to peony. Their hands and arms trembled under the stress. After a long struggle Weathers again brought his opponent's hand slowly onto the table. There was a murmur of applause from the spectators. The curate, who was standing beside the table, nodded his red head towards the victor and said with loutish familiarity:

"Ah! that's the knack!"

"What the hell do you know about it?" said Farrington fiercely, turning on the man. "What do you put in your gab for?"

"Sh, sh!" said O'Halloran, observing the violent expression of Farrington's face. "Pony up,[9] boys. We'll have just one little smahan more and then we'll be off."

A very sullen-faced man stood at the corner of O'Connell Bridge waiting for the little Sandymount tram to take him home. He was full of smoldering anger and revengefulness. He felt humiliated and discontented; he did not even feel drunk; and he had only twopence in his pocket. He cursed everything. He had done for himself in the office, pawned his watch, spent all his money; and he had not even got drunk. He began to feel thirsty again and he longed to be back again in the hot reeking public house. He had lost his reputation as a strong man, having been defeated twice by a mere boy. His heart swelled with fury, and when he thought of the woman in the big hat who had brushed against him and said *Pardon!* his fury nearly choked him.

His tram let him down at Shelbourne Road and he steered his great body along in the shadow of the wall of the barracks. He loathed returning to his home. When he went in by the side door he found the kitchen empty and the kitchen fire nearly out. He bawled upstairs:

"Ada! Ada!"

His wife was a little sharp-faced woman who bullied her husband when he was sober and was bullied by him when he was drunk. They had five children. A little boy came running down the stairs.

"Who is that?" said the man, peering through the darkness.

"Me, pa."

"Who are you? Charlie?"

"No, pa. Tom."

"Where's your mother?"

"She's out at the chapel."

"That's right. . . . Did she think of leaving any dinner for me?"

"Yes, pa. I—"

"Light the lamp. What do you mean by having the place in darkness? Are the other children in bed?"

The man sat down heavily on one of the chairs while the little boy lit the lamp. He began to mimic his son's flat accent, saying half to himself: *"At the chapel. At the chapel, if you please!"* When the lamp was lit he banged his fist on the table and shouted:

[9]**pony up:** pay what you owe.

"What's for my dinner?"

"I'm going . . . to cook it, pa," said the little boy.

The man jumped up furiously and pointed to the fire.

"On that fire! You let the fire out! By God, I'll teach you to do that again!"

He took a step to the door and seized the walking stick which was standing behind it.

"I'll teach you to let the fire out!" he said, rolling up his sleeve in order to give his arm free play.

The little boy cried *"O, pa!"* and ran whimpering round the table, but the man followed him and caught him by the coat. The little boy looked about him wildly but seeing no way of escape, fell upon his knees.

"Now, you'll let the fire out the next time!" said the man, striking at him vigorously with the stick. "Take that, you little whelp!"

The boy uttered a squeal of pain as the stick cut his thigh. He clasped his hands together in the air and his voice shook with fright.

"O, pa!" he cried. "Don't beat me, pa! And I'll . . . I'll say a *Hail Mary*[10] for you . . . . I'll say a *Hail Mary* for you, pa, if you don't beat me. . . . I'll say a *Hail Mary*. . . ."

[10]**Hail Mary:** Roman Catholic prayer.

Discuss

1. What are Farrington's working conditions?

2. Why does Farrington behave as he does on the job?

3. Why does Farrington ache for the comfort of the public house?

4. Are you surprised to discover that Farrington has a wife and children? If so, why?

Explore

1. Why is this story titled "Counterparts"?

2. What aspects of Farrington's behavior strongly suggest that he is an alcoholic?

3. Account for the way Farrington treats his son at the end of the story.

For Your Journal

1. Have you ever taken out your frustrations on someone else? How did you feel later?

2. Do some research into alcoholism. Find out its causes and the ways of treating alcoholics. Write up your discoveries as a report.

First Offense

Evan Hunter

Have you ever experienced the thrill of being scared and feeling tough at the same time? For example, you get called into the principal's office and, though deep inside you are worried, you put on a big act in front of your classmates. This act is called bravado, the pretense of not caring, of being able to handle punishment and danger. It is often a coverup for your real feelings. The main character in the following story seems to be a tough kid. Is he as tough as he seems? Is his act bravado?

HE SAT in the police van with the collar of his leather jacket turned up. He was seventeen years old. He carried his head high and erect because he knew he had a good profile. His hands were deep into his jacket pockets. There was excitement in his eyes, too, an almost holiday excitement. He tried to tell himself he was in trouble, but he couldn't quite believe it.

The desk sergeant had looked him over curiously.

"What's the matter, Fatty?" the boy asked.

The sergeant stared at him. "Put him away for the night," the sergeant said.

He'd slept overnight in the precinct cellblock, and he'd awakened with this strange excitement pulsing through his narrow body. It was the excitement that had caused his disbelief. He'd been in trouble before, but it had never felt like this. This was different. This was a ball, man. He was big-time now. They'd caught him and booked him, and he should have been scared but he was excited instead.

There was one other person in the van with him, a guy who'd spent the night in the cellblock, too. The guy was a bum, and his breath stank of cheap wine, but he was better than nobody to talk to.

"Hey!" he said. "Where are we going?"

"The lineup, kid," the bum said. "This your first time?"

"This's the first time I got caught," he answered cockily.

"All felonies go to the lineup," the bum told him. "You commit a felony?"

"Yeah," he said. What'd they have this bum in for anyway? Sleeping on a park bench?

"Well, that's why you're goin' to the lineup. They have guys from every detective squad in the city there, to look you over. So they'll remember you next time. They put you on a stage, and the Chief of Detectives starts firing questions at you. What's your name, kid?"

"What's it to you?"

"Don't get smart, punk, or I'll break your arm," the bum said.

He looked at the bum curiously. He was a pretty big guy, with a heavy growth of beard, and powerful shoulders. "My name's Stevie," he said.

"I'm Jim Skinner," the bum said. "When somebody's trying to give you advice, don't go hip on him. When they get you up there, you don't have to answer anything. They'll throw questions, but you don't have to answer. Did you make a statement at the scene?"

"No," he answered.

"Good. Then don't make no statement now, either. They can't force you to. Just keep your mouth shut, and don't tell them nothing."

"I ain't afraid. They know all about it anyway," Stevie said.

When they arrived at the Centre Street Headquarters, they put them in cells, awaiting the lineup which began at nine. At ten minutes to nine, they led him out of his cell, and the cop who'd arrested him took him into the special prisoner's elevator.

"How's it feel being an elevator boy?" he asked the cop.

The cop didn't answer him. They went upstairs to the big room where the lineup was being held. A detective in front of them was pinning on his shield so he could get past the cop at the desk. They crossed the large room, walking past the men sitting in folding chairs before the stage.

"Get a nice turnout, don't you?" Stevie said.

The blinds in the room had not been drawn yet, and Stevie could see everything clearly. The stage itself with the mike hanging from a narrow metal tube above; the height markers—four feet, five feet, six feet—behind the mike on the wide white wall. The men in the seats, he knew, were all detectives and his sense of importance suddenly flared again. These bulls[1] had come from all over the city just to look at him. Behind the bulls was a raised platform with a sort of stand on it. A mike rested on the stand, and a chair was behind it. This was where the chief bull would sit. There were uniformed cops stationed here and there around the room, and there was one man in civilian clothing who sat at a desk in front of the stage.

"Who's that?" Stevie asked the cop.

"Police stenographer," the cop answered. "He's going to take down your words."

They walked behind the stage, and Stevie watched as other felony offenders from all over the city joined them. There was one woman, but all the rest were men. They didn't look like much. He was better-looking than all of them, and the knowledge pleased him. Stevie looked around, spotted Skinner and walked over to him.

"What happens now?" he asked.

"They're going to pull the shades in a few minutes," Skinner said. "Then they'll turn on the spots and start the lineup. The spots won't blind you, but you won't be able to see the faces of any of the bulls out there."

"Who wants to see them mugs?" Stevie asked.

Skinner shrugged. "When your case is called, your arresting officer goes back and stands near the Chief of Detectives, just in case the Chief needs more dope from him. The Chief'll read off your name. He'll tell the bulls what they got you on,

[1] **bulls:** slang for police officers, a common mark of disfavor; the term was replaced by "pig" in the sixties and seventies.

and then he'll say either 'Statement' or 'No statement.' If you made a statement, chances are he won't ask many questions. If there's no statement, he'll fire questions like a machine gun. But you don't have to answer nothing."

"Then what?"

"When he's through, you go downstairs to get mugged and printed. Then they take you over to the Criminal Courts Building."

"You think there'll be reporters here?"

"Oh. There may be some reporters." Skinner paused. "Why? What'd you do?"

"It ain't so much what I done," Stevie said. "I was just wondering if we'd make the papers."

Skinner stared at him curiously. "This ain't as exciting as you think, kid. Take my word for it."

"Sure, you know all about it."

"You kill anybody?" asked Skinner.

"No," Stevie said.

"Assault?"

Stevie didn't answer.

"Whatever you done," Skinner advised, "and no matter how long you been doing it before they caught you, make like it's your first time. Tell them you done it, and then say you don't know why you done it, but you'll never do it again. It might help you, kid. You might get off with a suspended sentence."

"Yeah?"

"Sure. And then keep your nose clean afterwards, and you'll be okay."

"Keep my nose clean! Don't make me laugh, pal."

Skinner clutched Stevie's arm in a tight grip. "Kid, don't be a fool. If you can get out, get out now! I could have got out a hundred times, and I'm still with it, and it's no picnic. Get out before you get started."

"Knock it off there," the cop said. "We're ready to start."

"Take a look at your neighbors, kid," Skinner whispered. "Take a hard look. And then get out of it while you still can."

Stevie turned away from Skinner. Skinner whirled him around to face him again. "Kid," he said, "listen to me. Take my advice. I've been . . ."

"Knock it off!" the cop warned again.

He was suddenly aware of the fact that the shades had been drawn and the room was dim. It was very quiet out there, and he hoped they would take him first. What was Skinner talking about anyway? "Take a look at your neighbors, kid." The poor jerk probably had a wet brain. Why did the police bother with old drunks for anyway?

A uniformed cop led one of the men from behind the stage.

The man's eyes were very small, and he kept blinking them. He was bald at the back of his head, and he was wearing a Navy peacoat and dark tweed trousers, and his eyes were red-rimmed and sleepy-looking. He reached to the five-foot-six-inches marker on the wall behind him, and he stared out at the bulls, blinking.

"Assisi," the Chief of Detectives said, "Augustus. Thirty-three years old. Picked up in a bar on 43rd and Broadway, carrying a .45 Colt automatic. No statement. How about it, Gus? Were you carrying a gun?"

"Yes, I was carrying a gun."

"What were you doing with the gun, Gus?"

"I was just carrying it."

"Why?"

"Listen, I'm not going to answer any questions," Assisi said. "I want a lawyer."

"You'll get plenty of chances to have a lawyer," the Chief of Detectives said. "We just want to know what you were doing with a gun. You know that's against the law, don't you?"

"I've got a permit for the gun," Assisi said.

"We checked with Pistol Permits, and they say no. This is a Navy gun, isn't it?"

"Yeah, it's a Navy gun."

"Why were you carrying it around?"

"I like guns."

"The gun *was* loaded, wasn't it?"

"Yeah, it was loaded."

"We found a .38 in your room."

"It's no good. The firing mechanism is busted."

"You want a gun that works, is that it?"

"I didn't say that."

"Why do you need a gun that fires?"

"I was just carrying it. I didn't shoot anybody, did I?"

"No, you didn't. Were you planning on shooting somebody?"

"Sure," Assisi said. "That's just what I was planning."

"Who?"

"I don't know," Assisi said. "Anybody. The first guy I saw, all right? Everybody, all right? I was planning on wholesale murder."

"Not a murder, maybe, but a little larceny, huh? Where'd you get the gun?"

"In the Navy."

"You stole government property, is that it?"

"I found it."

"When'd you get out of the Navy?"

"Three months ago."

"You worked since?"

"No."

"Why'd you leave the Navy?"

Assisi hesitated for a long time.

"Why'd you leave the Navy?" the Chief of Detectives asked again.

"They kicked me out!" Assisi snapped.

"Why?"

Assisi did not answer.

"Why?"

There was silence in the darkened room. Stevie watched Assisi's face, the twitching mouth, the blinking eyelids.

"Next case," the Chief of Detectives said.

Steve watched as Assisi walked across the stage and down the steps on the other side, where the uniformed cop met him. He'd handled himself well, Assisi had. They'd rattled him a little at the end there, but on the whole he'd done a good job. So the guy was lugging a gun around, so what? He was right, wasn't he? He didn't shoot nobody, so what was all the fuss about? Cops!

A man and a woman walked past him and onto the stage. The man was very tall, topping the six-foot marker. The woman was shorter, a bleached blonde turning to fat.

"They picked them up together," Skinner whispered. "So they show them together. They figure a pair'll always work as a pair, usually."

"How'd you like that Assisi?" Stevie whispered back. "He really had them bulls on the run, didn't he?"

Skinner didn't answer. The Chief of Detectives cleared his throat.

"MacGregor, Peter, aged forty-five, and Anderson, Marcia, aged forty-two. Got them in a parked car on the Grand Concourse. Back seat of the car was loaded with goods including luggage, a typewriter, a portable sewing machine, and a fur coat. No statements. What about all that stuff, Pete?"

"It's mine."

"The fur coat, too."

"No, that's Marcia's."

"What about the stuff?" the Chief of Detectives said again.

"I told you," Pete said. "It's ours."

"What was it doing in the car?"

"Oh. Well, we were—uh . . ." The man paused for a long time. "We were going on a trip."

"Where to?"

"Where? Oh. To—uh . . ." Again he paused, frowning, and Stevie smiled, thinking what a clown this guy was. This guy couldn't tell a lie without having to think about it for an hour.

"Uh . . ." Pete said, still fumbling for words. "Uh . . . we were going to—uh . . . Denver."

"What for?"

"Oh, just a little pleasure trip, you know."

"How much money were you carrying when we picked you up?"

"Forty dollars."

"You were going to Denver on forty dollars?"

"Well it was fifty dollars. Yeah, it was more like fifty dollars."

"With a sewing machine, huh? You do a lot of sewing, Pete?"

"Marcia does."

"That right, Marcia?"

The blonde spoke in a high reedy voice. "Yeah, I do a lot of sewing."

"That fur coat, Marcia. Is it yours?"

"Sure."

"It has the initials G.D. on the lining. Those aren't your initials, are they, Marcia? Whose are they?"

"Search me. We bought that coat in a hock shop."

"What about that luggage. It had initials on it, too. And they weren't yours or Pete's. How about it?"

"We got that in a hock shop, too."

"And the typewriter?"

"That's Pete's."

"We're going to check all this stuff against our Stolen Goods list, you know that, don't you?"

"We got all that stuff in hock shops," Pete said. "If it's stolen, we don't know nothing about it."

"Your car was parked on the Grand Concourse. What were you doing there with a carload of stolen goods?"

"It wasn't stolen," Pete said.

"We were on our way to Yonkers," the woman said.

"I thought you were going to Denver."

"Yeah, but we had to get the car fixed first. There was something wrong with the . . ." She paused, turning to Pete. "What was it, Pete? That thing that was wrong?"

Pete waited a long time before answering. "Uh—the—uh . . . the flywheel, yeah. There's a garage up in Yonkers fixes them good, we heard. Flywheels, I mean."

"We found a wallet in your coat, Pete. It wasn't yours, was it?"

"No."

"Whose was it?"

"I don't know." He paused, then added, "There wasn't no money in it."

"No, but there was identification. A Mr. Simon Granger. Where'd you get it, Pete?"

"I found it in the subway. There wasn't no money in it."

"When's the last time you earned an honest dollar, Pete?"

Pete grinned, "Oh, about two, three years ago, I guess."

"Here're their records," the Chief of Detectives said. "Marcia, 1938, Sullivan Law; 1939, Concealing Birth of Issue; 1940, Possession of Narcotics—you still on the stuff, Marcia?"

"No."

"1943, Narcotics again; 1947—you had enough, Marcia?"

Marcia didn't answer.

"Pete," the Chief of Detectives said, "1940, Attempted Rape; 1941, Selective Service Act; 1942, dis cond; 1943, Attempted Burglary; 1947, Assault and Battery, did two years at Ossining."

"I never done no time," Pete said.

"According to this, you did."

"I never done no time," he insisted.

"Get them out of here," the Chief of Detectives said.

"See how long he kept them up there?" Skinner whispered. "He knows what they are, wants every bull in the city to recognize them if they . . ."

"Come on," a detective said, taking Skinner's arm.

Stevie watched as Skinner climbed the steps to the stage. Those two had really been something, all right. And just looking at them, you'd never know they were such operators. You'd never know they . . .

"Skinner, James. Aged fifty-one. Threw a garbage can through the plate glass window of a clothing shop on Third Avenue. Arresting officer found him inside the shop with a bundle of overcoats. No statement. That right, James?"

"I don't remember," Skinner said.

"You don't remember throwing that ash can through the window?"

"No, sir."

"Well, you must have done it, don't you think? The off-duty detective found you inside the store with the coats in your arms."

"I got only his word for that, sir."

"You've been here before, haven't you?"

"I don't remember, sir."

"What do you do for a living, James?"

"I'm unemployed, sir."

"When's the last time you worked?"

"I don't remember, sir."

"You don't remember much of anything, do you?"

"I have a poor memory, sir."

"Maybe the record has a better memory than you, James," the Chief of Detectives said. "I hardly know where to start, James. You haven't been exactly an ideal citizen."

"Haven't I, sir?"

"Here's as good a place as any: 1948, Assault and Robbery; 1951, Burglary; 1952, Assault and Robbery again. You're quite a guy, aren't you, James?"

"If you say so, sir."

"Maybe we should've started back a little further, huh, James? Here, on your record: 1938, convicted of first degree murder, sentenced to execution."

The detectives began murmuring among themselves. Stevie leaned forward to get a better look at this bum.

"What happened there, James?"

"What happened where, sir?"

"You were sentenced to death? How come you're still with us?"

"The case was appealed."

"And never retried?"

"No, sir."

"You're pretty lucky, aren't you?"

"I'm pretty unlucky, sir, if you ask me."

"Is that right? You cheat the chair, and you call that unlucky. Well, the law won't slip up this time."

"I don't know anything about law, sir."

"You don't, huh?"

"No, sir. I only know that if you want to get a police station into action, all you have to do is buy a cheap bottle of wine and drink it quiet, minding your own business."

"And you don't remember breaking into that store?"

"I don't remember anything."

"All right, next case."

Skinner turned his head slowly, and his eyes met Stevie's squarely. Again there was the same mute pleading in his eyes. He turned his head away and shuffled off the stage and down the steps into the darkness.

The cop's hand closed around Stevie's arm. For an instant, he didn't know what was happening, and then he realized his case was the next one. He shook off the cop's hand, squared his shoulders, lifted his head, and began climbing the steps.

He felt taller all at once. He felt like an actor.

The Chief of Detectives was reading off the information about him, but he didn't hear it. He kept looking at the lights, which were not really so bright, they didn't blind him at all. Didn't they have brighter lights? Couldn't they put more lights on him, so they could see him when he told his story?

He tried to make out the faces of the detectives, but he couldn't see them clearly. He glanced over his shoulder, trying to see how tall he was against the markers, and then he stood erect, his shoulders back, moving closer to the hanging mike, wanting to be sure his voice was heard when he began speaking.

". . . no statement," the Chief of Detectives concluded. There was a long pause, and Stevie waited, holding his breath. "This your first offense, Steve?" the Chief of Detectives asked.

"Don't you know?" Stevie answered.

"I'm asking you."

"Yeah, it's my first offense."

"You want to tell us all about it?"

"There's nothing to tell. You know the whole story, anyway."

"Sure, but do you?"

"What are you talking about?"

"Tell us the story, Steve."

"Whatya makin' a big federal case out of a lousy stickup for? Ain't you got nothing better to do with your time?"

"We've got plenty of time, Steve."

"Well, I'm in a hurry."

"You're not going any place, kid. Tell us about it."

"What's there to tell? There was a candy store stuck up, that's all."

"Did you stick it up?"

"That's for me to know and you to find out."

"We know you did."

"Then don't ask me stupid questions."

"Why'd you do it?"

"I ran out of butts."

"Come on, kid."

"I done it 'cause I wanted to."

"Why?"

"Look you caught me cold, so let's get this over with, huh? What are you wasting time with me for?"

"We want to hear what you've got to say. Why'd you pick this particular candy store?"

"I just picked it. I put slips in a hat and picked this one out."

"You didn't really, did you, Steve?"

"No, I didn't really. I picked it 'cause there's an old crumb who runs it, and I figured it was a push-over."

"What time did you enter the store, Steve?"

"The old guy told you all this already, didn't he? Look, I know I'm up here so you can get a good look at me. All right, take a good look, and let's get it over with."

"What time, Steve?"

"I don't have to tell you nothing."

"Except that we know it already."

"Then why do you want to hear it again? Ten o'clock, all right? How does that fit?"

"A little early, isn't it?"

"How's eleven? Try that one for size."

"Let's make it twelve, and we'll be closer."

"Make it whatever you want to," Stevie said, pleased with the way he was handling this. They knew all about it, anyway, so he might as well have himself a ball, show them they couldn't shove him around.

"You went into the store at twelve, is that right?"

"If you say so, Chief."

"Did you have a gun?"

"No."

"What then?"

"Nothing."

"Nothing at all?"

"Just me. I scared him with a dirty look, that's all."

"You had a switch knife, didn't you?"

"You found one on me, so why ask?"

"Did you use the knife?"

"No."

"You didn't tell the old man to open the cash register or you'd cut him up? Isn't that what you said?"

"I didn't make a tape recording of what I said."

"But you did threaten him with the knife. You did force him to open the cash register, holding the knife on him."

"I suppose so."

"How much money did you get?"

"You've got the dough. Why don't you count it?"

"We already have. Twelve dollars, is that right?"

"I didn't get a chance to count it. The Law showed."

"When did the Law show?"

"When I was leaving. Ask the cop who pinched me. He knows when."

"Something happened before you left, though."

"Nothing happened. I cleaned out the register and then blew. Period."

"Your knife had blood on it."

"Yeah? I was cleaning chickens last night."

"You stabbed the owner of that store, didn't you?"

"Me? I never stabbed nobody in my whole life."

"Why'd you stab him?"

"I didn't."

"Where'd you stab him?"

"I didn't stab him."

"We want you to tell us why you stabbed the owner of that store."

"And I told you I didn't stab him."

"He was taken to the hospital last night with six knife wounds. Now how about that, Steve?"

"Save your questioning for the Detective Squad Room. I ain't saying another word."

"Afraid he'd tell who held him up? Afraid he'd start yelling? What were you afraid of, kid?"

"I wasn't afraid of nothing. I told the old crumb to keep his mouth shut. He should have listened to me."

"He didn't keep his mouth shut?"

"No, he didn't keep his mouth shut. He started yelling. Right after I'd cleaned out the drawer. The damn jerk, for a lousy twelve bucks he starts yelling."

"What'd you do?"

"I hit him, and he still kept yelling. So—so I gave him the knife."

"Six times?"

"I don't know how many times. I just—gave it to him. He shouldn't have yelled. You ask him if I did any harm to him before that. Go ahead, ask him. He'll tell you. I didn't even touch the crumb before he started yelling. Go to the hospital and ask him if I touched him. Go ahead, ask him."

"We can't, Steve."

"Wh . . ."

"He died this morning."

"He . . ." For a moment, Stevie could not think clearly. Died? Is that what he'd said? The room was curiously still now. It had been silent before, but this was something else, something different, and the stillness suddenly chilled him. He looked down at his shoes.

"I—I didn't mean him to pass away," he mumbled.

The police stenographer looked up. "To what?"

"To pass away," a uniformed cop repeated, whispering.

"What?" the stenographer asked again.

"He didn't mean him to pass away!" the cop shouted.

The cop's voice echoed in the silent room. The stenographer bent his head and began scribbling in his pad.

"Next case," the Chief of Detectives said.

Stevie walked off the stage. He followed the cop to the door, and then walked with him to the elevator. They were both silent as the doors closed.

"You picked an important one for your first one," the cop said.

"He shouldn't have died on me," Stevie answered.

"You shouldn't have stabbed him," the cop said.

He tried to remember what Skinner had said to him before the lineup, but the noise of the elevator was loud in his ears, and he couldn't think clearly. He could only remember the word "neighbors" as the elevator dropped to the basement to join them.

Discuss

1. Stevie, a boy of seventeen, is excited because he's in the "big-time" now. What does he mean by big-time?

2. What is the reason for having a lineup? Why does Stevie ask if reporters will be at the lineup?

3. When Stevie insults the cop in the elevator, why doesn't the cop answer him?

4. Skinner tells Stevie to look at the other people in the lineup. Then a few of them are described. What should Stevie have been able to learn? What is Skinner trying to do?

5. In the lineup the police drag the story out of Stevie. What does he think the crime is? Why did Stevie pick the candy store to rob? How much money did he get from this robbery? Why did Stevie stab the old man?

6. You and Stevie discover something in the end. What is it? How does this knowledge affect Stevie? How did it, if at all, change your sympathies toward him?

Explore

1. When Skinner approaches Stevie with advice, you get a hint of why prison hardens many young criminals and makes them repeat offenders. Explain what probably happens in prison.

2. Why does the author place you in Stevie's thoughts?

3. Steve internally sneers at Skinner until he discovers something about him. What does Stevie's change in attitude after this discovery tell you about Stevie as a person?

4. When Skinner comes down from the lineup, his eyes meet Stevie's with mute pleading. What is he pleading with Stevie for?

5. There are several ironies in this story. One has to do with Skinner's advice that Stevie take a good look at his neighbors. Stevie's notion of the "big time" is ironic. And, there is irony in that Stevie blames someone else for his predicament. Explain these ironies more fully.

For Your Journal

Imagine yourself as a newspaper reporter. You've discovered the crime Stevie has committed; you've been at the lineup; you're interested in his personality, his background, his attitudes, and how he feels about his crime. You consider him representative of other street kids who grow up in certain neighborhoods. Write a news article on him. Tell about his home life and how he did in school; interview his teachers and his friends, to find out how they react to his crime.

Hostilities

*Many people believe that hate and
hostile behavior are unavoidable facts
of human relations. People have disagreements
which sometimes turn violent.
The most puzzling expression of the human
ability to hate is war, in which people
go far beyond verbal and physical attacks.
Whereas most killing is considered
a crime, killing in war is officially
sanctioned and justified. Why human beings
behave in this contradictory way baffles
psychologists and intrigues writers.
In conflict, writers often find elements of
tragedy combined with elements of heroism
and compassion. Ironically,
the experience of war sometimes brings out
the best in people. The literature
in this section deals with hostile actions
and their effects. Of course, war is
only one arena of hostile activity.
One poem in this section views nature
as an enemy, a contrast to
the usual view that nature is always good.*

The Sniper

Liam O'Flaherty

Liam O'Flaherty wrote this story a long time ago. If you are familiar with current international affairs and recognize the locale, you will note with sadness how little has changed and how little has been learned.

THE LONG June twilight faded into night. Dublin lay enveloped in darkness but for the dim light of the moon that shone through fleecy clouds, casting a pale light as of approaching dawn over the streets and the dark waters of the Liffey. Around the beleaguered Four Courts the heavy guns roared. Here and there through the city, machine guns and rifles broke the silence of the night, spasmodically, like dogs barking on lone farms. Republicans and Free Staters[1] were waging civil war.

On a roof top near O'Connell Bridge, a Republican sniper lay watching. Beside him lay his rifle and over his shoulders were slung a pair of field glasses. His face was the face of a student, thin and ascetic, but his eyes had the cold gleam of the fanatic. They were deep and thoughtful, the eyes of a man who is used to looking at death.

He was eating a sandwich hungrily. He had eaten nothing since morning. He had been too excited to eat. He finished the sandwich, and, taking a flask of whisky from his pocket, he took a short draught. Then he returned the flask to his pocket. He paused for a moment, considering whether he should risk a smoke. It was dangerous. The flash might be seen in the darkness and there were enemies watching. He decided to take the risk.

Placing a cigarette between his lips, he struck a match, inhaled the smoke hurriedly and put out the light. Almost immediately, a bullet flattened itself against the parapet[2] of the roof. The sniper took another whiff and put out the cigarette. Then he swore softly and crawled away to the left.

Cautiously he raised himself and peered over the parapet. There was a flash and a bullet whizzed over his head. He dropped immediately. He had seen the flash. It came from the opposite side of the street.

He rolled over the roof to a chimney stack in the rear, and slowly drew himself up behind it, until his eyes were level with the top of the parapet. There was nothing to be seen—just the dim outline of the opposite housetop against the blue sky. His enemy was under cover.

Just then an armored car came across the bridge and advanced slowly up the street. It stopped on the opposite side of the street, fifty yards ahead. The sniper could hear the dull panting of the motor. His heart beat faster. It was an enemy car. He wanted to fire, but he knew it was useless. His bullets would never pierce the steel that covered the gray monster.

Then round the corner of a side street came an old woman, her head covered by a tattered shawl. She began to talk to the man in the turret[3] of the car. She was pointing to the roof where the sniper lay. An informer.

The turret opened. A man's head and shoulders appeared, looking toward the sniper. The sniper raised his rifle and fired. The head fell heavily on the turret wall. The woman darted toward the side street. The sniper fired again. The woman whirled round and fell with a shriek into the gutter.

[1] **Republicans and Free Staters:** At the time of the civil war in this story, Ireland was part of Great Britain. The Free Staters wanted Ireland to be a separate country.
[2] **parapet:** low wall at the edge of a roof, balcony, or bridge.

[3] **turret:** the hatchway, or opening, on top of an armored vehicle.

Suddenly from the opposite roof a shot rang out and the sniper dropped his rifle with a curse. The rifle clattered to the roof. The sniper thought the noise would wake the dead. He stopped to pick the rifle up. He couldn't lift it. His forearm was dead. "I'm hit," he muttered.

Dropping flat onto the roof, he crawled back to the parapet. With his left hand he felt the injured right forearm. The blood was oozing through the sleeve of his coat. There was no pain—just a deadened sensation, as if the arm had been cut off.

Quickly he drew his knife from his pocket, opened it on the breastwork of the parapet, and ripped open the sleeve. There was a small hole where the bullet had entered. On the other side there was no hole. The bullet had lodged in the bone. It must have fractured it. He bent the arm below the wound. The arm bent back easily. He ground his teeth to overcome the pain.

Then taking out his field dressing, he ripped open the packet with his knife. He broke the neck of the iodine bottle and let the bitter fluid drip into the wound. A paroxysm of pain swept through him. He placed the cotton wadding over the wound and wrapped the dressing over it. He tied the ends with his teeth.

Then he lay still against the parapet, and, closing his eyes, he made an effort of will to overcome the pain.

In the street beneath all was still. The armored car had retired speedily over the bridge, with the machine gunner's head hanging lifeless over the turret. The woman's corpse lay still in the gutter.

The sniper lay still for a long time nursing his wounded arm and planning escape. Morning must not find him wounded on the roof. The enemy on the opposite roof covered his escape. He must kill that enemy and he could not use his rifle. He had only a revolver to do it. Then he thought of a plan.

Taking off his cap, he placed it over the muzzle of his rifle. Then he pushed the rifle slowly upward over the parapet, until the cap was visible from the opposite side of the street. Almost immediately there was a report, and a bullet pierced the center of the cap. The sniper slanted the rifle forward. The cap slipped down into the street. Then catching the rifle in the middle, the sniper dropped his left hand over the roof and let it hang, lifelessly. After a few moments he let the rifle drop to the street. Then he sank to the roof, dragging his hand with him.

Crawling quickly to the left, he peered up at the corner of the roof. His ruse[4] had succeeded. The other sniper, seeing the cap and rifle fall, thought that he had killed his man. He was now standing before a row of chimney pots, looking across, with his head clearly silhouetted against the western sky.

The Republican sniper smiled and lifted his revolver above the edge of the parapet. The distance was about fifty yards—a hard shot in the dim light, and his right arm was paining him like a thousand devils. He took a steady aim. His hand trembled with eagerness. Pressing his lips together he took a deep breath through his nostrils and fired. He was almost deafened with the report and his arm shook with the recoil.

Then when the smoke cleared he peered across and uttered a cry of joy. His enemy had been hit. He was reeling over the parapet in his death agony. He struggled to keep his feet, but he was slowly falling forward, as if in a dream. The rifle fell from his grasp, hit the parapet, fell over, bounded off the pole of a barber's shop beneath and then clattered on the pavement.

Then the dying man on the roof crumpled up and fell forward. The body turned over and over in space and hit the ground with a dull thud. Then it lay still.

The sniper looked at his enemy falling and he shuddered. The lust of battle died in him. He became bitten by remorse. The sweat stood out in beads on his forehead. Weakened by his wound and the long summer day of fasting and watching on the roof, he revolted from the sight of the shattered mass of his dead enemy. His teeth chattered, he began to gibber to himself, cursing the war, cursing himself, cursing everybody.

He looked at the smoking revolver in his hand, and with an oath he hurled it to the roof at his feet. The revolver went off with the concussion and the bullet whizzed past the sniper's head. He was frightened back to his senses by the shock. His nerves steadied. The cloud of fear scattered from his mind and he laughed.

Taking the whisky flask from his pocket, he emptied it at a draught. He felt reckless under the influence of the spirit. He decided to leave the roof now and look for his company commander, to report. Everywhere around was quiet. There was not much danger in going through the streets. He

[4]**ruse**: trick.

picked up his revolver and put it in his pocket. Then he crawled down through the skylight to the house underneath.

When the sniper reached the laneway on the street level, he felt a sudden curiosity as to the identity of the enemy sniper whom he had killed. He decided that he was a good shot, whoever he was. He wondered did he know him. Perhaps he had been in his own company before the split in the army. He decided to risk going over to have a look at him. He peered around the corner into O'Connell Street. In the upper part of the street there was heavy firing, but around here all was quiet.

The sniper darted across the street. A machine gun tore up the ground around him with a hail of bullets, but he escaped. He threw himself face downward beside the corpse. The machine gun stopped.

Then the sniper turned over the dead body and looked into his brother's face.

Discuss

1. Where is the civil war in this story taking place?

2. How bitter is the fighting in the civil war in this story? What factors appear to determine the degree of hatred?

3. What is a sniper?

4. In what part of the body does the sniper in this story get hit?

5. What trick does this sniper use to convince the other sniper that he is dead?

6. How does the trick work?

Explore

1. The sniper is described as having the face of a student and the eyes of a fanatic. How does his occupation as a student fit his fanatical dedication to a cause?

2. After he kills the other sniper, why does he feel remorse?

3. He recovers his composure but seems compelled to look at the man he has killed, even at the risk of his own life. How do you account for this action?

4. The last sentence makes an ironic point about civil warfare, which comes from the word "brother." Explain the irony and tell why the author's use of the word is significant.

5. On the basis of this story, how do you think the author feels about the civil war?

For Your Journal

1. What is happening in Northern Ireland's government today? Do your own research and write a report identifying issues related to hostility.

2. Someone once remarked that family quarrels are the most bitter. Do you agree? Why or why not?

The Man He Killed

Thomas Hardy

Can you imagine killing someone you have never met, someone who has never done you any harm? Isn't that what happens in a war? This poem by Thomas Hardy speculates about the curious ability of human beings to behave in such a cold-blooded way. Hardy never fought in a war, but he was well aware of the peculiar value system that permits a person to kill a total stranger without a pang of conscience.

"Had he and I but met
By some old ancient inn,
We should have sat us down to wet
Right many a nipperkin![1]

"But ranged as infantry,[2]
And staring face to face,
I shot at him as he at me,
And killed him in his place.

"I shot him dead because—
Because he was my foe,
Just so: my foe of course he was;
That's clear enough; although

"He thought he'd 'list, perhaps,
Off-hand like—just as I—
Was out of work—had sold his traps[3]—
No other reason why.

"Yes; quaint and curious war is!
You shoot a fellow down
You'd treat if met where any bar is,
Or help to half-a-crown."

[1]**nipperkin:** half pint of ale.
[2]**infantry:** soldiers on foot.
[3]**traps:** simple belongings.

Discuss

1. Why does Hardy specify that the speaker and his enemy were infantry?

2. In stanza three, which word tells you the speaker's reason for killing the stranger? Why is this word powerful?

Explore

1. Also in stanza three, notice how "because" is repeated. What effect does this manner of repetition produce?

2. Is the answer, "because he was my foe," satisfactory? How do you know?

3. Reread the last stanza. What is quaint about war?

4. The poem opens and closes with a bar scene. Does the speaker literally mean he would join any stranger in a drink of ale? Why or why not?

For Your Journal

Have you ever discovered that someone you thought you hated turned out to be a nice person? Write about this experience, telling how the change occurred.

War

Luigi Pirandello

No shooting. No scenes of violence. No blood and gore. Yet the effect of war
is apparent and very touching in this story. It is war as felt by parents.

THE PASSENGERS who had left Rome by the night express had had to stop until dawn at the small station of Fabriano in order to continue their journey by the small old-fashioned "local" joining the main line with Sulmona.

At dawn, in a stuffy and smoky second-class carriage in which five people had already spent the night, a bulky woman in deep mourning was hoisted in—almost like a shapeless bundle. Behind her—puffing and moaning, followed her husband—a tiny man, thin and weakly, his face death-white, his eyes small and bright and looking shy and uneasy.

Having at last taken a seat he politely thanked the passengers who had helped his wife and who had made room for her; then he turned round to the woman trying to pull down the collar of her coat and politely enquired:

"Are you all right, dear?"

The wife, instead of answering, pulled up her collar again to her eyes, so as to hide her face.

"Nasty world," muttered the husband with a sad smile.

And he felt it his duty to explain to his travelling companions that the poor woman was to be pitied for the war was taking away from her her only son, a boy of twenty to whom both had devoted their entire life, even breaking up their home at Sulmona to follow him to Rome where he had to go as a student, then allowing him to volunteer for war with an assurance, however, that at least for six months he would not be sent to the front and now, all of a sudden, receiving a wire saying that he was due to leave in three days' time and asking them to go and see him off.

The woman under the big coat was twisting and wriggling, at times growling like a wild animal,

feeling certain that all those explanations would not have aroused even a shadow of sympathy from those people who—most likely—were in the same plight as herself. One of them, who had been listening with particular attention, said:

"You should thank God that your son is only leaving now for the front. Mine has been sent there the first day of the war. He has already come back twice wounded and been sent back again to the front."

"What about me? I have two sons and three nephews at the front," said another passenger.

"Maybe, but in our case it is our *only* son," ventured the husband.

"What difference can it make? You may spoil your only son with excessive attentions, but you cannot love him more than you would all your other children if you had any. Paternal love is not like bread that can be broken into pieces and split amongst the children in equal shares. A father gives *all* his love to each one of his children without discrimination, whether it be one or ten, and if I am suffering now for my two sons, I am not suffering half for each of them but double . . ."

"True . . . true . . ." sighed the embarrassed husband, "but suppose (of course we all hope it will never be your case) a father has two sons at the front and he loses one of them, there is still one left to console him . . . while . . ."

"Yes," answered the other, getting cross, "a son left to console him but also a son left for whom he must survive, while in the case of the father of an only son if the son dies the father can die too and put an end to his distress. Which of the two positions is the worse? Don't you see how my case would be worse than yours?"

"Nonsense," interrupted another traveller, a fat, red-faced man with bloodshot eyes of the palest gray.

He was panting. From his bulging eyes seemed to spurt inner violence of an uncontrolled vitality which his weakened body could hardly contain.

"Nonsense," he repeated, trying to cover his mouth with his hand so as to hide the two missing front teeth. "Nonsense. Do we give life to our children for our own benefit?"

The other travellers stared at him in distress. The one who had had his son at the front since the first day of the war sighed: "You are right. Our children do not belong to us, they belong to the Country. . . ."

"Bosh," retorted the fat traveller. "Do we think of the Country when we give life to our children? Our sons are born because . . . well, because they must be born and when they come to life they take our own life with them. This is the truth. We belong to them but they never belong to us. And when they reach twenty they are exactly what we were at their age. We too had a father and mother, but there were so many other things as well . . . girls, cigarettes, illusions, new ties . . . and the Country, of course, whose call we would have answered—when we were twenty—even if father and mother had said no. Now, at our age, the love of our Country is still great, of course, but stronger than it is the love for our children. Is there any one of us here who wouldn't gladly take his son's place at the front if he could?"

There was a silence all round, everybody nodding as to approve.

"Why then," continued the fat man, "shouldn't we consider the feelings of our children when they are twenty? Isn't it *natural* that at their age they should consider the love for their Country (I am speaking of decent boys, of course) even greater than the love for us? Isn't it *natural* that it should be so, as after all they must look upon us as upon old boys who cannot move any more and must stay at home? If Country exists, if Country is a natural necessity like bread, of which each of us must eat in order not to die of hunger, somebody must go to defend it. And our sons go, when they are twenty, and they don't want tears, because if they die, they die inflamed and happy (I am speaking, of course, of decent boys). Now, if one dies young and happy, without having the ugly sides of life, the boredom of it, the pettiness, the bitterness of disillusion . . . what more can we ask for him?

Everyone should stop crying: everyone should laugh, as I do . . . or at least thank God—as I do—because my son, before dying, sent me a message saying that he was dying satisfied at having ended his life in the best way he could have wished. That is why, as you see, I do not even wear mourning. . . ."

He shook his light fawn coat as to show it; his livid lip over his missing teeth was trembling, his eyes were watery and motionless and soon after he ended with a shrill laugh which might well have been a sob.

"Quite so . . . quite so . . ." agreed the others.

The woman who, bundled in a corner under her coat, had been sitting and listening had—for the last three months—tried to find in the words of her husband and her friends something to console her in her deep sorrow, something that might show her how a mother should resign herself to send her son not even to death but to a probable danger of life. Yet not a word had she found amongst the many which had been said . . . and her grief had been greater in seeing that nobody—as she thought—could share her feelings.

But now the words of the traveller amazed and almost stunned her. She suddenly realized that it wasn't the others who were wrong and could not understand her but herself who could not rise up to the same height of those fathers and mothers willing to resign themselves, without crying, not only to the departure of their sons but even to their death.

She lifted her head, she bent over from her corner trying to listen with great attention to the details which the fat man was giving to his companions about the way his son had fallen as a hero, for his King and his Country, happy and without regrets. It seemed to her that she had stumbled into a world she had never dreamt of, a world so far unknown to her and she was so pleased to hear everyone joining in congratulating that brave father who could so stoically speak of his child's death.

Then suddenly, just as if she had heard nothing of what had been said and almost as if waking up from a dream, she turned to the old man, asking him:

"Then . . . is your son really dead?"

Everybody stared at her. The old man, too, turned to look at her, fixing his great, bulging, horribly watery light grey eyes, deep in her face. For some little time he tried to answer, but words failed him. He looked and looked at her, almost as if only then—at that silly, incongruous question—he had suddenly realized at last that his son was really dead . . . gone for ever . . . for ever. His face contracted, became horribly distorted, then he snatched in haste a handkerchief from his pocket and, to the amazement of everyone, broke into harrowing, heart-rending, uncontrollable sobs.

Discuss

1. A couple get on a train, and the husband explains why his wife is hiding her face. What explanation does he give?

2. This explanation sets off a conversation among the passengers. What does the conversation reveal about them all?

3. At first the fat man seems to accept his son's death without mourning. What is his explanation for doing so?

4. His words influence the woman whose son is about to be sent to the front. How does she now see her own behavior?

5. Why does she ask the fat man what appears to be an unnecessary question?

6. What happens after she asks the question?

Explore

1. This is a dramatic, though brief story. How does the author achieve the effects he does?

2. After the fat man makes a fine speech extolling his son's death and his own acceptance of it, one action suddenly wipes it all out. What does this action reveal?

For Your Journal

1. Analyze the fat man's argument that children do not exist for the sake of their parents.

2. Argue against the point of view claimed by the fat man.

Dulce et Decorum Est
Wilfred Owen

Coming after a period of relative tranquillity, World War I (1914–1918) was a shattering experience, especially for the front-line soldiers. They lived for weeks on end in trenches and underground dugouts. Covered with lice and scabies, a contagious skin disease, the soldiers had to endure artillery bombardments and attacks of poison gas. Massive frontal attacks by both sides resulted in thousands of deaths in a matter of minutes. Wilfred Owen, who wrote the following poem, was a young officer in this war. He died at the age of twenty-five, a few weeks before the war ended.

Bent double, like old beggars under sacks,
Knock-kneed, coughing like hags, we cursed through sludge,
Till on the haunting flares we turned our backs.
And towards our distant rest began to trudge.
Men marched asleep. Many had lost their boots,
But limped on, blood-shod. All went lame, all blind:
Drunk with fatigue: deaf even to the hoots
Of gas-shells dropping softly behind.

Gas! GAS! Quick, boys!—An ecstasy of fumbling,
Fitting the clumsy helmets just in time,
But someone still was yelling out and stumbling
And flound'ring like a man in fire or lime.[1]—
Dim through the misty panes and thick green light,
As under a green sea, I saw him drowning.
In all my dreams before my helpless sight
He plunges at me, guttering, choking, drowning.

[1] **lime:** calcium oxide, a compound used for burning up disposed matter. The effect here is also of the lime fruit's color—greenish mist.

(continued)

If in some smothering dreams, you too could pace
Behind the wagon that we flung him in,
And watch the white eyes writhing in his face,
His hanging face, like a devil's sick of sin,
If you could hear, at every jolt, the blood
Come gargling from the froth-corrupted lungs
Bitter as the cud[2]
Of vile, incurable sores on innocent tongues,—
My friend, you would not tell with such high zest
To children ardent for some desperate glory,
The old lie: *Dulce et decorum est*
Pro patria mori.[3]

[2]**cud:** food returned from the stomach to the mouth and chewed a second time.
[3]***Dulce et decorum est pro patria mori:*** a Latin quotation from the ancient poet Horace, meaning "It is sweet and proper to die for one's country."

Discuss

1. What image appears in the first line with the simile "old beggars under sacks"?

2. What don't men hear because they are so worn out? What are the "clumsy helmets"?

3. To be shod is to have shoes on. In line six, why is the term "blood-shod" so powerful?

4. Similes convey two powerful images in the second stanza. What are they?

Explore

1. What phrase of the poem sums up Owen's attitude toward warfare?

2. What image does Owen provide to support his attitude?

3. Notice Owen's use of the word "flung" in the last stanza. How do you picture the action?

4. The simile "like a devil's sick of sin" produces an interesting image. How do you interpret it?

For Your Journal

1. Come to grips with the last stanza. Picture the scene Owen describes, and then relate your reactions. What feelings would the experience arouse in you if you were the one pacing behind the wagon?

2. Could Owen's poem be considered unpatriotic? Why or why not? Write out your opinion of what patriotism is.

A Noiseless Flash

John Hersey

Hiroshima is known as the first city hit by an atomic bomb. Because the bomb has been dropped only twice, both times on Japan (the other city being Nagasaki) and during the forties, relatively few people today can recall its effects. Most people do know, however, that the nuclear weapons currently being developed in many places, including the United States, are many times more powerful than those first atomic bombs. As you read this excerpt from John Hersey's book *Hiroshima*, think of the devastation a bomb like that could cause in your home area. Can you even imagine what life would be like should such a catastrophe befall you?

AT EXACTLY fifteen minutes past eight in the morning, on August 6, 1945, Japanese time, at the moment when the atomic bomb flashed above Hiroshima, Miss Toshiko Sasaki, a clerk in the personnel department of the East Asia Tin Works, had just sat down at her place in the plant office and was turning her head to speak to the girl at the next desk. At that same moment, Dr. Masakazu Fujii was settling down cross-legged to read the Osaka *Asahi*[1] on the porch of his private hospital, overhanging one of the seven deltaic rivers which divide Hiroshima; Mrs. Hatsuyo Nakamura, a tailor's widow, stood by the window of her kitchen, watching a neighbor tearing down his house because it lay in the path of an air-raid-defense fire lane; Father Wilhelm Kleinsorge, a German priest of the Society of Jesus, reclined in his underwear on a cot on the top floor of his order's three-story mission house, reading a Jesuit magazine, *Stimmen der Zeit*; Dr. Terufumi Sasaki, a young member of the surgical staff of the city's large, modern Red Cross Hospital, walked along one of the hospital corridors with a blood specimen for a Wassermann test[2] in his hand; and the Reverend Mr. Kiyoshi Tanimoto, pastor of the Hiroshima Methodist Church, paused at the door of a rich man's house

in Koi, the city's western suburb, and prepared to unload a handcart full of things he had evacuated from town in fear of the massive B-29 raid which everyone expected Hiroshima to suffer. A hundred thousand people were killed by the atomic bomb, and these six were among the survivors. They still wonder why they lived when so many others died. Each of them counts many small items of chance or volition—a step taken in time, a decision to go indoors, catching one streetcar instead of the next—that spared him. And now each knows that in the act of survival he lived a dozen lives and saw more death than he ever thought he would see. At the time, none of them knew anything.

The Reverend Mr. Tanimoto got up at five o'clock that morning. He was alone in the parsonage, because for some time his wife had been commuting with their year-old baby to spend nights with a friend in Ushida, a suburb to the north. Of all the important cities of Japan, only two, Kyoto and Hiroshima, had not been visited in strength by B-*san*, or Mr. B, as the Japanese, with a mixture of respect and unhappy familiarity, called the B-29; and Mr. Tanimoto, like all his neighbors and friends, was almost sick with anxiety. He had heard uncomfortably detailed accounts of mass raids on Kure, Iwakuni, Tokuyama, and other nearby towns; he was sure Hiroshima's turn would come soon. He

[1]**Osaka *Asahi*:** a newspaper from the city of Osaka.
[2]**Wassermann test:** a blood test to discover syphilis, a veneral disease.

had slept badly the night before, because there had been several air-raid warnings. Hiroshima had been getting such warnings almost every night for weeks, for at that time the B-29s were using Lake Biwa, northeast of Hiroshima, as a rendezvous point, and no matter what city the Americans planned to hit, the Superfortresses[3] streamed in over the coast near Hiroshima. The frequency of the warnings and the continued abstinence of Mr. B with respect to Hiroshima had made its citizens jittery; a rumor was going around that the Americans were saving something special for the city.

Mr. Tanimoto is a small man, quick to talk, laugh, and cry. He wears his black hair parted in the middle and rather long; the prominence of the frontal bones just above his eyebrows and the smallness of his mustache, mouth, and chin give him a strange, old-young look, boyish and yet wise, weak and yet fiery. He moves nervously and fast, but with a restraint which suggests that he is a cautious, thoughtful man. He showed, indeed, just those qualities in the uneasy days before the bomb fell. Besides having his wife spend the nights in Ushida, Mr. Tanimoto had been carrying all the portable things from his church, in the close-packed residential district called Nagaragawa, to a house that belonged to a rayon manufacturer in Koi, two miles from the center of town. The rayon man, a Mr. Matsui, had opened his then unoccupied estate to a large number of his friends and acquaintances, so that they might evacuate whatever they wished to a safe distance from the probable target area. Mr. Tanimoto had had no difficulty in moving chairs, hymnals, Bibles, altar gear, and church records by pushcart himself, but the organ console and an upright piano required some aid. A friend of his named Matsuo had, the day before, helped him get the piano out to Koi; in return, he had promised this day to assist Mr. Matsuo in hauling out a daughter's belongings. That is why he had risen so early.

Mr. Tanimoto cooked his own breakfast. He felt awfully tired. The effort of moving the piano the day before, a sleepless night, weeks of worry and unbalanced diet, the cares of his parish—all combined to make him feel hardly adequate to the new day's work. There was another thing, too; Mr. Tanimoto had studied theology at Emory College, in Atlanta, Georgia; he had graduated in 1940; he spoke excellent English; he dressed in American clothes; he had corresponded with many American

friends right up to the time the war began; and among a people obsessed with a fear of being spied upon—perhaps almost obsessed himself—he found himself growing increasingly uneasy. The police had questioned him several times, and just a few days before, he had heard that an influential acquaintance, a Mr. Tanaka, a retired officer of the Toyo Kisen Kaisha steamship line, an anti-Christian, a man famous in Hiroshima for his showy philanthropies and notorious for his personal tyrannies, had been telling people that Tanimoto should not be trusted. In compensation, to show himself publicly a good Japanese, Mr. Tanimoto had taken on the chairmanship of his local *tonari-gumi*, or Neighborhood Association, and to his other duties and concerns this position had added the business of organizing air-raid defense for about twenty families.

Before six o'clock that morning, Mr. Tanimoto started for Mr. Matsuo's house. There he found that their burden was to be a *tansu*, a large Japanese cabinet, full of clothing and household goods. The two men set out. The morning was perfectly clear and so warm that the day promised to be uncomfortable. A few minutes after they started, the air-raid siren went off—a minute-long blast that warned of approaching planes but indicated to the people of Hiroshima only a slight degree of danger, since it sounded every morning at this time, when an American weather plane came over. The two men pulled and pushed the handcart through the city streets. Hiroshima was a fan-shaped city, lying mostly on the six islands formed by the seven estuarial rivers that branch out from the Ota River; its main commercial and residential districts, covering about four square miles in the center of the city, contained three-quarters of its population, which had been reduced by several evacuation programs from a wartime peak of 380,000 to about 245,000. Factories and other residential districts, or suburbs, lay compactly around the edges of the city. To the south were the docks, an airport, and the island-studded Inland Sea. A rim of mountains runs around the other three sides of the delta. Mr. Tanimoto and Mr. Matsuo took their way through the shopping center, already full of people, and across two of the rivers to the sloping streets of Koi, and up them to the outskirts and foothills. As they started up a valley away from the tight-ranked houses, the all-clear sounded. (The Japanese radar operators, detecting only three planes, supposed

[3]**superfortresses:** B-29 airplanes.

that they comprised a reconnaissance.[4] Pushing the handcart up to the rayon man's house was tiring, and the men, after they had maneuvered their load into the driveway and to the front steps, paused to rest awhile. They stood with a wing of the house between them and the city. Like most homes in this part of Japan, the house consisted of a wooden frame and wooden walls supporting a heavy tile roof. Its front hall, packed with rolls of bedding and clothing, looked like a cool cave full of fat cushions. Opposite the house, to the right of the front door, there was a large, finicky rock garden. There was no sound of planes. The morning was still; the place was cool and pleasant.

Then a tremendous flash of light cut across the sky. Mr. Tanimoto has a distinct recollection that it travelled from east to west, from the city toward the hills. It seemed a sheet of sun. Both he and Mr. Matsuo reacted in terror—and both had time to react (for they were 3,500 yards, or two miles, from the center of the explosion). Mr. Matsuo dashed up the front steps into the house and dived among the bedrolls and buried himself there. Mr. Tanimoto took four or five steps and threw himself between two big rocks in the garden. He bellied up very hard against one of them. As his face was against the stone, he did not see what happened. He felt a sudden pressure, and then splinters and pieces of board and fragments of tile fell on him. He heard no roar. (Almost no one in Hiroshima recalls hearing any noise of the bomb. But a fisherman in his sampan on the Inland Sea near Tsuzu, the man with whom Mr. Tanimoto's mother-in-law and sister-in-law were living, saw the flash and heard a tremendous explosion; he was nearly twenty miles from Hiroshima, but the thunder was greater than when the B-29s hit Iwakuni, only five miles away.)

When he dared, Mr. Tanimoto raised his head and saw that the rayon man's house had collapsed. He thought a bomb had fallen directly on it. Such clouds of dust had risen that there was a sort of twilight around. In panic, not thinking for the moment of Mr. Matsuo under the ruins, he dashed out into the street. He noticed as he ran that the concrete wall of the estate had fallen over—toward the house rather than away from it. In the street, the first thing he saw was a squad of soldiers who had been burrowing into the hillside opposite, making one of the thousands of dug-outs in which the Jap-

[4]reconnaissance: flight conducted to gather military information about an unfriendly nation.

anese apparently intended to resist invasion, hill by hill, life for life; the soldiers were coming out of the hole, where they should have been safe, and blood was running from their heads, chests, and backs. They were silent and dazed.

Under what seemed to be a local dust cloud, the day grew darker and darker.

At nearly midnight, the night before the bomb was dropped, an announcer on the city's radio station said that about two hundred B-29s were approaching southern Honshu and advised the population of Hiroshima to evacuate to their designated "safe areas." Mrs. Hatsuyo Nakamura, the tailor's widow, who lived in the section called Nobori-cho and who had long had a habit of doing as she was told, got her three children—a ten-year-old boy, Toshio, an eight-year-old girl, Yaeko, and a five-year-old girl, Myeko—out of bed and dressed them and walked with them to the military area known as the East Parade Ground, on the northeast edge of the city. There she unrolled some mats and the children lay down on them. They slept until about two, when they were awakened by the roar of the planes going over Hiroshima.

As soon as the planes had passed, Mrs. Nakamura started back with her children. They reached home a little after two-thirty and she immediately turned on the radio, which, to her distress, was just then broadcasting a fresh warning. When she looked at the children and saw how tired they were, and when she thought of the number of trips they had made in past weeks, all to no purpose, to the East Parade Ground, she decided that in spite of the instructions on the radio, she simply could not face starting out all over again. She put the children in their bedrolls on the floor, lay down herself at three o'clock, and fell asleep at once, so soundly that when planes passed over later, she did not waken to their sound.

The siren jarred her awake at about seven. She arose, dressed quickly, and hurried to the house of Mr. Nakamoto, the head of her Neighborhood Association, and asked him what she should do. He said that she should remain at home unless an urgent warning—a series of intermittent blasts of the siren—was sounded. She returned home, lit the stove in the kitchen, set some rice to cook, and sat down to read that morning's Hiroshima *Chugoku*. To her relief, the all-clear sounded at eight o'clock. She heard the children stirring, so she went and gave each of them a handful of peanuts and told them to stay on their bedrolls, because they were tired from the night's walk. She had hoped that they would go back to sleep, but the man in the house directly to the south began to make a terrible hullabaloo of hammering, wedging, ripping, and splitting. The prefectural government, convinced, as everyone in Hiroshima was, that the city would be attacked soon, had begun to press with threats and warnings for the completion of wide fire lanes, which, it was hoped, might act in conjunction with the rivers to localize any fires started by an incendiary raid; and the neighbor was reluctantly sacrificing his home to the city's safety. Just the day before, the prefecture had ordered all able-bodied girls from the secondary schools to spend a few days helping to clear these lanes, and they started work soon after the all-clear sounded.

Mrs. Nakamura went back to the kitchen, looked at the rice, and began watching the man next door. At first, she was annoyed with him for making so much noise, but then she was moved almost to tears by pity. Her emotion was specifically directed toward her neighbor, tearing down his home, board by board, at a time when there was so much unavoidable destruction, but undoubtedly she also felt a generalized, community pity, to say nothing of self-pity. She had not had an easy time. Her husband, Isawa, had gone into the Army just after Myeko was born, and she had heard nothing from or of him for a long time, until, on March 5, 1942, she received a seven-word telegram: "Isawa died an honorable death at Singapore."[5] She learned later that he had died on February 15th, the day Singapore fell, and that he had been a corporal. Isawa had been a not particularly prosperous tailor, and his only capital was a Sankoku sewing machine. After his death, when his allotments stopped coming, Mrs. Nakamura got out the machine and began to take in piecework herself, and since then had supported the children, but poorly, by sewing.

As Mrs. Nakamura stood watching her neighbor, everything flashed whiter than any white she had ever seen. She did not notice what happened to the man next door; the reflex of a mother set her in motion toward her children. She had taken a single step (the house was 1,350 yards, or three-quarters of a mile, from the center of the explosion) when something picked her up and she

seemed to fly into the next room over the raised sleeping platform, pursued by parts of her house.

Timbers fell around her as she landed, and a shower of tiles pommelled her; everything became dark, for she was buried. The debris did not cover her deeply. She rose up and freed herself. She heard a child cry, "Mother, help me!," and saw her youngest—Myeko, the five-year-old—buried up to her breast and unable to move. As Mrs. Nakamura started frantically to claw her way toward the baby, she could see or hear nothing of her other children.

In the days right before the bombing, Dr. Masakazu Fujii, being prosperous, hedonistic,[6] and at the time not too busy, had been allowing himself the luxury of sleeping until nine or nine-thirty, but fortunately he had to get up early the morning the bomb was dropped to see a house guest off on a train. He rose at six, and half an hour later walked with his friend to the station, not far away, across two of the rivers. He was back home by seven, just as the siren sounded its sustained warning. He ate breakfast and then, because the morning was already hot, undressed down to his underwear and went out on the porch to read the paper. This porch—in fact, the whole building—was curiously constructed. Dr. Fujii was the proprietor of a peculiarly Japanese institution: a private, single-doctor hospital. This building, perched beside and over the water of the Kyo River, and next to the bridge of the same name, contained thirty rooms for thirty patients and their kinfolk—for, according to Japanese custom, when a person falls sick and goes to a hospital, one or more members of his family go and live there with him, to cook for him, bathe, massage, and read to him, and to offer incessant familial sympathy, without which a Japanese patient would be miserable indeed. Dr. Fujii had no beds—only straw mats—for his patients. He did, however, have all sorts of modern equipment: an X-ray machine, diathermy apparatus, and a fine tiled laboratory. The structure rested two-thirds on the land, one-third on piles over the tidal waters of the Kyo. This overhang, the part of the building where Dr. Fujii lived, was queer-looking, but it was cool in summer and from the porch, which faced away from the center of the city, the prospect of the river, with pleasure boats drifting up and down it, was always refreshing. Dr. Fujii had occasionally had anxious moments when the Ota and its mouth

[5]**Singapore:** an island then part of Malaya (now Malaysia); captured by Japanese troops in 1942.

[6]**hedonistic:** habitually pleasure-seeking.

branches rose to flood, but the piling was apparently firm enough and the house had always held.

Dr. Fujii had been relatively idle for about a month because in July, as the number of untouched cities in Japan dwindled and as Hiroshima seemed more and more inevitably a target, he began turning patients away, on the ground that in case of a fire raid he would not be able to evacuate them. Now he had only two patients left—a woman from Yano, injured in the shoulder, and a young man of twenty-five recovering from burns he had suffered when the steel factory near Hiroshima in which he worked had been hit. Dr. Fujii had six nurses to tend his patients. His wife and children were safe; his wife and one son were living outside Osaka, and another son and two daughters were in the country on Kyushu. A niece was living with him, and a maid and a manservant. He had little to do and did not mind, for he had saved some money. At fifty, he was healthy, convivial, and calm, and he was pleased to pass the evenings drinking whiskey with friends, always sensibly and for the sake of conversation. Before the war, he had affected brands imported from Scotland and America; now he was perfectly satisfied with the best Japanese brand, Suntory.

Dr. Fujii sat down cross-legged in his underwear on the spotless matting of the porch, put on his glasses, and started reading the Osaka *Asahi*. He liked to read the Osaka news because his wife was there. He saw the flash. To him—faced away from the center and looking at his paper—it seemed a brilliant yellow. Startled, he began to rise to his feet. In that moment (he was 1,550 yards from the center), the hospital leaned behind his rising and, with a terrible ripping noise, toppled into the river. The Doctor, still in the act of getting to his feet, was thrown forward and around and over; he was buffeted and gripped; he lost track of everything, because things were so speeded up; he felt the water.

Dr. Fujii hardly had time to think that he was dying before he realized that he was alive, squeezed tightly by two long timbers in a V across his chest, like a morsel suspended between two huge chopsticks—held upright, so that he could not move, with his head miraculously above water and his torso and legs in it. The remains of his hospital were all around him in a mad assortment of splintered lumber and materials for the relief of pain. His left shoulder hurt terribly. His glasses were gone.

Father Wilhelm Kleinsorge, of the Society of Jesus, was, on the morning of the explosion, in rather frail condition. The Japanese wartime diet had not sustained him, and he felt the strain of being a foreigner in an increasingly xenophobic[7] Japan; even a German, since the defeat of the Fatherland, was unpopular. Father Kleinsorge had, at thirty-eight, the look of a boy growing too fast— thin in the face, with a prominent Adam's apple, a hollow chest, dangling hands, big feet. He walked clumsily, leaning forward a little. He was tired all the time. To make matters worse, he had suffered for two days, along with Father Cieslik, a fellow-priest, from a rather painful and urgent diarrhea, which they blamed on the beans and black ration bread they were obliged to eat. Two other priests then living in the mission compound, which was in the Nobori-cho section—Father Superior LaSalle and Father Schiffer—had happily escaped this affliction.

Father Kleinsorge woke up about six the morning the bomb was dropped, and half an hour later—he was a bit tardy because of his sickness— he began to read Mass in the mission chapel, a small Japanese-style wooden building which was without pews, since its worshippers knelt on the usual Japanese matted floor, facing an altar graced with splendid silks, brass, silver, and heavy embroideries. This morning, a Monday, the only worshippers were Mr. Takemoto, a theological student living in the mission house; Mr. Fukai, the secretary of the diocese; Mrs. Murata, the mission's devoutly Christian housekeeper; and his fellow-priests. After Mass, while Father Kleinsorge was reading the Prayers of Thanksgiving, the siren sounded. He stopped the service and the missionaries retired across the compound to the bigger building. There, in his room on the ground floor, to the right of the front door, Father Kleinsorge changed into a military uniform which he had acquired when he was teaching at the Rokko Middle School in Kobe and which he wore during air-raid alerts.

After an alarm, Father Kleinsorge always went out and scanned the sky, and in this instance, when he stepped outside, he was glad to see only the single weather plane that flew over Hiroshima each day about this time. Satisfied that nothing would happen, he went in and breakfasted with the other Fathers on substitute coffee and ration bread, which, under the circumstances, was especially re-

[7]**xenophobic:** fearful of strangers.

pugnant to him. The Fathers sat and talked awhile, until, at eight, they heard the all-clear. They went then to various parts of the building. Father Schiffer retired to his room to do some writing. Father Cieslik sat in his room in a straight chair with a pillow over his stomach to ease his pain, and read. Father Superior LaSalle stood at the window of his room, thinking. Father Kleinsorge went up to a room on the third floor, took off all his clothes except his underwear, and stretched out on his right side on a cot and began reading his *Stimmen der Zeit*.

After the terrible flash—which, Father Kleinsorge later realized, reminded him of something he had read as a boy about a large meteor colliding with the earth—he had time (since he was 1,400 yards from the center) for one thought: A bomb has fallen directly on us. Then, for a few seconds or minutes, he went out of his mind.

Father Kleinsorge never knew how he got out of the house. The next things he was conscious of were that he was wandering around in the mission's vegetable garden in his underwear, bleeding slightly from small cuts along his left flank; that all the buildings round about had fallen down except the Jesuits' mission house, which had long before been braced and double-braced by a priest named Gropper, who was terrified of earthquakes; that the day had turned dark; and that Murata-*san*, the housekeeper, was nearby, crying over and over, "*Shu Jesusu, awaremi tamai!* Our Lord Jesus, have pity on us!"

On the train on the way into Hiroshima from the country, where he lived with his mother, Dr. Terufumi Sasaki, the Red Cross Hospital surgeon, thought over an unpleasant nightmare he had had the night before. His mother's home was in Mukaihara, thirty miles from the city, and it took him two hours by train and tram to reach the hospital. He had slept uneasily all night and had awakened an hour earlier than usual, and, feeling sluggish and slightly feverish, had debated whether to go to the hospital at all; his sense of duty finally forced him to go, and he had started out on an earlier train than he took most mornings. The dream had particularly frightened him because it was so closely associated, on the surface at least, with a disturbing actuality. He was only twenty-five years old and had just completed his training at the Eastern Medical University, in Tsingtao, China. He was something of an idealist and was much dis-

tressed by the inadequacy of medical facilities in the country town where his mother lived. Quite on his own, and without a permit, he had begun visiting a few sick people out there in the evenings, after his eight hours at the hospital and four hours' commuting. He had recently learned that the penalty for practicing without a permit was severe; a fellow-doctor whom he had asked about it had given him a serious scolding. Nevertheless, he had continued to practice. In his dream, he had been at the bedside of a country patient when the police and the doctor he had consulted burst into the room, seized him, dragged him outside, and beat him up cruelly. On the train, he just about decided to give up the work in Mukaihara, since he felt it would be impossible to get a permit, because the authorities would hold that it would conflict with his duties at the Red Cross Hospital.

At the terminus, he caught a streetcar at once. (He later calculated that if he had taken his customary train that morning, and if he had had to wait a few minutes for the streetcar, as often happened, he would have been close to the center at the time of the explosion and would surely have perished.) He arrived at the hospital at seven-forty and reported to the chief surgeon. A few minutes later, he went to a room on the first floor and drew blood from the arm of a man in order to perform a Wassermann test. The laboratory containing the incubators for the test was on the third floor. With the blood specimen in his left hand, walking in a kind of distraction he had felt all morning, probably because of the dream and his restless night, he started along the main corridor on his way toward the stairs. He was one step beyond an open window when the light of the bomb was reflected, like a gigantic photographic flash, in the corridor. He ducked down on one knee and said to himself, as only a Japanese would, "Sasaki, *gambare!* Be brave!" Just then (the building was 1,650 yards from the center), the blast ripped through the hospital. The glasses he was wearing flew off his face; the bottle of blood crashed against one wall; his Japanese slippers zipped out from under his feet— but otherwise, thanks to where he stood, he was untouched.

Dr. Sasaki shouted the name of the chief surgeon and rushed around to the man's office and found him terribly cut by glass. The hospital was in horrible confusion: heavy partitions and ceilings had fallen on patients, beds had overturned, windows had blown in and cut people, blood was spattered on the walls and floors, instruments were everywhere, many of the patients were running about screaming, many more lay dead. (A colleague working in the laboratory to which Dr. Sasaki had been walking was dead; Dr. Sasaki's patient, whom he had just left and who a few moments before had been dreadfully afraid of syphilis, was also dead.) Dr. Sasaki found himself the only doctor in the hospital who was unhurt.

Dr. Sasaki, who believed that the enemy had hit only the building he was in, got bandages and began to bind the wounds of those inside the hospital; while outside, all over Hiroshima, maimed and dying citizens turned their unsteady steps toward the Red Cross Hospital to begin an invasion that was to make Dr. Sasaki forget his private nightmare for a long, long time.

Miss Toshiko Sasaki, the East Asia Tin Works clerk, who is not related to Dr. Sasaki, got up at three o'clock in the morning on the day the bomb fell. There was extra housework to do. Her eleven-month-old brother, Akio, had come down the day before with a serious stomach upset; her mother had taken him to the Tamura Pediatric Hospital and was staying there with him. Miss Sasaki, who was about twenty, had to cook breakfast for her father, a brother, a sister, and herself, and—since the hospital, because of the war, was unable to provide food—to prepare a whole day's meals for her mother and the baby, in time for her father, who worked in a factory making rubber earplugs for artillery crews, to take the food by on his way to the plant. When she had finished and had cleaned and put away the cooking things, it was nearly seven. The family lived in Koi, and she had a forty-five-minute trip to the tin works, in the section of town

called Kannonmachi. She was in charge of the personnel records in the factory. She left Koi at seven, and as soon as she reached the plant, she went with some of the other girls from the personnel department to the factory auditorium. A prominent local Navy man, a former employee, had committed suicide the day before by throwing himself under a train—a death considered honorable enough to warrant a memorial service, which was to be held at the tin works at ten o'clock that morning. In the large hall, Miss Sasaki and the others made suitable preparations for the meeting. This work took about twenty minutes.

Miss Sasaki went back to her office and sat down at her desk. She was quite far from the windows, which were off to her left, and behind her were a couple of tall bookcases containing all the books of the factory library, which the personnel department had organized. She settled herself at her desk, put some things in a drawer, and shifted papers. She thought that before she began to make entries in her lists of new employees, discharges, and departures for the Army, she would chat for a moment with the girl at her right. Just as she turned her head away from the windows, the room was filled with a blinding light. She was paralyzed by fear, fixed still in her chair for a long moment (the plant was 1,600 yards from the center).

Everything fell, and Miss Sasaki lost consciousness. The ceiling dropped suddenly and the wooden floor above collapsed in splinters and the people up there came down and the roof above them gave way; but principally and first of all, the bookcases right behind her swooped forward and the contents threw her down, with her left leg horribly twisted and breaking underneath her. There, in the tin factory, in the first moment of the atomic age, a human being was crushed by books.

Discuss

1. During which war was the atomic bomb dropped on Hiroshima?

2. Six people are named in the first paragraph of this excerpt. Why?

3. Why did the people of Hiroshima feel jittery before the atomic bomb was dropped?

4. Mr. Tanimoto was a Christian. How do you know?

5. How far from the center of the explosion were Mr. Tanimoto and Mr. Matsuo? What did each do in response to the flash of the bomb? Which of the two survived?

6. What had happened to Mrs. Nakamura's husband? How far from the center of the explosion was her house?

7. How far was Dr. Fujii from the center?

8. Who was Father Kleinsorge? How far from the center was he?

Explore

1. Why is this excerpt titled "A Noiseless Flash"?

2. Why does Hersey write about individual cases?

3. Why does Hersey provide so many details of these people's activities immediately before the bombing?

4. Explain the last sentence of the excerpt.

For Your Journal

1. Research and analyze the bombings of Hiroshima and Nagasaki. How did the effects of the explosions differ in each city? What were the most important factors in the decisions to drop the bombs? Do you think the United States did the right thing in bombing those cities? Why or why not?

2. How do you think your country would fare if attacked with nuclear weapons today? Do you think anybody would survive a nuclear attack? Describe what you think might happen before, during, and after the explosion to various members of your family and your community. What chance do you believe there would be of rebuilding the area?

The Death of the Ball Turret Gunner
Randall Jarrell

A bit of background will help you appreciate the tremendous power of this very short poem which takes place during World War II. Bombers known as flying fortresses needed men with machine guns in ball turrets, domed structures which could swivel to track oncoming enemy fighter planes. Most flights were long and the gunner in the ball turret sat hunched over his weapon, swathed in warm clothing because it was quite cold at the height he flew. Several bombers flew in formation to protect one another. But the group was vulnerable to the machine guns of fighter planes from above, below, and the sides.

From my mother's sleep I fell into the State,
And I hunched in its belly till my wet fur froze.
Six miles from earth, loosed from its dream of life,
I woke to black flak[1] and the nightmare fighters.
When I died they washed me out of the turret with a hose.

[1]**flak:** the fire and explosion of antiaircraft guns.

Discuss

1. In the first line, what is the State the speaker fell into?

2. What is his wet fur? Why does his fur freeze?

3. Why does the speaker refer to his combat with the fighters as an awakening?

4. Why are they nightmare fighters?

5. What picture does the last line give you?

Explore

1. There is a comparison and a contrast between the speaker's connection to his mother and his connection to his aircraft. Explain.

2. What is the speaker dreaming of high above the earth?

3. Why is a dead man the speaker?

4. Does this poem support war or oppose war? How do you know?

For Your Journal

1. What is your response to this poem? Do you feel revulsion or antagonism because it is too explicit or seemingly unpatriotic? Do you identify with the unknown and unnamed ball turret gunner? If you were in the armed forces today, would you consider being the modern-day equivalent of a ball turret gunner? Whatever your response, explain it.

2. Do you know any people who fought in recent wars: World War II, the Korean police action, the war in Vietnam? If you do, interview them for their reactions. See if you can speak to several veterans to get contrasting views, especially between those who were in actual combat and those who weren't. Is there a difference in how they look back on their experiences? Would they want to repeat them? Record what they say.

Sea Lullaby

Elinor Wylie

Although nature itself is impersonal—that is, its doings really happen without preplanning, without some mind at work saying "now I'm going to produce a hurricane"—people project onto nature human characteristics and often think of nature as being hostile to human well-being. Notice how this way of thinking pervades the poem you are about to read.

The old moon is tarnished
With smoke of the flood,
The dead leaves are varnished
With color like blood,

A treacherous smiler
With teeth white as milk,
A savage beguiler[1]
In sheathing of silk,

The sea creeps to pillage,[2]
She leaps on her prey;
A child of the village
Was murdered today.

She came up to meet him
In a smooth golden cloak,
She choked him and beat him
To death, for a joke.

Her bright locks were tangled,
She shouted for joy,
With one hand she strangled
A strong little boy.

Now in silence she lingers
Beside him all night
To wash her long fingers
In silvery light.

[1]**beguiler:** deceiver, traitor.
[2]**pillage:** to plunder, rob, lay waste to.

Discuss

1. The title of this poem is intriguing. Why a lullaby?

2. What image of the sea is presented in the poem?

Explore

1. The portrayal of the sea is unusual. More often, it is seen as romantic, life-sustaining, and helpful. Why do you think the poet has a negative view of the sea?

2. This poem uses personification to create an effect. What human characteristics does the sea display?

3. What is horrible in the attitude of the sea, along with the act it commits?

4. In stanza four what is the golden cloak?

For Your Journal

1. Which strikes you as more horrible, the death of the ball turret gunner or the death of the child by drowning? Explain your reasoning.

2. Do you know of a tragic event as devastating as the one described in this poem? If you are lucky enough to be unacquainted with such a tragedy, pick up the newspaper and find one. React to it by writing an essay or poem about the accident.

I Will Fight No More Forever
Chief Joseph

One of the briefest, most eloquent statements ever recorded on the subject of war was made by Chief Joseph, or Hinmatonyalatkit, of the Nez Percé. In 1877 Chief Joseph resisted the U.S. government's attempt to move his people onto a reservation in Idaho. For over a year, he baffled U.S. forces, as he struggled to lead his people across the border into Canada. At one point, he relaxed the pace, believing incorrectly that he had crossed the border. He was surprised and defeated. His statement of surrender is a message to all people.

I AM TIRED of fighting. Our chiefs are killed. Looking Glass is dead. Toohulsote is dead. The old men are all dead. It is the young men who say no and yes. He who led the young men is dead. It is cold and we have no blankets. The little children are freezing to death. My people, some of them, have run away to the hills and have no blankets, no food. No one knows where they are—perhaps they are freezing to death. I want to have time to look for my children and see how many of them I can find. Maybe I shall find them among the dead. Hear me, my chiefs, I am tired. My heart is sad and sick. From where the sun now stands I will fight no more forever.

Discuss

1. What does it mean to say, "I will fight no more forever"?

2. Is this a wise commitment, or not? When is it wise? When not?

Explore

1. In your opinion, would it have been better for Chief Joseph to sacrifice all his people for a principle? Why or why not?

2. Chief Joseph's statement reveals that he had to give up resisting the U.S. government. What outcome of such resistance do you think he—like other Native Americans—had hoped for before he made this commitment to peace?

For Your Journal

1. Argue for or against the pacifist point of view.

2. Write about life from a Native American point of view today. Explain why you feel mistreated and discriminated against. If possible, include your suggestion for how to correct old wrongs.

Glossary of Key Literary Terms

Alliteration. Repetition of a consonant sound at the beginning of two or more words.

> Then all smiles stopped together. There she stands
> —Robert Browning

Allusion. Reference to a person, place or event of historical, literary, or mythological importance.

> Or like stout Cortez when with eagle eyes
>   He stared at the Pacific
> —John Keats

In this instance, the allusion to Cortez as the discoverer of the Pacific Ocean was wrong; Vasco de Balboa was the first European to see the Pacific.

Ballad. A brief poem often sung to music that usually tells a story. Such poems are usually passed on by word of mouth from singer to singer, and their authors are unknown, as is the case with "The Big Rock Candy Mountains."

Biography. An account of a person's life prepared by someone else. Usually book-length, biographies also appear in shorter forms as profiles and sketches. When the account of a person's life is written by the subject, it is called an **autobiography**. "Equal in Paris" by James Baldwin is an autobiographical sketch.

Blank verse. Unrhymed verse having five metrical feet and ten syllables, alternately unstressed and stressed.

> Ŏ más|těrs , lórds | ănd rúl| eřs ín | ăll lánds,
> Hŏw wíll | thĕ Fú|tŭre réck| ŏn wíth|this mán?
> —Edwin Markham

Characterization. Methods by which a writer reveals the significance of a person in a literary work. Writers reveal this significance by describing the appearance of the person, by showing the actions of the person, by describing the person's attitudes, and, in some cases, by the name the person is given.

Dialogue. Conversation recorded in writing. In a short story like "Counterparts" by James Joyce, the dialogue is enclosed in quotation marks. In a play like *The Long Christmas Dinner* by Thornton Wilder, quotation marks are not used and the speaker's name appears before each line.

Diction. Choice of words. Diction helps to distinguish one author's writing from another's.

Epic. Long narrative poem, usually written in formal, dignified language, celebrating the adventures of a hero of history or of legend.

Essay. A brief composition in prose that usually takes up a single topic and often expresses a personal viewpoint. The term *essay* covers a variety of styles and subject matter—from the persuasive analysis of Gloria Steinem's "The Time Factor" to the objective exposition of "Eleven Blue Men" by Berton Roueché.

Foreshadowing. Anticipation or hints of what is to come later in a narrative. Near the beginning of the story "Sucker" by Carson McCullers, Pete says, "If a person admires you a lot you despise him and don't care—and it is the person who doesn't notice you that you are apt to admire." The author is foreshadowing what happens to Sucker, Pete, and Maybelle as the plot develops.

Free verse. Poetry that has no regular pattern of rhyme or rhythm. "The Centaur" by May Swenson is written in free verse.

Imagery. Mental pictures produced by words and phrases.

> a red wheel
> barrow
> glazed with rain
> water
> —William Carlos Williams

The term *imagery* is also applied to non-visual images, words that stimulate a response of the senses.

> I'd wake and hear the cold splintering, breaking.
> —Robert Hayden

Irony. There are three different but related kinds of irony—verbal irony, irony of situation, and dramatic irony.

Verbal irony is lying, saying something that is not true. But it is lying in a special way. The writer who uses verbal irony does not want to deceive. In fact, the writer hopes that the reader will be smart enough to recognize the difference between what is said and what is meant. Here's an example of verbal irony, some advice on how to select a title for a scientific article.

> Ignore the reader whenever possible. If the proposed title means something to you, stop right there; think no further. If the title baffles or misleads the reader, you have won the first round.
> —Paul W. Merrill

Merrill's underlying meaning is almost the opposite of his stated meaning. He is really urging scientific writers to be clear.

A second kind of irony, irony of situation, depends upon an unexpected turn of events. At one point in Thornton Wilder's play *The Long Christmas Dinner*, Charles Bayard says, "Perhaps an occasional war isn't so bad after all. It clears up a lot of poisons that collect in nations. It's like a boil." But then his son is killed, and Charles is no longer glib about the benefits of war. In contrast, he can only stammer to his wife, "My dear, my dear."

Dramatic irony is the third kind of irony. It is created when the reader or audience knows more about the given situation than the characters involved in it. For example, in Shakespeare's *Romeo and Juliet*, the audience knows that Juliet is not dead, only sleeping. Romeo, however, believes she is dead and as a result takes his life.

All three kinds of irony make use of contrast— between what is said and what is meant, between what is expected and what happens, between what is believed and what is known.

Lyric. Originally, a poem sung to the accompaniment of a lyre. The term *lyric* is now applied to any short, nonnarrative poem presenting a speaker who expresses intense personal feeling. William Carlos Williams' poem "The Red Wheelbarrow" is a lyric as is John Keats's "On First Looking into Chapman's Homer."

Metaphor. A comparison between objects that are dissimilar.

> **Life** is the **fruit** she longs to hand you,
> Ripe on a plate.
> —Phyllis McGinley

Meter. The rhythm of regular verse is measured according to its pattern of stressed and unstressed syllables. Here is a line of verse, with its syllables marked for stress (´) or the lack of it (˘).

> Ĭ tóok | thĕ óne | lĕss trávell | ĕd bý
> —Robert Frost

Notice how the syllables are divided in this line. They are divided into *feet,* the basic unit of meter. A foot consists of one stressed syllable and one or more unstressed syllables. Notice also how the word *travelled* is divided. The first syllable is part of one foot; the second, part of another. A foot with an unstressed syllable followed by a stressed one is called an *iamb*. A line with four feet in it is called *tetrameter*. Putting the name of the foot and the name for the line together, you get iambic tetrameter. Besides the iamb, some other commonly used feet in English verse are the following:

Trochee is the reverse of an iamb, having a stressed syllable followed by an unstressed syllable (fóot băll).

Anapest has three syllables, two unstressed followed by a stressed syllable (nŏt ăt áll).

Dactyl also has three syllables, one stressed followed by two unstressed syllables (mús ĭ căl)

The most common number of syllables in English verse is ten. A line of ten syllables, or five feet, is called *pentameter*. A line of six feet is called *hexameter*.

Monologue. A long passage in a literary work spoken by one person. A dramatic monologue, such as "My Last Duchess" by Robert Browning, may use a speaker talking to a silent listener to reveal a tragic situation.

Mood. The atmosphere in a literary work that creates certain expectations in the mind of the reader about what will happen. Mood may be described generally as optimistic or pessimistic and specifically as happy or sad, funny or sinister, calm or oppressive.

Myth. A narrative, often anonymous, dealing with the actions of supernatural creatures and human heroes. Myths often serve to explain the origins of some natural phenomena. One myth, for example, tells how humans acquired fire after it was stolen from the gods by Prometheus. Although modern people may not believe in the literal truth of ancient myths, myths still have strong appeal, and many modern writers employ myths in their works. Tennyson's "Ulysses" tells the story of the ancient hero in his old age.

Narration. The kind of writing that tells a story. Usually, events in a narrative are told in the order of their happening, whether the narrative is factual, like a biography, or imagined, like a novel.

Onomatopoeia. Words whose sounds echo their meaning. Examples of such words are *boom, burp, fizz,* and *sizzle.*

Persona. Usually applied to the first-person narrator of fiction or to the speaker of a lyric poem. Originally, the term referred to the mask worn by an actor in classical drama. *Persona* is now used to distinguish between the author and the character created to speak the author's words. In "My Last Duchess," the speaker and the author of the poem are separate and distinct. The speaker is Robert Browning's *persona.*

Personification. A word or a phrase that attributes human qualities to a thing or an idea. In the following lines, the sea is personified as a predator:

> A treacherous smiler
> With teeth white as milk,
> A savage beguiler
> In sheathing of silk,
> The sea creeps to pillage
> —Elinor Wylie

Plot. The arrangement a writer gives to events in drama, fiction, or narrative poetry. A plot has three parts—a beginning, a middle, and an end. Thus, a plot will be made up of at least three events. Plot is not the same as narrative. A news story is a narrative without a plot—a string of events recorded in their order of happening. A short story is a narrative with a plot, one event grows out of another. In formal criticism, the beginning of a plot is called the *exposition,* the middle concludes with the *climax,* and the end is called the *denouement.*

Point of view. The way a story is told, how it is presented to the reader. In a story told from the first-person point of view, the narrator is a character in the story and speaks as "I." The narrator may be either a major or minor character. A story told from this point of view is limited to what the narrator knows, thinks, and sees. In the story "Charles" by Shirley Jackson, Laurie's mother is a first-person narrator. In third-person point of view, the narrator is not a character in the story. A story told in the third person is sometimes *limited.* The narrator only sets the scene and reports what the characters say and do but not what they think and feel. However, with the third-person point of view, the narrator can enter the minds of the characters and tell readers what they are thinking. This kind of narrator is called an *omniscient narrator.* The narrator of "A Sudden Trip Home in the Spring" by Alice Walker is an omniscient narrator.

Rhyme. Most English rhymes are *masculine.* That is, the sounds coming before the stressed vowels are different, but the stressed vowels and any sounds following them are the same. The words *door* and *floor* are masculine rhyme. If the final syllables are unstressed, the rhyme is *feminine.* The words *sorrow* and *borrow* are feminine rhyme. Both feminine and masculine rhymes are considered *full rhyme.*

In additon to full rhyme, there is *sight rhyme, assonance, consonance,* and *identical rhyme.* For the most part, these other kinds of rhyme are used to avoid the heavy effect sometimes produced by continuous full rhymes.

Examples of sight rhyme are *own/crown, love/move,* and *blood/stood.* These words look as though they rhyme but do not. Examples of assonance are *cat/man* and *sank/hand.* The vowel sounds in each pair are the same, but the following consonants are different.

Examples of consonance are *add/read* and *road/blood.* In these pairs, the vowel sounds differ, but the following consonants are the same.

Examples of identical rhyme are *blue/blew, rain/reign,* and *sea/see.* These words are spelled differently but pronounced the same.

Rhyme scheme. The scheme of a verse is usually shown with letters, a different letter being used each time a new rhyme is introduced.

I shall be telling this with a sigh	a
Somewhere ages and ages hence:	b
Two roads diverged in a wood, and I—	a
I took the one less travelled by,	a
And that has made all the difference.	b

—Robert Frost

Satire. Verse or prose that ridicules institutions, people, or customs. "Report on the Barnhouse Effect" by Kurt Vonnegut, Jr., ridicules the short-sighted self-interest of government bureaucracies. "As Best She Could" by Don Jones heaps scorn on the insensitive treatment of human needs by welfare agencies.

Setting. The place and time of a story, play, narrative poem, or essay. The setting is more critical in some works of literature than in others. In James Baldwin's essay "Equal in Paris," the setting is crucial; being in Paris, with its different culture, and becoming entangled in its legal system, Baldwin finds himself in an unfamiliar situation and has difficulty in coping.

Simile. A comparison between objects that are dissimilar using the words *like* or *as.*

My hair flopped to the side
like the mane of a horse in the wind.

—May Swenson

Sonnet. A poem of fourteen lines, usually written in iambic pentameter, following a conventional pattern of rhymes. There are two basic forms of the sonnet—the Italian and the English. The Italian sonnet is divided into two parts. The first part is the *octave* and consists of eight lines that rhyme *a-b-b-a-a-b-b-a.* The

Basic Sonnet Forms

	Italian		English	
	Petrarchan	Miltonic	Shakespearean	Spenserian
octave	a b b a a b b a	a b b a a b b a	quatrain: a b a b	a b a b
	(break)	(no break)	quatrain: c d c d	b c b c
sestet	c d e c d e	c d c or c d c e	quatrain: e f e f	c d c d
			couplet: g g	e e
number of rhymes				
5	4	5	7	5

second part, the *sestet,* consists of six lines that rhyme either *c-d-e-c-d-e* or *c-d-c-d-c-d.* "On First Looking into Chapman's Homer" by John Keats is an example of the Italian sonnet.

The English sonnet, also called the Shakespearean sonnet, consists of three quatrains (sets of four lines), each with its own rhyme scheme, plus a couplet (two lines). The couplet acts as a sort of punch line, summing up what has gone before.

A variation on each of the basic forms exists. The Miltonic sonnet is a variation of the Italian sonnet. The Spenserian sonnet is a variation on the English sonnet. The previous chart illustrates the differences between the forms of the sonnet.

Stanza. A grouping of lines within a poem, often determined by the rhyme scheme. Some stanzas have a fixed number of lines. The *ballad stanza,* for example, has four lines and is called a *quatrain.* A stanza of two lines is called a *couplet.* Stanzas of free verse vary in the number of their lines.

Style. The selection and arrangement of words in a piece of writing. The term is also used to describe a writer's characteristic use of language—for example, "the direct, lucid, honest style of George Orwell."

Symbol. An object or event in a work of literature that has a range of meanings beyond itself. The road in Robert Frost's poem "The Road Not Taken" is both a literal road and one that symbolizes a decision taken early in life.

Theme. The general meaning of a literary work that rises out of its subject. The subject of Robert Browning's "My Last Duchess" is the Duke of Ferrara showing his art collection to a visitor. One theme of this poem is the cruelty and egotism a sophisticated person shows toward a simple, warm, and uncalculating person. Themes are sometimes difficult to state exactly, and a given literary work may actually have several themes.

Tone. The author's attitude toward his or her subject as reflected in the work. The tone of a literary work may be described as funny or serious, comic or tragic, sarcastic or reverent, or by whatever words seem appropriate.

Villanelle. A lyric poem made up of five stanzas of three lines each plus a final stanza of four lines. In the first five stanzas, the rhyme scheme is *a-b-a;* in the final stanza, it is *a-b-a-a.* The villanelle also uses a refrain, two lines repeated four times. Dylan Thomas's poem "Do not go gentle into that good night" is a villanelle. The form began as a round-song for farm laborers, and the name comes from the Latin word *villa,* meaning "farm."